Storage Networks Explained

Storage Networks Explained
Basics and Application of Fibre Channel SAN, NAS, iSCSI and InfiniBand

Ulf Troppens, Rainer Erkens

IBM TotalStorage Interoperability Center, Mainz, Germany

Wolfgang Müller

IBM Software Development Open Systems, Mainz, Germany

Translated by Rachel Waddington, Member of the Institute of Translating and Interpreting

John Wiley & Sons, Ltd

First published under the title *Speichernetze. Grundlagen und Einsatz von Fibre Channel SAN, NAS, iSCSI und InfiniBand*, ISBN: 3-89864-135-X by dpunkt.verlag GmbH
© dpunkt.verlag GmbH, Heidelberg, Germany, 2003

Copyright © 2004   for the English translation: John Wiley & Sons Ltd
The Atrium, Southern Gate, Chichester,
West Sussex PO19 8SQ, England

Telephone (+44) 1243 779777

Email (for orders and customer service enquiries): cs-books@wiley.co.uk
Visit our Home Page on www.wileyeurope.com or www.wiley.com

Reprinted September 2005, August and December 2006, May 2007, July 2008

Other Wiley Editorial Offices

John Wiley & Sons Inc., 111 River Street, Hoboken, NJ 07030, USA

Jossey-Bass, 989 Market Street, San Francisco, CA 94103-1741, USA

Wiley-VCH Verlag GmbH, Boschstr. 12, D-69469 Weinheim, Germany

John Wiley & Sons Australia Ltd, 33 Park Road, Milton, Queensland 4064, Australia

John Wiley & Sons (Asia) Pte Ltd, 2 Clementi Loop #02-01, Jin Xing Distripark, Singapore 129809

John Wiley & Sons Canada Ltd, 22 Worcester Road, Etobicoke, Ontario, Canada M9W 1L1

British Library Cataloguing in Publication Data

A catalogue record for this book is available from the British Library

ISBN 13: 978-0-470-86182-0 (H/B)

Typeset in 10/12pt Times by Laserwords Private Limited, Chennai, India
Printed and bound in Great Britain by CPI Antony Rowe, Chippenham, Wiltshire

For Silke, Hannah, Nina, and Julia
You keep showing me what really matters in life.

For Christina, Edith, and Heribert
For the love and constant support you have given me.

For Christel
Only your patience and your understanding have made my contribution
to this book possible.

Contents

About the authors

Ulf Troppens (left) and **Rainer Erkens** (centre) are employed at IBM TotalStorage Interoperability Centre in Mainz, a testing, development and demonstration laboratory for storage products and storage networks. Both authors work at the interface between technology and customers. Their duties include the testing of new products and the validation of concepts on the basis of customer environments set up in the laboratory. They present the latest hardware and software products in the field of storage networks to customers and discuss the set up test environment with them.

Ulf Troppens studied Computer Science at the University of Karlsruhe until 1995. Since 1989 he has been primarily involved in the administration of Unix systems, storage systems, data and storage networks and distributed applications. In April 2004 Ulf joined Wolfgang's team to help with the roll-out of a software for tape library virtualization.

Rainer Erkens studied Mathematics at the University of Mainz until 2000. His experience in the management of computers and the management of distributed applications goes back to 1992. Since 2000 he has been working primarily with storage systems and storage networks. In February 2004 he was appointed to Chairman of the SNIA Europe Solutions Committee.

Wolfgang Müller (right) is currently working as a software architect in the Storage Software Development Department at IBM in Mainz, Germany, where the focus is on software development projects supporting open standards such as SMI-S/CIM/WBEM and IEEE 1244. He received his Dipl.-Inform.(FH) degree in computer science from the University of Applied Sciences, Darmstadt, Germany, in 1993.

Foreword by Tom Clark

It is gratifying to see *Storage Networks Explained* appear in this new English translation. The fact that this work originally appeared in German and is now available in English translation is a testimony to the global adoption of SAN technology and the proliferation of SAN expertise internationally. Ulf Troppens, Rainer Erkens, and Wolfgang Müller have created an invaluable resource for understanding and implementing efficient storage networking solutions. Although this work does not claim to provide detailed blueprints for SANs, it provides a wealth of practical information for leveraging the benefits that SANs provide for storage data, including storage consolidation, high availability access to data, and data protection via data copy and tape backup.

The migration from fixed, direct-attached storage to storage networking has had a major impact on the IT community over the past decade. The first-generation Fibre Channel SANs that were initially adopted by large enterprises have now spread to a much wider market of enterprise branches and small and medium businesses. At the same time, entirely new technologies have emerged within storage networking such as IP SANs, storage virtualization, and comprehensive SAN management based on CIM and SMI-S. These new SAN technologies are helping to drive storage networking into the mainstream while delivering more productive applications based on SAN intelligence and storage-process automation. Although it has taken several years to overcome basic transport, interoperability, and management issues in storage networking, the ideal of a storage utility seems now within reach.

Like other technologies before it, SAN technology is quickly evolving towards its own demise as a separate discipline. This will not occur through disappearance from the market, but through universal and ubiquitous adoption across the entire market. Just as Gigabit Ethernet over long distances is gradually obscuring the difference between LANs and WANs, the melding of Fibre Channel and IP storage technologies will obscure the difference between LANs, WANs, and SANs. Eventually, there will just be 'the network' that will offer extremely high performance and resiliency where required to service a wide variety of applications, including storage data transport and high availability access.

Storage Networks Explained provides the basic knowledge to understand the various technical components of both conventional and new SAN solutions, as well as practical guidelines for aligning technical solutions with the business objectives of data availability and preservation. Troppens, Erkens, and Müller apply technical explanations as needed to assist the reader in differentiating between the many options available for SANs but avoid burdening the work with excessive granular detail. This helps the reader to focus on what is most relevant for making SAN technology decisions. Customers do not, after all, deploy technology for technology's sake but to solve real and pressing business problems.

By concentrating on the practical benefits of SANs for applications and business processes, this book is an essential resource for managers, administrators, and SAN architects who have day-to-day responsibility for aligning the appropriate technologies to specific business problems.

Tom Clark
Seattle, Washington
Former Board Member, Storage Networking Industry Association (SNIA)
Author: *Designing Storage Area Networks Second Edition* and *IP SANs: A Guide to iSCSI, iFCP and FCIP Protocols for IP Storage Area Networks*

Foreword to the German Edition by Hermann Strass

The subject of storage networks is particularly topical at the moment and for a number of reasons will remain so for a very long time to come. Storage networking technology brings with it fundamental new structures and procedures that will continue to be of great importance for the foreseeable future regardless of incremental differences and changes in products. A book on this subject is therefore of particular importance in these fast-moving times.

This book is based upon the experience of the two authors (Wolfgang joined the other two authors for the English edition of this book), who work with the subject matter on a daily basis. It provides system administrators and system architects in particular, with the tools for the optimal selection and the cost-effective use of this partially new technology, the use and operation of which currently seem indispensable in view of the ever-growing storage quantities in companies. The technology of networked storage is associated with demonstrable decisive cost savings. Therefore, growth continues even in an unfavourable economic climate.

Storage quantities are growing because we are currently tending to work in colour, in three-dimension and in digital format to a much greater extent than was the case a few years ago. Furthermore, there are now legal regulations in the European Union and in other countries that make the electronic/digital storage of all business data compulsory. The archiving of old business events in files in printed format is no longer sufficient to comply with the law. And data quantities continue to increase in both good times and bad: even lost orders and the related data have to be stored electronically. These legal regulations thus ensure that a certain amount of growth in data quantities is inevitable.

In the past, data was stored upon disk and tape drives connected directly to the server. Storage was operated as a peripheral to the computer. Access rights, virus protection and other functions could thus be performed on the computer (server) in question. For reasons that will be described in detail in this book, this way of working is no longer practical today. Storage is therefore detached from the servers and brought together to form a dedicated storage network. This gives rise to a fundamentally different way of working. The new procedures that this requires have been and will continue to be further developed and introduced now and in the future. Data storage thus has its own value. It is no longer a question of attaching a further disk drive to a server.

Nowadays, stored data and the information that it contains are the prized possessions for a company. The computers (servers) necessary for data processing can be purchased at any time, by the dozen or in greater quantities, in the form of individual blade servers or packed in cabinets, they can be integrated into a LAN and defective units can be exchanged. However, if stored data is lost, getting it back is infinitely more expensive and time-consuming – if it is indeed possible to restore some or all of the data. Data generally also has to be available around the clock. Data networks must, therefore, be designed with built-in redundancy and for high availability.

These and related topics are considered in detail in this book. The approach is based only to a certain degree upon the current state of the art. More important in this context is the description of the underlying topics and their interdependencies. This extends beyond the scope of even more lengthy magazine articles and will continue to be topical even in the future.

The requirements imposed upon storage networks are fundamentally different from the requirements made of the local networks (LANs) used in the past. Therefore, storage networks have up until now almost exclusively used the Fibre Channel technology that was specially developed for them as a connection technology. However, storage networking is no short-term fad and efforts are currently under way to use existing network technologies (e.g. Ethernet/LAN/TCP-IP) and emerging technologies (e.g. InfiniBand). Under certain circumstances this is a completely worthwhile alternative. The book highlights which selection criteria play a role in this context. It is not usually technical details or prejudices that are decisive here, but usage requirements, the available infrastructure and devices and a careful estimate of the future development in companies. This book will therefore be a valuable aid in the structural planning and selection of devices and software.

Overall, this book is an excellent work, which explains the subject comprehensively, in detail and with a good technical foundation. It is to be hoped that the book gains a wide circulation, particularly as it corrects a great many half-truths and prejudices.

Hermann Strass

Hermann Strass is an author and a consultant on new technologies, in particular bus architectures, mass storage, industrial networks and automation. He is a member of national and international standardization committees and Technical Coordinator of the VMEbus International Trade Association (VITA) in Europe.

Preface by the Authors

This Preface answers the following main questions:

- What does this book deal with?
- Who should read this book?
- How should this book be read?
- Who has written this book?

What does this book deal with?

The technology of Storage Area Networks (SANs) fundamentally changes the architecture of IT systems. In conventional IT systems, storage devices are connected to servers by means of SCSI cables. The idea behind storage networks is that these SCSI cables are replaced by a network, which is installed in addition to the existing LAN. Server and storage devices can exchange data over this new network using the SCSI protocol. Storage networks have long been a known quantity in the world of mainframes. Fibre Channel, iSCSI and Network Attached Storage (NAS) are now also taking storage networks into the field of Open Systems (Unix, Windows NT/2000/2003, OS/400, Novell Netware, MacOS). The term 'Unix' for us also encompasses the Linux operating system, which is sometimes presented separately in such itemizations.

Storage networks are becoming a fundamental technology like databases or LANs. According to market research, in 2004 over 70% of external storage will be realized in the form of storage networks. The term 'external storage' is used here to mean storage that is accommodated in a different enclosure to the server itself. Consequently, anyone who is involved in the planning or the operation of IT systems requires a basic knowledge of the principles and the use of storage networks. They are thus becoming as omnipresent as SCSI, but are more complex than LANs and TCP/IP.

The book is divided into two parts. Part I deals with fundamental technologies relating to storage networks. It guides the reader from the structure and operating method of storage devices through I/O techniques and I/O protocols to the file systems and storage virtualization.

Part II introduces applications that utilize the new functions of storage networks and intelligent storage subsystems. The focus is upon the sharing of resources that can be accessed via the storage network and upon server and application clusters, web applications and data protection (backup). Further focal points are the administration of storage networks and the administration of removable media. Last but not least, the SNIA Shared Storage Model provides a reference model to describe storage networks.

At the end of the book we have added a glossary, an index and an annotated bibliography, which in addition to further literature also highlights numerous freely available sources on the Internet.

Section 1.4 sets out in detail the structure of the book and the relationships between the individual chapters. Figure 1.7 on page 8 illustrates the structure of the book. At this point, it is worth casting a glance at this illustration. Note that the illustration also describes the subjects that we will not be covering.

Who should read this book?

Our approach is, first, to explain the basic techniques behind storage networks and, secondly, to show how these new techniques help to overcome problems in current IT systems. The book is equally suitable for beginners with basic IT knowledge and for old hands. It is more an introduction to the basic concepts and techniques than a technical reference work. The target group thus includes:

- system administrators
- system architects
- decision makers
- students.

After reading the whole book you will be familiar with

- the concepts of storage networks and their basic techniques
- usage options for storage networks
- proposed solutions for the support of business processes with the aid of storage networks
- the advantages of storage networks
- new possibilities opened up by storage networks.

How should this book be read?

There are two possible ways of reading this book. Those who are interested exclusively in the concepts and the possibilities for the use of storage networks should read Chapter 1 ('Introduction'), Chapter 5 ('Virtualization') and the Part II; any missing technical fundamentals can be looked up in the first part as required. Anyone who is also interested in the technical foundations of storage networks should read the book from start to finish.

Who has written this book?

Two of us, Ulf Troppens and Rainer Erkens, work at the IBM TotalStorage Interoperability Centre in Mainz, a testing and demonstration centre for storage networks. In our daily work we install and configure hardware and software for storage networks. We tell customers about suitable products and explain the concepts that underlie the products. We also discuss with customers how storage networks can help solve problems in their current IT systems. We are therefore very well acquainted with the questions that customers ask about storage networks, both those with experience in storage networks and beginners. We therefore believe that our daily work has helped us to structure the content of this book and to select the subjects that are important to the readers of a book on storage networks. Wolfgang Müller joined the authors for the English edition of this book. Wolfgang is the architect in charge of a removable media management system developed at the IBM Software Development Open Systems Lab in Mainz, Germany. He provides in-depth knowledge on tape and tape management.

Our intention has been to take off our 'IBM hats' and write this book from an unbiased viewpoint. Of course, as employees of IBM, experience and opinions have flowed into this book that have been formed in our daily work. Despite this, the book is our personal work and has no connection with IBM apart from our employee relationship. In particular, this book does not present any official opinions of IBM.

Acknowledgements

To conclude the preface we would like to thank a few people who have made a significant contribution to this book. From a chronological point of view we should first mention the editors of *iX* magazine and the readers' department of dpunkt.verlag, who set the whole thing in motion in March 2001 with the question 'Could you see yourselves writing a book on the subject of storage in the network?'

Regarding content, our colleagues from the IBM Mainz storage community, especially the former SAN Lab and the current TotalStorage Interoperability Centre deserve mention: without the collaboration on storage hardware and software with customers and employees of partner companies, business partners and IBM, and without the associated knowledge exchange, we would lack the experience and knowledge that we have been able to put into this book. The list of people in question is much too long for us to include it here. The co-operation of one of the three authors with the students of the BAITI 2000 course of the Berufsakademie Mannheim (University of Applied Science Mannheim), from whom we have learnt that we have to explain subjects such as 'RAID', 'disk subsystems', 'instant copy', 'remote mirroring' and 'file server', was also valuable from a didactic point of view.

With regard to quality control, we thank our proof-readers Axel Köster, Bernd Blaudow, Birgit Bäuerlein, Frank Krämer, Gaetano Bisaz, Hermann Strass, Jürgen Deicke, Julia Neumann, Michael Lindner, Michael Riepe, Peter Münch, René Schönfeldt, Steffen Fischer, Susanne Nolte, Thorsten Schäfer, Uwe Harms and Willi Gardt as well as our helpers at dpunkt.verlag, whose names we do not know. We should emphasize in particular the many constructive suggestions for improvement by Susanne Nolte, who also contributed a few paragraphs on 'DAFS', and the numerous comments from our colleagues Axel Köster and Jürgen Deicke and our manuscript reader René Schönfeldt. In this connection, the efforts of Jürgen Deicke and Tom Clark should also be mentioned regarding the 'SNIA Recommended Reading' logo, which is printed on the front cover of the book.

With regard to the English edition of this book we have to thank even more people: First of all, we would like to thank René Schönfeldt from dpunkt.verlag for convincing Birgit Gruber from Wiley & Sons to invest in the translation. We greatly appreciate Birgit Gruber for taking a risk on the translation project and having so much patience with all our editorial changes. Rachel Waddington did an outstanding job of translating the text and all figures from German into English. Last but not least, we would like to thank Daniel Gill for leading the production process including copy-editing and typesetting and we would like to thank the team at Laserwords for typesetting the whole book.

Finally, the support of our parents, parents-in-law and partners should be mentioned. I, Wolfgang Müller, would like to thank my fiancée Christel for her patience, her emotional support and for many more reasons than there is room in these notes to list. And I, Ulf Troppens, would like at this point to thank my dear wife Silke, who has taken many household and family duties off my hands and thus given me the time that I needed to write this book, for her support. And I, Rainer Erkens, would like to thank my dear partner Christina, who never lost the view for the worldly things and thus enabled me to travel untroubled through the world of storage networks, for her support. We are pleased that we now have more time for children, family and friends. May we have many more happy and healthy years together.

Mainz, April 2004   Ulf Troppens
                                                                          Rainer Erkens
                                                                        Wolfgang Müller

List of Figures and Tables

FIGURES

TABLES

1

Introduction

The purpose of this chapter is to convey the basic idea underlying this book. To this end we will first describe conventional server-centric IT architecture and sketch out its limitations (Section 1.1). We will then introduce the alternative approach of storage-centric IT architecture (Section 1.2), explaining its advantages using the case study 'Replacing a Server with Storage Networks' (Section 1.3). Finally, we explain the structure of the entire book and discuss which subjects are not covered (Section 1.4).

1.1 SERVER-CENTRIC IT ARCHITECTURE AND ITS LIMITATIONS

In conventional IT architectures, storage devices are normally only connected to a single server (Figure 1.1). To increase fault-tolerance, storage devices are sometimes connected to two servers, with only one server actually able to use the storage device at any one time. In both cases, the storage device exists only in relation to the server to which it is connected. Other servers cannot directly access the data; they always have to go through the server that is connected to the storage device. This conventional IT architecture is therefore called server-centric IT architecture. In this approach, servers and storage devices are generally connected together by SCSI cables.

As mentioned above, in conventional server-centric IT architecture storage devices exist only in relation to the one or two servers to which they are connected. The failure of both of these computers would make it impossible to access this data. Most companies find this unacceptable: at least some of the company data (for example, patient files, websites) must be available around the clock.

Storage Networks Explained   U. Troppens R. Erkens W. Müller
© 2004 John Wiley & Sons, Ltd   ISBN: 0-470-86182-7

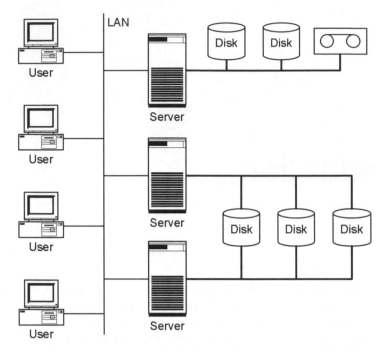

Figure 1.1 In a server-centric IT architecture storage devices exist only in relation to servers

Although the storage density of hard disks and tapes is increasing all the time due to ongoing technical development, the need for installed storage is increasing even faster. Consequently, it is necessary to connect ever more storage devices to a computer. This throws up the problem that each computer can accommodate only a limited number of I/O cards (for example, SCSI cards). Furthermore, the length of SCSI cables is limited to a maximum of 25 m. This means that the storage capacity that can be connected to a computer using conventional technologies is limited. Conventional technologies are therefore no longer sufficient to satisfy the growing demand for storage capacity.

In server-centric IT environments the storage device is statically assigned to the computer to which it is connected. In general, a computer cannot access storage devices that are connected to a different computer. This means that if a computer requires more storage space than is connected to it, it is no help whatsoever that another computer still has attached storage space, which is not currently used (Figure 1.2).

Last, but not least, storage devices are often scattered throughout an entire building or branch. Sometimes this is because new computers are set up all over the campus without any great consideration and then upgraded repeatedly. Alternatively, computers may be consciously set up where the user accesses the data in order to reduce LAN data traffic. The result is that the storage devices are distributed throughout many rooms, which are neither protected against unauthorized access nor sufficiently air-conditioned. This may sound over-the top, but many system administrators could write a book about replacing defective hard disks that are scattered all over the country.

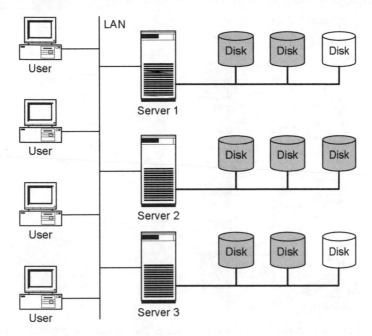

Figure 1.2   The storage capacity on server 2 is full. It cannot make use of the fact that there is still storage space free on server 1 and server 3

1.2   STORAGE-CENTRIC IT ARCHITECTURE AND ITS ADVANTAGES

Storage networks can solve the problems of server-centric IT architecture that we have just discussed. Furthermore, storage networks open up new possibilities for data management. The idea behind storage networks is that the SCSI cable is replaced by a network that is installed in addition to the existing LAN and is primarily used for data exchange between computers and storage devices (Figure 1.3).

In contrast to server-centric IT architecture, in storage networks storage devices exist completely independently of any computer. Several servers can access the same storage device directly over the storage network without another server having to be involved. Storage devices are thus placed at the centre of the IT architecture; servers, on the other hand, become an appendage of the storage devices that 'just process data'. IT architectures with storage networks are therefore known as storage-centric IT architectures.

When a storage network is introduced, the storage devices are usually also consolidated. This involves replacing the many small hard disks attached to the computers with a large disk subsystem. Disk subsystems currently (end of 2003) have a maximum storage capacity of several ten terabytes. The storage network permits all computers to access the disk subsystem and share it. Free storage capacity can thus be flexibly assigned to the computer that needs it at the time. In the same manner, many small tape libraries can be replaced by one big one.

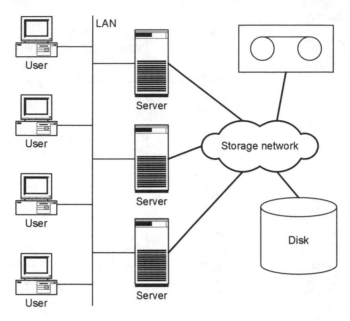

Figure 1.3 In storage-centric IT architecture the SCSI cables are replaced by a network. Storage devices now exist independently of a server

More and more companies are converting their IT systems to a storage-centric IT architecture. It has now become a permanent component of large data centres and the IT systems of large companies. In our experience, more and more medium-sized companies and public institutions are now considering storage networks. Even today, most storage capacity is no longer fitted into the case of a server (internal storage device), but has its own case (external storage device). Depending upon the source, it is predicted that by the end of 2004 two-thirds of external storage capacity will be connected by means of storage networks.

1.3 CASE STUDY: REPLACING A SERVER WITH STORAGE NETWORKS

In the following we will illustrate some advantages of storage-centric IT architecture using a case study: in a production environment an application server is no longer powerful enough. The ageing computer must be replaced by a higher-performance device. Whereas such a measure can be very complicated in a conventional, server-centric IT architecture, it can be carried out very elegantly in a storage network.

1. Before the exchange, the old computer is connected to a storage device via the storage network, which it uses partially (Figure 1.4 shows stages 1, 2 and 3).

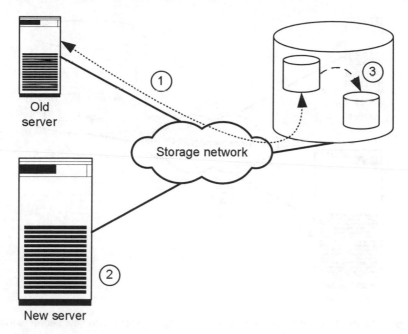

Figure 1.4   The old server is connected to a storage device via a storage network (1). The new server is assembled and connected to the storage network (2). To generate test data the production data is copied within the storage device (3)

2. First, the necessary application software is installed on the new computer. The new computer is then set up at the location at which it will ultimately stand. With storage networks it is possible to set up the computer and storage device several kilometres apart.

3. Next, the production data for generating test data within the disk subsystem is copied. Modern storage systems can (practically) copy even terabyte-sized data files within seconds. This function is called instant copy and is explained in more detail in Chapter 2 ('Intelligent disk subsystems').
   To copy data it is often necessary to shut down the applications, so that the copied data is in a consistent state. Consistency is necessary to permit the application to resume operation with the data. Some applications are also capable of keeping a consistent state on the disk during operation (online back-up mode of database systems, snapshots of file systems).

4. Then the copied data is assigned to the new computer and the new computer is tested intensively (Figure 1.5). If the storage system is placed under such an extreme load by the tests that its performance is no longer sufficient for the actual application, the data must first be transferred to a second storage system by means of remote mirroring. Remote mirroring is also explained in more detail in Chapter 2 ('Intelligent disk subsystems').

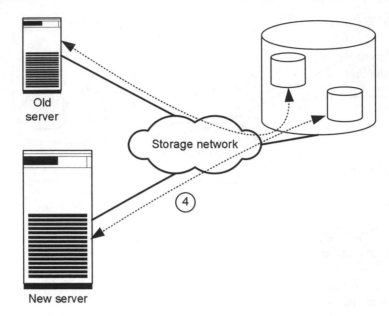

Figure 1.5   Old server and new server share the storage system. The new server is intensively tested using the copied production data (4)

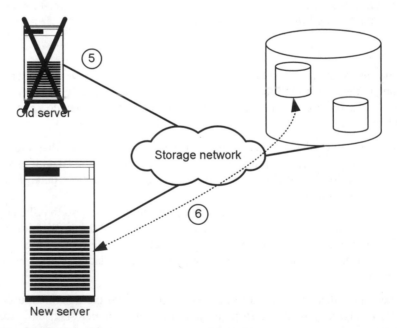

Figure 1.6   Finally, the old server is powered down (5) and the new server is started up with the production data (6)

5. After successful testing, both computers are shut down and the production data assigned to the new server. The assignment of the production data to the new server also takes just a few seconds (Figure 1.6 shows steps 5 and 6).

6. Finally, the new server is restarted with the production data.

1.4   THE STRUCTURE OF THE BOOK

One objective of this book is to graphically explain the benefits of storage networks. In order to provide an introduction to this subject, this chapter has presented a few fundamental problems of conventional server-centric IT architecture and concluded by mentioning a few advantages of storage-centric IT architecture based upon the equipment of an application server. The remaining chapters deal with the concepts and techniques that have already been sketched out and discuss further case studies in detail. The book is structured around the path from the storage device to the application (Figure 1.7, page 8).

In modern IT systems, data is normally stored on hard disks and tapes. It is more economical to procure and manage a few large storage systems than several small ones. This means that the individual disk drives are being replaced by disk subsystems. In contrast to a file server, an intelligent disk subsystem can be visualized as a hard disk server; other servers can use these hard disks that are exported via the storage network just as they can use locally connected disk drives. Chapter 2 shows what modern disk subsystems can do in addition to the instant copy and remote mirroring functions mentioned above. The hardware of tapes and tape libraries changes only slightly as a result of the transition to storage networks, so we only touch upon this subject in the book. In Section 6.2.2 we will discuss the sharing of large tape libraries by several servers and access to these over a storage network and Chapter 9 will present the management of removable media including – among other removable media – tapes and tape libraries.

Fibre Channel has established itself as a technology with which storage networks can be efficiently realized for both open systems (Unix, Windows NT/2000/2003, Novell Netware, MacOS, OS/400) and mainframes. iSCSI is currently receiving a lot of attention as an alternative to Fibre Channel. In contrast to Fibre Channel, which defines a new transmission technology, iSCSI is based upon the proven TCP/IP and Gigabit Ethernet. iSCSI thus has the potential to supersede Fibre Channel in the long term. Furthermore, a third network technology will soon be available. This technology is InfiniBand and is suitable for the realization of block-oriented storage networks. In all probability, InfiniBand will replace the PCI bus in large servers by a serial network. Fibre Channel, iSCSI (or more generally: IP Storage) and InfiniBand are the subject of Chapter 3.

File systems are of interest in this book for two reasons. First, preconfigured file servers, also known as Network Attached Storage (NAS), have established themselves as an important building block for current IT systems. Storage networks can also be realized using NAS servers. In contrast to the block-oriented data traffic of Fibre Channel and iSCSI, in this approach whole files or file fragments are transferred.

So-called shared-disk file systems represent the other interesting development in the field of file systems. In shared-disk file systems, several computers can access the same

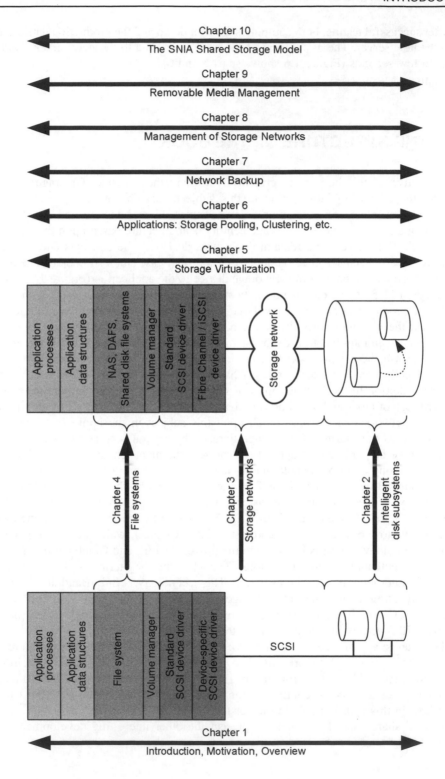

data area in an intelligent disk subsystem over the storage network. The performance of shared-disk file systems is currently significantly better than those of NFS, CIFS, AppleTalk or the above-mentioned NAS servers. Examples of problems are discussed on the basis of shared-disk file systems that must also be solved in the same manner for comparable applications such as parallel databases. Chapter 4 deals with Network Attached Storage (NAS) and shared-disk file systems.

The first four chapters of the book discuss fundamental components and technologies with regard to storage networks. As storage networks have become more widespread, it has become clear that the implementation of a storage network alone is not sufficient to make efficient use of the resources of ever growing storage networks. Chapter 5 sketches out the difficulties associated with the use of storage networks and it introduces storage virtualization – an approach that aims to reduce the total cost of ownership (TCO) for assessing and managing huge amounts of data. It further discusses possible locations for the realization of storage virtualization and discusses various alternative approaches to storage virtualization such as virtualization on block level and virtualization on file level or symmetric and asymmetric storage virtualization.

The first chapters introduce a whole range of new technologies. In Chapter 6 we turn our attention to the application of these new techniques. This chapter uses many case studies to show how storage networks help in the design of IT systems that are more flexible and more fault-tolerant than conventional server-centric IT systems.

Data protection (Back-up) is a central application in every IT system. Using network back-up systems it is possible to back up heterogeneous IT environments with several thousands of computers largely automatically. Chapter 7 explains the fundamentals of network back-up and shows how these new techniques help to back up data even more efficiently. Once again, this clarifies the limitations of server-centric IT architecture and the benefits of the storage-centric IT architecture.

Storage networks are complex systems made up of numerous individual components. As one of the first steps in the management of storage networks it is necessary to understand the current state. This calls for tools that help to answer such questions as 'which server occupies how much space on which disk subsystem?', 'which servers are connected to my storage network at all?', 'which hardware components are in use and how great is the load upon the network?'. In this connection the monitoring of the storage network with regard to faults and performance and capacity bottlenecks of file systems is also important. The

---

Figure 1.7 The book is divided into two main parts. The first section discusses the fundamental techniques that underlie storage networks. Individually, these are intelligent disk subsystems (Chapter 2), block-oriented storage networks (Chapter 3) and file systems (Chapter 4). Furthermore, we outline how virtualization can help to manage storage resources more efficiently (Chapter 5). The second part discusses the application of these new technologies. Individually, standard applications such as storage pooling and clustering (Chapter 6) and back-up (Chapter 7) are discussed. Those chapters illustrate how storage networks help in the development of IT systems that are more flexible, more fault-tolerant and more powerful than traditional systems. Then the management of storage networks (Chapter 8) and the management of removable media (Chapter 9) are discussed. Finally, the SNIA Shared Storage Model (Chapter 10) is presented

second step relates to the automation of the management of storage networks: important subjects are rule-based error handling and the automatic allocation of free storage capacity. Chapter 8 deals in detail with the management of storage networks and in this connection also discusses standards such as SNMP, CIM/WBEM and SMI-S (Bluefin).

Removable media represent a central component of the storage architecture of large data centres. Storage networks allow several servers, and thus several different applications, to share media and libraries. Therefore, the management of removable media in storage networks is becoming increasingly important. Chapter 9 deals with the requirements of removable media management and it introduces the IEEE 1244 Standard for Removable Media Management.

Storage networks are a complex subject area. There is still a lack of unified terminology, with different manufacturers using the same term to refer to different features and, conversely, describing the same feature using different terms. As a result, it is often unclear what kind of a product is being offered by a manufacturer and which functions a customer can ultimately expect from this product. It is thus difficult for the customer to compare the products of the individual manufacturers and to work out the differences between the alternatives on offer. For this reason, the Technical Council of the Storage Networking Industry Association (SNIA) has introduced the so-called Shared Storage Model in 2001 in order to unify the terminology and descriptive models used by the storage network industry. We introduce this model in Chapter 10.

What doesn't this book cover?

In order to define the content it is also important to know which subjects are not covered:

- Specific products:
  Product lifecycles are too short for specific products to be discussed in a book. Products change, concepts do not.
- Economic aspects:
  This book primarily deals with the technical aspects of storage networks. It discusses concepts and approaches to solutions. Prices change very frequently, concepts do not.
- Excessively technical details:
  The book is an introduction to storage networks. It does not deal with the details necessary for the development of components for storage networks. The communication of the overall picture is more important to us.
- The planning and implementation of storage networks:
  Planning and implementation require knowledge of specific products, but products change very frequently. Planning and implementation require a great deal of experience. This book, on the other hand, is designed as an introduction. Inexperienced readers should consult experts when introducing a storage network. Furthermore, a specific implementation must always take into account the specific environment in question. It is precisely this that this book cannot do.

Part I
Technologies for Storage Networks

2
Intelligent Disk Subsystems

Hard disks and tapes are currently the most important media for the storage of data. When storage networks are introduced, the existing small storage devices are replaced by a few large storage systems (storage consolidation). For example, individual hard disks and small disk stacks are replaced by large disk subsystems that can store between a few hundred gigabytes and several ten terabytes of data, depending upon size. Furthermore, they have the advantage that functions such as high availability, high performance, instant copies and remote mirroring are available at a reasonable price even in the field of open systems (Unix, Windows NT/2000, OS/400, Novell Netware, MacOS). The administration of a few large storage systems is significantly simpler, and thus cheaper, than the administration of many small disk stacks. However, the administrator must plan what he is doing more precisely when working with large disk subsystems. This chapter describes the functions of such modern disk subsystems.

This chapter begins with an overview of the internal structure of a disk subsystem (Section 2.1). We then go on to consider the hard disks used inside the system and the configuration options for the internal I/O channels (Section 2.2). The controller represents the control centre of a disk subsystem. Disk subsystems without controllers are called JBODs (Just a Bunch of Disks); JBODs provide only an enclosure and a common power supply for several hard disks (Section 2.3). So-called RAID controllers bring together several physical hard disks to form virtual hard disks that are faster and more fault-tolerant than individual physical hard disks (Sections 2.4 and 2.5). Some RAID controllers use a cache to further accelerate write and read access to the server (Server 2.6). In addition, intelligent controllers provide services such as instant copy and remote mirroring (Section 2.7). The conclusion to this chapter summarizes the measures discussed for increasing the fault-tolerance of intelligent disk subsystems (Section 2.8).

Storage Networks Explained   U. Troppens R. Erkens W. Müller
© 2004 John Wiley & Sons, Ltd   ISBN: 0-470-86182-7

2.1 ARCHITECTURE OF INTELLIGENT DISK SUBSYSTEMS

In contrast to a file server, a disk subsystem can be visualized as a hard disk server. Servers are connected to the connection port of the disk subsystem using standard I/O techniques such as SCSI, Fibre Channel or iSCSI and can thus use the storage capacity that the disk subsystem provides (Figure 2.1). The internal structure of the disk subsystem is completely hidden from the server, which sees only the hard disks that the disk subsystem provides to the server.

The connection ports are extended to the hard disks of the disk subsystem by means of internal I/O channels (Figure 2.2). In most disk subsystems there is a controller between the connection ports and the hard disks. The controller can significantly increase the data availability and data access performance with the aid of a so-called RAID procedure (RAID = Redundant Array of Independent Disks). Furthermore, some controllers realize the copying services instant copy and remote mirroring and further additional services. The controller uses a cache in an attempt to accelerate read and write accesses to the server.

All sizes of disk subsystems are available. Small disk subsystems have one to two connections for servers or storage networks, six to eight hard disks and – depending

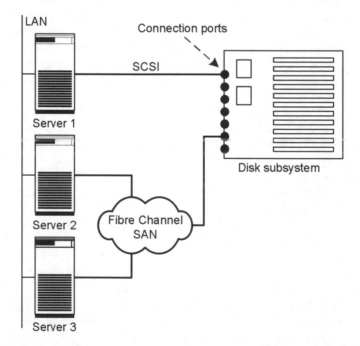

Figure 2.1 Servers are connected to a disk subsystem using standard I/O techniques. The figure shows a server that is connected by SCSI. Two others are connected by Fibre Channel SAN

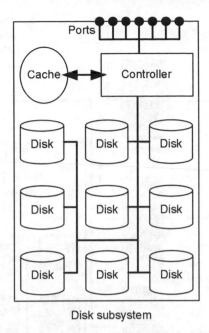

Disk subsystem

Figure 2.2 Servers are connected to the disk subsystems via the ports. Internally, the disk subsystem consists of hard disks, a controller, a cache and internal I/O channels

upon disk capacity – a storage capacity of around 500 gigabytes. Large disk subsystems have several ten ports for servers or storage networks, redundant controllers and several internal I/O channels. Connection via a storage network means that a significantly greater number of servers can access the disk subsystem. Large disk subsystems can store several ten terabytes of data and – depending upon the manufacturer – weigh a few tons. The dimensions of a large disk subsystem are comparable with those of a wardrobe.

Figure 2.2 shows a simplified schematic representation. The architecture of real disk subsystems is more complex and varies greatly. Ultimately, however, it will always include the components shown in Figure 2.2. The simplified representation in Figure 2.2 provides a sufficient basis for the further discussion in the book.

Regardless of storage networks, most disk subsystems have the advantage that free disk space can be flexibly assigned to each server connected to the disk subsystem (storage pooling). Figure 2.3 refers back once again to the example of Figure 1.2 on page 3. In Figure 1.2 it is not possible to assign more storage to server 2, even though free space is available on servers 1 and 3. In Figure 2.3 this is not a problem. All servers are either directly connected to the disk subsystem or indirectly connected via a storage network. In this configuration each server can be assigned free storage. Incidentally, free storage capacity should be understood to mean both hard disks that have already been installed and have not yet been used and also free slots for hard disks that have yet to be installed.

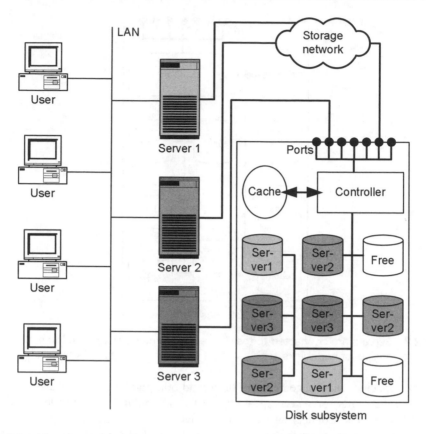

Figure 2.3 All servers share the storage capacity of a disk subsystem. Each server can be assigned free storage more flexibly as required

2.2 HARD DISKS AND INTERNAL I/O CHANNELS

The controller of the disk subsystem must ultimately store all data on physical hard disks. Standard hard disks that range in size from 18 GB to 250 GB are currently (2003) used for this purpose. Since the maximum number hard disks that can be used is often limited, the size of the hard disk used gives an indication of the maximum capacity of the overall disk subsystem.

When selecting the size of the internal physical hard disks it is necessary to weigh the requirements of maximum performance against those of the maximum capacity of the overall system. With regard to performance it is often beneficial to use smaller hard disks at the expense of the maximum capacity: given the same capacity, if more hard disks are available in a disk subsystem, the data is distributed over several hard disks and thus the overall load is spread over more arms and read/write heads and usually over more I/O channels (Figure 2.4). For most applications, medium-sized hard disks are sufficient. Only for applications with extremely high performance requirements should smaller hard disks

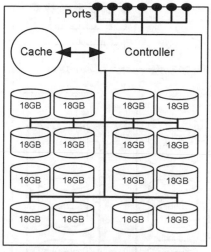
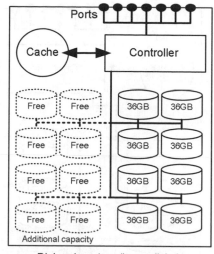

Disk subsystem (small disks)   Disk subsystem (large disks)

Figure 2.4   If small internal hard disks are used, the load is distributed over more hard disks and thus over more read and write heads. On the other hand, the maximum storage capacity is reduced, since in both disk subsystems only 16 hard disks can be fitted

be considered. However, consideration should be given to the fact that more modern, larger hard disks generally have shorter seek times and larger caches, so it is necessary to carefully weigh up which hard disks will offer the highest performance for a certain load profile in each individual case.

Standard I/O techniques such as SCSI and Fibre Channel, to an increasing degree SATA (Serial ATA) and sometimes also SSA (Serial Storage Architecture) are very often used for the internal I/O channels between connection ports and controller and between controller and internal hard disks. Sometimes, however, proprietary – i.e. manufacturer-specific – I/O technologies are used. Regardless of the I/O technology used, the I/O channels can be designed with built-in redundancy in order to increase the fault-tolerance of the disk subsystem. The following cases can be differentiated here:

- Active
  In active cabling the individual physical hard disks are only connected via one I/O channel (Figure 2.5, left). If this access path fails, then it is no longer possible to access the data.

- Active/passive
  In active/passive cabling the individual hard disks are connected via two I/O channels (Figure 2.5, right). In normal operation the controller communicates with the hard disks via the first I/O channel and the second I/O channel is not used. In the event of the failure of the first I/O channel, the disk subsystem switches from the first to the second I/O channel.

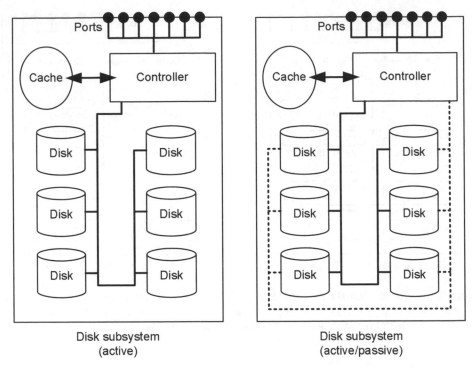

Disk subsystem
(active)

Disk subsystem
(active/passive)

Figure 2.5 In active cabling all hard disks are connected by a just one I/O channel. In active/passive cabling all hard disks are additionally connected by a second I/O channel. If the primary I/O channel fails, the disk subsystem switches to the second I/O channel

- Active/active (no load sharing)
  In this cabling method the controller uses both I/O channels in normal operation (Figure 2.6, left). The hard disks are divided into two groups: in normal operation the first group is addressed via the first I/O channel and the second via the second I/O channel. If one I/O channel fails, both groups are addressed via the other I/O channel.

- Active/active (load sharing)
  In this approach all hard disks are addressed via both I/O channels in normal operation (Figure 2.6, right). The controller divides the load dynamically between the two I/O channels so that the available hardware can be optimally utilized. If one I/O channel fails, then the communication goes through the other channel only.

Active cabling is the simplest and thus also the cheapest to realize but offers no protection against failure. Active/passive cabling is the minimum needed to protect against failure, whereas active/active cabling with load sharing best utilizes the underlying hardware.

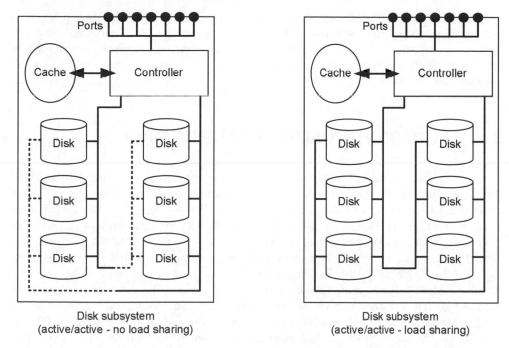

Disk subsystem
(active/active - no load sharing)

Disk subsystem
(active/active - load sharing)

Figure 2.6   Active/active cabling (no load sharing) uses both I/O channels at the same time. However, each disk is addressed via one I/O channel only, switching to the other channel in the event of a fault. In active/active cabling (load sharing) hard disks are addressed via both I/O channels

2.3   JBOD: JUST A BUNCH OF DISKS

If we compare disk subsystems with regard to their controllers we can differentiate between three levels of complexity: (1) no controller; (2) RAID controller (Sections 2.4 and 2.5); and (3) intelligent controller with additional services such as instant copy and remote mirroring (Section 2.7).

If the disk subsystem has no internal controller, it is only an enclosure full of disks (Just a Bunch of Disks, JBOD). In this instance, the hard disks are permanently fitted into the enclosure and the connections for I/O channels and power supply are taken outwards at a single point. Therefore, a JBOD is simpler to manage than a few loose hard disks. Typical JBOD disk subsystems have space for 8 or 16 hard disks. A connected server recognizes all these hard disks as independent disks. Therefore, 16 device addresses are required for a JBOD disk subsystem incorporating 16 hard disks. In some I/O techniques such as SCSI and Fibre Channel arbitrated loop (Section 3.3.6), this can lead to a bottleneck at device addresses.

In contrast to intelligent disk subsystems, a JBOD disk subsystem in particular is not capable of supporting RAID or other forms of virtualization. If required, however, these can be realized outside the JBOD disk subsystem, for example, as software in the server (Section 5.1) or as an independent virtualization entity in the storage network (Section 5.6.3).

2.4   STORAGE VIRTUALIZATION USING RAID

A disk subsystem with a RAID controller offers greater functional scope than a JBOD disk subsystem. RAID was originally developed at a time when hard disks were still very expensive and less reliable than they are today. RAID was originally called 'Redundant Array of Inexpensive Disks'. Today RAID stands for 'Redundant Array of Independent Disks'. Disk subsystems that support RAID are sometimes also called RAID arrays.

RAID has two main goals: to increase performance by striping and to increase fault-tolerance by redundancy. Striping distributes the data over several hard disks and thus distributes the load over more hardware. Redundancy means that additional information is stored so that the operation of the application itself can continue in the event of the failure of a hard disk. You cannot increase the performance of an individual hard disk any more than you can improve its fault-tolerance. Individual physical hard disks are slow and have a limited life-cycle. However, through a suitable combination of physical hard disks it is possible to significantly increase the fault-tolerance and performance of the system as a whole.

The bundle of physical hard disks brought together by the RAID controller are also known as virtual hard disks. A server that is connected to a RAID system sees only the virtual hard disk; the fact that the RAID controller actually distributes the data over several physical hard disks is completely hidden to the server (Figure 2.7). This is only visible to the administrator from outside.

A RAID controller can distribute the data that a server writes to the virtual hard disk amongst the individual physical hard disks in various manners. These different procedures are known as RAID levels. Section 2.5 explains various RAID levels in detail.

One factor common to almost all RAID levels is that they store redundant information. If a physical hard disk fails, its data can be reconstructed from the hard disks that remain intact. The defective hard disk can even be replaced by a new one during operation if a disk subsystem has the appropriate hardware. Then the RAID controller reconstructs the data of the exchanged hard disk. This process remains hidden to the server apart from a possible reduction in performance: the server can continue to work uninterrupted on the virtual hard disk.

Modern RAID controllers initiate this process automatically. This requires the definition of so-called hot spare disks (Figure 2.8). The hot spare disks are not used in normal operation. If a disk fails, the RAID controller immediately begins to copy the data of the remaining intact disk onto a hot spare disk. After the replacement of the defective disk, this is included in the pool of hot spare disks. Modern RAID controllers can manage a

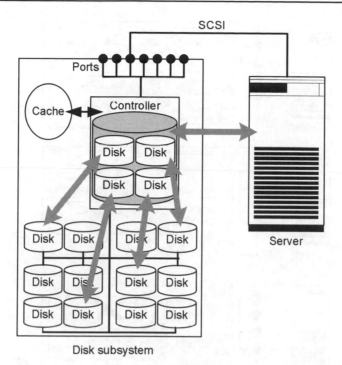

Figure 2.7   The RAID controller combines several physical hard disks to create a virtual hard disk. The server sees only a single virtual hard disk. The controller hides the assignment of the virtual hard disk to the individual physical hard disks

common pool of hot spare disks for several virtual RAID disks. Hot spare disks can be defined for all RAID levels that offer redundancy.

The recreation of the data from a defective hard disk takes place at the same time as write and read operations of the server to the virtual hard disk, so that from the point of view of the server, performance reductions at least can be observed. Modern hard disks come with self-diagnosis programs that report an increase in write and read errors to the system administrator in plenty of time: 'Caution! I am about to depart this life. Please replace me with a new disk. Thank you!' To this end, the individual hard disks store the data with a redundant code such as the Hamming code. The Hamming code permits the correct recreation of the data, even if individual bits are changed on the hard disk. If the system is looked after properly you can assume that the installed physical hard disks will hold out for a while. Therefore, for the benefit of higher performance, it is generally an acceptable risk to give access by the server a higher priority than the recreation of the data of an exchanged physical hard disk.

A further side-effect of the bringing together of several physical hard disks to form a virtual hard disk is the higher capacity of the virtual hard disks. As a result, less device addresses are used up in the I/O channel and thus the administration of the server is also simplified, because less hard disks (drive letters or volumes) need to be used.

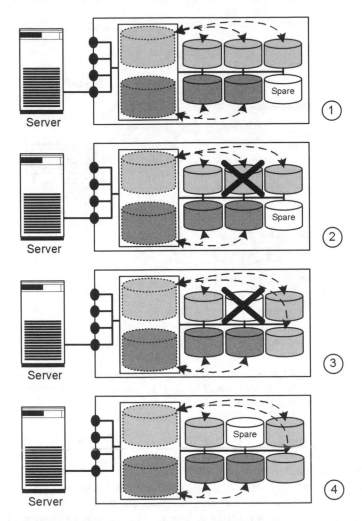

Figure 2.8 Hot spare disk: the disk subsystem provides the server with two virtual disks for which a common hot spare disk is available (1). Due to the redundant data storage the server can continue to process data even though a physical disk has failed, at the expense of a reduction in performance (2). The RAID controller recreates the data from the defective disk on the hot spare disk (3). After the defective disk has been replaced a hot spare disk is once again available (4)

2.5 DIFFERENT RAID LEVELS IN DETAIL

RAID has developed since its original definition in 1987. Due to technical progress some RAID levels are now practically meaningless, whilst others have been modified or added at a later date. This section introduces the RAID levels that are currently the most significant in practice. We will not introduce RAID levels that represent manufacturer-specific variants and variants that only deviate slightly from the basic forms mentioned in the following.

2.5.1 RAID 0: block-by-block striping

RAID 0 distributes the data that the server writes to the virtual hard disk onto one physical hard disk after another block-by-block (block-by-block striping). Figure 2.9 shows a RAID array with four physical hard disks. In Figure 2.9 the server writes the blocks A, B, C, D, E, etc. onto the virtual hard disk one after the other. The RAID controller distributes the sequence of blocks onto the individual physical hard disks: it writes the first block, A, to the first physical hard disk, the second block, B, to the second physical hard disk, block C to the third and block D to the fourth. Then it begins to write to the first physical hard disk once again, writing block E to the first disk, block F to the second, and so on.

RAID 0 increases the performance of the virtual hard disk as follows: the individual hard disks can exchange data with the RAID controller via the I/O channel significantly more quickly than they can write to or read from the rotating disk. In Figure 2.9 the RAID controller sends the first block, block A, to the first hard disk. This takes some time to write the block to the disk. Whilst the first disk is writing the first block to the physical hard disk, the RAID controller is already sending the second block, block B,

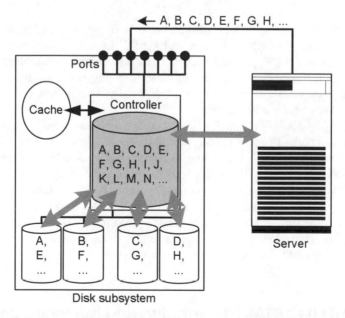

Figure 2.9 RAID 0 (striping): as in all RAID levels, the server sees only the virtual hard disk. The RAID controller distributes the write operations of the server amongst several physical hard disks. Parallel writing means that the performance of the virtual hard disk is higher than that of the individual physical hard disks

to the second hard disk and block C to the third hard disk. In the meantime the first two physical hard disks are still engaged in depositing their respective blocks onto the physical hard disk. If the RAID controller now sends block E to the first hard disk, then this has written block A at least partially, if not entirely, to the physical hard disk.

In the example, the throughput can thus be approximately quadrupled: individual hard disks currently (2003) achieve a throughput of around 50 MByte/s. The four physical hard disks achieve a total throughput of around 4×50 MByte/s ≈ 200 MByte/s. Current I/O techniques such as SCSI or Fibre Channel achieve a throughput of 160 MByte/s or 200 MByte/s. If the RAID array consisted of just three physical hard disks the total throughput of the hard disks would be the limiting factor. If, on the other hand, the RAID array consisted of five physical hard disks the I/O path would be the limiting factor. With five or more hard disks, therefore, performance increases are only possible if the hard disks are connected to different I/O paths so that the load can be striped not only over several physical hard disks, but also over several I/O paths.

RAID 0 increases the performance of the virtual hard disk, but not its fault-tolerance. If a physical hard disk is lost, all the data on the virtual hard disk is lost. To be precise, therefore, the 'R' for 'Redundant' in RAID is incorrect in the case of RAID 0, with 'RAID 0' standing instead for 'zero redundancy'.

2.5.2   RAID 1: block-by-block mirroring

In contrast to RAID 0, in RAID 1 fault-tolerance is of primary importance. The basic form of RAID 1 brings together two physical hard disks to form a virtual hard disk by mirroring the data on the two physical hard disks. If the server writes a block to the virtual hard disk, the RAID controller writes this block to both physical hard disks (Figure 2.10). The individual copies are also called mirrors. Normally, two or sometimes three copies of the data are kept (three-way mirror).

In a normal operation with pure RAID 1, performance increases are only possible in read operations. After all, when reading the data the load can be divided between the two disks. However, this gain is very low in comparison to RAID 0. When writing with RAID 1 it tends to be the case that reductions in performance may even have to be taken into account. This is because the RAID controller has to send the data to both hard disks. This disadvantage can be disregarded for an individual write operation, since the capacity of the I/O channel is significantly higher than the maximum write speed of the two hard disks put together. However, the I/O channel is under twice the load, which hinders other data traffic using the I/O channel at the same time.

2.5.3   RAID 0+1/RAID 10: striping and mirroring combined

The problem with RAID 0 and RAID 1 is that they increase either performance (RAID 0) or fault-tolerance (RAID 1). However, it would be nice to have both performance and

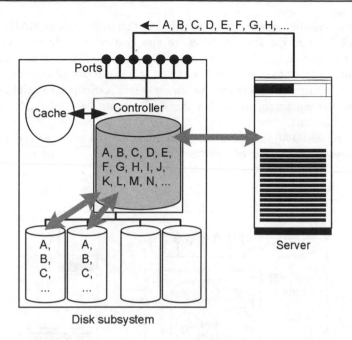

← A, B, C, D, E, F, G, H, ...

Ports

Cache

Controller

A, B, C, D, E, F, G, H, I, J, K, L, M, N, ...

A, B, C, ...

A, B, C, ...

Server

Disk subsystem

Figure 2.10 RAID 1 (mirroring): as in all RAID levels, the server sees only the virtual hard disk. The RAID controller duplicates each of the server's write operations onto two physical hard disks. After the failure of one physical hard disk the data can still be read from the other disk

fault-tolerance. This is where RAID 0+1 and RAID 10 come into play. These two RAID levels combine the ideas of RAID 0 and RAID 1.

RAID 0+1 and RAID 10 each represent a two-stage virtualization hierarchy. Figure 2.11 shows the principle behind RAID 0+1 (mirrored stripes). In the example, eight physical hard disks are used. The RAID controller initially brings together each four physical hard disks to form a total of two virtual hard disks that are only visible within the RAID controller by means of RAID 0 (striping). In the second level, it consolidates these two virtual hard disks into a single virtual hard disk by means of RAID 1 (mirroring); only this virtual hard disk is visible to the server.

In RAID 10 (striped mirrors) the sequence of RAID 0 (striping) and RAID 1 (mirroring) is reversed in relation to RAID 0+1 (mirrored stripes). Figure 2.12 shows the principle underlying RAID 10 based again on eight physical hard disks. In RAID 10 the RAID controller initially brings together the physical hard disks in pairs by means of RAID 1 (mirroring) to form a total of four virtual hard disks that are only visible within the RAID controller. In the second stage, the RAID controller consolidates these four virtual hard disks into a virtual hard disk by means of RAID 0 (striping). Here too, only this last virtual hard disk is visible to the server.

In both RAID 0+1 and RAID 10 the server sees only a single hard disk, which is larger, faster and more fault-tolerant than a physical hard disk. We now have to ask the question: which of the two RAID levels, RAID 0+1 or RAID 10, is preferable?

The question can be answered by considering that when using RAID 0 the failure of a hard disk leads to the loss of the entire virtual hard disk. In the example relating to RAID 0+1 (Figure 2.11) the failure of a physical hard disk is thus equivalent to the effective failure of four physical hard disks (Figure 2.13). If one of the other four physical hard disks is lost, then the data is lost. In principle it is sometimes possible to reconstruct the data from the remaining disks, but the RAID controllers available on the market cannot do this particularly well.

In the case of RAID 10, on the other hand, after the failure of an individual physical hard disk, the additional failure of a further physical hard disk – with the exception of the

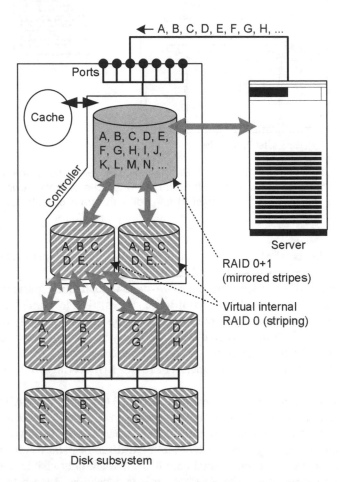

Figure 2.11   RAID 0+1 (mirrored stripes): as in all RAID levels, the server sees only the virtual hard disk. Internally, the RAID controller realizes the virtual disk in two stages: In the first stage it brings together every four physical hard disks into one virtual hard disk that is only visible within the RAID controller by means of RAID 0 (striping). In the second stage it consolidates these two virtual hard disks by means of RAID 1 (mirroring) to form the hard disk that is visible to the server

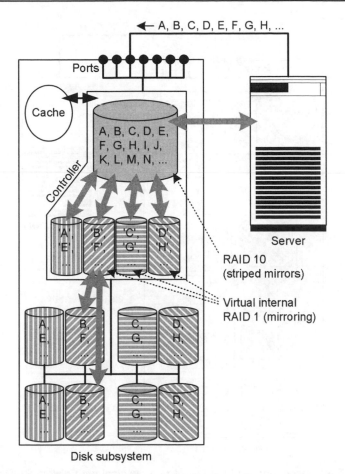

A, B, C, D, E, F, G, H, ...

Ports

Cache

Controller

A, B, C, D, E,
F, G, H, I, J,
K, L, M, N, ...

Server

RAID 10
(striped mirrors)

Virtual internal
RAID 1 (mirroring)

Disk subsystem

Figure 2.12 RAID 10 (striped mirrors): as in all RAID levels, the server sees only the virtual hard disk. Here too, we proceed in two stages. The sequence of striping and mirroring is reversed in relation to RAID 0+1. In the first stage the controller links every two physical hard disks by means of RAID 1 (mirroring) to a virtual hard disk, which it unifies by means of RAID 0 (striping) in the second stage to form the hard disk that is visible to the server

corresponding mirror – can be withstood (Figure 2.14). RAID 10 thus has a significantly higher fault-tolerance than RAID 0+1. In addition, the cost of restoring the RAID system after the failure of a hard disk is much lower in the case of RAID 10 than RAID 0+1. In RAID 10 only one physical hard disk has to be recreated. In RAID 0+1, on the other hand, a virtual hard disk must be recreated that is made up of four physical disks. However, the cost of recreating the defective hard disk can be significantly reduced because a physical hard disk is exchanged as a preventative measure when the number of read errors start to increase. In this case it is sufficient to copy the data from the old disk to the new.

However, things look different if the performance of RAID 0+1 is compared with the performance of RAID 10. In Section 5.1 we discuss a case study in which the use of RAID 0+1 is advantageous.

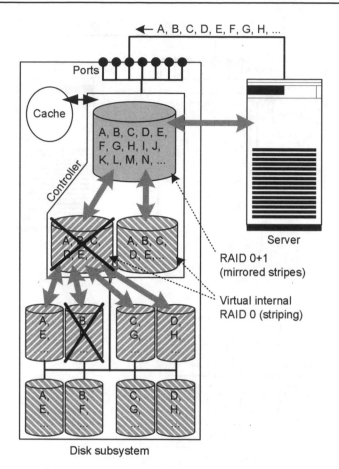

Figure 2.13 The consequences of the failure of a physical hard disk in RAID 0+1 (mirrored stripes) are relatively high in comparison to RAID 10 (striped mirrors). The failure of a physical hard disk brings about the failure of the corresponding internal RAID 0 disk, so that in effect half of the physical hard disks have failed. The restoration of the data from the failed disk is expensive

With regard to RAID 0+1 and RAID 10 it should be borne in mind that the two RAID procedures are often confused. Therefore the answer 'We use RAID 10!' or 'We use RAID 0+1' does not always provide the necessary clarity. In discussions it is better to ask if mirroring takes place first and the mirror is then striped or if striping takes place first and the stripes are then mirrored.

2.5.4 RAID 4 and RAID 5: parity instead of mirroring

RAID 10 provides excellent performance at a high level of fault-tolerance. The problem with this is that mirroring using RAID 1 means that all data is written to the physical hard disk twice. RAID 10 thus doubles the required storage capacity.

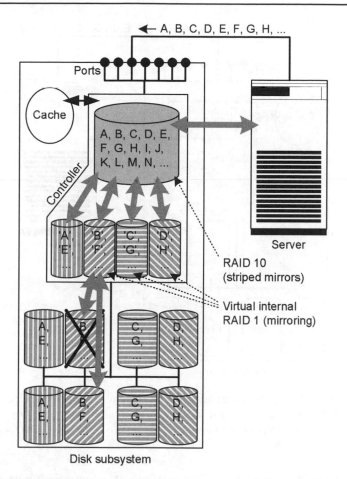

Figure 2.14 In RAID 10 (striped mirrors) the consequences of the failure of a physical hard disk are not as serious as in RAID 0+1 (mirrored stripes). All virtual hard disks remain intact. The restoration of the data from the failed hard disk is simple

The idea of RAID 4 and RAID 5 is to replace all mirror disks of RAID 10 with a single parity hard disk. Figure 2.15 shows the principle of RAID 4 based upon five physical hard disks. The server again writes the blocks A, B, C, D, E, etc. to the virtual hard disk sequentially. The RAID controller stripes the data blocks over the first four physical hard disks. Instead of mirroring all data onto the further four physical hard disks, as in RAID 10, the RAID controller calculates a parity block for every four blocks and writes this onto the fifth physical hard disk. For example, the RAID controller calculates the parity block P_{ABCD} for the blocks A, B, C and D. If one of the four data disks fails, the RAID controller can reconstruct the data of the defective disks using the three other data disks and the parity disk. In comparison to the examples in Figures 2.11 (RAID 0+1) and 2.12 (RAID 10), RAID 4 saves three physical hard disks. As in all other RAID levels, the server again sees only the virtual disk, as if it were a single physical hard disk.

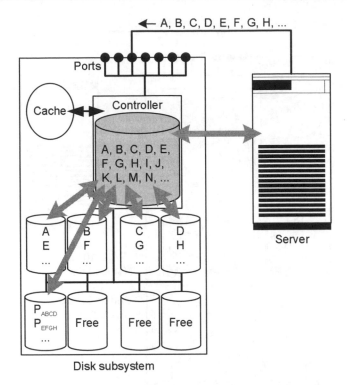

Disk subsystem

Figure 2.15 RAID 4 (parity disk) is designed to reduce the storage requirement of RAID 0+1 and RAID 10. In the example, the data blocks are distributed over four physical hard disks by means of RAID 0 (striping). Instead of mirroring all data once again, only a parity block is stored for each four blocks

From a mathematical point of view the parity block is calculated with the aid of the logical XOR operator (Exclusive OR). In the example from Figure 2.15, for example, the equation P_{ABCD} = A XOR B XOR C XOR D applies.

The space saving offered by RAID 4 and RAID 5, which remains to be discussed, comes at a price in relation to RAID 10. Changing a data block changes the value of the associated parity block. This means that each write operation to the virtual hard disk requires (1) the physical writing of the data block, (2) the recalculation of the parity block and (3) the physical writing of the newly calculated parity block. This extra cost for write operations in RAID 4 and RAID 5 is called the write penalty of RAID 4 or the write penalty of RAID 5.

The cost for the recalculation of the parity block is relatively low due to the mathematical properties of the XOR operator. If the block A is overwritten by block $\tilde{A}$ and Δ is the difference between the old and new data block, then Δ = A XOR $\tilde{A}$. The new parity block $\tilde{P}$ can now simply be calculated from the old parity block P and Δ, i.e. $\tilde{P}$ = P XOR Δ. Proof of this property can be found in Appendix A. Therefore, if P_{ABCD} is the parity block for the data blocks A, B, C and D, then after the data block A has been changed, the new parity block can be calculated without knowing the remaining blocks

B, C and D. However, the old block A must be read in before overwriting the physical hard disk in the controller, so that this can calculate the difference Δ.

When processing write commands for RAID 4 and RAID 5 arrays, RAID controllers use the above-mentioned mathematical properties of the XOR operation for the recalculation of the parity block. Figure 2.16 shows a server that changes block D on the virtual hard disk. The RAID controller reads the data block and the associated parity block from the disk in question into its cache. Then it uses the XOR operation to calculate the difference between the old and the new parity block, i.e. $\Delta = D \text{ XOR } \tilde{D}$, and from this the new parity block $\tilde{P}_{ABCD}$ by means of $\tilde{P}_{ABCD} = P_{ABCD} \text{ XOR } \Delta$. Therefore it is not necessary to read in all four associated data blocks to recalculate the parity block. To conclude the write operation to the virtual hard disk, the RAID controller writes the new data block and the recalculated parity block onto the physical hard disks in question.

Good RAID 4 and RAID 5 implementations are capable of reducing the write penalty even further for certain load profiles. For example, if large data quantities are written

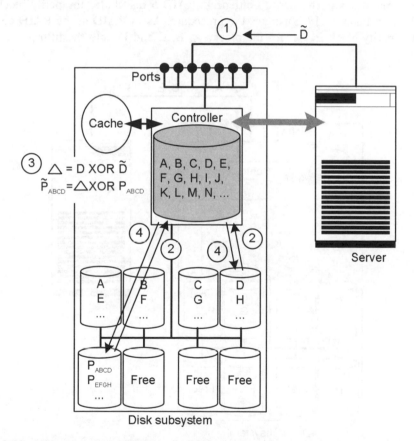

Figure 2.16 Write penalty of RAID 4 and RAID 5: the server writes a changed data block (1). The RAID controller reads in the old data block and the associated old parity block (2) and calculates the new parity block (3). Finally it writes the new data block and the new parity block onto the physical hard disk in question (4)

sequentially, then the RAID controller can calculate the parity blocks from the data flow without reading the old parity block from the disk. If, for example, the blocks E, F, G and H in Figure 2.15 are written in one go, then the controller can calculate the parity block P_{EFGH} from them and overwrite this without having previously read in the old value. Likewise, a RAID controller with a suitably large cache can hold frequently changed parity blocks in the cache after writing to the disk, so that the next time one of the data blocks in question is changed there is no need to read in the parity block. In both cases the I/O load is now lower than in the case of RAID 10. In the example only five physical blocks now need to be written instead of eight as is the case with RAID 10.

RAID 4 saves all parity blocks onto a single physical hard disk. For the example in Figure 2.15 this means that the write operations for the data blocks are distributed over four physical hard disks. However, the parity disk has to handle the same number of write operations all on its own. Therefore, the parity disk become the performance bottleneck of RAID 4 if there are a high number of write operations.

To get around this performance bottleneck, RAID 5 distributes the parity blocks over all hard disks. Figure 2.17 illustrates the procedure. As in RAID 4, the RAID controller writes the parity block P_{ABCD} for the blocks A, B, C and D onto the fifth physical hard

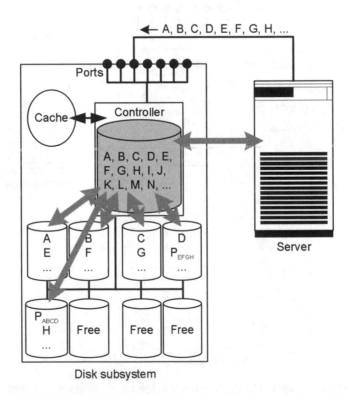

Figure 2.17 RAID 5 (striped parity): in RAID 4 each write access by the server is associated with a write operation to the parity disk for the comparison of parity information. RAID 5 distributes the load of the parity disk over all physical hard disks

disk. Unlike RAID 4, however, in RAID 5 the parity block P_{EFGH} moves to the fourth physical hard disk for the next four blocks E, F, G, H.

RAID 4 and RAID 5 distribute the data blocks over many physical hard disks. Therefore, the read performance of RAID 4 and RAID 5 is as good as that of RAID 0 and almost as good as that of RAID 10. As discussed, the write performance of RAID 4 and RAID 5 suffers from the write penalty; in RAID 4 there is an additional bottleneck caused by the parity disk. Therefore, RAID 4 is seldom used in practice because RAID 5 accomplishes more than RAID 4 with the same technical resources (see also Section 2.5.6).

RAID 4 and RAID 5 can withstand the failure of a physical hard disk. The use of parity blocks means that the data on the defective hard disk can be restored with the aid of the other hard disk. In contrast to RAID 10, the failure of a second physical hard disk always leads to data loss. Some RAID 5 variants get around this by simply keeping a second parity disk so that the data is doubly protected.

In RAID 4 and RAID 5 the restoration of a defective physical hard disk is significantly more expensive than is the case for RAID 1 and RAID 10. In the latter two RAID levels only the mirror of the defective disk needs to be copied to the replaced disk. In RAID 4 and RAID 5, on the other hand, the RAID controller has to read the data from all disks, use this to recalculate the lost data blocks and parity blocks, and then write these blocks to the replacement disk. As in RAID 0+1 this high cost can be avoided by replacing a physical hard disk as a precaution as soon as the rate of read errors increases. If this is done, it is sufficient to copy the data from the hard disk to be replaced onto the new hard disk.

If the fifth physical hard disk has to be restored in the examples from Figure 2.15 (RAID 4) and Figure 2.17 (RAID 5), the RAID controller must first read the blocks A, B, C and D from the physical hard disks, recalculate the parity block P_{ABCD} and then write to the exchanged physical hard disk. If a data block has to be restored, only the calculation rule changes. If, in the example, the third physical hard disk is to be recreated, the controller would first have to read in the blocks A, B, D and P_{ABCD}, use these to reconstruct block C and write this to the replaced disk.

2.5.5　RAID 2 and RAID 3

When introducing the RAID levels we are sometimes asked: 'and what about RAID 2 and RAID 3?'. The early work on RAID began at a time when disks were not yet very reliable: bit errors were possible that could lead to a written 'one' being read as 'zero' or a written 'zero' being read as 'one'. In RAID 2 the Hamming code is used, so that redundant information is stored in addition to the actual data. This additional data permits the recognition of read errors and to some degree also makes it possible to correct them. Today, comparable functions are performed by the controller of each individual hard disk, which means that RAID 2 no longer has any practical significance.

Like RAID 4 or RAID 5, RAID 3 stores parity data. RAID 3 distributes the data of a block amongst all the disks of the RAID 3 system so that, in contrast to RAID 4 or RAID 5, all disks are involved in every read or write access. RAID 3 only permits the reading

and writing of whole blocks, thus dispensing with the write penalty that occurs in RAID
4 and RAID 5. The writing of individual blocks of a parity group is thus not possible.
In addition, in RAID 3 the rotation of the individual hard disks is synchronized so that
the data of a block can truly be written simultaneously. RAID 3 was for a long time
called the recommended RAID level for sequential write and read profiles such as data
mining and video processing. Current hard disks come with a large cache of their own,
which means that they can temporarily store the data of an entire track, and they have
significantly higher rotation speeds than the hard disks of the past. As a result of these
innovations, other RAID levels are now suitable for sequential load profiles, meaning that
RAID 3 is becoming less and less important.

2.5.6 A comparison of the RAID levels

The various RAID levels raise the question of which RAID level should be used when.
Table 2.1 compares the criteria of fault-tolerance, write performance, read performance
and space requirement for the individual RAID levels. The evaluation of the criteria can
be found in the discussion in the previous sections.

*CAUTION PLEASE: The comparison of the various RAID levels discussed in this
section is only applicable to the theoretical basic forms of the RAID level in question.
In practice, manufacturers of disk subsystems have design options in*

- *the selection of the internal physical hard disks;*
- *the I/O technique used for the communication within the disk subsystem;*
- *the use of several I/O channels;*
- *the realization of the RAID controller;*
- *the size of the cache; and*
- *the cache algorithms themselves.*

*The performance data of the specific disk subsystem must be considered very carefully
for each individual case. For example, in the previous chapter measures were discussed*

Table 2.1 The table compares the theoretical basic forms of the various RAID levels. In
practice there are very marked differences in the quality of the implementation of RAID
controllers

RAID level	Fault-tolerance	Read performance	Write performance	Space requirement
RAID 0	none	good	very good	minimal
RAID 1	high	poor	poor	high
RAID 10	very high	very good	good	high
RAID 4	high	good	very very poor	low
RAID 5	high	good	very poor	low

that greatly reduce the write penalty of RAID 4 and RAID 5. Specific RAID controllers
may implement these measures, but they do not have to.

Subject to the above warning, RAID 0 is the choice for applications for which the maximum write performance is more important than protection against the failure of a disk. Examples are the storage of multimedia data for film and video production and the recording of physical experiments in which the entire series of measurements has no value if all measured values cannot be recorded. In this case it is more beneficial to record all of the measured data on a RAID 0 array first and then copy it after the experiment, for example on a RAID 5 array. In databases, RAID 0 is used as a fast store for segments in which intermediate results for complex requests are to be temporarily stored. However, as a rule hard disks tend to fail at the most inconvenient moment so database administrators only use RAID 0 if it is absolutely necessary, even for temporary data.

With RAID 1, performance and capacity are limited because only two physical hard disks are used. RAID 1 is therefore a good choice for small databases for which the configuration of a virtual RAID 5 or RAID 10 disk would be too large. A further important field of application for RAID 1 is in combination with RAID 0.

RAID 10 is used in situations where high write performance and high fault-tolerance are called for. For a long time it was recommended that database log files be stored on RAID 10. Databases record all changes in log files so this application has a high write component. After a system crash the restarting of the database can only be guaranteed if all log files are fully available. Manufacturers of storage systems disagree as to whether this recommendation is still valid as there are now fast RAID 4 and RAID 5 implementations.

RAID 4 and RAID 5 save disk space at the expense of a poorer write performance. For a long time the rule of thumb was to use RAID 5 where the ratio of read operations to write operations is $70:30$. At this point we wish to repeat that there are now storage systems on the market with excellent write performance that store the data internally using RAID 4 or RAID 5.

2.6   CACHING: ACCELERATION OF HARD DISK ACCESS

In all fields of computer systems, caches are used to speed up slow operations by operating them from the cache. Specifically in the field of disk subsystems, caches are designed to accelerate write and read accesses to physical hard disks. In this connection we can differentiate between two types of cache: (1) cache on the hard disk (Section 2.6.1) and (2) cache in the RAID controller. The cache in the RAID controller is subdivided into write cache (Section 2.6.2) and read cache (Section 2.6.3).

2.6.1   Cache on the hard disk

Each individual hard disk comes with a very small cache. This is necessary because the transfer rate of the I/O channel to the disk controller is significantly higher than the speed at which the disk controller can write to or read from the physical hard disk. If a server or a RAID controller writes a block to a physical hard disk, the disk controller stores this in its cache. The disk controller can thus write the block to the physical hard disk in its own time whilst the I/O channel can be used for data traffic to the other hard disk. Many RAID levels use precisely this state of affairs to increase the performance of the virtual hard disk.

Read access is accelerated in a similar manner. If a server or an intermediate RAID controller wishes to read a block, it sends the address of the requested block to the hard disk controller. The I/O channel can be used for other data traffic while the hard disk controller copies the complete block from the physical hard disk into its cache at a slower data rate. The hard disk controller transfers the block from its cache to the RAID controller or to the server at the higher data rate of the I/O channel.

2.6.2   Write cache in the controller of the disk subsystem

In addition to the cache of the individual hard drives many disk subsystems come with their own cache, which in some models is gigabytes in size. As a result it can buffer much greater data quantities than the cache on the hard disk. The write cache should have a battery back-up and ideally be mirrored. The battery back-up is necessary to allow the data in the write cache to survive a power cut. A write cache with battery back-up can significantly reduce the write penalty of RAID 4 and RAID 5, particularly for sequential write access (cf. Section 2.5.4 'RAID 4 and RAID 5: parity instead of mirroring'), and smooth out load peaks.

Many applications do not write data at a continuous rate, but in batches. If a server sends several data blocks to the disk subsystem, the controller initially buffers all blocks into a write cache with a battery back-up and immediately reports back to the server that all data has been securely written to the drive. The disk subsystem then copies the data from the write cache to the slower physical hard disk in order to make space for the next write peak.

2.6.3   Read cache in the RAID controller

The acceleration of read operations is difficult in comparison to the acceleration of write operations using cache. To speed up read access by the server, the disk subsystem's controller must copy the relevant data blocks from the slower physical hard disk to the fast cache before the server requests the data in question.

The problem with this is that it is very difficult for the disk subsystem's controller to work out in advance what data the server will ask for next. The controller in the disk subsystem knows neither the structure of the information stored in the data blocks nor the access pattern that an application will follow when accessing the data. Consequently, the controller can only analyse past data access and use this to extrapolate which data blocks the server will access next. In sequential read processes this prediction is comparatively simple, in the case of random access it is almost impossible. As a rule of thumb, good RAID controllers manage to provide around 40% of the requested blocks from the read cache in mixed read profiles.

The disk subsystem's controller cannot further increase the ratio of read access provided from the cache (pre-fetch hit rate), because it does not have the necessary application knowledge. Therefore, it is often worthwhile realizing a further cache within applications. For example, after opening a file, file systems can load all blocks of the file into the main memory; the file system knows the structures that the files are stored in. File systems can thus achieve a prefetch hit rate of 100%. However, it is impossible to know whether the expense for the storage of the blocks is worthwhile in an individual case, since the application may not actually request further blocks of the file.

2.7   INTELLIGENT DISK SUBSYSTEMS

Intelligent disk subsystems represent the third level of complexity for controllers after JBODs and RAID arrays. The controllers of intelligent disk subsystems offer additional functions over and above those offered by RAID. In the disk subsystems that are currently available on the market these functions are usually instant copies (Section 2.7.1), remote mirroring (Section 2.7.2) and LUN masking (Section 2.7.3).

2.7.1   Instant copies

Instant copies can practically copy data sets of several terabytes within a disk subsystem in a few seconds. Virtual copying means that disk subsystems fool the attached servers into believing that they are capable of copying such large data quantities in such a short space of time. The actual copying process takes significantly longer. However, the same server, or a second server, can access the practically copied data after a few seconds (Figure 2.18).

Instant copies are used, for example, for the generation of test data, for the back-up of data and for the generation of data copies for data mining. Based upon the case study in Section 1.3 it was shown that when copying data using instant copies, attention should be paid to the consistency of the copied data. Sections 7.8.5 and 7.10.3 discuss in detail the interaction of applications and storage systems for the generation of consistent instant copies.

There are numerous alternative implementations for instant copies. One thing that all implementations have in common is that the pretence of being able to copy data in a matter of seconds costs resources. All realizations of instant copies require controller computing time and cache and place a load on internal I/O channels and hard disks. The different implementations of instant copy force the performance down at different times. However, it is not possible to choose the most favourable implementation alternative depending upon the application used because real disk subsystems only ever realize one implementation alternative of instant copy.

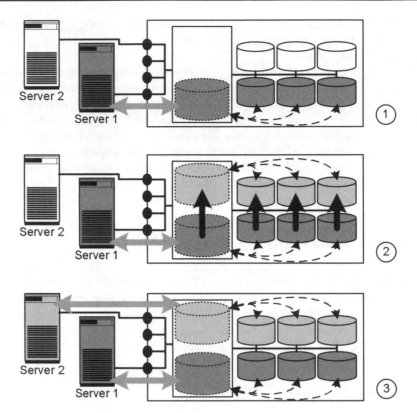

Figure 2.18 Instant copies can practically copy several terabytes of data within a disk subsystem in a few seconds: server 1 works on the original data (1). The original data is practically copied in a few seconds (2). Then server 2 can work with the data copy, whilst server 1 continues to operate with the original data (3)

In the following, two implementation alternatives will be discussed that function in very different ways. At one extreme the data is permanently mirrored (RAID 1 or RAID 10). Upon the copy command both mirrors are separated: the separated mirrors can then be used independently of the original. After the separation of the mirror the production data is no longer protected against the failure of a hard disk. Therefore, to increase data protection, three mirrors are often kept prior to the separation of the mirror (three-way mirror), so that the production data is always mirrored after the separation of the copy.

At the other extreme, no data at all is copied prior to the copy command, only after the instant copy has been requested. To achieve this, the controller administers two data areas, one for the original data and one for the data copy generated by means of instant copy. The controller must ensure that during write and read access operations to original data or data copies the blocks in question are written to or read from the data areas in question. In some implementations it is permissible to write to the copy, in some it is not. Some implementations copy just the blocks that have actually changed (partial copy), others copy all blocks as a background process until a complete copy of the original data has been generated (full copy).

In the following, the case differentiations of the controller will be investigated in more detail based upon the example from Figure 2.18. We will first consider access by server 1 to the original data. Read operations are completely unproblematic; they are always served from the area of the original data. Handling write operations is trickier. If a block is changed for the first time since the generation of the instant copy, the controller must first copy the old block to the data copy area so that server 2 can continue to access the old data set. Only then may it write the changed block to the original data area. If a block that has already been changed in this manner has to be written again, it must be written to the original data area. The controller may not even back up the previous version of the block to the data copy area because otherwise the correct version of the block would be overwritten.

The case differentiations for access by server 2 to the data copy generated by means of instant copy are somewhat simpler. In this case, write operations are unproblematic: the controller always writes all blocks to the data copy area. On the other hand, for read operations it has to establish whether the block in question has already been copied or not. This determines whether it has to read the block from the original data area or read it from the data copy area and forward it to the server.

2.7.2   Remote mirroring

Instant copies are excellently suited for the copying of data sets within disk subsystems. However, they can only be used to a limited degree for data protection. Although data copies generated using instant copy protect against application errors (accidental deletion of a file system) and logical errors (errors in the database program), they do not protect against the failure of a disk subsystem. Something as simple as a power failure can prevent access to production data and data copies for several hours. A fire in the disk subsystem would destroy original data and data copies. For data protection, therefore, the proximity of production data and data copies is fatal.

Remote mirroring offers protection against such catastrophes. Modern disk subsystems can now mirror their data, or part of their data, independently to a second disk subsystem, which is a long way away. The entire remote mirroring operation is handled by the two participating disk subsystems. Remote mirroring is invisible to application servers and does not consume their resources. However, remote mirroring requires resources in the two disk subsystems and in the I/O channel that connects the two disk subsystems together, which means that reductions in performance can sometimes make their way through to the application.

Figure 2.19 shows an application that is designed to achieve high availability using remote mirroring. The application server and the disk subsystem, plus the associated data, are installed in the primary data centre. The disk subsystem independently mirrors the application data onto the second disk subsystem that is installed 50 kilometres away in the back-up data centre by means of remote mirroring. Remote mirroring ensures that the application data in the back-up data centre is always kept up-to-date with the time

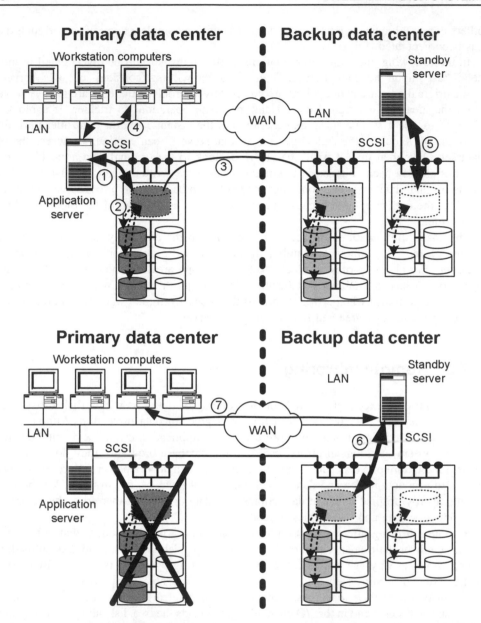

Figure 2.19 High availability with remote mirroring: (1) The application server stores its data on a local disk subsystem. (2) The disk subsystem saves the data to several physical drives by means of RAID. (3) The local disk subsystem uses remote mirroring to mirror the data onto a second disk subsystem located in the back-up data centre. (4) Users use the application via the LAN. (5) The stand-by server in the back-up data centre is used as a test system. The test data is located on a further disk subsystem. (6) If the first disk subsystem fails, the application is started up on the stand-by server using the data of the second disk subsystem. (7) Users use the application via the WAN

interval for updating the second disk subsystem being configurable. If the disk subsystem in the primary data centre fails, the back-up application server in the back-up data centre can be started up using the data of the second disk subsystem and the operation of the application can be continued. The I/O techniques required for the connection of the two disk subsystems will be discussed in the next chapter.

We can differentiate between synchronous and asynchronous remote mirroring. In synchronous remote mirroring the first disk subsystem sends the data to the second disk subsystem first before it acknowledges a server's write command. By contrast, asynchronous remote mirroring acknowledges a write command immediately; only then does it send the copy of the block to the second disk subsystem.

Figure 2.20 illustrates the data flow of synchronous remote mirroring. The server writes block A to the first disk subsystem. This stores the block in its write cache and immediately sends it to the second disk subsystem, which also initially stores the block in its write cache. The first disk subsystem waits until the second reports that it has written the block. The question of whether the block is still stored in the write cache of the second disk subsystem or has already been written to the hard disk is irrelevant to the first disk subsystem. It does not acknowledge to the server that the block has been written until it has received confirmation from the second disk subsystem that this has written the block.

Synchronous remote mirroring has the advantage that the copy of the data held by the second disk subsystem is always up-to-date. This means that if the first disk subsystem fails, the application can continue working with the most recent data set by utilizing the data on the second disk subsystem.

The disadvantage is that copying the data from the first disk subsystem to the second and sending the write acknowledgement back from the second to the first increases the response time of the first disk subsystem to the server. However, it is precisely this response time that determines the throughput of applications such as databases and file systems. An important factor for the response time is the signal transit time between the two disk subsystems. After all, their communication is encoded in the form of physical signals, which propagate at a certain speed. The propagation of the signals from one disk subsystem to another simply costs time. As a rule of thumb, it is worth using synchronous remote mirroring if the cable lengths from the server to the second disk subsystem via the first are a maximum of 6–10 kilometres.

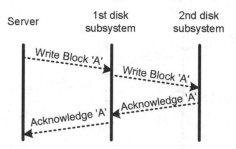

Figure 2.20 In synchronous remote mirroring a disk subsystem does not acknowledge write operations until it has saved a block itself and received write confirmation from the second disk subsystem

If we want to mirror the data over longer distances, then we have to switch to asynchronous remote mirroring. Figure 2.21 illustrates the data flow in asynchronous remote mirroring. In this approach the first disk subsystem acknowledges the receipt of data as soon as it has been temporarily stored in the write cache. The first disk subsystem does not send the copy of the data to the second disk subsystem until later. The write confirmation of the second disk subsystem to the first is not important to the server that has written the data.

The price of the rapid response time achieved using asynchronous remote mirroring is obvious. In contrast to synchronous remote mirroring, in asynchronous remote mirroring there is no guarantee that the data on the second disk subsystem is up-to-date. This is precisely the case if the first disk subsystem has sent the write acknowledgement to the server but the block has not yet been saved to the second disk subsystem.

If we wish to mirror data over long distances but do not want to use only asynchronous remote mirroring it is necessary to use three disk subsystems (Figure 2.22). The first two may be located just a few kilometres apart, so that synchronous remote mirroring can be used between the two. In addition, the data of the second disk subsystem is mirrored onto a third by means of asynchronous remote mirroring. However, this solution comes at a

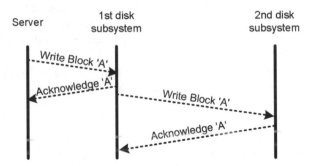

Figure 2.21 In asynchronous remote mirroring one disk subsystem acknowledges a write operation as soon as it has saved the block itself

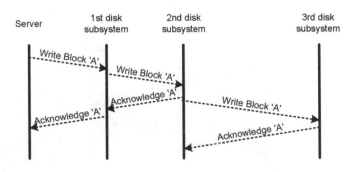

Figure 2.22 The combination of synchronous and asynchronous remote mirroring means that rapid response times can be achieved in combination with mirroring over long distances

price: for most applications the cost of data protection would exceed the costs that would be incurred after data loss in the event of a catastrophe. This approach would therefore only be considered for very important applications.

2.7.3 LUN masking

So-called LUN masking brings us to the third important function – after instant copy and remote mirroring – that intelligent disk subsystems offer over and above that offered by

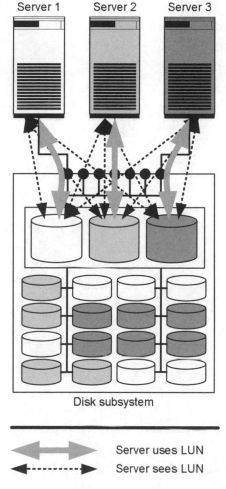

Figure 2.23 Chaos: each server works to its own virtual hard disk. Without LUN masking each server sees all hard disks. A configuration error on server 1 can destroy the data on the other two servers. The data is thus poorly protected

RAID. LUN masking limits the access to the hard disks that the disk subsystem exports to the connected server.

A disk subsystem makes the storage capacity of its internal physical hard disks available to servers by permitting access to individual physical hard disks, or to virtual hard disks created using RAID, via the connection ports. Based upon the SCSI protocol, all hard disks – physical and virtual – that are visible outside the disk subsystem are also known as LUN (Logical Unit Number).

Without LUN masking every server would see all hard disks that the disk subsystem provides. Figure 2.23 shows a disk subsystem without LUN masking to which three servers are connected. Each server sees all hard disks that the disk subsystem exports outwards. As a result, considerably more hard disks are visible to each server than is necessary.

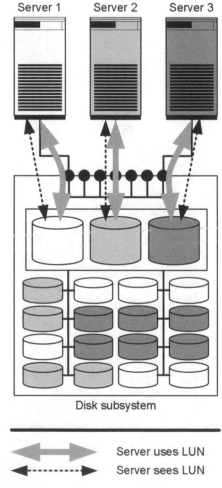

Figure 2.24 Order: each server works to its own virtual hard disk. With LUN masking, each server sees only its own hard disks. A configuration error on server 1 can no longer destroy the data of the two other servers. The data is now protected

In particular, on each server those hard disks that are required by applications that run on a different server are visible. This means that the individual servers must be very carefully configured. In Figure 2.23 an erroneous formatting of the disk LUN 3 of server 1 would destroy the data of the application that runs on server 3. In addition, some operating systems are very greedy: when booting up they try to draw to them each hard disk that is written with the signature (label) of a foreign operating system.

Without LUN masking, therefore, the use of the hard disk must be very carefully configured in the operating systems of the participating servers. LUN masking brings order to this chaos by assigning the hard disks that are externally visible to servers. As a result, it limits the visibility of exported disks within the disk subsystem. Figure 2.24 shows how LUN masking brings order to the chaos of Figure 2.23. Each server now sees only the hard disks that it actually requires. LUN masking thus acts as a filter between the exported hard disks and the accessing servers.

It is now no longer possible to destroy data that belongs to applications that run on another server. Configuration errors are still possible, but the consequences are no longer so devastating. Furthermore, configuration errors can now be more quickly traced since the information is bundled within the disk subsystem instead of being distributed over all servers.

We differentiate between port-based LUN masking and server-based LUN masking. Port-based LUN masking is the 'poor man's LUN masking', it is found primarily in low-end disk subsystems. In port-based LUN masking the filter only works using the granularity of a port. This means that all servers connected to the disk subsystem via the same port see the same disks.

Server-based LUN masking offers more flexibility. In this approach every server sees only the hard disks assigned to it, regardless of which port it is connected via or which other servers are connected via the same port.

2.8 AVAILABILITY OF DISK SUBSYSTEMS

Disk subsystems are assembled from standard components, which have a limited fault-tolerance. In this chapter we have shown how these standard components are combined in order to achieve a level of fault-tolerance for the entire disk subsystem that lies significantly above the fault-tolerance of the individual components. Today, disk subsystems can be constructed so that they can withstand the failure of any component without data being lost or becoming inaccessible. We can also say that such disk subsystems have no 'single point of failure'.

The following list describes the individual measures that can be taken to increase the availability of data:

• The data is distributed over several hard disks using RAID processes and supplemented by further data for error correction. After the failure of a physical hard disk, the data of the defective hard disk can be reconstructed from the remaining data and the additional data.

- Individual hard disks store the data using the so-called Hamming code. The Hamming code allows data to be correctly restored even if individual bits are changed on the hard disk. Self-diagnosis functions in the disk controller continuously monitor the rate of bit errors and the physical variables (temperature sensors, spindle vibration sensors). In the event of an increase in the error rate, hard disks can be replaced before data is lost.

- Each internal physical hard disk can be connected to the controller via two internal I/O channels. If one of the two channels fails, the other can still be used.

- The controller in the disk subsystem can be realized by several controller instances. If one of the controller instances fails, one of the remaining instances takes over the tasks of the defective instance.

- Other auxiliary components such as power supplies, batteries and fans can often be duplicated so that the failure of one of the components is unimportant. When connecting the power supply it should be ensured that the various power cables are at least connected through various fuses. Ideally, the individual power cables would be supplied via different external power networks; however, in practice this is seldom realizable.

- Server and disk subsystem are connected together via several I/O channels. If one of the channels fails, the remaining ones can still be used.

- Instant copies can be used to protect against logical errors. For example, it would be possible to create an instant copy of a database every hour. If a table is 'accidentally' deleted, then the database could revert to the last instant copy in which the database is still complete.

- Remote mirroring protects against physical damage. If, for whatever reason, the original data can no longer be accessed, operation can continue using the data copy that was generated using remote mirroring.

This list shows that disk subsystems can guarantee the availability of data to a very high degree. Despite everything it is in practice sometimes necessary to shut down and switch off a disk subsystem. In such cases, it can be very tiresome to co-ordinate all project groups to a common waiting window, especially if these are distributed over different time zones.

Further important factors for the availability of an entire IT system are the availability of the applications or the application server itself and the availability of the connection between application servers and disk subsystems. Chapter 6 shows how multipathing can improve the connection between servers and storage systems and how clustering can increase the fault-tolerance of applications.

2.9 SUMMARY

Large disk subsystems have a storage capacity of several ten terabytes that is often shared by several servers. The administration of a few large disk subsystems that are used by several servers is more flexible and cheaper than the administration of many individual disks or many small disk stacks. Large disk subsystems are assembled from standard components such as disks, RAM and CPU. Skillful combining of standard components and additional software can make the disk subsystem as a whole significantly more high-performance and more fault-tolerant than its individual components.

A server connected to a disk subsystem sees only the physical and virtual hard disks that the disk subsystem exports via the connection ports and makes available to it by LUN masking. The internal structure is completely hidden to the server. The controller is the control centre of the disk subsystem. The sole advantage of disk subsystems without a controller (JBODs) is that they are simpler to handle than the corresponding number of separate disks without a common enclosure. RAID controllers offer clear advantages over JBODs. They bring together several physical hard disks to form virtual hard disks that can be significantly higher-performance, more fault-tolerant and larger than an individual physical hard disk. In addition to RAID, intelligent controllers realize the copying functions of instant copy and remote mirroring plus LUN masking. With instant copy, data sets up to several terabytes in size can be practically copied within a disk subsystem in a few seconds. Remote mirroring mirrors the data of one disk subsystem to another without server resources being required for this.

Disk subsystems can thus take on many tasks that were previously performed within the operating system. As a result, more and more functions are being moved from the operating system to the storage systems, meaning that intelligent storage systems are moving into the centre of the IT architecture (storage-centric IT architecture). Storage systems and servers are connected together by means of block-oriented I/O techniques such as SCSI, Fibre Channel and iSCSI. These will be described in detail in the next chapter.

3

I/O Techniques

Computers generate, process and delete data. However, they can only store data for very short periods. Therefore, computers move data to storage devices such as tape libraries and the disk subsystems discussed in the previous chapter for long-term storage and fetch it back from these storage media for further processing. So-called I/O techniques realize the data exchange between computers and storage devices. This chapter describes I/O techniques that are currently in use or that the authors believe will very probably be used in the coming years.

This chapter first considers the I/O path from the CPU to the storage system (Section 3.1). An important technique for the realization of the I/O path is SCSI (Section 3.2). To be precise, SCSI defines a medium (SCSI cable) and a communication protocol (SCSI protocol). The idea of Fibre Channel SAN is to replace the SCSI cable by a network that is realized using Fibre Channel technology: servers and storage devices exchange data as before using SCSI commands, but the data is transmitted via the Fibre Channel network instead of via the SCSI cable (Sections 3.3, 3.4). An alternative to Fibre Channel SAN is IP storage. Like Fibre Channel, IP storage connects several servers and storage devices via a network on which data exchange takes place using the SCSI protocol. In contrast to Fibre Channel, however, the devices are connected by TCP/IP and Ethernet (Section 3.5). With InfiniBand, networks move even closer to the CPU. The objective of InfiniBand is to replace the PCI bus in the computer by a serial network (Section 3.6). These new transfer technologies (Fibre Channel, Gigabit Ethernet and in particular InfiniBand) form the basis for lightweight communication connections such as Virtual Interfaces (VI) and Remote Direct Memory Access (RDMA), which permit the fast and efficient exchange of data (Section 3.7). Finally we present an emerging protocol family which combines these lightweight communication connections with TCP/IP. Namely we present RDMA over TCP, the Socket Direct Protocol (SDP) and the iSCSI Extension for RDMA (iSER) (Section 3.8).

Storage Networks Explained   U. Troppens R. Erkens W. Müller
© 2004 John Wiley & Sons, Ltd   ISBN: 0-470-86182-7

3.1 THE PHYSICAL I/O PATH FROM THE CPU TO THE STORAGE SYSTEM

In the computer, one or more CPUs process data that is stored in the CPU cache or in the main memory (Random Access Memory, RAM). CPU cache and main memory are very fast; however, they cannot store data after the power has been switched off. Furthermore, main memory is expensive in comparison to disk and tape storage. Therefore, the data is moved from the main memory to the storage devices such as disk subsystems and tape libraries via system bus, host bus and I/O bus (Figure 3.1). Although storage devices are slower than CPU cache and main memory, they compensate for this by being cheaper and

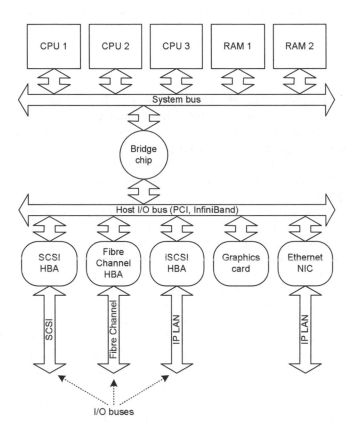

Figure 3.1 The physical I/O path from the CPU to the storage system consists of system bus, host I/O bus and I/O bus. More recent technologies such as InfiniBand, Fibre Channel and iSCSI replace individual buses with a serial network. For historic reasons the corresponding connections are still called host I/O bus or I/O bus

by their ability to store data even when the power is switched off. Incidentally, the same I/O path also exists within a disk subsystem between the connection ports and the disk subsystem controller and between the controller and the internal hard disk (Figure 3.2).

At the heart of the computer, the system bus ensures the rapid transfer of data between CPUs and main memory. The system bus must be timed at a very high frequency so that it can supply the CPU with data sufficiently quickly. It is realized in the form of printed conductors on the main circuit board. Due to physical properties, high system speeds require short printed conductors. Therefore, the system bus is kept as short as possible and thus connects only CPUs and main memory.

In modern computers as many tasks as possible are moved to special processors such as graphics processors in order to free up the CPU for the processing of the application. These cannot be connected to the system bus due to the physical limitations mentioned above. Therefore, most computer architectures realize a second bus, the so-called host I/O bus. So-called bridge communication chips provide the connection between system bus and host I/O bus. Peripheral Component Interconnect (PCI) is currently the most widespread technology for the realization of host I/O buses. InfiniBand is an emerging technology that will very probably replace the parallel PCI bus by a serial network (Section 3.6).

Device drivers are responsible for the control of and communication with peripheral devices of all types. The device drivers for storage devices are partially realized in the form of software that is processed by the CPU. However, part of the device driver for the communication with storage devices is almost always realized by firmware that is processed by special processors (Application Specific Integrated Circuits, ASICs). These ASICs are currently partially integrated into the main circuit board, such as on-board SCSI controllers, or connected to the main board via add-on cards (PCI cards). These add-on cards are usually called network cards (Network Interface Controller, NIC) or simply controllers. Storage devices are connected to the server via the host bus adapter (HBA) or via the on-board controller. The communication connection between controller and peripheral device is called the I/O bus.

The most important technologies for I/O buses are currently SCSI (Small Computer System Interface) and Fibre Channel. SCSI defines a parallel bus that can connect up to 16 servers and storage devices with one another. Fibre Channel, on the other hand, defines different topologies for storage networks that can connect several millions of servers and storage devices. As an alternative to Fibre Channel, the industry is currently experimenting with different options for the realization of storage networks by means of

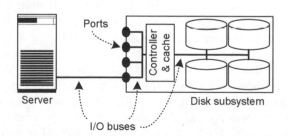

Figure 3.2 The same I/O techniques are used within a disk subsystem as those used between server and disk subsystem

TCP/IP and Ethernet (IP storage). It is worth noting that all new technologies continue
to use the SCSI protocol for device communication.

The Virtual Interface Architecture (VIA) is a further I/O protocol. The VIA permits
rapid and CPU-saving data exchange between two processes that run on two different
servers or storage devices. In contrast to the I/O techniques discussed previously the
Virtual Interface Architecture defines only a protocol. As a medium it requires the existence of a powerful and low-error communication path, which is realized, for example, by
means of Fibre Channel, Gigabit Ethernet or InfiniBand. VIA could become an important
technology for storage networks and server clusters.

There are numerous other I/O bus technologies on the market that will not be discussed
further in this book, for example, Serial Storage Architecture (SSA), IEEE 1394 (Apple's
Firewire, Sony's i.Link), High-Performance Parallel Interface (HIPPI), Advanced Technology Attachment (ATA)/Integrated Drive Electronics (IDE), Serial ATA (SATA) and
Universal Serial Bus (USB). All have in common that they are either used by very
few manufacturers or are not powerful enough for the connection of servers and storage
devices. Some of these technologies can form small storage networks. However, none is
anywhere near as flexible and scalable as the Fibre Channel and IP Storage technologies
described in this book.

3.2 SCSI

The Small Computer System Interface (SCSI) was for a long time *the* technology for I/O
buses in Unix and PC servers, is still very important today and will presumably remain
so for a good many years to come. The first version of the SCSI standard was released in
1986. Since then SCSI has been continuously developed in order to keep it abreast with
technical progress.

3.2.1 SCSI basics

As a medium, SCSI defines a parallel bus for the transmission of data with additional
lines for the control of communication. The bus can be realized in the form of printed
conductors on the circuit board or as a cable. Over time, numerous cable and plug types
have been defined that are not directly compatible with one another (Table 3.1). A so-
called daisy chain can connect up to 16 devices together (Figure 3.3).

The SCSI protocol defines how the devices communicate with each other via the SCSI
bus. It specifies how the devices reserve the SCSI bus and in which format data is
transferred. The SCSI protocol has been further developed over the years. For example,
a server could originally only begin a new SCSI command when the previous SCSI
command had been acknowledged by the partner; however, precisely this overlapping of
SCSI commands is the basis for the performance increase achieved by RAID. Today it
is even possible using asynchronous I/O to initiate several write or read commands to a
storage device at the same time.

Table 3.1 SCSI: maximum cable lengths, transmission speeds

SCSI version	MByte/s	Bus width	Max. no. of devices	Single ended (SE)	High Voltage Differential (HVD)	Low Voltage Differential (LVD)
SCSI-2	5	8	8	6 m	25 m	–
Wide Ultra SCSI	40	16	16	–	25 m	–
Wide Ultra SCSI	40	16	8	1.5 m	–	–
Wide Ultra SCSI	40	16	4	3 m	–	–
Ultra2 SCSI	40	8	8	–	25 m	12 m
Wide Ultra2 SCSI	80	16	16	–	25 m	12 m
Ultra3 SCSI	160	16	16	–	–	12 m
Ultra320 SCSI	320	16	16	–	–	12 m

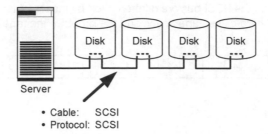

- Cable: SCSI
- Protocol: SCSI

Figure 3.3 An SCSI bus connects one server to several peripheral devices by means of a daisy chain. SCSI defines both the characteristics of the connection cable and also the transmission protocol

The SCSI protocol introduces SCSI IDs (sometimes also called target ID or just ID) and Logical Unit Numbers (LUN) for the addressing of devices. Each device in the SCSI bus must have an unambiguous ID, with the host bus adapter in the server requiring its own ID. Depending upon the version of the SCSI standard, a maximum of 8 or 16 IDs are permitted per SCSI bus. Storage devices such as RAID disk subsystems, intelligent disk subsystems or tape libraries can include several subdevices, such as virtual hard disks, tape drives or a media changer to insert the tapes, which means that the IDs would be used up very quickly. Therefore, so-called LUNs were introduced in order to address subdevices within larger devices (Figure 3.4). A server can be equipped with several SCSI controllers. Therefore, the operating system must note three things for the differentiation of devices – the controller ID, SCSI ID and LUN.

The priority of SCSI IDs is slightly trickier. Originally, the SCSI protocol permitted only eight IDs, with the ID '7' having the highest priority. More recent versions of the SCSI protocol permit 16 different IDs. For reasons of compatibility the IDs '7' to '0' should retain the highest priority, so that the IDs '15' to 8' have a lower priority (Figure 3.5).

Devices (servers and storage devices) must reserve the SCSI bus (arbitrate) before they may send data through it. During the arbitration of the bus, the device that has the highest

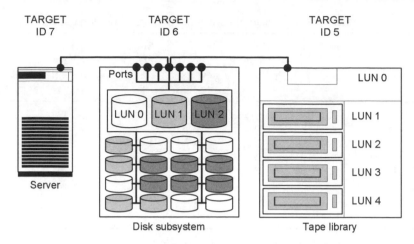

Figure 3.4   Devices on the SCSI bus are differentiated by means of target IDs. Components within devices (virtual hard disks, tape drives and the robots in the tape library) by LUNs

Figure 3.5   SCSI Target IDs with a higher priority win the arbitration of the SCSI bus

priority SCSI ID always wins. In the event that the bus is heavily loaded, this can lead to devices with lower priorities never being allowed to send data. The SCSI arbitration procedure is therefore 'unfair'.

3.2.2   SCSI and storage networks

SCSI is only suitable for the realization of storage networks to a limited degree. First, a SCSI daisy chain can only connect a very few devices with each other. Although it is theoretically possible to connect several servers to a SCSI bus, this does not work very well in practice. Clusters with so-called twin-tailed SCSI cables and a stand-by server have proved their worth in increasing the availability of data and the applications based upon it (Figure 3.6). Both servers can access the shared storage devices, with only one server having active access to the data at any time. If this server fails, then the stand-by server actively accesses the storage device and continues to operate the application.

Second, the maximum lengths of SCSI buses greatly limit the construction of storage networks. Large disk subsystems have over 30 connection ports for SCSI cables, so that several dozen servers can access them (Figure 3.7), and many of the advantages of storage-centric IT architectures can be achieved with this layout. However,

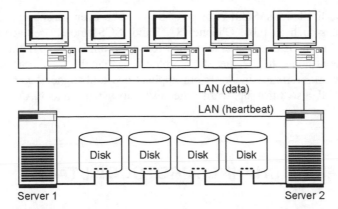

Figure 3.6 In twin-tailed SCSI cabling only one server is active. The second server takes over the devices if the first server fails

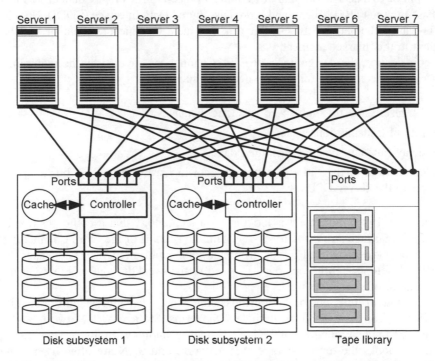

Figure 3.7 SCSI SANs can be built up using multi-port storage systems. The dimensions of servers and storage devices and the length restrictions of the SCSI cable make construction difficult. SCSI SANs are difficult to administer, less flexible and only scalable to a limited degree

due to the dimensions of disk subsystems, tape libraries and servers and the length limits of SCSI buses, constructing the configuration shown in Figure 3.7 using real devices is a challenge. Although it is possible to extend the length of the SCSI buses with so-called link extenders, the use of a large number of link extenders is unwieldy.

Despite these limitations, SCSI is of great importance even for storage-centric IT systems. Techniques such as Fibre Channel SAN and iSCSI merely replace the SCSI bus by a network; the SCSI protocol is still used for communication over this network. The advantage of continuing to use the SCSI protocol is that the transition of SCSI cables to storage networks remains hidden from applications and higher layers of the operating system. SCSI also turns up within the disk subsystems and NAS servers used in storage networks.

3.3   THE FIBRE CHANNEL PROTOCOL STACK

Fibre Channel is currently *the* technique for the realization of storage networks. Interestingly, Fibre Channel was originally developed as a backbone technology for the connection of LANs. The original development objective for Fibre Channel was to supersede Fast-Ethernet (100 Mbit/s) and Fibre Distributed Data Interface (FDDI). Now it looks as if Gigabit Ethernet and 10 Gigabit Ethernet have become prevalent or will become prevalent in this market segment.

By coincidence, the design goals of Fibre Channel are covered by the requirements of a transmission technology for storage networks such as:

- serial transmission for high speed and long distances;
- low rate of transmission errors;
- low delay (latency) of the transmitted data;
- implementation of the Fibre Channel protocol in hardware on host bus adapter cards to free up the server CPUs.

In the early 1990s, Seagate was looking for a technology that it could position against IBM's Serial Storage Architecture (SSA). With the support of the Fibre Channel industry, Fibre Channel was expanded by the arbitrated loop topology, which is cheaper than the originally developed fabric topology. This led to the breakthrough of Fibre Channel for the realization of storage networks.

Fibre Channel is only one of the transmission technologies with which storage area networks (SANs) can be realized. Nevertheless, the terms 'Storage Area Network' and 'SAN' are often used synonymously with Fibre Channel technology. In discussions, newspaper articles and books the terms 'storage area network' and SAN are often used to mean a storage area network that is built up using Fibre Channel. The advantages of storage area networks and server-centric IT architectures can, however, also be achieved using other technologies for storage area networks, for example, iSCSI.

In this book we have taken great pains to express ourselves precisely. We do not use the terms 'storage area network' and 'SAN' on their own. For unambiguous differentiation we always also state the technology, for example, 'Fibre Channel SAN' or 'iSCSI SAN'. In statements about storage area networks in general that are independent of a specific technology we use the term 'storage network'. We use the term 'Fibre Channel' without the suffix 'SAN' when we are referring to the transmission technology that underlies a Fibre Channel SAN.

For the sake of completeness we should also mention that the three letters 'SAN' are also used as an abbreviation for 'System Area Network'. A System Area Network is a network with a high bandwidth and a low latency that serves as a connection between computers in a distributed computer system. In this book we have never used the abbreviation SAN in this manner. However, it should be noted that the VIA standard, for example, does use this second meaning of the abbreviation 'SAN'.

The Fibre Channel protocol stack is subdivided into five layers (Figure 3.8). The lower four layers, FC-0 to FC-3 define the fundamental communication techniques, i.e. the physical levels, the transmission and the addressing. The upper layer, FC-4, defines how application protocols (upper layer protocols, ULPs) are mapped on the underlying Fibre Channel network. The use of the various ULPs decides, for example, whether a real Fibre Channel network is used as an IP network, a Fibre Channel SAN (i.e. as a storage network) or both at the same time. The link services and fabric services are located quasi-adjacent to the Fibre Channel protocol stack. These services will be required in order to administer and operate a Fibre Channel network.

Basic knowledge of the Fibre Channel standard helps to improve understanding of the possibilities for the use of Fibre Channel for a Fibre Channel SAN. This section (Section 3.3) explains technical details of the Fibre Channel protocol. We will restrict the level of detail to the parts of the Fibre Channel standard that are helpful in the administration or the design of a Fibre Channel SAN. Building upon this, the next section (Section 3.4) explains the use of Fibre Channel for storage networks.

3.3.1   Links, ports and topologies

The Fibre Channel standard defines three different topologies: fabric, arbitrated loop and point-to-point (Figure 3.9). Point-to-point defines a bi-directional connection between two devices. Arbitrated loop defines a unidirectional ring in which only two devices can ever exchange data with one another at any one time. Finally, fabric defines a network in which several devices can exchange data simultaneously at full bandwidth. A fabric basically requires one or more Fibre Channel switches connected together to form a control centre between the end devices. Furthermore, the standard permits the connection of one or more arbitrated loops to a fabric. The fabric topology is the most frequently used of all topologies, and this is why more emphasis is placed upon the fabric topology than on the two other topologies in the following.

Common to all topologies is that devices (servers, storage devices and switches) must be equipped with one or more Fibre Channel ports. In servers, the port is generally realized by means of so-called host bus adapters (HBAs, for example, PCI cards) that are also fitted in the server. A port always consists of two channels, one input and one output channel.

The connection between two ports is called a link. In the point-to-point topology and in the fabric topology the links are always bi-directional: in this case the input channel and the output channel of the two ports involved in the link are connected together by

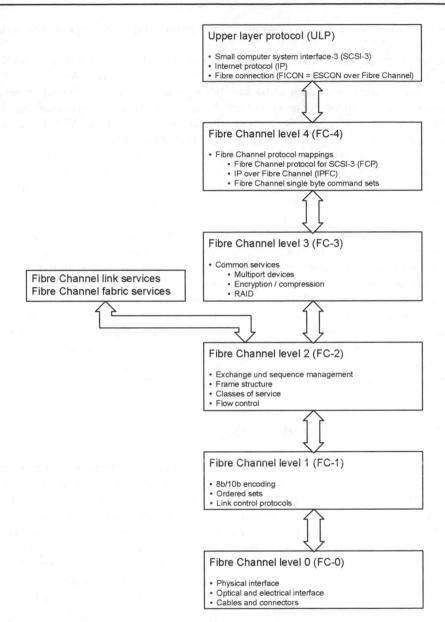

Figure 3.8   The Fibre Channel protocol stack is divided into two parts: the lower four layers (FC-0 to FC-3) realize the underlying Fibre Channel transmission technology. The link services and the fabric services help to administer and configure the Fibre Channel network. The upper layer (FC-4) defines how the application protocols (for example, SCSI and IP) are mapped on a Fibre Channel network

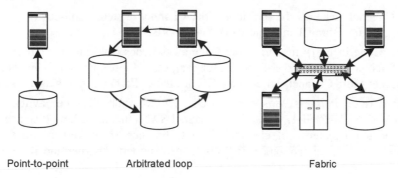

Point-to-point   Arbitrated loop   Fabric

Figure 3.9   The fabric topology is the most flexible and scalable Fibre Channel topology

a cross, so that every output channel is connected to an input channel. On the other hand, the links of the arbitrated loop topology are unidirectional: each output channel is connected to the input channel of the next port until the circle is closed. The cabling of an arbitrated loop can be simplified with the aid of a hub. In this configuration the end devices are bi-directionally connected to the hub; the wiring within the hub ensures that the unidirectional data flow within the arbitrated loop is maintained.

The fabric and arbitrated loop topologies are realized by different, incompatible protocols. We can differentiate between the following port types with different capabilities:

- N-Port (Node_Port): originally the communication of Fibre Channel was developed around N-Ports and F-Ports, with 'N' standing for 'node' and 'F' for 'fabric'. An N-Port describes the capability of a port as an end device (server, storage device), also called node, to participate in the fabric topology or to participate in the point-to-point topology as a partner.

- F-Port (Fabric_Port): F-Ports are the counterpart to N-Ports in the Fibre Channel switch. The F-port knows how it can pass a frame that an N-Port sends to it through the Fibre Channel network on to the desired end device.

- L-Port (Loop_Port): the arbitrated loop uses different protocols for data exchange than the fabric. An L-Port describes the capability of a port to participate in the arbitrated loop topology as an end device (server, storage device). More modern devices are now fitted with NL-Ports instead of L-Ports. Nevertheless, old devices that are fitted with an L-Port are still encountered in practice.

- NL_Port (Node_Loop_Port): an NL-Port has the capabilities of both an N-Port and an L-port. An NL-Port can thus be connected both in a fabric and in an arbitrated loop. Most modern host bus adapter cards are equipped with NL-Ports.

- FL-Port (Fabric_Loop_Port): an FL-Port allows a fabric to connect to a loop. However, this is far from meaning that end devices in the arbitrated loop can communicate with end devices in the fabric. More on the subject of connecting fabric and arbitrated loop can be found in Section 3.4.3.

- E-Port (Expansion_Port): two Fibre Channel switches are connected together by E-Ports. E-Ports transmit the data from end devices that are connected to two different

Fibre Channel switches. In addition, Fibre Channel switches smooth out information over the entire Fibre Channel network via E-ports.

- G-Port (Generic_Port): modern Fibre Channel switches configure their ports automatically. Such ports are called G-Ports. If, for example, a Fibre Channel switch is connected to a further Fibre Channel switch via a G-Port, the G-Port configures itself as an E-Port.

- B-Port (Bridge_Port): B-Ports serve to connect two Fibre Channel switches together via ATM or SONET/SDH. Thus Fibre Channel SANs that are a long distance apart can be connected together using classical WAN techniques. In future versions of the Fibre Channel standard we can expect B-Ports to also support Ethernet and IP.

Some Fibre Channel switches have further, manufacturer-specific port types over and above those in the Fibre Channel standard: these port types provide additional functions. When using such port types, it should be noted that you can sometimes bind yourself to the Fibre Channel switches of a certain manufacturer, which cannot subsequently be replaced by Fibre Channel switches of a different manufacturer.

3.3.2 FC-0: cables, plugs and signal encoding

FC-0 defines the physical transmission medium (cable, plug) and specifies which physical signals are used to transmit the bits '0' and '1'. In contrast to the SCSI bus, in which each bit has its own data line plus additional control lines. Fibre Channel transmits the bits sequentially via a single line. In general, buses come up against the problem that the signals have a different transit time on the different data lines (skew), which means that the speed can only be increased to a limited degree in buses. The different signal transit times can be visualized as the hand rail in an escalator that runs faster or slower than the escalator stairs themselves.

Fibre Channel therefore transmits the bits serially. This means that, in contrast to the parallel bus, a high transfer rate is possible even over long distances. The high transfer rate of serial transmission more than compensates for the parallel lines of a bus. Transfer rates of 200 MByte/s are currently (2003) standard; we expect that in 2004 the first products will support 400 MByte/s and 1 GByte/s. When considering the transfer rate it should be noted that in the fabric and point-to-point topologies the transfer is bi-directional and full-duplex, which means that today the transfer rate of 200 MByte/s is available in each direction.

Fibre Channel defines various cable types (Table 3.2) for copper and fiber-optic cable, where the higher speeds only support fiber-optic. Various plug types are defined both for copper cable and for fiber-optic cable. Figure 3.10 shows various plug types for fiber-optic cable. Apart from their different dimensions, no technical advantages are associated with the various types.

Copper cables are subdivided into 'intracabinct' cables and 'intercabinet' cables. Intra-cabinet cables are designed for cabling within an enclosure, they are less well shielded against electromagnetic interference – and thus cheaper – than intercabinet cable, which can be used to connect up devices outside the limits of enclosures.

Table 3.2   Fibre Channel defines various cable types. The cheapest cable type for the desired connection length can be selected. Today (2003) all products support a transfer rate of 200 MByte/s

Medium	100 MByte/s	200 MByte/s	400 MByte/s	1 GByte/s (Seriell)	1 GByte/s (4 Lane)	1 GByte/s (CWDM)
Copper intracabinet	24 m	–	–			
Copper intercabinet	59 m	–	–	–	–	–
Fiber-optic 62.5 micron	300 m	90 m	50 m	33 m	75 m	290 m
Fiber-optic 50 micron	500 m	300 m	175 m	82 m	150 m	290 m
Fibre-optic 50 micron (High bandwidth)	–	–	–	300 m	300 m	550 m
Fiber-optic 9 micron	10,000 m	2,000 m	2,000 m	10,000 m	–	10,000 m

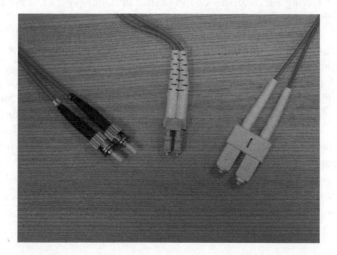

Figure 3.10   Three different plug types for fiber-optic cable

Fiber-optic cables are more expensive than copper cables. They do, however, have some advantages:

- greater distances possible than with copper cable;
- insensitivity to electromagnetic interference;
- no electromagnetic radiation;
- no electrical connection between the devices;
- no danger of 'cross-talking'.

Different cable and plug types are also defined for fiber-optic cable. Cables for long distances are more expensive than those for short distances. The definition of various cables makes it possible to choose the most economical technology for each distance to be bridged.

With 1 GByte Fibre Channel there will be some innovations in fiber-optic cables. First, a new cable type has been introduced – the 50 micron high bandwidth cable – with which greater distances can be spanned than with a conventional 50 micron cable. Second, it will be possible to multiplex the data stream over four connections. This may occur first by distributing the data over four fiber-optic pairs (4 lines). In another variant, Coarse Wavelength Division Multiplexing (CWDM), these four physical lines are replaced by four signals in different frequency ranges, so that one physical pair of lines is sufficient. In practice, we will have to wait and see which of these different cable variants the industry will actually support with real products for 1 GByte Fibre Channel.

For all media, the Fibre Channel standard demands that a single bit error may occur at most once in every 10^{12} transmitted bits. On average, this means that for a 100 Mbit/s connection under full load a bit error may occur only every 16.6 minutes. The error recognition and handling mechanisms of the higher protocol layers are optimized for the maintenance of this error rate. Therefore, when installing a Fibre Channel network it is recommended that the cable is properly laid so that the bit error rate of 10^{12} is, where possible, also achieved for connections from end device to end device, i.e. including all components connected in between such as repeaters and switches.

The distance information in Table 3.2 specifies the minimum distances at which the error rate can reliably be kept within the stipulated figure, given the current state of technology and proper laying of the cable during the timeframe the standard was ratified. Technical improvements and proper laying of the cable make it possible for even greater distances to be bridged in actual installations. Today (2003), distances up to several 10 kilometres are supported for 200 MByte/s. The reduction in the supported cable lengths could represent a problem when upgrading the equipment of an existing Fibre Channel SAN to a higher speed, thus it should be checked in advance, whether a given distance can be bridged at the higher speed as well.

3.3.3   FC-1: 8b/10b encoding, ordered sets and link control protocol

FC-1 defines how data is encoded before it is transmitted via a Fibre Channel cable (8b/10b encoding). FC-1 also describes certain transmission words (ordered sets) that are required for the administration of a Fibre Channel connection (link control protocol).

8b/10b encoding

In all digital transmission techniques, transmitter and receiver must synchronize their clock-pulse rates. In parallel buses the bus rate is transmitted via an additional data line. By contrast, in the serial transmission used in Fibre Channel only one data line is available through which the data is transmitted. This means that the receiver must regenerate the transmission rate from the data stream.

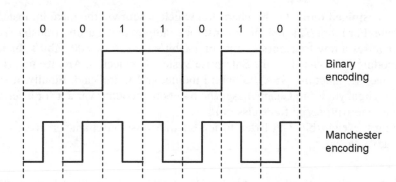

Figure 3.11 In Manchester encoding at least one signal change takes place for every bit transmitted

The receiver can only synchronize the rate at the points where there is a signal change in the medium. In simple binary encoding (Figure 3.11) this is only the case if the signal changes from '0' to '1' or from '1' to '0'. In Manchester encoding there is a signal change for every bit transmitted. Manchester encoding therefore creates two physical signals for each bit transmitted. It therefore requires a transfer rate that is twice as high as that for binary encoding. Therefore, Fibre Channel – like many other transmission techniques – uses binary encoding, because at a given rate of signal changes more bits can be transmitted than is the case for Manchester encoding.

The problem with this approach is that the signal steps that arrive at the receiver are not always the same length (jitter). This means that the signal at the receiver is sometimes a little longer and sometimes a little shorter (Figure 3.12). In the escalator analogy this means that the escalator bucks. Jitter can lead to the receiver losing synchronization with the received signal. If, for example, the transmitter sends a sequence of ten zeros, the receiver cannot decide whether it is a sequence of nine, ten or eleven zeros.

If we nevertheless wish to use binary encoding, then we have to ensure that the data stream generates a signal change frequently enough that jitter cannot strike. The so-called 8b/10b encoding represents a good compromise. 8b/10b encoding converts an eight-bit

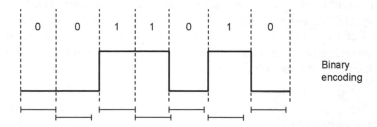

Figure 3.12 Due to physical properties the signals are not always the same length at the receiver (jitter)

byte to be transmitted into a ten-bit character, which is sent via the medium instead of the eight-bit byte. For Fibre Channel this means, for example, that a useful transfer rate of 100 MByte/s requires a raw transmission rate of 1 Gbit/s instead of 800 Mbit/s. Incidentally, 8b/10b encoding is also used for the Enterprise System Connection Architecture (ESCON), Serial Storage Architecture (SSA), Gigabit Ethernet and InfiniBand. Finally, it should be noted that 1 Gigabyte Fibre Channel uses the 64b/66b encoding variant for a certain cable type (single lane with serial transmission).

Expanding the eight-bit data bytes to ten-bit transmission character gives rise to the following advantages:

- In 8b/10b encoding, of all available ten-bit characters, only those that generate a bit sequence that contains a maximum of five zeros one after the other or five ones one after the other for any desired combination of the ten-bit character are selected. Therefore, a signal change takes place at the latest after five signal steps, so that the clock synchronization of the receiver is guaranteed.

- A bit sequence generated using 8b/10b encoding has a uniform distribution of zeros and ones. This has the advantage that only small direct currents flow in the hardware that processes the 8b/10b encoded bit sequence. This makes the realization of Fibre Channel hardware components simpler and cheaper.

- Further ten-bit characters are available that do not represent eight-bit data bytes. These additional characters can be used for the administration of a Fibre Channel link.

Ordered sets

Fibre Channel aggregates four ten-bit transmission characters to form a 40-bit transmission word. The Fibre Channel standard differentiates between two types of transmission word: data words and ordered sets. Data words represent a sequence of four eight-bit data bytes. Data words may only stand between a Start-of-Frame delimiter (SOF delimiter) and an End-of-Frame delimiter (EOF delimiter).

Ordered sets may only stand between an EOF delimiter and a SOF delimiter, with SOFs and EOFs themselves being ordered sets. All ordered sets have in common that they begin with a certain transmission character, the so-called K28.5 character. The K28.5 character includes a special bit sequence that does not occur elsewhere in the data stream. The input channel of a Fibre Channel port can therefore use the K28.5 character to divide the continuous incoming bit stream into 40 bit transmission words when initializing a Fibre Channel link or after the loss of synchronization on a link.

Link control protocol

With the aid of ordered sets, FC-1 defines various link level protocols for the initialization and administration of a link. The initialization of a link is the prerequisite for data exchange by means of frames. Examples of link level protocols are the initialization and arbitration of an arbitrated loop.

3.3.4 FC-2: data transfer

FC-2 is the most comprehensive layer in the Fibre Channel protocol stack. It determines how larger data units (for example, a file) are transmitted via the Fibre Channel network. It regulates the flow control that ensures that the transmitter only sends the data at a speed that the receiver can process it. And it defines various service classes that are tailored to the requirements of various applications.

Exchange, sequence and frame

FC-2 introduces a three-layer hierarchy for the transmission of data (Figure 3.13). At the top layer a so-called exchange defines a logical communication connection between two end devices. For example, each process that reads and writes data could be assigned its own exchange. End devices (servers and storage devices) can simultaneously maintain several exchange relationships, even between the same ports. Different exchanges help the FC-2 layer to deliver the incoming data quickly and efficiently to the correct receiver in the higher protocol layer (FC-3).

A sequence is a larger data unit that is transferred from a transmitter to a receiver. Only one sequence can be transferred after another within an exchange. FC-2 guarantees that sequences are delivered to the receiver in the same order they were sent from the transmitter; hence the name 'sequence'. Furthermore, sequences are only delivered to the next protocol layer up when all frames of the sequence have arrived at the receiver (Figure 3.13). A sequence could represent the writing of a file or an individual database transaction.

A Fibre Channel network transmits control frames and data frames. Control frames contain no useful data, they signal events such as the successful delivery of a data frame. Data frames transmit up to 2112 bytes of useful data. Larger sequences therefore have to be broken down into several frames. Although it is theoretically possible to agree upon different maximum frame sizes, this is hardly ever done in practice.

A Fibre Channel frame consists of a header, useful data (payload) and a CRC checksum (Figure 3.14). In addition, the frame is bracketed by a Start-of-Frame delimiter (SOF) and an End-of-Frame delimiter (EOF). Finally, six filling words must be transmitted by means of a link between two frames. In contrast to Ethernet and TCP/IP, Fibre Channel is an integrated whole: the layers of the Fibre Channel protocol stack are so well harmonized with one another that the ratio of payload to protocol overhead is very efficient at up to 98%. The CRC checking procedure is designed to recognize all transmission errors if the underlying medium does not exceed the specified error rate of 10^{-12}.

Error correction takes place at sequence level: if a frame of a sequence is wrongly transmitted, the entire sequence is retransmitted. At gigabit speed it is more efficient to resend a complete sequence than to extend the Fibre Channel hardware so that individual lost frames can be resent and inserted in the correct position. The underlying protocol

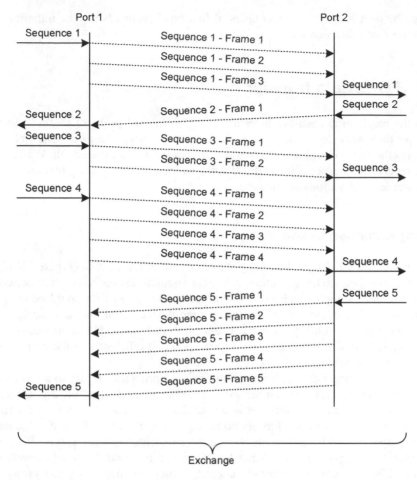

Figure 3.13 One sequence is transferred after another within an exchange. Large sequences are broken down into several frames prior to transmission. On the receiver side, a sequence is not delivered to the next highest protocol layer (FC-3) until all the frames of the sequence have arrived

layer must maintain the specified maximum error rate of 10^{-12} so that this procedure is efficient.

Flow control

Flow control ensures that the transmitter only sends data at a speed that the receiver can receive it. Fibre Channel uses the so-called credit model for this. Each credit represents the capacity of the receiver to receive a Fibre Channel frame. If the receiver awards the

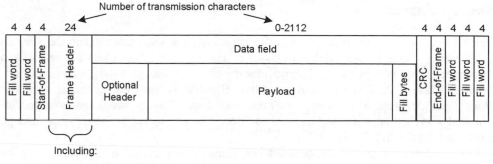

Including:
- Frame Destination Address (D_ID)
- Frame Source Address (S_ID)
- Sequence ID
- Number of the frame within the sequence
- Exhange ID

Figure 3.14 The Fibre Channel frame format

transmitter a credit of '4', the transmitter may only send the receiver four frames. The transmitter may not send further frames until the receiver has acknowledged the receipt of at least some of the transmitted frames.

FC-2 defines two different mechanisms for flow control: end-to-end flow control and link flow control (Figure 3.15). In end-to-end flow control two end devices negotiate the end-to-end credit before the data exchange. The end-to-end flow control is realized on the host bus adapter cards of the end devices. By contrast, link flow control takes place at each physical connection. This is achieved by two communicating ports negotiating the buffer-to-buffer credit. This means that the link flow control also takes place at the Fibre Channel switches.

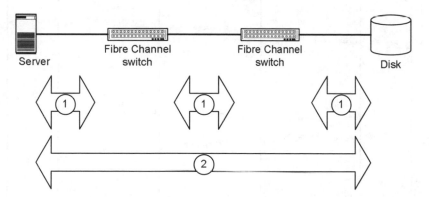

Figure 3.15 In link flow control the ports negotiate the buffer-to-buffer credit at each link (1). By contrast, in end-to-end flow control the end-to-end credit is only negotiated between the end devices (2)

Service classes

The Fibre Channel standard defines six different service classes for data exchange between end devices. Three of these defined classes (Class 1, Class 2 and Class 3) are realized in products available on the market, with hardly any products providing the connection-oriented Class 1. Almost all new Fibre Channel products (host bus adapters, switches, storage devices) support the service classes Class 2 and Class 3, which realize a packet-oriented service (datagram service). In addition, Class F serves for the data exchange between the switches within a fabric.

Class 1 defines a connection-oriented communication connection between two node ports: a Class 1 connection is opened before the transmission of frames. This specifies a route through the Fibre Channel network. Thereafter, all frames take the same route through the Fibre Channel network so that frames are delivered in the sequence in which they were transmitted. A Class 1 connection guarantees the availability of the full bandwidth. A port thus cannot send any other frames while a Class 1 connection is open.

Class 2 and Class 3, on the other hand, are packet-oriented services (datagram services): no dedicated connection is built up, instead the frames are individually routed through the Fibre Channel network. A port can thus maintain several connections at the same time. Several Class 2 and Class 3 connections can thus share the bandwidth.

Class 2 uses end-to-end flow control and link flow control. In Class 2 the receiver acknowledges each received frame (acknowledgement, Figure 3.16). This acknowledgement is used both for end-to-end flow control and for the recognition of lost frames. A

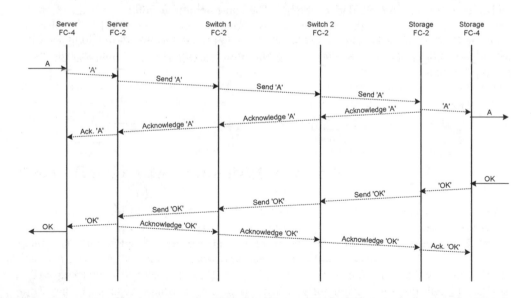

Figure 3.16 Class 2: each Fibre Channel frame transmitted is acknowledged within the FC-2 layer. The acknowledgement aids the recognition of lost frames (see Figure 3.18) and the end-to-end flow control. The link flow control and the conversion of sequences to frames are not shown

missing acknowledgement leads to the immediate recognition of transmission errors by FC-2, which are then immediately signalled to the higher protocol layers. The higher protocol layers can thus initiate error correction measures straight away (Figure 3.18). Users of a Class 2 connection can demand the delivery of the frames in the correct order.

Class 3 achieves less than Class 2: frames are not acknowledged (Figure 3.17). This means that only link flow control takes place, not end-to-end flow control. In addition, the higher protocol layers must notice for themselves whether a frame has been lost. The loss of a frame is indicated to higher protocol layers by the fact that an expected sequence is not delivered because it has not yet been completely received by the FC-2 layer. A switch may dispose of Class 2 and Class 3 frames if its buffer is full. Due to greater time-out values in the higher protocol layers it can take much longer to recognize the loss of a frame than is the case in Class 2 (Figure 3.19).

We have already stated that in practice only Class 2 and Class 3 are important. In practice the service classes are hardly ever explicitly configured, meaning that in current Fibre Channel SAN implementations the end devices themselves negotiate whether they communicate by Class 2 or Class 3. From a theoretical point of view the two service classes differ in that Class 3 sacrifices some of the communication reliability of Class 2 in favour of a less complex protocol. Class 3 is currently the most frequently used service class. This may be because the current Fibre Channel SANs are still very small, so that frames are very seldom lost or overtake each other. The linking of current Fibre Channel SAN islands to a large SAN could lead to Class 2 playing a greater role in future due to its faster error recognition.

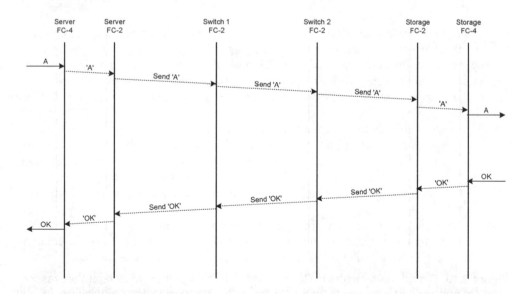

Figure 3.17 Class 3: transmitted frames are not acknowledged in the FC-2 layer. Lost frames must be recognized in the higher protocol layers (see Figure 3.19). The link flow control and the conversion of sequences to frames are not shown

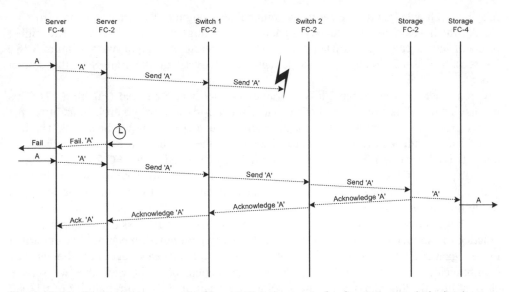

Figure 3.18 Transmission error in Class 2: the time-outs for frames are relatively short on the FC-2 layer. Missing acknowledgements are thus quickly recognized within the FC-2 layer of the transmitter and signalled to the higher protocol levels. The higher protocol layers are responsible for the error processing. In the figure the lost frame is simply resent. The link flow control and the conversion of sequences to frames are not shown

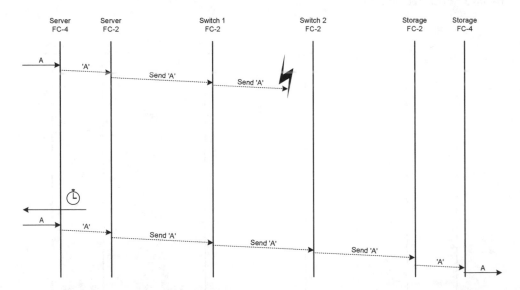

Figure 3.19 Transmission errors in Class 3: here too the higher protocol layers are responsible for error processing. The time-outs in the higher protocol layers are relatively long in comparison to the time-outs in the FC-2 layer. In Class 3 it thus take significantly longer before there is a response to a lost frame. In the figure the lost frame is simply resent. The link flow control and the conversion of sequences to frames are not shown

3.3.5   FC-3: common services

FC-3 has been in its conceptual phase since 1988; in currently available products FC-3 is empty. The following functions are being discussed for FC-3:

- Striping manages several paths between multiport end devices. Striping could distribute the frames of an exchange over several ports and thus increase the throughput between the two devices.
- Multipathing combines several paths between two multiport end devices to form a logical path group. Failure or overloading of a path can be hidden from the higher protocol layers.
- Compressing the data to be transmitted, preferably realized in the hardware on the host bus adapter.
- Encryption of the data to be transmitted, preferably realized in the hardware on the host bus adapter.
- Finally, mirroring and other RAID levels are the last example that are mentioned in the Fibre Channel standard as possible functions of FC-3.

However, the fact that these functions are not realized within the Fibre Channel protocol does not mean that they are not available at all. For example, multipathing functions are currently provided both by suitable additional software in the operating system (Section 6.3.1) and also by some more modern Fibre Channel switches (ISL Trunking).

3.3.6   Link services: login and addressing

Link services and the fabric services discussed in the next section stand next to the Fibre Channel protocol stack. They are required to operate data traffic over a Fibre Channel network. Activities of these services do not result from the data traffic of the application protocols. Instead, these services are required to manage the infrastructure of a Fibre Channel network and thus the data traffic on the level of the application protocols. For example, at any given time the switches of a fabric know the topology of the whole network.

Login

Two ports have to get to know each other before application processes can exchange data over them. To this end the Fibre Channel standard provides a three-stage login mechanism (Figure 3.20):

1. Fabric login (FLOGI)
   The fabric login establishes a session between an N-Port and a corresponding F-Port. The fabric login takes place after the initialization of the link and is an absolute prerequisite for the exchange of further frames. The F-Port assigns the N-Port a dynamic

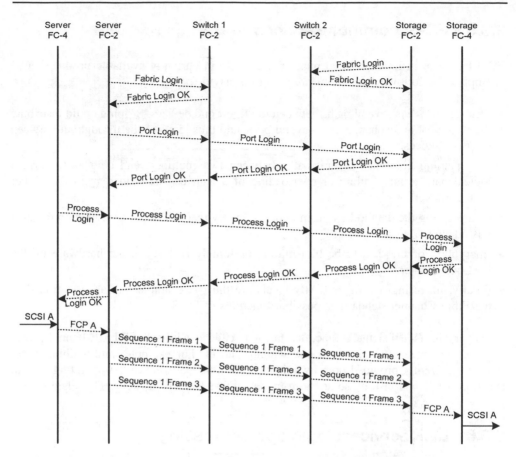

Figure 3.20 Fabric login, N-Port login and process login are the prerequisites for data exchange

address. In addition, service parameters such as the buffer-to-buffer credit are negotiated. The fabric login is crucial for the point-to-point topology and for the fabric topology. An N-Port can tell from the response of the corresponding port whether it is a fabric topology or a point-to-point topology. In arbitrated loop topology the fabric login is optional.

2. N-Port login (PLOGI)
   N-Port login establishes a session between two N-ports. The N-Port login takes place after the fabric login and is a compulsory prerequisite for the data exchange at FC-4 level. N-Port login negotiates service parameters such as end-to-end credit. N-Port login is optional for Class 3 communication and compulsory for all other service classes.

3. Process login (PRLI)
   Process login establishes a session between two FC-4 processes that are based upon two different N-Ports. These could be system processes in Unix systems and system partitions in mainframes. Process login takes place after the N-Port login. Process login

is optional from the point of view of FC-2. However, some FC-4 protocol mappings call for a process login for the exchange of FC-4-specific service parameters.

Addressing

Fibre Channel differentiates between addresses and names. Fibre Channel devices (servers, switches, ports) are differentiated by a 64-bit identifier. The Fibre Channel standard defines different name formats for this. Some name formats guarantee that such a 64-bit identifier will only be issued once world-wide. Such identifiers are thus also known as World Wide Names (WWPN). On the other hand, 64-bit identifiers that can be issued several times in separate networks are simply called Fibre Channel Names (FCN).

In practice this fine distinction between WWN and FCN is hardly ever noticed, with all 64-bit identifiers being called WWNs. In the following we comply with the general usage and use only the term WWN.

World Wide Names are differentiated into World Wide Port Names (WWPNs) and World Wide Node Names (WWNNs). As the name suggests, every port is assigned its own World Wide Name in the form of a World Wide Port Name and in addition the entire device is assigned its own World Wide Name in the form of a World Wide Node Name. The differentiation between World Wide Node Name and World Wide Port Name allows us to determine which ports belong to a common multiport device in the Fibre Channel network. Examples of multiport devices are intelligent disk subsystems with several Fibre Channel ports or servers with several Fibre Channel host bus adapter cards. WWNNs could also be used to realize services such as striping over several redundant physical paths within the Fibre Channel protocol. As discussed above (Section 3.3.5, 'FC-3: common services'), the Fibre Channel standard unfortunately does not support these options, so that such functions are implemented in the operating system or by manufacturer-specific expansions of the Fibre Channel standard.

In the fabric, each 64-bit World Wide Port Name is automatically assigned a 24-bit port address (N-Port identifier, N-Port_ID) during fabric login. The 24-bit port addresses are used within a Fibre Channel frame for the identification of transmitter and receiver of the frame. The port address of the transmitter is called the Source Identifier (S_ID) and that of the receiver the Destination Identifier (D_ID). The 24-bit addresses are hierarchically structured and mirror the topology of the Fibre Channel network. As a result, it is a simple matter for a Fibre Channel switch to recognize which port it must send an incoming frame to from the destination ID (Figure 3.21). Some of the 24-bit addresses are reserved for special purposes, so that 'only' 15.5 million addresses remain for the addressing of devices.

In the arbitrated loop every 64-bit World Wide Port Name is even assigned only an eight-bit address, the so-called Arbitrated Loop Physical Address (AL_PA). Of the 256 possible eight-bit addresses, only those for which the 8b/10b encoded transmission word contains an equal number of zeros and ones may be used. Some ordered sets for the configuration of the arbitrated loop are parametrized using AL_PAs. Only by limiting the values for AL_PAs is it possible to guarantee a uniform distribution of zeros and ones in the whole data stream. After the deduction of a few of these values for the control

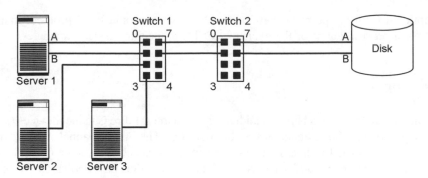

Port_ID	WWPN	WWNN	Device
010000	20000003 EAFE2C31	2100000C EAFE2C31	Server 1, Port A
010100	20000003 C10E8CC2	2100000C EAFE2C31	Server 1, Port B
010200	10000007 FE667122	10000007 FE667122	Server 2
010300	20000003 3CCD4431	2100000A EA331231	Server 3
020600	20000003 EAFE4C31	50000003 214CC4EF	Disk, Port B
020700	20000003 EAFE8C31	50000003 214CC4EF	Disk, Port A

Figure 3.21 Fibre Channel differentiates end devices using World Wide Node Names (WWPN). Each connection port is assigned its own World Wide Port Name (WWPN). For addressing in the fabric WWNNs or WWPNs are converted into shorter Port_IDs that reflect the network topology

of the arbitrated loop, 127 addresses of the 256 possible addresses remain. One of these addresses is reserved for a Fibre Channel switch so only 126 servers or storage devices can be connected in the arbitrated loop.

3.3.7 Fabric services: name server and co

In a fabric topology the switches manage a range of information that is required for the operation of the fabric. This information is managed by the so-called fabric services. All services have in common that they are addressed via FC-2 frames and can be reached by defined addresses (Table 3.3). In the following we introduce the fabric login server, the fabric controller and the name server.

The fabric login server processes incoming fabric login requests under the address '0×FF FF FE'. All switches must support the fabric login under this address.

The fabric controller manages changes to the fabric under the address '0×FF FF FD'. N-Ports can register for state changes in the fabric controller (State Change Registration, SCR). The fabric controller then informs registered N-Ports of changes to the fabric (Registered State Change Notification, RSCN). Servers can use this service to monitor their storage devices.

The name server (Simple Name Server to be precise) administers a database on N-Ports under the address '0×FF FF FC'. It stores information such as port WWN, node WWN, port address, supported service classes, supported FC-4 protocols, etc. N-Ports can register

Table 3.3 The Fibre Channel standard specifies the addresses at which the auxiliary services for the administration and configuration of the Fibre Channel network can be addressed

Address	Description
0×FF FF FF	Broadcast addresses
0×FF FF FE	Fabric Login Server
0×FF FF FD	Fabric Controller
0×FF FF FC	Name Server
0×FF FF FB	Time Server
0×FF FF FA	Management Server
0×FF FF F9	Quality of Service Facilitator
0×FF FF F8	Alias Server
0×FF FF F7	Security Key Distribution Server
0×FF FF F6	Clock Synchronization Server
0×FF FF F5	Multicast Server
0×FF FF F4	Reserved
0×FF FF F3	Reserved
0×FF FF F2	Reserved
0×FF FF F1	Reserved
0×FF FF F0	Reserved

their own properties with the name server and request information on other N-Ports. Like all services, the name server appears as an N-Port to the other ports. N-Ports must log on with the name server by means of port login before they can use its services.

3.3.8 FC-4 and ULPs: application protocols

The layers FC-0 to FC-3 discussed previously serve solely to connect end devices together by means of a Fibre Channel network. However, the type of data that end devices exchange via Fibre Channel connections remains open. This is where the application protocols (upper layer protocols, ULPs) come into play. A specific Fibre Channel network can serve as a medium for several application protocols, for example, SCSI and IP.

The task of the FC-4 protocol mappings is to map the application protocols onto the underlying Fibre Channel network. This means that the FC-4 protocol mappings support the API of existing protocols upwards in the direction of the operating system and realize these downwards in the direction of the medium via the Fibre Channel network (Figure 3.22). The protocol mappings determine how the mechanisms of Fibre Channel are used in order to realize the application protocol by means of Fibre Channel. For example, they specify which service classes will be used and how the data flow in the application protocol will be projected onto the exchange sequence frame mechanism of Fibre Channel. This mapping of existing protocols aims to ease the transition to Fibre Channel networks: ideally, no further modifications are necessary to the operating system except for the installation of a new device driver.

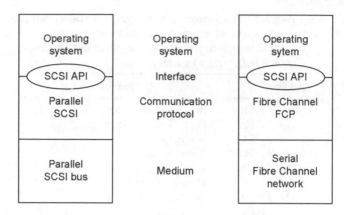

Figure 3.22   Fibre Channel FCP makes its services available to the operating system via the SCSI API. The purpose of this is to ease the transition from SCSI to Fibre Channel SAN

The application protocol for SCSI is called simply Fibre Channel Protocol (FCP). FCP maps the SCSI protocol onto the underlying Fibre Channel network. For the connection of storage devices to servers the SCSI cable is therefore replaced by a Fibre Channel network. The SCSI protocol operates as before via the new Fibre Channel medium to exchange data between server and storage. It is therefore precisely at this point that the transition from server-centric IT architecture to storage-centric IT-architecture takes place. Thus it is here that the Fibre Channel network becomes a Fibre Channel SAN.

The idea of the FCP protocol is that the system administrator merely installs a new device driver on the server and this realizes the FCP protocol. The operating system recognizes storage devices connected via Fibre Channel as SCSI devices, which it addresses like 'normal' SCSI devices. This emulation of traditional SCSI devices should make it possible for Fibre Channel SANs to be simply and painlessly integrated into existing hardware and software.

The FCP driver has to achieve a great deal: SCSI uses parallel cables; daisy chain connects several devices together via a SCSI bus. By contrast, in Fibre Channel the data transmission takes place serially. The parallel transmission via the SCSI bus must therefore be serialized for the Fibre Channel SAN, so that the bits are transferred one after the other. Likewise, FCP must map the daisy chain of the SCSI bus onto the underlying Fibre Channel topology. For example, the scanning for devices on a SCSI bus or the arbitration of the SCSI bus requires a totally different logic compared to the same operations in a Fibre Channel network.

A further application protocol is IPFC: IPFC uses a Fibre Channel connection between two servers as a medium for IP data traffic. To this end, IPFC defines how IP packets will be transferred via a Fibre Channel network. Like all application protocols, IPFC is realized as a device driver in the operating system. The connection into the local IP configuration takes place using 'ipconfig' or 'ifconfig'. The IPFC driver then addresses the Fibre Channel host bus adapter card in order to transmit IP packets over Fibre Channel. The IP data traffic over Fibre Channel plays a less important role both in comparison to SCSI over Fibre Channel and in comparison to IP data traffic over Gigabit Ethernet.

Fibre Connection (FICON) is a further important application protocol. FICON maps the ESCON protocol (Enterprise System Connection) used in the world of mainframes onto Fibre Channel networks. Using ESCON it has been possible to realize storage networks in the world of mainframes since the 1990s. Fibre Channel is therefore taking the old familiar storage networks from the world of mainframes into the Open System world (Unix, Windows NT/2000, OS/400, Novell, MacOS) and both worlds can even realize their storage networks on a common infrastructure.

The Fibre Channel standard also defines a few more application protocols. Particularly worth a mention is the Virtual Interface Architecture (VIA, Section 3.7). VIA describes a very lightweight protocol that is tailored to the efficient communication within server clusters. With VIA it will in future be possible to construct systems of servers and storage devices in which the boundaries between servers and storage devices disappear to an ever greater degree.

3.4 FIBRE CHANNEL SAN

The previous section introduced the fundamentals of the Fibre Channel protocol stack. This section expands our view of Fibre Channel with the aim of realizing storage networks with Fibre Channel. To this end, we will first consider the three Fibre Channel topologies point-to-point, fabric and arbitrated loop more closely (Sections 3.4.1. to 3.4.3). We will then introduce some hardware components that are required for the realization of a Fibre Channel SAN (Section 3.4.4). Building upon this, the networking of small storage network islands to form a large SAN will be discussed (Section 3.4.5). Finally, the question of interoperability in Fibre Channel SANs will be explained (Section 3.4.6).

3.4.1 Point-to-point topology

The point-to-point topology connects just two devices and is not expandable to three or more devices. For storage networks this means that the point-to-point topology connects a server to a storage device. The point-to-point topology may not be very exciting, but it offers two important advantages compared to SCSI cabling. First, significantly greater cable lengths are possible with Fibre Channel than with SCSI because Fibre Channel supports distances up to ten kilometres without repeaters, whilst SCSI supports only up to 25 metres. Second, Fibre Channel defines various fiber-optic cables in addition to copper cables. Optical transmission via fiber-optic is robust in relation to electromagnetic interference and does not emit electromagnetic signals. This is particularly beneficial in technical environments.

Fibre Channel cables are simpler to lay than SCSI cables. For example, the SCSI SAN shown in Figure 3.7 can very simply be realized using the point-to-point topology. Application servers for the control of production can be set up close to the production machines and the data of the application server can be stored on the shared storage systems, which are located in a room that is protected against unauthorized access and physical influences such as fire, water and extremes of temperature.

3.4.2 Fabric topology

The fabric topology is the most flexible and scalable of the three Fibre Channel topologies. A fabric consists of one or more Fibre Channel switches connected together. Servers and storage devices are connected to the fabric by the Fibre Channel switches. In theory a fabric can connect together up to 15.5 million end devices. However, Fibre Channel SANs connected to several hundreds of end devices are currently (2003) still the exception. Most installations use two to four switches. There are, however, a few 'power users', who operate significantly larger Fibre Channel SANs.

End Devices (servers and storage devices) connected to the various Fibre Channel switches can exchange data by means of switch-to-switch connections (inter-switch links, ISLs). Several inter-switch links can be installed between two switches in order to increase the bandwidth. A transmitting end device only needs to know the Node_ID of the target device; the necessary routing of the Fibre Channel frame is taken care of by the Fibre Channel switches. Fibre Channel switches generally support so-called cut-through routing: cut-through routing means that a Fibre Channel switch forwards an incoming frame before it has been fully received.

The latency describes the period of time that a component requires to transmit a signal or the period of time that a component requires to forward a frame. Figure 3.23 compares the latency of different Fibre Channel SAN components. Light requires approximately 25 microseconds to cover a distance of ten kilometres. A ten kilometre-long Fibre Channel cable thus significantly increases the latency of an end-to-end connection. For hardware

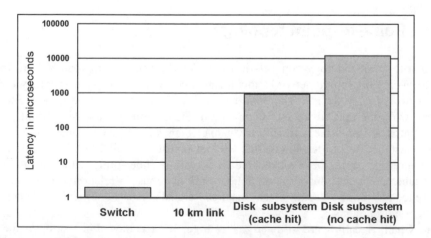

Figure 3.23 The latency of the Fibre Channel switches is low in comparison to the latency of the end devices. The latency of a 10 km link in comparison to the latency of a switch is worth noting (note the logarithmic scale of the y-axis!)

components the rule of thumb is that a Fibre Channel switch can forward a frame in two
to four microseconds; a Fibre Channel host bus adapter requires two to four milliseconds
to process it. Additional Fibre Channel switches between two end devices therefore only
increase the latency of the network to an insignificant degree.

One special feature of the fabric is that several devices can send and receive data
simultaneously at the full data rate. All devices thus have the full bandwidth available
to them at the same time. Figure 3.24 shows a Fibre Channel SAN with three servers
and three storage devices, in which each server works to its own storage device. Each of
the three logical connections over the Fibre Channel SAN has the full bandwidth of 200
MByte/s available to them.

A prerequisite for the availability of the full bandwidth is good design of the Fibre
Channel network. Figure 3.25 shows a similar structure to that in Figure 3.24, the only
difference is that the single switch has been replaced by two switches, which are connected
via one inter-switch link (ISL). It is precisely this inter-switch link that represents the
limiting factor because all three logical connections now pass through the same inter-
switch link. This means that all three connections have, on average, only a third of the
maximum bandwidth available to them. Therefore, despite cut-through routing, switches
have a certain number of buffers (frame buffers) available to them, with which they can
temporarily bridge such bottlenecks. However, the switch must still reject valid frames if
the flow control does not engage quickly enough.

In addition to routing, switches realize the basic services of aliasing, name server and
zoning. As described in Section 3.3.6, end devices are differentiated using 64-bit World
Wide Node Names (WWNNs) or by 64-bit World Wide Port Names (WWPNs) and
addressed via 24-bit port addresses (N-Port_ID). To make his job easier the administrator
can issue alias names to WWNs and ports.

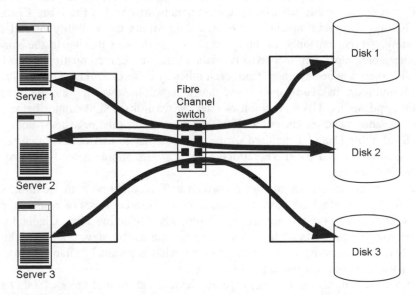

Figure 3.24 The switch can enable several connections at full bandwidth. The fabric thus
has a higher total throughput (aggregate bandwidth) than the individual links

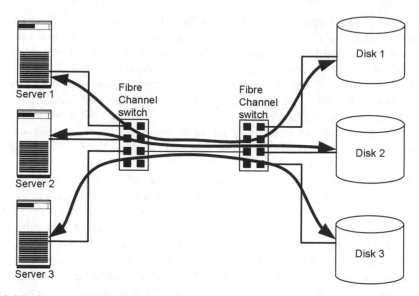

Figure 3.25 Inter-switch links (ISLs) quickly become performance bottlenecks: the total throughput of the three connections is limited by the ISL

The name server supplies information about all end devices connected to the Fibre Channel SAN (Section 3.3.7). If an end device is connected to a switch, it reports to this and registers itself with the name server. At the same time it can ask the name server which other devices are still connected to the SAN. The name server administers end devices that are currently active; switched off end devices are not listed in the name server.

Finally, zoning makes it possible to define subnetworks within the Fibre Channel network. This has two main advantages. First, zoning limits the visibility of end devices. With zoning, servers can only see and access storage devices that lie in the same zone. Zoning therefore helps to protect sensitive data. Furthermore, incompatible Fibre Channel host bus adapters can be separated from each other by different zones. Second, individual ports of a multiport disk subsystem – and thus a certain bandwidth – can be reserved for important applications. The bandwidth of inter-switch links (ISLs) cannot be reserved in this manner since switches currently (2003) do not support this, or at least not officially. Although the Fibre Channel standard defines service classes that reserve a certain bandwidth (Classes 1, 4 and 6), these service classes are not implemented in most current Fibre Channel devices.

There are many variants of zoning, for which unfortunately no consistent terminology exists. Different manufacturers use the same term for different types of zoning and different terms for the same type of zoning. Therefore, when selecting Fibre Channel switches do not let yourself get fobbed off with statements such as 'the device supports hard zoning'. Rather, it is necessary to ask very precisely what is meant by 'hard zoning'. In the following we introduce various types of zoning.

In zoning, the administrator brings together devices that should see each other in Fibre Channel SAN into a zone, whereby zones can overlap. Zones are described by World Wide Node Names, World Wide Port Names, port addresses or by their alias names. The description on the basis of WWNNs and WWPNs has the advantage that zoning is robust in relation to changes in cabling: it does not need to be changed for a device to be plugged into a different switch port. By contrast, zoning on the basis of port addresses must be altered since every port in the switch has a different port address.

Soft zoning restricts itself to the information of the name server. If an end device asks the name server about other end devices in the Fibre Channel network, it is only informed of the end devices with which it shares at least one common zone. If, however, an end device knows the address (Port_ID) of another device, it can still communicate with it. Soft zoning thus does not protect access to sensitive data. Soft zoning is problematic in relation to operating systems that store the WWNs of Fibre Channel devices that have been found in an internal database or in which WWNs are announced in configuration files because this means that WWNs remain known to the operating system even after a system reboot. Thus in soft zoning operating systems continue to have access to all known devices despite changes to the zoning, regardless of whether they lie in a common zone or not.

Hard zoning offers better protection. In hard zoning only devices that share at least one common zone can actually communicate with one another. Both hard zoning and soft zoning can be based upon port addresses or WWNs. Nevertheless, port-based zoning is sometimes known as hard zoning.

Some more modern Fibre Channel switches support LUN masking – described in Section 2.7.3 in relation to disk subsystems – within the switch. To achieve this they read the first bytes of the payload of each Fibre Channel frame. Although reading part of the Fibre Channel payload increases the latency of a Fibre Channel switch, this increase in latency is so minimal that it is insignificant in comparison to the latency of the host bus adapter in the end devices.

So-called virtual storage area networks (virtual SAN, VSAN) represent a further innovation. In this technique, several ports or WWNs and thus several end devices of a Fibre Channel fabric, are grouped together to form a virtual fabric. This means that several virtual Fibre Channel fabrics that are logically separate from one another can be operated over one physical Fibre Channel network. In addition, separate fabric services such as name server and zoning are realized for each virtual storage network. In addition to pure zoning, virtual storage networks thus not only limit the mutual visibility of end devices but also the mutual visibility of the fabric configuration. This is particularly advantageous in installations which aim to offer storage services for various customers over a consolidated infrastructure. Here, in particular, it is not desirable for a customer to be able to read which end devices belonging to other customers are still connected in the storage network, or even change their configuration, over the name server.

3.4.3 Arbitrated loop topology

An arbitrated loop connects servers and storage devices by means of a ring. Data transmission in the ring can only take place in one direction. At any one time only two devices can exchange data with one another – the others have to wait until the arbitrated loop becomes free. Therefore, if six servers are connected to storage devices via an arbitrated loop, each server has on average only one-sixth of the maximum bandwidth. Instead of 200 MByte/s it can, on average, only send and receive data at 33.3 MByte/s.

In general, hubs are used to simplify the cabling (Figure 3.26). To increase the size of the arbitrated loop several hubs can be cascaded together (Figure 3.27). Hubs are invisible to the connected end devices. The arbitrated loop is less scalable and flexible than the fabric: a maximum of 126 servers and storage devices can be connected in an arbitrated loop. In addition, a switch can connect a loop to a fabric.

Arbitrated loops do not support any additional services such as aliasing, routing, name server and zoning. Therefore, the components for arbitrated loops are significantly cheaper than the components for a fabric. The price advantage of the arbitrated loop has helped the Fibre Channel technology to finally make a breakthrough. The fabric topology is now increasingly displacing the arbitrated loop due to its better scalability in the sense of the number of connected devices and the higher aggregated bandwidth of the storage

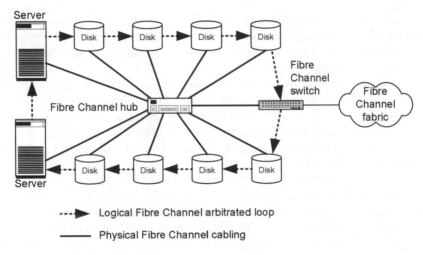

Figure 3.26 Fibre Channel hubs simplify the cabling of Fibre Channel arbitrated loops. A switch can connect a loop to a fabric

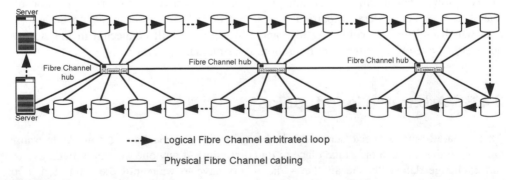

Figure 3.27 An arbitrated loop can span several hubs (cascading)

network as a whole. In new installations arbitrated loop is seldom used for the connection of servers and storage devices, for example in the connection of individual hard disks or individual tape drives that are fitted with Fibre Channel ports instead of SCSI ports. However, for cost reasons the arbitrated loop still remains important for the realization of I/O buses within disk subsystems (Figure 3.2).

Arbitrated loops are subdivided into public loops and private loops (Figure 3.28). A private loop is closed in on itself; a public loop is connected to a fabric by a switch. Physically, a public loop can be connected to a fabric via several Fibre Channel switches. However, in an arbitrated loop only one switch can be active at any one time. The other switches serve merely to increase the fault-tolerance if one switch fails.

The connection of an arbitrated loop to a fabric via a Fibre Channel switch is, however, not enough to permit communication between end devices in the loop and end devices in the fabric. A device in a public arbitrated loop can only communicate with devices in the fabric if it controls both the arbitrated loop protocol and the fabric protocol. This means that the end device must have an NL-port. End devices connected to NL-Ports in arbitrated loops are called public loop devices. Figure 3.29 shows the communication of a public loop device with a device in the fabric.

Unlike public loop devices, private loop devices only have an L-Port. They therefore control only the arbitrated loop protocol. Private loop devices thus cannot be connected to a fabric and cannot communicate with devices in the fabric if they are connected in a public loop.

So-called emulated loops can help here. Emulated loops are manufacturer-specific upgrades produced by the Fibre Channel switch manufacturer that are not compatible

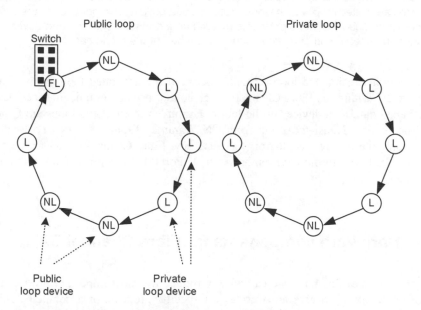

Figure 3.28 In contrast to private loops, public loops are connected to a fabric via a switch. Public loop devices master both the fabric and the loop protocol; private loop devices master only the loop protocol

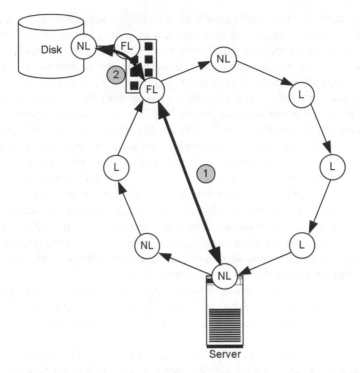

Disk

Server

Figure 3.29 For the communication from loop to fabric the public loop device must first arbitrate the arbitrated loop with the loop protocols and build up a connection to the switch (1). From there it can use the fabric protocols to build up a connection to the end device (2). The loop cannot be used by other devices during this time but the fabric can

with one another. Emulated loops translate between the arbitrated loop protocol and the fabric protocol within the Fibre Channel switch so that private loop devices can neverthe-less exchange data with devices in the fabric. Examples of emulated loops are Quickloop from Brocade and Translated Loop from CNT/Inrange. Emulated loops no longer play an important role in new installations because new Fibre Channel devices are generally fitted with NL-Ports. In old devices, however, L-Ports that cannot be exchanged are still encountered.

3.4.4   Hardware components for Fibre Channel SAN

Within the scope of this book we can only introduce the most important product groups. It is not worth trying to give an overview of specific products or a detailed description of individual products due to the short product cycles. This section mentions once again some product groups that have been discussed previously and introduces some product groups that have not yet been discussed.

It is self-evident that servers and storage devices are connected to a Fibre Channel network. In the server this can be achieved by fitting the host bus adapter cards (HBAs) of different manufacturers, with each manufacturer offering different HBAs with differing performance features. In storage devices the same HBAs are normally used. However, the manufacturers of storage devices restrict the selection of HBAs.

Of course, cables and connectors are required for cabling. In Section 3.3.2 we discussed different copper and fiber-optic cables and their properties. Various connector types are currently on offer for all cable types. It may sound banal, but in practice the installation of a Fibre Channel SAN is sometimes delayed because the connectors on the cable do not fit the connectors on the end devices, hubs and switches and a suitable adapter is not to hand.

A further, initially improbably, but important device is the so-called Fibre Channel-to-SCSI bridge. As the name suggests, a Fibre Channel-to-SCSI bridge creates a connection between Fibre Channel and SCSI (Figure 3.30). These bridges have two important fields of application. First, old storage devices often cannot be converted from SCSI to Fibre Channel. If the old devices are still functional they can continue to be used in the Fibre Channel SAN by the deployment of a Fibre Channel-to-SCSI bridge. Second, new tape libraries in particular often initially only support SCSI; the conversion to Fibre Channel is often not planned until later. With a Fibre Channel-to-SCSI bridge the newest tape libraries can be operated directly in a Fibre Channel SAN and Fibre Channel connections retrofitted as soon as they become available. Unfortunately, the manufacturers have not agreed upon a consistent name for this type of device. In addition to Fibre Channel-to-SCSI bridge, terms such as SAN router or storage gateway are also common.

The switch is the control centre of the fabric topology. It provides routing and aliasing, name server and zoning functions. Fibre Channel switches support both cut-through routing and the buffering of frames. In new switches a number of ports between eight and about 250 and a data transfer rate of 200 MByte/s should currently (2003) be viewed as standard. In Fibre Channel SANs that have already been installed, however, a large base of switches exists that still work at 100 MByte/s.

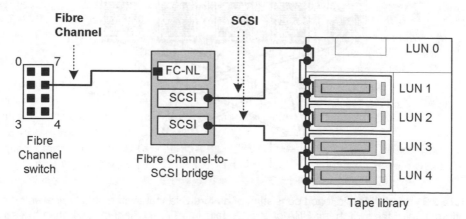

Figure 3.30 Fibre Channel-to-SCSI bridges translate between Fibre Channel FCP and SCSI. This makes it possible to connect old SCSI devices into a Fibre Channel SAN

Resilient, enterprise-class switches are commonly referred to as 'directors', named after the switching technology used in mainframe ESCON cabling. Like Fibre Channel switches they provide routing, alias names, name server and zoning functions. Fibre Channel directors are designed to avoid any single point of failure, having for instance two backplanes and two controllers. Current directors (2003) have between 64 and 256 ports.

Designing a SAN often raises the question whether several complementary switches or a single director should be preferred. As described, directors are more fault-tolerant than switches, but they are more expensive per port. Therefore, designers of small entry-level SANs commonly choose two complementary Fibre Channel switches, with mutual traffic fail-over in case of a switch or a I/O path failure (Figure 3.31). Designers of larger Fibre Channel SANs often favour directors due to the number of ports currently available per device and the resulting layout simplicity. However, this argument in favour of directors becomes more and more obsolete since today switches with a greater number of ports are available as well.

SANs running especially critical applications, e.g. stock market banking or flight control, would use complementary directors with mutual traffic failover, even though these directors already avoid internal single points of failure. This is similar to wearing trousers with a belt and braces in addition: protecting against double or triple failures. In less critical cases, a single director or a dual complementary switch solution will be considered sufficient.

If we disregard the number of ports and the cost, the decision for a switch or a director in an Open Systems Fibre Channel network primarily comes down to fault-tolerance of

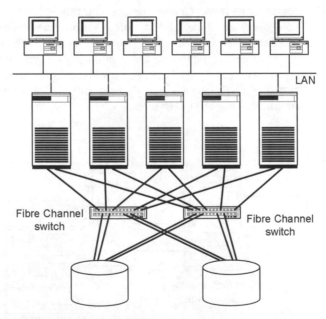

Figure 3.31 A dual fabric, each consisting of a Fibre Channel switch, is a typical entry-level configuration. If the switch, an HBA or a cable fails in a Fibre Channel SAN, then the server can still access the data via the second SAN. Likewise, zoning errors are isolated to one of the two SANs

an individual component. For the sake of simplicity we will use the term 'Fibre Channel switch' throughout this book in place of 'Fibre Channel switch or Fibre Channel director'.

A hub simplifies the cabling of an arbitrated loop. Hubs are transparent from the point of view of the connected devices. This means that hubs send on the signals of the connected devices; in contrast to a Fibre Channel switch, however, the connected devices do not communicate with the hub. Hubs change the physical cabling from a ring to a star-shape. Hubs bridge across defective and switched-off devices, so that the physical ring is maintained for the other devices. The arbitrated loop protocol is located above this cabling.

Hubs are divided into unmanaged hubs, managed hubs and switched hubs. Unmanaged hubs are the cheap version of hubs: they can only bridge across switched-off devices. However, they can neither intervene in the event of protocol infringements by an end device nor indicate the state of the hub or the arbitrated loop to the outside world. This means that an unmanaged hub cannot itself notify the administrator if one of its components is defective. A very cost-conscious administrator can build up a small SAN from PC systems, JBODs and unmanaged hubs. However, the upgrade path to a large Fibre Channel SAN is difficult: in larger Fibre Channel SANs it is questionable whether the economical purchase costs compensate for the higher administration costs.

In contrast to unmanaged hubs, managed hubs have administration and diagnosis functions like those that are a matter of course in switches and directors. Managed hubs monitor the power supply, serviceability of fans, temperature, and the status of the individual ports. In addition, some managed hubs can, whilst remaining invisible to the connected devices, intervene in higher Fibre Channel protocol layers, for example, to deactivate the port of a device that frequently sends invalid Fibre Channel frames. Managed hubs, like switches and directors, can inform the system administrator about events via serial interfaces, Telnet, HTTP and SNMP (see also Chapter 8).

Finally, the switched hub is mid-way between a hub and a switch. In addition to the properties of a managed hub, with a switched hub several end devices can exchange data at full bandwidth. Fibre Channel switched hubs are cheaper than Fibre Channel switches, so in some cases they represent a cheap alternative to switches. However, it should be noted that only 126 devices can be connected together via hubs and that services such as aliasing and zoning are not available. Furthermore, the protocol cost for the connection or the removal of a device in a loop is somewhat higher than in a fabric (keyword 'Loop Initialisation Primitive Sequence', 'LIP').

Finally, so-called link extenders should also be mentioned. Fibre Channel supports a maximum cable length of several ten kilometres (Section 3.3.2). A link extender can increase the maximum cable length of Fibre Channel by transmitting Fibre Channel frames using MAN/WAN techniques such as ATM, SONET or TCP/IP (Figure 3.32). When using link extenders it should be borne in mind that long distances between end devices significantly increase the latency of a connection. Time-critical applications such as database transactions should therefore not run over a link extender. On the other hand, Fibre Channel SANs with link extenders offer new possibilities for applications such as back-up, data sharing and asynchronous data mirroring.

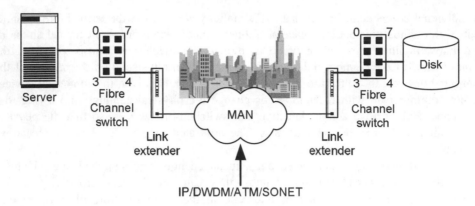

Figure 3.32 A link extender can connect two storage networks over long distances

3.4.5 InterSANs

Fibre Channel SAN is a comparatively new technology. In many data centres in which Fibre Channel SANs are used, it is currently (2003) more likely that there will be several islands of small Fibre Channel SANs than one large Fibre Channel SAN (Figure 3.33). Over 80% of the installed Fibre Channel SANs consist only of up to four Fibre Channel switches. A server can only indirectly access data stored on a different SAN via the LAN and a second server. The reasons for the islands of small Fibre Channel SANs are that they are simpler to manage than one large Fibre Channel SAN and that it was often unnecessary to install a large one.

Originally, Fibre Channel SAN was used only as an alternative to SCSI cabling. Until now the possibility of flexibly dividing the capacity of a storage device between several servers (storage pooling) and the improved availability of dual SANs have been the main reasons for the use of Fibre Channel SANs. Both can be realized very well with several small Fibre Channel SAN islands. However, more and more applications are now exploiting the possibilities offered by a Fibre Channel SAN. Applications such as back-up

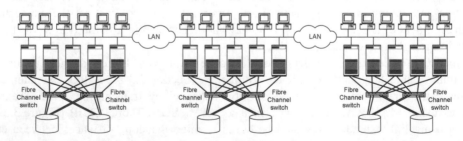

Figure 3.33 Current IT environments (2003) consist almost exclusively of small Fibre Channel SANs that are designed with built-in redundancy. If a server has to access storage devices that are connected to a different SAN, it has to take the indirect route via the LAN and a further server

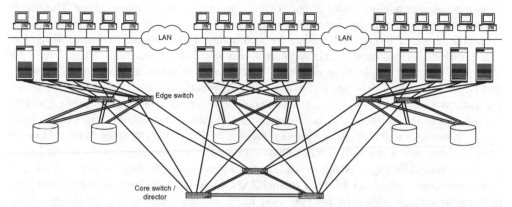

Figure 3.34 More and more applications are exploiting the new possibilities offered by Fibre Channel SAN. In order to make better use of the new possibilities of storage networks it is necessary to connect the individual SAN islands

(Chapter 7), remote data mirroring and data sharing over Fibre Channel SAN (Chapter 6) and storage virtualization (Chapter 5) require that all servers and storage devices are connected via a single SAN.

Incidentally, the connection of Fibre Channel SANs to form a large SAN could be one field of application in which a Fibre Channel director is preferable to a Fibre Channel switch (Figure 3.34). As yet these connections are generally not critical. In the future, however, this could change (extreme situation: virtualization over several data centres). In our opinion these connection points between two storage networks tend to represent a single point of failure, so they should be designed to be particularly fault-tolerant.

3.4.6 Interoperability of Fibre Channel SAN

Fibre Channel SANs are currently being successfully used in production environments. Nevertheless, interoperability is an issue with Fibre Channel SAN, as in all new cross-manufacturer technologies. When discussing the interoperability of Fibre Channel SAN we must differentiate between the interoperability of the underlying Fibre Channel network layer, the interoperability of the Fibre Channel application protocols, such as FCP (SCSI over Fibre Channel) and the interoperability of the applications running on the Fibre Channel SAN.

The interoperability of Fibre Channel SAN stands and falls by the interoperability of FCP. FCP is the protocol mapping of the FC-4 layer, which maps the SCSI protocol on a Fibre Channel network (Section 3.3.8).

The FCP is a complex piece of software that can only be implemented in the form of a device driver. The implementation of hardware-like device drivers alone is a task that attracts errors as if by magic. The developers of FCP device drivers must therefore test extensively and thoroughly.

Two general conditions make it more difficult to test the FCP device driver. The server initiates the data transfer by means of the SCSI protocol; the storage device only responds to the requests of the server. However, the idea of storage networks is to consolidate storage devices, i.e. for many servers to share a few large storage devices. Therefore, with storage networks a single storage device must be able to serve several parallel requests from different servers simultaneously. For example, it is typical for a server to be exchanging data with a storage device just when another server is scanning the Fibre Channel SAN for available storage devices. This situation requires end devices to be able to multitask. When testing multitasking systems the race conditions of the tasks to be performed come to bear: just a few milliseconds delay can lead to a completely different test result.

The second difficulty encountered during testing is due to the large number of components that come together in a Fibre Channel SAN. Even when a single server is connected to a single storage device via a single switch, there are numerous possibilities that cannot all be tested. If, for example, a Windows server is selected, there is still the choice between NT, 2000 and 2003, each with different service packs. Several manufacturers offer several different models of the Fibre Channel host bus adapter card in the server. If we take into account the various firmware versions for the Fibre Channel host bus adapter cards we find that we already have more than 50 combinations before we even select a switch.

Companies want to use their storage network to connect servers and storage devices from various manufacturers, some of which are already present. The manufacturers of Fibre Channel components (servers, switches and storage devices) must therefore perform interoperability tests in order to guarantee that these components work with devices from third-party manufacturers. Right at the top of the priority list are those combinations that are required by most customers, because this is where the expected profit is the highest. The result of the interoperability test is a so-called support matrix. It specifies, for example, which storage device supports which server model with which operating system versions and Fibre Channel cards. Manufacturers of servers and storage devices often limit the Fibre Channel switches that can be used.

Therefore, before building a Fibre Channel SAN you should carefully check whether the manufacturers in question state that they support the planned configuration. If the desired configuration is not listed, you can negotiate with the manufacturer regarding the payment of a surcharge to secure manufacturer support. Although non-supported configurations can work very well, if problems occur, you are left without support in critical situations. If in any doubt you should therefore look for alternatives right at the planning stage.

All this seems absolutely terrifying at first glance. However, manufacturers now support a number of different configurations. If the manufacturers' support matrices are taken into consideration, robust Fibre Channel SANs can now be operated. The operation of up-to-date operating systems such as Windows NT/2000, AIX, Solaris, HP-UX and Linux is particularly unproblematic.

Fibre Channel SANs are based upon Fibre Channel networks. The incompatibility of the fabric and arbitrated loop topologies and the networking of fabrics and arbitrated loops has already been discussed in Section 3.4.3. Within the fabric, the incompatibility of the Fibre Channel switches from different manufacturers should also be mentioned. At the end of 2003 we still recommend that when installing a Fibre Channel SAN only the switches and directors of a single manufacturer are used. Even though routing between switches and directors of different manufacturers may work as expected, and basic functions of the fabric topology such as aliasing, name server and zoning work well across different vendors in so-called 'compatibility modes'. But bear in mind that there is still only a very small installed base of mixed switch vendor configurations. A standard has been passed that addresses the interoperability of these basic functions, meaning that it is now just a matter of time before these basic functions work across every manufacturers' products. However, for new functions such as SAN security, inter-switch-link trunking or B-Ports, teething troubles with interoperability must once again be expected.

In general, applications can be subdivided into higher applications that model and support the business processes and system-based applications such as file systems, databases and back-up systems. The system-based applications are of particular interest from the point of view of storage networks and storage management. The compatibility of network file systems such as NFS and CIFS is now taken for granted and hardly ever queried. As storage networks penetrate into the field of file systems, cross-manufacturer standards are becoming ever more important in this area too. A first offering is Network Data Management Protocol (NDMP, Section 7.9.4) for the back-up of NAS servers. Further down the road we expect also a customer demand for cross-vendor standards in the emerging field of storage virtualization (Chapter 5).

The subject of interoperability will preoccupy manufacturers and customers in the field of storage networks for a long time to come. Virtual Interface Architecture (VIA), Infini-Band and Remote Direct Memory Access (RDMA) represent emerging new technologies that must also work in a cross-manufacturer manner. The same applies for Internet SCSI (iSCSI) and its variants like iSCSI Extensions over RDMA (iSER). iSCSI transmits the SCSI protocol via TCP/IP and, for example, Ethernet. Just like FCP, iSCSI has to serialize the SCSI protocol bit-by-bit and map it onto a complex network topology. Interoperability will therefore also play an important role in iSCSI.

3.5   IP STORAGE

Fibre Channel SANs are currently (2003) being successfully implemented in production environments. Nevertheless, the industry is at pains to establish storage networks based upon IP (IP storage) and Ethernet as an alternative to Fibre Channel. This section first introduces various protocols for the transmission of storage data traffic via TCP/IP (Section 3.5.1). Then we explain to what extent TCP/IP and Ethernet are suitable transmission techniques for storage networks at all (Section 3.5.2). Finally, we discuss a migration path from SCSI and Fibre Channel to IP storage (Section 3.5.3).

3.5.1   IP storage standards: iSCSI, iFCP, mFCP, FCIP and iSNS

Three protocols are available for transmitting storage data traffic over TCP/IP: Internet SCSI (iSCSI), Internet FCP (iFCP) and Fibre Channel over IP (FCIP) – not to be confused with IPFC. They form the family of IP-based storage protocols that are also known as IP storage. These standards have in common that in one form or another they transmit SCSI over IP and thus in practice usually over Ethernet. Although we do not yet know which of these standards will dominate the IP storage market, if we look at the products announced by manufacturers we find that iSCSI and FCIP are currently receiving the most attention.

'Storage over IP (SoIP)' is sometimes called a standard in association with IP storage. This is incorrect: SoIP is a product from Nishan Technologies (acquired by McData Corporation in September 2003) that, according to the manufacturer, is compatible with various IP storage standards.

The basic idea behind Internet SCSI (iSCSI) is to transmit the SCSI protocol over TCP/IP (Figure 3.35). iSCSI thus takes a similar approach to Fibre Channel SAN, the difference being that in iSCSI a TCP/IP/Ethernet connection replaces the SCSI cable. Just like Fibre Channel SAN, iSCSI has to be installed in the operating system as a device driver. Like FCP, this realizes the SCSI protocol and maps the SCSI daisy chain onto a TCP/IP network.

Although the Internet Engineering Task Force (IETF) did not ratify the iSCSI standard until the beginning of 2003, there are already (end of 2003) end devices that directly support iSCSI and more and more reputable manufacturers are announcing the appearance of iSCSI products. As one option, conventional Ethernet network cards can be used on the servers, for which an additional iSCSI driver is installed that realizes the protocols in the form of software, thereby placing a load on the server CPU. As an alternative, iSCSI HBAs are available, which – in a similar manner to the TCP/IP offload engines – realize the iSCSI/TCP/IP/Ethernet protocol stack in the form of hardware. Initial measurements on iSCSI HBAs (network cards that handle a large part of the iSCSI/TCP/IP/Ethernet protocol stack on the network card) show that the load on the server CPU can be significantly reduced by offloading the protocol processing into hardware. Therefore, iSCSI HBAs can be used for high performance requirements, whereas conventional, and thus significantly cheaper, Ethernet cards are sufficient for low and possibly even average performance requirements. It is feasible that later versions of the iSCSI standard will also be based upon UDP/IP, IP or in the forms of SDP and iSER on Remote Direct Memory Access (RDMA, Section 3.7).

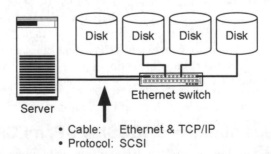

Figure 3.35 Like Fibre Channel, iSCSI replaces the SCSI cable by a network over which the SCSI protocol is run. In contrast to Fibre Channel, TCP/IP and Ethernet are used as the transmission technology

In production environments, the use of iSCSI is still largely limited to the connection of iSCSI servers to Fibre Channel storage devices over an iSCSI-to-Fibre Channel gateway. Since many manufacturers are only just launching the first versions of their iSCSI devices and drivers onto the market, incompatibilities are currently unavoidable. Therefore, iSCSI is currently only used in niche markets. A common example is the booting of diskless servers over iSCSI. They take their hard disks, including boot image and operating system, from a Fibre Channel disk subsystem via iSCSI-to-Fibre Channel gateway by means of iSCSI (Figure 3.36). Such a shifting of the storage capacity from internal hard drives to external disk subsystems brings with it the normal cost benefits associated with storage networks. Manufacturer-specific techniques are currently still being used for this. The IETF is now working on the standardization of booting by means of iSCSI.

In contrast to iSCSI, which defines a new protocol mapping of SCSI on TCP/IP, Internet FCP (iFCP) describes the mapping of Fibre Channel FCP on TCP/IP. The idea is to protect the investment in a large number of Fibre Channel devices that have already been installed and merely replace the Fibre Channel network infrastructure by an IP/Ethernet network infrastructure. The developers of iFCP expect that this will provide cost benefits in relation to a pure Fibre Channel network. For the realization of iFCP, LAN switches must either provide a Fibre Channel F-Port or an FL-Port. Alternatively, Fibre Channel FCP-to-iFCP gateways could also be used (Figure 3.37).

The difference between Metro FCP (mFCP) and iFCP is that mFCP is not based upon TCP/IP but on UDP/IP. This means that mFCP gains performance at the expense of the reliability of the underlying network connection. The approach of replacing TCP/IP by UDP/IP has proved itself many times. For example, NFS was originally based upon TCP/IP, but today it can be based upon TCP/IP or UDP/IP. Error correction mechanisms in the application protocol (in this case NFS or mFCP) ensure that no data is lost. This is only worthwhile in low-error networks such as LANs.

In order to provide fabric services, iFCP/mFCP must evaluate the Fibre Channel frames received from the end devices and further process these accordingly. It forwards useful data for a different end device to the appropriate gateway or switch via TCP/IP. Likewise,

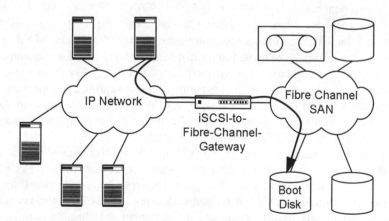

Figure 3.36 When booting over iSCSI the internal hard disk and the FC host bus adapter can be dispensed with

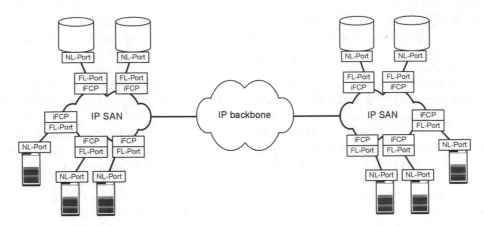

Figure 3.37 iFCP is a gateway protocol that connects Fibre Channel devices via a TCP/IP network

it also has to map infrastructure services of the fabric such as zoning and name service on TCP/IP.

In our opinion, the benefits of iFCP and mFCP remain to be proved. Both protocols make a very elegant attempt to protect investments that have already been made by connecting existing Fibre Channel storage devices into IP-based storage networks. Furthermore, the use of iFCP/mFCP makes it possible to reach back to the fully developed techniques, services and management tools of an IP network. However, iFCP and mFCP are complex protocols that have to be intensively tested before cross-manufacturer compatibility can be ensured. iFCP and mFCP offer few new benefits for the transmission of Fibre Channel FCP over IP: today, Fibre Channel-to-iSCSI gateways and the FCIP mentioned below provide alternative methods of connecting existing Fibre Channel devices over IP. Therefore, the benefits, and thus the future, of iFCP/mFCP remain dubious in view of the required implementation and testing cost for the manufacturer of iFCP/mFCP components.

The third protocol for IP storage, Fibre Channel over IP (FCIP), was designed as a supplement to Fibre Channel, in order to remove the distance limitations of Fibre Channel. Companies are increasingly requiring longer distances to be spanned, for example for data mirroring or to back-up data to back-up media that is a long way from the production data in order to prevent data loss in the event of large-scale catastrophes. Until now, such requirements meant that either the tapes had to be sent to the back-up data centre by courier or comparatively expensive and difficult to manage WAN techniques such as Dark Fiber, DWDM or SONET/SDH had to be used.

FCIP represents an alternative to the conventional WAN techniques: it is a tunnelling protocol that connects two Fibre Channel islands together over a TCP/IP route (Figure 3.38). FCIP thus creates a point-to-point connection between two Fibre Channel SANs and simply compresses all Fibre Channel frames into TCP/IP packets. The use of FCIP remains completely hidden from the Fibre Channel switches, so both of the Fibre Channel SANs connected using FCIP merge into a large storage network. Additional services and drivers are unnecessary.

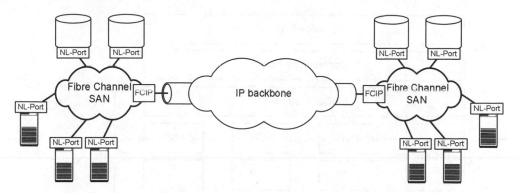

Figure 3.38 FCIP is a tunnelling protocol that connects two Fibre Channel SANs by means of TCP/IP

A further advantage of FCIP compared to the connection of Fibre Channel networks using conventional WAN techniques lies in the encryption of the data to be transmitted. Whereas encryption techniques are still in their infancy in Dark Fibre, DWDM and SONET/SDH, the encryption of the data traffic between two IP routers by means of IPSec has now become a standard technique.

Currently, many manufacturers have announced the expansion of their product portfolio to include FCIP or have already brought this onto the market. The passing of the FCIP standard by the IETF is still awaited (end of 2003). Only then can work on the interoperability of the FCIP components of different manufacturers be driven forward. Until then, FCIP-to-Fibre Channel gateways from the same manufacturer will have to be used at both ends of a FCIP route.

A common feature of all the protocols introduced here is that they transmit SCSI data traffic over IP in one form or another. In addition to the data transmission, a service is required to help scan for devices or communication partners in the IP network and to query device properties. Internet Storage Name Service (iSNS) is a standard that defines precisely such a service. iSNS is a client-server application, in which the clients register their attributes with the server, which for its part informs clients about changes to the topology. Both iSCSI and iFCP integrate iSNS. FCIP does not need to do this because it only provides a transmission route between two Fibre Channel SANs and thus has the same function as a Fibre Channel cable.

iSCSI, iFCP and FCIP are similar protocols that can easily be mistaken for one another. Therefore it makes sense to contrast these protocols once again from different points of view. Figure 3.39 compares the protocol stacks of the different approaches: FCP is realized completely by Fibre Channel protocols. FCIP creates a point-to-point connection between two Fibre Channel SANs, with all Fibre Channel frames simply being packetized in TCP/IP packets. iFCP represents an expansion of FCIP, since it not only tunnels Fibre Channel frames, but also realizes fabric services such as routing, name server and zoning over TCP/IP. Finally, iSCSI is based upon TCP/IP without any reference to Fibre Channel. Table 3.4 summarizes which parts of the protocol stack in question are realized by Fibre Channel and which by TCP/IP/Ethernet. Finally, Figure 3.40 compares the frame formats.

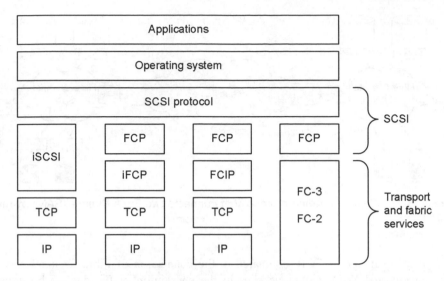

Figure 3.39 All protocols are addressed from the operating system via SCSI

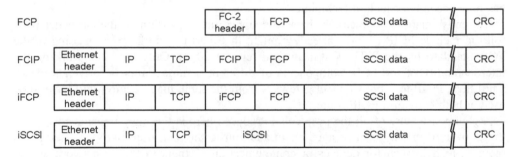

Figure 3.40 Fibre Channel FCP has the lowest protocol overhead in comparison to the IP-based SCSI protocols

Table 3.4 In contrast to FCIP, iFCP manages without Fibre Channel networks

	Terminal	Fabric services	Transport
FCP	Fibre Channel	Fibre Channel	Fibre Channel
FCIP	Fibre Channel	Fibre Channel	IP/Ethernet
iFCP	Fibre Channel	IP/Ethernet	IP/Ethernet
iSCSI	IP/Ethernet	IP/Ethernet	IP/Ethernet

3.5.2 TCP/IP and Ethernet as an I/O technology

From a technical point of view, Fibre Channel has some advantages in relation to IP storage: the Fibre Channel protocol stack is integrated and thus very efficient. In comparison to Fibre Channel, TCP/IP has a significantly higher protocol overhead. Furthermore, Fibre Channel has for some years been successfully used in production environments. By contrast, IP storage has not yet stood the test of time: the iSCSI standard was only passed by the IETF at the beginning of 2003. The ratification of FCIP is expected to take place in 2004. As a result, there are currently very few production environments in which one of the new IP storage protocols is used.

In what follows we will describe the reasons why we nevertheless believe that IP storage will establish itself as an important technique for storage networks in a few years time. To this end, we will first explain the advantages and disadvantages of IP storage and then show in Section 3.5.3 a migration path from Fibre Channel to IP storage.

Proponents of IP storage cite the following advantages in relation to Fibre Channel:

• common network for LAN, MAN, WAN, SAN, voice and probably video;
• standardization and maturity of technology since TCP/IP and Ethernet have been in use for decades;
• more personnel are available with TCP/IP knowledge than with knowledge of Fibre Channel;
• TCP/IP have no distance limits;
• cheaper hardware, since competition is greater in the field of TCP/IP than Fibre Channel due to the higher market volume;
• availability of administration tools for TCP/IP networks.

In the following we will discuss how these supposed advantages of IP storage are not as clear-cut as they might appear. However, we let us first also mention the supposed disadvantages of IP storage:

• lack of standardization of IP storage;
• lack of interoperability of IP storage;
• high CPU use for SAN data traffic via TCP/IP;
• greater TCP/IP overhead, since the protocol is not designed for mass data;
• high latency of TCP/IP/Ethernet switches;
• low exploitation of the bandwidth of Ethernet (20–30%) due to the typical collisions for Ethernet.

In what follows we will also investigate the listed disadvantages, some of which contradict the advantages of IP storage that are often put forward.

It is correct that when using IP storage LAN, MAN, WAN and SAN can be operated via common physical IP networks (Figure 3.41). However, it should be borne in mind

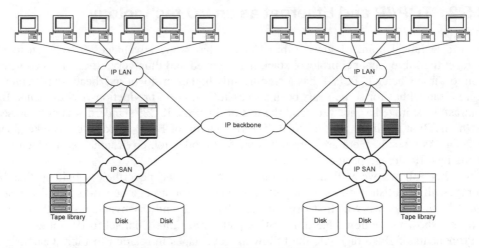

Figure 3.41 With IP storage LAN, MAN, WAN and SAN can be based upon a common network infrastructure. In practice, the LAN is usually heavily loaded for the data traffic between clients and servers, which means that a further LAN must be installed for SAN data traffic. LANs and SANs can be connected via the same IP backbone

that in many environments the LAN-MAN-WAN network is already working at its limit. This means that when using IP storage, just as when using Fibre Channel SAN, additional network capacity must be installed. It is questionable whether it is organizationally possible for the IP network for LAN to be managed by the same people who manage the IP network for IP storage: with LAN, access to data is restricted by the applications so that the LAN administrator cannot simply access confidential data. In IP storage, on the other hand, the administrator can access significantly more data.

Nevertheless, there is increasingly a trend towards handling all data traffic over IP and Ethernet. Conventional data networks use almost traditional TCP/IP and its application protocols such as HTTP, FTP, NFS, CIFS or SMTP. In pilot projects Gigabit Ethernet is already being used for the networking of schools, authorities and households in Metropolitan Area Networks (MANs). It is therefore easily possible that Gigabit Ethernet will at some point supersede DSL for connecting companies, authorities and households to the broadband Internet (the Internet of the future). In addition, telephoning over IP (Voice of IP, VoIP) has been in use in new office buildings for some time. If locations a long distance apart frequently have to be in telephone contact, telephoning over the Internet can save an immense amount of money.

The standardization of all data traffic – from telephony through LAN to storage networks – to IP networks would have certain advantages. If only IP networks were used in office buildings, the available bandwidth could be provided to different types of data traffic as required. In an extreme case, the capacity could be used for different purposes depending upon the time of day, for example, for telephone calls during the day and for network back-up during the night.

In addition, many companies rent dedicated IP connections for the office data traffic, which are idle during the night. FCIP allows the network capacity to be used to copy data without renting additional lines. When writing tapes over a Gigabit Ethernet line of ten kilometres in length by FCIP, a throughput of 30 to 40 MByte/s has been measured. A higher throughput was limited by the tape drive used. Considerable cost savings are thus possible with FCIP because the WAN connections that are already available and occasionally not used can also be used.

Furthermore, the standardization of all communications to TCP/IP/Ethernet ensures further cost savings because the market volume of TCP/IP/Ethernet components is significantly greater than that of any other network technology segment. For example, the development and testing cost for new components is distributed over a much larger number of units. This gives rise to greater competition and ultimately to lower prices for Ethernet components than for Fibre Channel components. However, high-end LAN switches and high-end LAN routers also come at a price, so we will have to wait and see how great the price advantage is.

The availability of personnel with knowledge of the necessary network technology is a point in favour of IP and Gigabit Ethernet. IP and Ethernet have been in use for LANs for many years. Knowledge regarding these technologies is therefore widespread. Fibre Channel, on the other hand, is a young technology that is mastered by few people in comparison to IP and Ethernet. There is nothing magical about learning to use Fibre Channel technology. However, it costs money and time for the training of staff, which is usually not necessary for IP and Ethernet. However, training is also necessary for IP SANs, for example for iSCSI and iSCSI SAN concepts.

It is correct to say that there are currently (2003) very few tools on the market that can help in the management of a heterogeneous Fibre Channel SAN. There are hardly any tools that show the topology of a Fibre Channel SAN, in which the network components and end devices of different manufacturers are used. The administration tools for TCP/IP networks are much broader here. However, here too expansions are necessary. For example, for storage administration we need to know which servers use which storage devices and how great the load is on the storage devices in question as a result of read and write access. Although it is currently possible to find this out for individual servers, there are no tools that help to determine the storage resource consumption of all servers in a heterogeneous environment (Chapter 8).

In connection with IP storage, the vision is sometimes put forward that servers will store their data on storage systems that export virtual hard disks on the Internet – TCP/IP makes this possible. However, we have to keep in mind the fact that the Internet today has a high latency and the transmission rates achieved sometimes fluctuate sharply. This means that storage servers on the Internet are completely unsuitable for time-critical I/O accesses such as database transactions. Even if the performance of the Internet infrastructure increases, the transmission of signals over long distances costs time. For this reason, a database server in London will never access virtual hard disks in New York. This scenario is therefore only of interest for services that tolerate a higher network latency, such as the copying, back-up, replication or asynchronous mirroring of data.

Like Fibre Channel FCP, IP storage has to serialize the SCSI protocol and map it onto IP, TCP/IP or UDP/IP. Precisely this standardization is still in progress: different approaches to IP storage are currently being standardized for iSCSI, iFCP, mFCP and FCIP. These standards must first be implemented by various manufacturers and tested for interoperability. Anyone who wishes to use storage networks today (2003) is therefore forced to use Fibre Channel or put up with the proprietary IP storage solutions of individual manufacturers.

The assertion that IP storage will have no interoperability problems because the underlying TCP/IP technology has been in use for decades is nonsense. The protocols based upon TCP/IP such as iSCSI or iFCP have to work together in a cross-manufacturer manner just like Fibre Channel SAN. In addition, there is generally room for interpretation in the implementation of a standard. Experiences with Fibre Channel show that, despite standardization, comprehensive interoperability testing is indispensable (Section 3.4.6). Interoperability problems should therefore be expected in the first supposedly standard-compliant products from different manufacturers.

It is correct that TCP/IP data traffic is very CPU-intensive. Figure 3.42 compares the CPU load of TCP/IP and Fibre Channel data traffic. The reason for the low CPU load of Fibre Channel is that a large part of the Fibre Channel protocol stack is realized on the Fibre Channel host bus adapter. By contrast, in current network cards a large part of the TCP/IP protocol stack is processed on the server CPU. The communication between the Ethernet network card and the CPU takes place via interrupts. This costs additional computing power, because every interrupt triggers an expensive process change in the operating system. However, more and more manufacturers are now offering so-called TCP/IP offload engines (TOEs). These are network cards that handle most of the TCP/IP protocol stack and thus greatly free up the CPU. Now even the first prototypes for iSCSI HBAs are available, which in addition to TCP/IP also realize the iSCSI protocol in hardware. Measurements have shown that the CPU load can be significantly reduced.

The Fibre Channel protocol stack is a integrated whole. As a result, cut-through routing is comparatively simple to realize for Fibre Channel switches. By contrast, TCP/IP

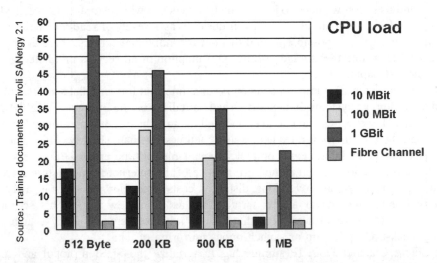

Figure 3.42 TCP/IP data traffic places a load on the server CPU. The CPU load of Fibre Channel is low because its protocol is mainly processed on the host bus adapter. (The *y*-axis shows the CPU load of a 400 MHz CPU)

and Ethernet were developed independently and not harmonized to one another. In the TCP/IP/Ethernet protocol stack the IP layer is responsible for the routing. So-called level 3 routers permit the use of cut-through routing by analysing the IP data traffic and then realizing the cut-through routing a layer below on the Ethernet layer. It is therefore highly probable that the latency of an Ethernet/IP switch will always be poorer than the latency of a Fibre Channel switch. How relevant this is to the performance of IP storage is currently unknown: Figure 3.23 shows that in today's Fibre Channel SANs the latency of the switches is insignificant in comparison to the latency of the end devices. The economic advantages of IP storage discussed above would presumably be negated if IP storage required different IP/Ethernet switches than the switches for LAN/MAN/WAN data traffic.

Proponents of Fibre Channel sometimes assert that TCP/IP and Ethernet is inefficient where there are several simultaneous transmitters because in this situation the collisions that occur in Ethernet lead to the medium only being able to be utilized at 20–30%. This statement is simply incorrect. Today's Ethernet switches are full duplex just like Fibre Channel switches. Full duplex means that several devices can exchange data in pairs using the full bandwidth, without interfering with each other.

To summarize the discussion above, IP storage will at least fulfil the performance requirements of many average applications. The question of to what degree IP storage is also suitable for central applications with extremely high performance requirements has yet to be answered. Since no practical experience is available regarding this question, only theoretical considerations are possible.

An I/O technique for high performance applications must guarantee a high throughput at a low CPU load and a low latency (delay) of data transmission. As discussed, even now the CPU load is under control with iSCSI HBAs. More bandwidth will very soon also be available between servers and storage devices than can be processed with the current level of technology. If the manufacturers stick to their announcements and launch the first 10-Gigabit Ethernet components for storage networks onto the market in 2004, it will be possible by means of trunking to bring together several 10-Gigabit Ethernet connections into one virtual connection that provides an even greater bandwidth.

It is more difficult to make predictions regarding the effect of the latency of IP storage, which will probably be higher, on the performance of applications. We will have to wait for relevant experiences in production environments. The current reference installations are not yet sufficient to make a comprehensive judgement that is proven by practical experience. Furthermore, in the more distant future we can hope for improvements if techniques such as Remote Direct Access Memory (RDMA), Virtual Interfaces (VI) and InfiniBand are drawn into storage networks, and protocols such as iSCSI, iSER and SDP are based directly upon these new techniques (Sections 3.6, 3.7 and 3.8).

There is still a long way to go before IP storage can be viewed as a serious alternative to Fibre Channel SAN for the realization of storage networks. There are some technical tasks to be dealt with that do not require a supreme engineering achievement, but simply have to be done. Many reputable manufacturers have announced the appearance of IP storage products, so it is now just a matter of time before IP storage becomes a serious alternative to Fibre Channel SAN. We believe that IP storage will gain a large share of the market for storage networks in a few years due to the economic advantages over Fibre

Channel discussed above. In our opinion IP storage has the potential to marginalize Fibre Channel in the long term, like the technologies of ATM and FDDI that once had similar ambitions. It would not be the first time that Ethernet has prevailed.

3.5.3   Migration from SCSI and Fibre Channel to IP storage

These days, anyone investing in a storage network wants to be able to make use of his investment for as long as possible. This means that he should first of all invest in technologies that solve today's problems. Second, he should invest in technologies that have a long life cycle ahead of them. Finally, he not only has to purchase hardware and software, but also train his staff appropriately and gather experience in production environments.

For anyone who wishes to use storage networks today (2003) it is almost impossible to avoid Fibre Channel. IP storage may have a great deal of potential but there are only a few products on the market. Anyone implementing IP storage today will be forced to tie themselves to one manufacturer: it is unlikely that products from different manufacturers will be interoperable until the relevant standards have been passed and the cross-vendor interoperability of IP storage components has been tested. IP storage is therefore only suitable in exceptional cases or for pilot installations or as extension to an already existing Fibre Channel SAN. In environments where no databases are connected via storage networks, Network Attached Storage (NAS, Section 4.2.2) provides an alternative to Fibre Channel SAN.

In the coming one to two years (2004 and 2005) Fibre Channel will remain the only alternative for storage networks with high performance requirements. During this period, in our estimate, numerous IP storage products will come onto the market that represent cheap and production-ready alternatives to Fibre Channel SAN for storage networks with low and medium performance requirements. For high performance requirements we will have to wait for appropriate iSCSI host bus adapters, which handle a large part of the protocol stack on the network card and thus free up the server CPU.

For local storage networks, Fibre Channel is currently the right choice in almost all situations. It is the only technology for storage networks that is used very successfully on a large scale in production environments. The comprehensive use of IP storage, on the other hand, is imminent. Nevertheless, you can invest in Fibre Channel components today with an easy mind. They will still be able to be operated in a subsequent transition to IP storage, for example, using iSCSI-to-Fibre Channel gateways.

Even today, despite the lack of a standard, FCIP is suitable for the connection of two Fibre Channel SANs over a TCP/IP route. However, FCIP components from the same manufacturer must be used at both ends of the connection. Due to the teething troubles described, iSCSI is suitable as an expansion of existing FC-SANs for certain sub-requirements.

Figure 3.43 shows a possible migration path from Fibre Channel SAN to IP storage. In the first stage, iSCSI-to-Fibre Channel gateways and FCIP-to-Fibre Channel gateways are required so that, for example, a server connected via iSCSI can back up its data over the storage network onto a tape library connected via Fibre Channel. Currently (2003) it

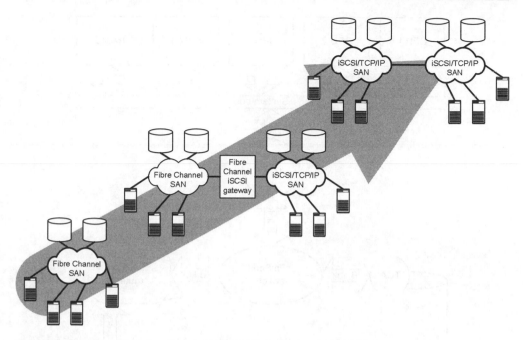

Figure 3.43   Possible migration path from Fibre Channel to iSCSI

looks like a good idea to invest further in existing Fibre Channel infrastructure and to additionally try out iSCSI and the integration of iSCSI and Fibre Channel in pilot projects. After an extended period of usage in practice we can prove whether IP storage represents an alternative to Fibre Channel SAN and to what extent IP storage will establish itself alongside Fibre Channel. Only when it has been proven in practice that IP storage (iSCSI in Figure 3.42) also fulfils the highest performance requirements will IP storage possibly marginalize Fibre Channel over time.

3.6   INFINIBAND

In the near future, Fibre Channel and Ethernet will support transmission rates of 10 Gbit/s and above. Consequently, the host I/O bus in the computer must be able to transmit data at the same rate. However, like all parallel buses, the transmission rate of the PCI bus can only be increased to a limited degree (Section 3.3.2). InfiniBand represents an emerging I/O technology that will probably supersede the PCI bus in high-end servers.

InfiniBand replaces the PCI bus with a serial network (Figure 3.44). In InfiniBand the devices communicate by means of messages, with an InfiniBand switch forwarding the data packets to the receiver in question. The communication is full duplex and a transmission rate of 2.5 Gbit/s in each direction is supported. If we take into account the fact that, like Fibre Channel, InfiniBand uses 8b/10b encoding, this yields a net data

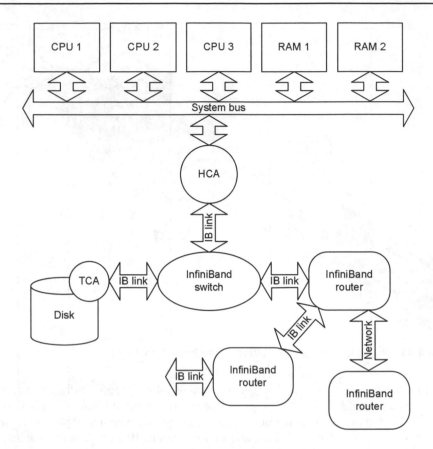

Figure 3.44 InfiniBand replaces the PCI bus by a serial network

rate of 250 MByte/s per link and direction. InfiniBand makes it possible to bundle four or twelve links so that a transmission rate of 10 Gbit/s (1 GByte/s net) or 30 Gbit/s (3 GByte/s net) is achieved in each direction. It can be expected that InfiniBand will initially only be used in high-end servers and that the PCI bus will, for now, remain the choice for all other computers.

As a medium, InfiniBand defines various copper and fiber-optic cables. A maximum length of 17 metres is specified for copper cable and up to 10,000 metres for fiber-optic cable. There are also plans to realize InfiniBand directly upon the circuit board using conductor tracks.

The end points in an InfiniBand network are called channel adapters. InfiniBand differentiates between Host Channel Adapters (HCAs) and Target Channel Adapters (TCAs). HCAs bridge between the InfiniBand network and the system bus to which the CPUs and the main memory (RAM) are connected. TCAs make a connection between InfiniBand networks and peripheral devices that are connected via SCSI, Fibre Channel or Ethernet. In comparison to PCI, HCAs correspond with the PCI bridge chips and TCAs correspond with the Fibre Channel host bus adapter cards or the Ethernet network cards.

InfiniBand has the potential to completely change the architecture of servers and storage devices. We have to consider this: network cards and host bus adapter cards can be located 100 metres apart. This means that mainboards with CPU and memory, network cards, host bus adapter cards and storage devices are all installed individually as physically separate, decoupled devices. These components are connected together over a network. Today it is still unclear which of the three transmission technologies will prevail in which area.

Figure 3.45 shows what such an interconnection of CPU, memory, I/O cards and storage devices might look like. The computing power of the interconnection is provided by two CPU & RAM modules that are connected via a direct InfiniBand link for the benefit of lightweight interprocess communication. Peripheral devices are connected via the InfiniBand network. In the example a tape library is connected via Fibre Channel and the disk subsystem is connected directly via InfiniBand. If the computing power of the interconnection is no longer sufficient a further CPU & RAM module can be added.

Intelligent disk subsystems are becoming more and more powerful and InfiniBand facilitates fast communication between servers and storage devices that reduces the load on the CPU. It is therefore at least theoretically feasible for subfunctions such as the

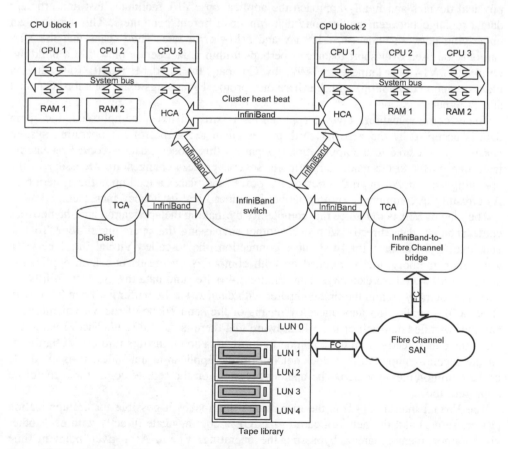

Figure 3.45   InfiniBand could radically change the architecture of server clusters

caching of file systems or the lock synchronization of shared disk file systems to be implemented directly on the disk subsystem or on special processors (Chapter 4).

Right from the start, the InfiniBand protocol stack was designed so that it could be realized efficiently. A conscious decision was made only to specify performance features that could be implemented in the hardware. Nevertheless, the InfiniBand standard incorporates performance features such as flow control, zoning and various service classes. However, we assume that in InfiniBand – as in Fibre Channel – not all parts of the standard will be realized in the products.

3.7 VIRTUAL INTERFACES AND REMOTE DIRECT MEMORY ACCESS (RDMA)

With the Virtual Interface Architecture we move away from the communication between physical devices and finally approach the applications. VIA facilitates fast and efficient data exchange between applications that run on different computers. This requires an underlying network with a low latency and a low error rate. This means that the VIA can only be used over short distances, perhaps within a data centre or within a building. Originally, VIA was launched in 1997 by Compaq, Intel and Microsoft. Today it is a fixed component of InfiniBand. Furthermore, protocol mappings exist for Fibre Channel and Ethernet.

Today communication between applications is still relatively complicated. Incoming data is accepted by the network card, processed in the kernel of the operating system and finally delivered to the application. As part of this process, data is copied repeatedly from one buffer to the next. Furthermore, several process changes are necessary in the operating system. All in all this costs CPU power and places a load upon the system bus. As a result the communication throughput is reduced and its latency increased.

The idea of VIA is to reduce this complexity by making the application and the network card exchange data directly with one another, bypassing the operating system. To this end, two applications initially set up a connection, the so-called Virtual Interface (VI): a common memory area is defined on both computers by means of which application and local network card exchange data (Figure 3.46). To send data the application fills the common memory area in the first computer with data. After the buffer has been filled with all data, the application announces by means of the send queue of the Virtual Interface and the so-called doorbell of the VI hardware that there is data to send. The VI hardware reads the data directly from the common memory area and transmits it to the VI hardware on the second computer. This does not inform the application until all data is available in the common memory area. The operating system on the second computer is therefore bypassed, too.

The Virtual Interface (VI) is the mechanism that makes it possible for the application (VI consumer) and the network card (VI NIC) to communicate directly with each other via common memory areas, bypassing the operating system. At a given point in time a Virtual Interface is connected with a maximum of one other Virtual Interface. Virtual

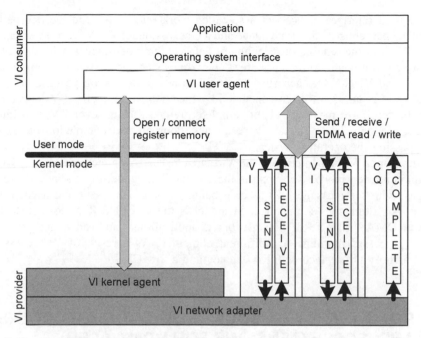

Figure 3.46 The Virtual Interface Architecture (VIA) allows applications and VI network cards to exchange data, bypassing the operating system

Interfaces therefore only ever allow point-to-point communication with precisely one remote Virtual Interface.

A VI provider consists of the underlying physical hardware (VI Network Interface Controller, VI NIC) and a device driver (kernel agent). Examples of VI NICs are VI-capable Fibre Channel host bus adapters, VI-capable Ethernet network cards and InfiniBand host channel adapters. The VI NIC realizes the Virtual Interfaces and completion queues and transmits the data to other VI NICs. The kernel agent is the device driver of a VI NIC that is responsible for the management of Virtual Interfaces. Its duties include the generation and removal of Virtual Interfaces, the opening and closing of VI connections to remote Virtual Interfaces, memory management and error handling. In contrast to communication over the Virtual Interface and the completion queue, communication with the kernel agent is associated with the normal overhead such as process switching. This extra cost can, however, be disregarded because after the Virtual Interface has been set up by the kernel agent all data is exchanged over the Virtual Interface.

Applications and operating systems that communicate with each other via Virtual Interfaces are called VI consumers. Applications generally use a Virtual Interface via an intermediate layer such as sockets or MPI. Access to a Virtual Interface is provided by the user agent. The user agent first of all contacts the kernel agent in order to generate a Virtual Interface and to connect this to a Virtual Interface on a remote device (server, storage device). The actual data transfer then takes place via the Virtual Interface as described above, bypassing the operating system, meaning that the transfer is quick and the load on the CPU is lessened.

The Virtual Interface consists of a so-called work queue pair and the doorbells. The work queue pair consists of a send queue and a receive queue. The VI consumer can charge the VI NIC with the sending or receiving of data via the work queues, with the data itself being stored in a common memory area. The requests are processed asynchronously. VI consumer and VI NIC let each other know when new requests are pending or when the processing of requests has been concluded by means of a doorbell. A VI consumer can bundle the receipt of messages about completed requests from several Virtual Interfaces in a common completion queue. Work queues, doorbell and completion queue can be used bypassing the operating system.

Building upon Virtual Interfaces, the Virtual Interface Architecture defines two different communication models. It supports the old familiar model of sending and receiving messages, with the messages in this case being asynchronous sent and asynchronously received. An alternative communication model is the so-called Remote Direct Memory Access (RDMA). Using RDMA, distributed applications can read and write memory areas of processes running on a different computer. As a result of VI, access to the remote memory takes place with low latency and a low CPU load.

3.8   RDMA OVER TCP, SOCKET DIRECT PROTOCOL (SDP) AND iSCSI EXTENSIONS FOR RDMA (iSER)

It has already been proved that RDMA can improve the performance of commercial applications, but none of these RDMA-enabled applications is commercially successful. This is mostly due to the fact that today (2003) RDMA-capable network cards are not interoperable and thus add costs for owning and managing RDMA-enabled applications. Therefore in May 2002 several companies founded the RDMA Consortium (www.rdmaconsortium.org) to standardize the RDMA protocol suite. The consortium has standardized all interfaces required to implement the software and the hardware for RDMA over TCP. In addition to that, it has been defined two upper layer protocols – the Socket Direct Protocol (SDP) and the iSCSI Extension for RDMA (iSER) – which exploit RDMA for fast and CPU light communication. The consortium has forwarded all specifications to the IETF and intends to complete its activity when these standards have been ratified as Internet standards.

RDMA over TCP offloads much of TCP protocol processing overhead from the CPU to the Ethernet network card. Furthermore, each incoming network packet has enough information, thus its payload can be placed directly to the proper destination memory location, even when packets arrive out of order. That means RDMA over TCP gains the benefits of the Virtual Interface Architecture whilst it uses the existing TCP/IP/Ethernet network infrastructure. RDMA over TCP is layered on top of TCP, needs no modification of the TCP/IP protocol suite and thus can benefit from underlying protocols like IPsec.

RDMA over TCP has some advantages in comparison to TCP/IP Offload Engines (TOEs). TOEs move the load for TCP protocol processing from the CPU to the network card, but the zero copy of incoming data streams is very proprietary in the TOE design, the operating systems interfaces, and the applications communication model. Thus in many cases, TOEs do not support a zero copy model for incoming data. RDMA over TCP benefits from its superior specification, thus a combination of TCP Offload Engines and RDMA provides the optimal architecture for high speed networking by reducing the CPU load and avoiding the need for copying data buffers. The RDMA consortium expects that the first RDMA-enabled network interface controllers (RNIC) will enter the market in 2004.

RDMA over TCP, VI Architecture and InfiniBand each specify a form of RDMA, but these are not exactly the same. The aim of VI Architecture is to specify a form of RDMA without specifying the underlying transport protocol. On the other hand, InfiniBand specifies an underlying transmission technique which is optimized to support RDMA semantics. Finally, RDMA over TCP specifies a layer which will interoperate with the standard TCP/IP protocol stack. As a result, the protocol verbs of each RDMA variant are slightly different, thus these RDMA variants are not interoperable.

However, the RDMA Consortium specified two upper layer protocols which utilize RDMA over TCP. The Socket Direct Protocol (SDP) represents an approach to accelerate TCP/IP communication. SDP maps the socket API of TCP/IP onto RDMA over TCP so that protocols based upon TCP/IP such as NFS and CIFS can benefit from RDMA without being modified. SDP benefits from offloading much of the TCP/IP protocol processing burden from CPU and its ability to avoid copying packets from buffer to buffer. It is very interesting to observe that applications using SDP think that they are using native TCP when the real transport of the data is performed by an integration of RDMA and TCP.

iSCSI Extension for RDMA (iSER) is the second upper layer protocol specified by the RDMA consortium. It is an extension of the iSCSI protocol (Section 3.5.1) which enables iSCSI to benefit from RDMA eliminating TCP/IP processing overhead on generic RNICs. This is important as Ethernet and therefore iSCSI approach 10 GBit/s in 2004. iSER is not a replacement for iSCSI, it is complementary. iSER requires iSCSI components such as login negotiation, discovery, security and boot. It only changes the data mover model of iSCSI. It is expected the iSCSI end nodes and iSCSI/iSER end nodes will be interoperable. During iSCSI login both end nodes will exchange characteristics, thus each node is clearly aware of the other's node transport capabilities.

RDMA is not yet widespread in current applications; however, it opens up new possibilities for the implementation of distributed synchronization mechanisms for caching and locking in databases and file systems. We expect that the completed standardization of RDMA over TCP will boost the adoption of RDMA-enabled applications in the next years. All distributed applications will benefit from RDMA-enabled transport via SDP and iSER whilst the applications itself remain unchanged. Furthermore, communication intensive applications will be adapted to utilize the native RDMA communication, for instance, file systems, databases, and applications in parallel computing. Section 4.2.5 shows in the example of the Direct Access File System (DAFS) how RDMA changes the design of network file systems.

3.9 SUMMARY

I/O techniques connect the CPU to the main memory and the peripheral devices. In the past, I/O technologies were based upon the bus architecture. Buses are subdivided into system buses, host I/O buses and I/O buses. The most important I/O buses for servers are SCSI, Fibre Channel and the family of IP storage protocols. SCSI makes it possible to address storage devices in a block-oriented manner via targets and LUNs. The SCSI protocol is also encountered in Fibre Channel and IP storage: these two new transmission technologies replace the SCSI cable by a serial network and continue to use the SCSI protocol over this network. Fibre Channel is a new transmission technology that is particularly well suited to storage networks. With point-to-point, arbitrated loop and fabric it defines three different network topologies that – in the case of the fabric – can connect together up to 15.5 million servers and storage devices. IP storage takes a similar approach to Fibre Channel. However, in contrast to Fibre Channel it is based upon the tried and tested TCP/IP, and thus mainly upon Ethernet. Anyone today (2003) who wants to implement block-oriented storage networks must take Fibre Channel as the basis. In the near future, IP storage will probably establish itself as an alternative to Fibre Channel. The most important host I/O bus technology today is the PCI bus. However, PCI is slowly coming up against its physical limits, which means that it can no longer keep up with the throughput of networks such as Fibre Channel and Ethernet. InfiniBand, which can probably replace the PCI bus in high-end servers with a serial network, can help here. The Virtual Interface Architecture (VIA) represents a technology that allows distributed applications to exchange data quickly and in a manner that lessens the load on the CPU by bypassing the operating systems of the computers. Finally, the standardization of RDMA over TCP and its application protocols SDP and iSER will adapt the TCP protocol and the iSCSI protocol for the requirements of a 10 GBit/s network technology.

With the disk subsystems discussed in the previous chapter and the Fibre Channel and IP storage I/O techniques discussed in this chapter we have introduced the technologies that are required to build storage-centric IT systems. However, intelligent disk subsystems and storage networks represent only the physical basis for storage-centric IT systems. Ultimately, software that exploits the new storage-centric infrastructure and thus fully develops its possibilities will also be required. Therefore, in the next chapter we show how intelligent disk subsystems and storage networks can change the architecture of file systems.

4

File Systems and Network Attached Storage (NAS)

Disk subsystems provide block-oriented storage. For end users and for higher applications the handling of blocks addressed via cylinders, tracks and sectors is very cumbersome. File systems therefore represent an intermediate layer in the operating system that provides users with the familiar directories or folders and files and stores these on the block-oriented storage media so that they are hidden to the end users. This chapter introduces the basics of files systems and shows the role that they play in connection with storage networks.

This chapter first of all describes the fundamental requirements that are imposed upon file systems (Section 4.1). Then network file systems, file servers and the Network Attached Storage (NAS) product category are introduced (Section 4.2). We will then show how shared disk file systems can achieve a significantly higher performance than classical network file systems (Section 4.3). The chapter concludes with a comparison with block-oriented storage networks (Fibre Channel SAN, iSCSI SAN) and Network Attached Storage (NAS) (Section 4.4).

4.1 LOCAL FILE SYSTEMS

File systems form an intermediate layer between block-oriented hard disks and applications, with a volume manager often being used between the file system and the hard disk (Figure 4.1). Together, these manage the blocks of the disk and make these available to users and applications via the familiar directories and files.

Storage Networks Explained   U. Troppens R. Erkens W. Müller
© 2004 John Wiley & Sons, Ltd   ISBN: 0-470-86182-7

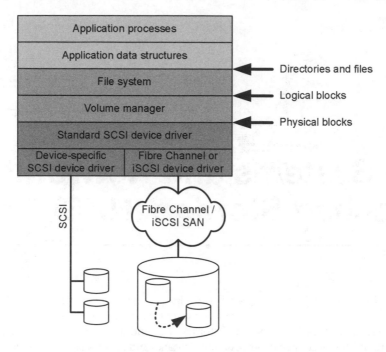

Figure 4.1 File system and volume manager manage the blocks of the block-oriented hard disks. Applications and users thus use the storage capacity of the disks via directories and files

4.1.1   File systems and databases

File systems and volume manager provide their services to numerous applications with various load profiles. This means that they are generic applications; their performance is not generally optimized for a specific application.

Database systems such as DB2 or Oracle can get around the file system and manage the blocks of the hard disk themselves (Figure 4.2). As a result, although the performance of the database can be increased, the management of the database is more difficult. In practice, therefore, database systems are usually configured to store their data in files that are managed by a file system. If more performance is required for a specific database, database administrators generally prefer to pay for higher performance hardware than to reconfigure the database to store its data directly upon the block-oriented hard disks.

4.1.2   Journaling

In addition to the basic services, modern file systems provide three functions – journaling, snapshots and dynamic file system expansion. Journaling is a mechanism that guarantees the consistency of the file system even after a system crash. To this end, the file system

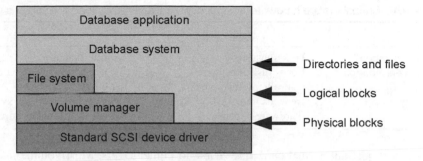

Figure 4.2   To increase performance, databases can get around the file system and manage the blocks themselves

first of all writes every change to a log file that is invisible to applications and end users, before making the change in the filesystem itself. After a system crash the file system only has to run through the end of the log file in order to recreate the consistency of the file system.

In file systems without journaling, typically older file systems like Microsoft's FAT32 file system or the UFS file system that is widespread in Unix systems, the consistency of the entire file system has to be checked after a system crash (file system check); in large file systems this can take several hours. In file systems without journaling it can therefore take several hours after a system crash – depending upon the size of the file system – before the data and thus the applications are back in operation.

4.1.3   Snapshots

Snapshots represent the same function as the instant copies function that is familiar from disk subsystems (cf. Section 2.7.1). Snapshots freeze the state of a file system at a given point in time. Applications and end users can access the frozen copy via a special path. As is the case for instant copies, the creation of the copy only takes a few seconds. Likewise, when creating a snapshot, care should be taken to ensure that the state of the frozen data is consistent.

Table 4.1 compares instant copies and snapshots. An important advantage of snapshots is that they can be realized with any hardware. On the other hand, instant copies within a disk subsystem place less load on the CPU and the buses of the server, thus leaving more system resources for the actual applications.

4.1.4   Volume manager

The volume manager is an intermediate layer within the operating system between the file system or database and the actual hard disks. The most important basic function of the volume manager is to aggregate several hard disks to form a large virtual hard

Table 4.1 Snapshots are hardware-independent, however, they load the server's CPU

	Instant copy	Snapshot
Place of realization	Disk subsystem	File system
Resource consumption	Loads disk subsystem's controller and its buses	Loads server's CPU and all buses
Availability	Depends upon disk subsystem (hardware-dependent)	Depends upon file system (hardware-independent)

disk and make just this virtual hard disk visible to higher layers. Most volume managers provide the option of breaking this virtual disk back down into several smaller virtual hard disks and enlarging or reducing these (Figure 4.3). This virtualization within the volume manager makes it possible for system administrators to quickly react to changed storage requirements of applications such as databases and file systems.

The volume manager can, depending upon its implementation, provide the same functions as a RAID controller (Section 2.4) or an intelligent disk subsystem (Section 2.7). As in snapshots, here too functions such as RAID, instant copies and remote mirroring are realized in a hardware-independent manner in the volume manager. Likewise, a RAID

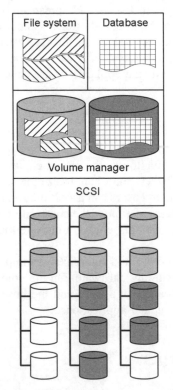

Figure 4.3 The volume manager aggregates physical hard disks into virtual hard disks, which it can break back down into smaller virtual hard disks. In the illustration one virtual hard disk is used directly from a database, the others are shared between two file systems

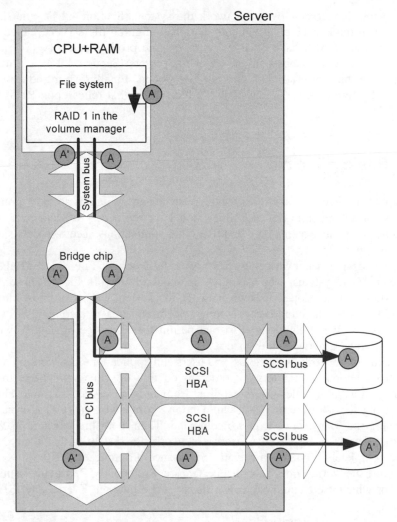

Figure 4.4 RAID in the volume manager loads the buses and CPU of the server. In RAID 1, for example, each block written by the file system must be passed through all the buses twice

controller or an intelligent disk subsystem can take the pressure off the resources of the server if the corresponding functions are moved to the storage devices. The realization of RAID in the volume manager loads not only on the server's CPU, but also on its buses (Figure 4.4).

4.2 NETWORK FILE SYSTEMS AND FILE SERVERS

Network file systems are the natural extension of local file systems. End users and applications can access directories and files that are physically located on a different

computer – the file server – over a network file system (Section 4.2.1). File servers are
so important in modern IT environments that preconfigured file servers, called Network
Attached Storage (NAS), have emerged as a separate product category (Section 4.2.2).
We highlight the performance bottlenecks of file servers (Section 4.2.3) and discuss the
possibilities for the acceleration of network file systems. Finally, we introduce the Direct
Access File System (DAFS), a new network file system that relies upon RDMA and VI
instead of TCP/IP.

4.2.1 Basic principle

The metaphor of directories and files for the management of data is so easy to understand
that it was for a long time the prevailing model for the access of data over networks.
So-called network file systems give end users and applications access to data stored on a
different computer (Figure 4.5).

The first widespread network file system was the Network File System (NFS) developed by Sun Microsystems, which is now *the* standard network file system on all Unix
systems. Microsoft developed its own network file system – the Common Internet File
System (CIFS) – for its Windows operating system and this is incompatible with NFS.
Today, various software solutions exist that permit the exchange of data between Unix
and Windows over a network file system.

With the aid of network file systems, end users and applications can work on a common
data set from various computers. In order to do this on Unix computers the system
administrator must link a file system exported from an NFS server into the local directory
structure using the `mount` command. On Windows computers, any end user can do this
himself using the Map Network Drive command. Then, both in Unix and in Windows,
the fact that data is being accessed from a network file system, rather than a local file
system, is completely hidden apart from performance differences.

Long before the World Wide Web, the File Transfer Protocol (FTP) provided a mechanism
by means of which users could exchange files over the Internet. Even today, FTP servers

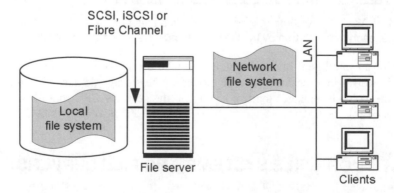

Figure 4.5 Network file systems make local files and directories available over the LAN.
Several end users can thus work on common files (for example, project data, source code)

remain an important means of distributing freely available software and freely available documents. Unlike network file systems, access to FTP servers is clearly visible to the end user. Users require a special FTP client with which they can copy back and forwards between the FTP server and their local computer.

The Hyper Text Markup Language (HTML) and the Hyper Text Transfer Protocol (HTTP) radically changed the usage model of the Internet. In contrast to FTP, the data on the Internet is linked together by means of HTML documents. The user on the Internet no longer accesses individual files, instead he 'surfs' the World Wide Web (WWW). He views HTML documents on his browser that are sometimes statically available on a HTTP server in the form of files or today are increasingly dynamically generated. Currently, graphic HTTP clients – the browsers – without exception have an integrated FTP client, with which they can easily 'download' files.

4.2.2 Network Attached Storage (NAS)

File servers are so important in current IT environments that they have developed into an independent product group in recent years. Network Attached Storage (NAS) is the name for preconfigured file servers. They consist of one or more internal servers, preconfigured disk capacity and usually a stripped-down or special operating system (Figure 4.6).

NAS servers are usually connected via Ethernet to the LAN, where they provide their disk space as file servers. Web servers represent a further important field of application for NAS servers. By definition, the clients are located at the other end of the WAN so there is no alternative to communication over IP. Large NAS servers offer additional functions such as snapshots, remote mirroring and back-up over Fibre Channel SAN.

NAS servers were specially developed for file sharing. This has two advantages: since, by definition, the purpose of NAS servers is known, NAS operating systems can be significantly better optimized than generic operating systems. This means that NAS servers can operate more quickly than file servers on comparable hardware that are based upon a generic operating system.

The second advantage of NAS is that NAS servers provide Plug&Play file systems, i.e. connect – power up – use. In contrast to a generic operating system all functions can be removed that are not necessary for the file serving. NAS storage can therefore excel due to low installation and maintenance costs, which takes the pressure off system administrators.

NAS servers are very scalable. For example the system administrator can attach a dedicated NAS server for every project or for every department. In this manner it is simple to expand large websites. E-mail file system full? No problem, I simply provide another NAS server for the next 10,000 users in my Ethernet. However, this approach can become a management nightmare if the storage requirement is very large, thus dozens of NAS servers are required.

One disadvantage of NAS servers is the unclear upgrade path. For example, the internal server cannot simply be replaced by a more powerful server because this goes against the principle of the preconfigured file server. The upgrade options available in this situation are those offered by the manufacturer of the NAS server in question.

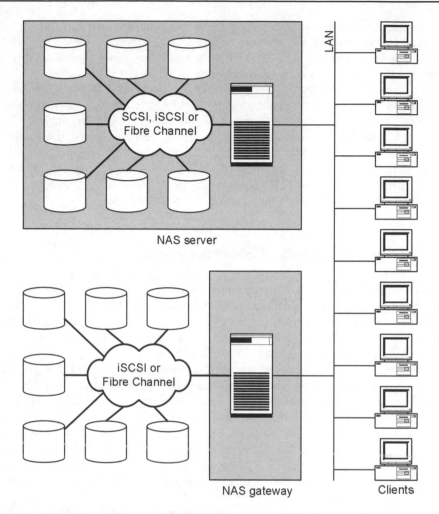

Figure 4.6 A NAS server is a preconfigured file server with internal hard disks, which makes its storage capacity available via LAN. A NAS gateway is a preconfigured file server that provides the storage capacity available in the storage network via the LAN

Performance bottlenecks for more I/O-intensive applications such as databases, back-up, batch processes or multimedia applications represent a further important disadvantage of NAS servers. These are described in the following subsection.

4.2.3 Performance bottlenecks in file servers

Current NAS servers and NAS gateways, as well as classical file servers, provide their storage capacity via conventional network file systems such as NFS and CIFS or Internet protocols such as FTP and HTTP. Although these may be suitable for classical file sharing, such protocols are not powerful enough for I/O-intensive applications such as databases or video processing. Nowadays, therefore, I/O-intensive databases draw their storage from disk subsystems rather than file servers.

Let us assume for a moment that a user wishes to read a file on an NFS client, which is stored on a NAS server with internal SCSI disks. The NAS server's operating system first of all loads the file into the main memory from the hard disk via the SCSI bus, the PCI bus and the system bus, only to forward it from there to the network card via the system bus and the PCI bus. The data is thus shovelled through the system bus and the PCI bus on the file server twice (Figure 4.7). If the load on a file server is high enough, its buses can thus become a performance bottleneck.

When using classical network file systems the data to be transported is additionally copied from the private storage area of the application into the buffer cache of the kernel on the transmitting computer before this copies the data via the PCI bus into the packet buffer of the network card. Every single copying operation increases the latency of the communication, the load on the CPU due to costly process changes between application processes and kernel processes, and the load on the system bus between CPU and main memory.

The file is then transferred from the network card to the NFS client via IP and Gigabit Ethernet. At the current state of technology most Ethernet cards can only handle a small part of the TCP/IP protocol independently, which means that the CPU itself has to handle the rest of the protocol. The communication from the Ethernet card to the CPU is initiated by means of interrupts. Taken together, this can cost a great deal of CPU time (cf. Section 3.5.2, 'TCP/IP and Ethernet as an I/O technology').

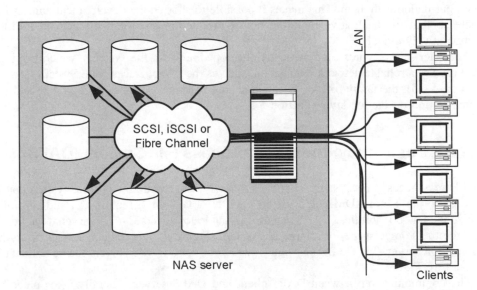

Figure 4.7 The file server becomes like the eye of the needle: en route between hard disk and client all data passes through the internal buses of the file server twice

4.2.4   Acceleration of network file systems

If we look at the I/O path from the application to the hard disks connected to a NAS server (Figure 4.15 on page 130), there are two places to start from to accelerate file sharing: (1) the underlying communication protocol (TCP/IP); and (2) the network file system (NFS, CIFS) itself.

TCP/IP was originally developed to achieve reliable data exchange via unreliable transport routes. The TCP/IP protocol stack is correspondingly complex and CPU-intensive. This can be improved first of all by so-called TCP/IP offload engines (TOEs), which in contrast to conventional network cards process a large part of the TCP/IP protocol stack on their own processor and thus significantly reduce the load on the server CPU (Section 3.5.2).

It would be even better to get rid of TCP/IP all together. This is where communication techniques such as Virtual Interfaces (VI) and Remote Direct Memory Access (RDMA) come into play (Chapter 3.7). Today there are various approaches for accelerating network file systems with VI and RDMA. The Socket Direct Protocol (SDP) represents an approach which combines the benefits of TOEs and RDMA-enabled transport (Section 3.7). Hence, protocols based on TCP/IP such as NFS and CIFS can – without modification – benefit via SDP from RDMA-enabled transport.

Other approaches map existing network file systems directly onto RDMA. For example, a subgroup of the Storage Networking Industry Association (SNIA) is working on the protocol mapping of NFS on RDMA. Likewise, it would also be feasible for Microsoft to develop a CIFS implementation that uses RDMA instead of TCP/IP as the communication protocol. The advantage of this approach is that the network file systems NFS or CIFS that have matured over the years merely have a new communication mechanism put underneath them. This makes it possible to shorten the development and testing cycle so that the qualitative requirements of production environments can be fulfilled comparatively quickly.

A greater step is represented by newly developed network file systems, which from the start require a reliable network connection, such as the Direct Access File System (DAFS, Section 4.2.5), the family of the so-called shared disk file systems (Section 4.3) and the virtualization on the file-level (Section 5.5).

4.2.5   Case study: the Direct Access File System (DAFS)

The Direct Access File System (DAFS) is a newly developed network file system that is tailored to the use of RDMA. It is based upon NFS version 4, requires VI and can fully utilize its new possibilities. DAFS makes it possible for several DAFS servers together to provide the storage space for a large file system (Figure 4.8). It remains hidden from the application server – as the DAFS client – which of these DAFS servers the actual data is located in (Figure 4.9).

The communication between DAFS client and DAFS server generally takes place by means of RDMA. The use of RDMA means that access to data that lies upon a DAFS server is nearly as quick as access to local data. In addition, typical file system operations

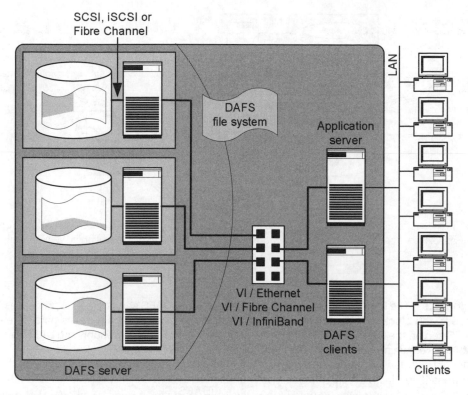

Figure 4.8   A DAFS file system can extend over several DAFS servers. All DAFS servers and DAFS clients are connected via a VI-capable network such as InfiniBand, Fibre Channel or Ethernet

such as the address conversion of files to SCSI block addresses, which naturally also require the CPU, are offloaded from the application server to the DAFS server.

An important function of file sharing in general is the synchronization of simultaneous accesses to file entries – i.e. metadata such as file names, access rights, etc. – and file contents, in order to protect the consistency of the data and metadata. DAFS makes it possible to cache the locks at the client side so that a subsequent access to the same data requires no interaction with the file server. If a node requires the lock entry of a different node, then this transmits the entry without time-out. DAFS uses lease-based locking in order to avoid the permanent blocking of a file due to the failure of a client. Furthermore, it possesses recovery mechanisms in case the connection between DAFS client and DAFS server is briefly interrupted or a different server from the cluster has to step in. Similarly, DAFS takes over the authentication of client and server and furthermore can also authenticate individual users in relation to a client-server session.

Two approaches prevail in the discussion about the client implementation. It can either be implemented as a shared library (Unix) or DLL (Windows) in the user space or as a kernel module (Figure 4.10). In the user space variant – known as uDAFS – the DAFS library instructs the kernel to set up an exclusive end-to-end connection with the

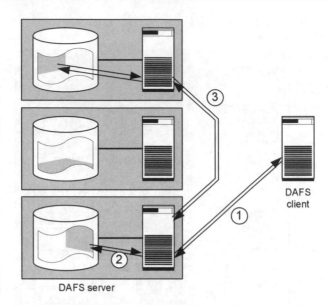

Figure 4.9 The DAFS client communicates with just one DAFS server (1). This processes file access, the blocks of which it manages itself (2). In the case of data that lies on a different DAFS server, the DAFS server forwards the storage access to the corresponding DAFS server, with this remaining hidden from the DAFS client

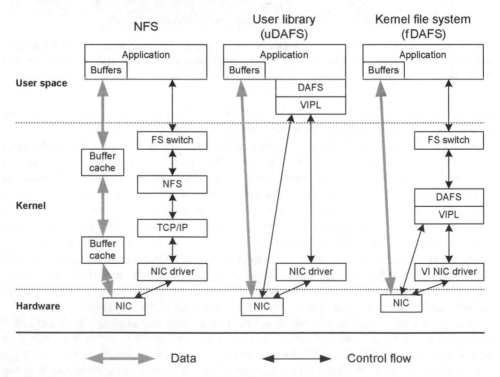

Figure 4.10 A comparison between NFS, uDAFS and fDAFS

DAFS server for each system call (or for each API call under Windows) by means of a VI provider layer (VIPL), which is also realized as a library in user space. The VI-capable NIC guarantees the necessary protection against accesses or faults caused by other processes. The user space implementation can utilize the full potential of DAFS to increase the I/O performance because it completely circumvents the kernel. If offers the application explicit control over the access of the NIC to its private storage area. Although control communication takes place between the VI provider layer in the user space and the VI-NIC driver in the kernel, the CPU cost that this entails can be disregarded due to the low data quantities.

The disadvantage of the methods is the lack of compatibility with previous applications, which without exception require an upgrade in order to use DAFS. Such a cost is only justified for applications for which a high I/O performance is critical.

In the second, kernel-based variant the implementation is in the form of a loadable file system module (fDAFS) underneath the Virtual File System (VFS layer) for Unix or as an Installable File System (IFS) for Windows. Each application can address the file system driver as normal by means of the standard system calls and VFS or API calls and the I/O manager; DAFS then directs a query to the DAFS server. The I/O performance is slowed due to the fact that all file system accesses run via the VFS or the I/O manager because this requires additional process changes between user and kernel processes. On the other hand, there is compatibility with all applications.

Some proponents of DAFS claim to have taken measurements in prototypes showing that data access over DAFS is quicker than data access on local hard disks. In our opinion this comparison is dubious. The DAFS server also has to store data to hard disks. We find it barely conceivable that disk access can be quicker on a DAFS server than on a conventional file server.

Nevertheless, DAFS-capable NAS servers could potentially support I/O-intensive applications such as databases, batch processes or multi-media applications. Integration with RDMA makes it irrelevant whether the file accesses take place via a network. The separation between databases and DAFS servers even has the advantage that the address conversion of files to SCSI block addresses is offloaded from the database server to the DAFS server, thus reducing the load on the database server's CPU.

However, file servers and database servers will profit equally from InfiniBand, VI and RDMA. There is therefore the danger that a DAFS server will only be able to operate very few databases from the point of view of I/O, meaning that numerous DAFS servers may have to be installed. A corresponding number of DAFS-capable NAS servers could be installed comparatively quickly. However, the subsequent administrative effort could be considerably greater.

The development of DAFS was primarily advanced by the company Network Appliance, an important NAS manufacturer. The standardization of the DAFS protocol for communication between server and client and the DAFS API for the use of the file system by applications was performed by the DAFS Collaborative (www.dafscollaborative.org). Since the release of Version 1.0 in September 2001 (protocol) and in November 2001 (API) the standardization efforts have slowed down. Initially the DAFS standard was submitted to the IETF in September 2001, but it did not get enough support across the storage industry. Instead of this we can observe more activity for an alternative approach, the enablement of NFS to run RDMA-native and the adding of DAFS-like local sharing semantics.

DAFS is an interesting approach to the use of NAS servers as storage for I/O-intensive applications. Due to a lack of standardization and widespread support across the industry, current DAFS offerings (2003) should be considered as a temporary solution for specific environments until alternatives like NFS over RDMA and CIFS over RDMA emerge. Furthermore, iSCSI is of interest to those who see DAFS as a way of avoiding an investment in Fibre Channel, the more so because iSCSI – just like NFS and CIFS – can benefit from TCP/IP Offload Engines, the Socket Direct Protocol (SDP) and a direct mapping of iSCSI on RDMA (iSER) (Section 3.7). Shared-disk file systems (Section 4.3) also offer a solution for high-speed file sharing and in addition to that, storage virtualization (Chapter 5) provides high-speed file sharing while it addresses the increasingly expensive management of storage and storage networks as well.

4.3   SHARED DISK FILE SYSTEMS

The greatest performance limitation of NAS servers and self-configured file servers is that each file must pass through the internal buses of the file servers twice before the files arrive at the computer where they are required (Figure 4.7). Even DAFS and its alternatives like NFS over RDMA cannot get around this 'eye of the needle'.

With storage networks it is possible for several computers to access a storage device simultaneously. The I/O bottleneck in the file server can be circumvented if all clients fetch the files from the disk directly via the storage network (Figure 4.11).

The difficulty here: today's file systems consider their storage devices as local. They concentrate upon the caching and the aggregation of I/O operations; they increase performance by reducing the number of disk accesses needed.

So-called shared disk file systems can deal with this problem. Integrated into them are special algorithms that synchronize the simultaneous accesses of several computers to common disks. As a result, shared disk file systems make it possible for several computers to access files simultaneously without causing version conflict.

To achieve this, shared disk file systems must synchronize write accesses in addition to the functions of local file systems. It should be ensured locally that new files are written to different areas of the hard disk. It must also be ensured that cache entries are marked as invalid. Let us assume that two computers each have a file in their local cache and one of the computers changes the file. If the second computer subsequently reads the file again it may not take the now invalid copy from the cache.

The great advantage of shared disk file systems is that the computers accessing files and the storage devices in question now communicate with each other directly. The diversion via a central file server, which represents the bottleneck in conventional network file systems and also in DAFS and RDMA-enabled NFS, is no longer necessary.

In addition, the load on the CPU in the accessing machine is reduced because communication via Fibre Channel places less of a load on the processor than communication

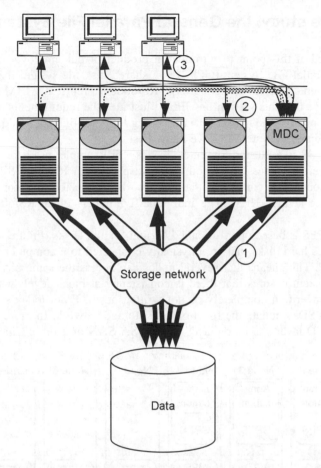

Figure 4.11   In a shared disk file system all clients can access the disks directly via the storage network (1). LAN data traffic is now only necessary for the synchronization of the write accesses (2). The data of a shared disk file system can additionally be exported over the LAN in the form of a network file system with NFS or CIFS (3)

via IP and Ethernet. The sequential access to large files can thus more than make up for the extra cost for access synchronization. On the other hand, in applications with many small files or in the case of many random accesses within the same file, we should check whether the use of a shared disk file system is really worthwhile.

One side-effect of file sharing over the storage network is that the availability of the shared disk file system can be better than that of conventional network file systems. This is because a central file server is no longer needed. If a machine in the shared disk file system cluster fails, then the other machines can carry on working. This means that the availability of the underlying storage devices largely determines the availability of shared disk file systems.

4.3.1   Case study: the General Parallel File System (GPFS)

We have decided at this point to introduce a product of our employer, IBM, for once. The General Parallel File System (GPFS) is a shared disk file system that has for many years been used on cluster computers of type RS/6000 SP (currently IBM eServer Cluster 1600). We believe that this section on GPFS illustrates the requirements of a shared disk file system very nicely. The reason for introducing GPFS at this point is quite simply that it is the shared disk file system that we know best.

The RS/6000 SP is a cluster computer. It was, for example, used for Deep Blue, the computer that beat the chess champion Gary Kasparov. An RS/6000 SP consists of up to 512 conventional AIX computers that can also be connected together via a so-called high performance switch (HPS). The individual computers of an RS/6000 SP are also called nodes.

Originally GPFS is based upon so-called Virtual Shared Disks (Figure 4.12). The VSD subsystem makes hard disks that are physically connected to a computer visible to other nodes of the SP. This means that several nodes can access the same physical hard disk. The VSD subsystem ensures that there is consistency at block level, which means that a block is either written completely or not written at all. From today's perspective we could say that VSDs emulate the function of a storage network. In more recent versions of GPFS the VSD layer can be replaced by an SSA SAN or a Fibre Channel SAN.

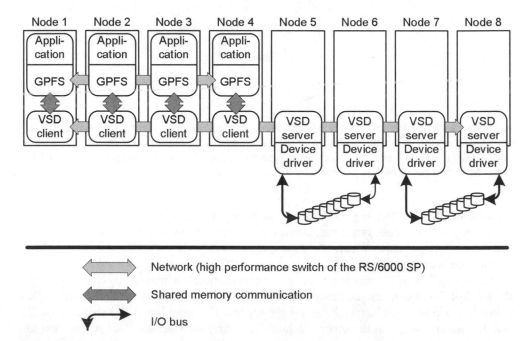

Figure 4.12   Applications see the GPFS file system like a local file system. The GPFS file system itself is a distributed application that synchronizes parallel accesses. The VSD subsystem permits access to hard disks regardless of where they are physically connected

GPFS uses the VSDs to ensure the consistency of the file system, i.e. to ensure that the metadata structure of the file system is maintained. For example, no file names are allocated twice. Furthermore, GPFS realizes some RAID functions such as the striping and mirroring of data and metadata.

Figure 4.12 illustrates two benefits of shared disk file systems. First, they can use RAID 0 to stripe the data over several hard disks, host bus adapters and even disk subsystems, which means that shared disk file systems can achieve a very high throughput. All applications that have at least a partially sequential access pattern profit from this.

Second, the location of the application becomes independent of the location of the data. In Figure 4.12 the system administrator can start applications on the four GPFS nodes that have the most resources (CPU, main memory, buses) available at the time. A so-called workload manager can move applications from one node to the other depending upon load. In conventional file systems this is not possible. Instead, applications have to run on the nodes on which the file system is mounted since access via a network file system such as NFS or CIFS is generally too slow.

The unusual thing about GPFS is that there is no individual file server. Each node in the GPFS cluster can mount a GPFS file system. For end users and applications the GPFS file system behaves – apart from its significantly better performance – like a conventional local file system.

GPFS introduces the so-called node set as an additional management unit. Several node sets can exist within a GPFS cluster, with a single node only ever being able to belong to a maximum of one node set (Figure 4.13). GPFS file systems are only ever visible within a node set. Several GPFS file systems can be active in every node set.

The GPFS Daemon must run on every node in the GPFS cluster. GPFS is realized as distributed application, with all nodes in a GPFS cluster having the same rights and duties. In addition, depending upon the configuration of the GPFS cluster, the GPFS Daemon must take on further administrative functions over and above the normal tasks of a file system.

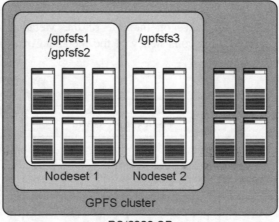

Figure 4.13 GPFS introduces the node sets as an additional management unit. GPFS file systems are visible to all nodes of a node set

In the terminology of GPFS the GPFS Daemon can assume the following roles:

- Configuration Manager
  In every node set one GPFS Daemon takes on the role of the Configuration Manager. The Configuration Manager determines the File System Manager for every file system and monitors the so-called quorum. The quorum is a common procedure in distributed systems that maintains the consistency of the distributed application in the event of a network split. For GPFS more than half of the nodes of a node set must be active. If the quorum is lost in a node set, the GPFS file system is automatically deactivated (unmount) on all nodes of the node set.

- File System Manager
  Every file system has its own File System Manager. Its tasks include the following:
  - configuration changes of the file system;
  - management of the hard disk blocks;
  - token administration;
  - management and monitoring of the quota; and
  - security services.

  Token administration is particularly worth highlighting. One of the design objectives of GPFS is the support of parallel applications that read and modify common files from different nodes. Like every file system, GPFS buffers files or file fragments in order to increase performance. GPFS uses a token mechanism in order to synchronize the cache entries on various computers in the event of parallel write and read accesses (Figure 4.14). However, this synchronization only ensures that GPFS behaves precisely in the same way as a local file system that can only be mounted on one computer. This means that in GPFS – as in every file system – parallel applications still have to synchronize the accesses to common files, for example, by means of locks.

- Metadata Manager
  Finally, one GPFS Daemon takes on the role of the Metadata Manager for every open file. GPFS guarantees the consistency of the metadata of a file because only the

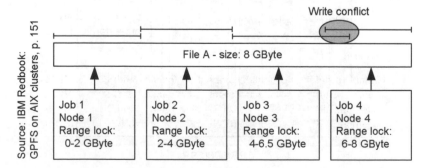

Figure 4.14 GPFS synchronizes write accesses for file areas. If several nodes request the token for the same area, GPFS knows that it has to synchronize cache entries

Metadata Manager may change a file's metadata. Generally, the GPFS Daemon of the node on which the file has been open for the longest is the Metadata Manager for the file. The assignment of the Metadata Manager of a file to a node can change in relation to the access behaviour of the applications.

The example of GPFS shows that a shared disk file system has to achieve a great deal more than a conventional local file system, which is only managed on one computer. GPFS has been used successfully on the RS/6000 SP for some years. The complexity of shared disk file systems is illustrated by the fact that IBM is only gradually transferring the GPFS file system to other operating systems such as Linux, which is strategically supported by IBM, and to new I/O technologies such as Fibre Channel.

4.4 COMPARISON: NAS, FIBRE CHANNEL SAN AND ISCSI SAN

Fibre Channel SAN, iSCSI SAN and NAS are three techniques with which storage networks can be realized. Figure 4.15 compares the I/O paths of the three techniques and Table 4.2 summarizes the most important differences.

In contrast to NAS, in Fibre Channel and iSCSI the data exchange between servers and storage devices takes place in a block-based fashion. Storage networks are more difficult

Table 4.2 Comparison of Fibre Channel, iSCSI and NAS

	Fibre channel	iSCSI	NAS
Protocol	FCP (SCSI)	iSCSI (SCSI)	NFS, CIFS, HTTP
Network	Fibre Channel	TCP/IP	TCP/IP
Source/target	Server/storage device	Server/storage device	Client/NAS server, application server/NAS server
Transfer objects	Device blocks	Device blocks	Files, file fragments
Access via the storage device	Directly via Fibre Channel	Directly via iSCSI	Indirectly via the NAS-internal computer
Embedded file system	No	No	Yes
Pre-fetch hit rate	40%	40%	100%
Configuration	By end user (flexible)	By end user (flexible)	Preconfigured by NAS manufacturers (Plug&Play)
Suitability for databases	Yes	To a limited degree (2003)	T a limited degree
Production-readiness	Yes	To a limited degree (2003)	Yes

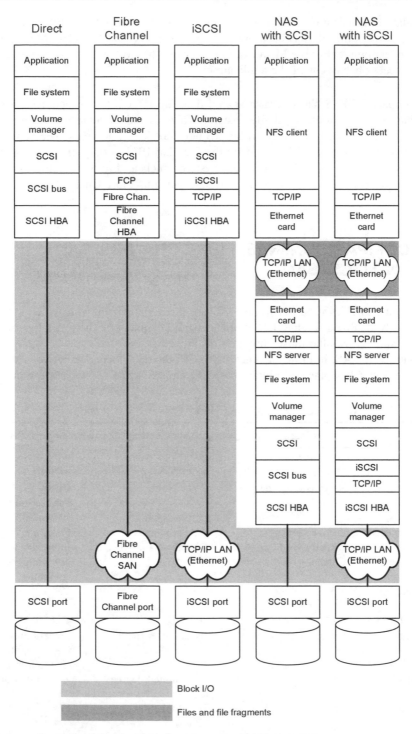

Figure 4.15 Comparison of the different I/O paths of SCSI, iSCSI, Fibre Channel and NAS

to configure. On the other hand, Fibre Channel at least supplies optimal performance for the data exchange between server and storage device.

NAS servers, on the other hand, are turnkey file servers. They can only be used as file servers, but they do this very well. NAS servers have only limited suitability as data storage for databases due to lack of performance. Storage networks can be realized with NAS servers by installing an additional LAN between NAS server and the application servers (Figure 4.16). In contrast to Fibre Channel and iSCSI this storage network transfers files or file fragments.

One supposed advantage of NAS is that NAS servers at first glance have a higher prefetch hit rate than disk subsystems connected via Fibre Channel or iSCSI (or just SCSI). However, it should be borne in mind that NAS servers work at file system level and disk subsystems only at block level. A file server can move the blocks of an opened file from the hard disk into the main memory and thus operate subsequent file accesses more quickly from the main memory.

Disk subsystems, on the other hand, have a prefetch hit rate of around 40% because they only know blocks; they do not know how the data (for example, a file system or database) is organized in the blocks. A self-configured file server or a NAS server that uses hard disks in the storage network can naturally implement its own prefetch strategy in addition to the prefetch strategy of the disk subsystem and, just like a NAS server, achieve a prefetch hit rate of 100%.

As yet, only Fibre Channel and NAS have been successfully implemented in production environments. Fibre Channel satisfies the highest performance requirements – it is currently (2003) the only transmission technique for storage networks that is suitable for I/O intensive databases. Since 2002, iSCSI has slowly been moving into production environments. It is said that iSCSI is initially being used for applications with low or medium performance requirements. It remains to be seen in practice whether iSCSI also satisfies high performance requirements (cf. Section 3.5.2, 'TCP/IP and Ethernet as an I/O technology'). NAS is excellently suited to web servers and for the file sharing of work groups. With RDMA-enabled NFS and CIFS, NAS could also establish itself as a more convenient data store for databases.

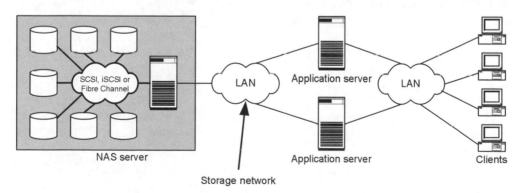

Figure 4.16 For performance reasons a separate LAN, which serves as a storage network, is installed here between the NAS server and the application servers

4.5 SUMMARY

Hard disks provide their storage in the form of blocks that are addressed via cylinders, sectors and tracks. File systems manage the blocks of the hard disks and make their storage capacity available to users in the form of directories and files. Network file systems and shared disk file systems make it possible to access to the common data set from various computers. Modern file systems have additional functions, which can increase the availability of data in various situations. Journaling ensures that file systems become available again quickly after a system crash; snapshots allows data sets to be practically copied within a few seconds; the volume manager makes it possible to react to changed storage requirements without interrupting operation. Network file systems export local file systems over the LAN so that it is possible to work on a common data set from different computers. The performance of network file systems is limited by two factors: (1) all data accesses to network file systems have to pass through a single file server; and (2) current network file systems such as NFS and CIFS and the underlying network protocols are not suitable for a high throughput. We introduced two approaches to circumventing these performance bottlenecks: RDMA-enabled file systems such as the Direct Access File System (DAFS) and shared disk file systems such as the General Parallel File System (GPFS). Network Attached Storage (NAS) represents a new product category. NAS servers are preconfigured file servers, the operating systems of which have been optimized for the tasks of file servers. Storage networks can also be realized with NAS servers. However, current NAS servers are not suitable for providing storage space for I/O intensive databases.

In the previous chapters we have introduced all the necessary techniques for storage networks. Many of these techniques deal with the virtualization of storage resources like RAID, instant copy, remote mirroring, volume manager, file systems, and file system snapshots. All these virtualization techniques have in common that they present given storage resources to the upper layers as logical resources which are easier to use and administrate and which very often are also more performant and more failure tolerant. The next chapter will discuss how the concept of storage virtualization changes in a storage-centric IT architecture.

5

Storage Virtualization

Although the cost of storage has fallen considerably in recent years, at the same time the need for storage has risen immensely, so that we can observe of a real data explosion. The administrative costs associated with these quantities of data should not, however, increase to the same degree. The introduction of storage networks is a first step towards remedying the disadvantages of the server-centric IT architecture (Section 1.1). Whereas in smaller environments the use of storage networks is completely adequate for the mastery of data, practical experience has shown that, in large environments, a storage network alone is not sufficient to efficiently manage the ever-increasing volumes of data.

In this chapter we will introduce the storage virtualization in the storage network, an approach that has the potential to get to grips with the management of large quantities of data. The basic idea behind storage virtualization is to move the storage virtualization functions from the servers (volume manager, file systems) and disk subsystems (caching, RAID, instant copy, remote mirroring, LUN masking) into the storage network (Figure 5.1). This creates a new virtualization entity which, as a result of its positioning in the storage network, spans all servers and storage systems. This new virtualization in the storage network permits the full utilization of the potential of a storage network with regard to the efficient use of resources and data, the improvement of performance and protection against failures.

As an introduction into storage virtualization we repeat the I/O path from the disk to the main memory: Section 5.1 contrasts the virtualization variants discussed so far once again. Then we describe the difficulties relating to storage administration and the requirements of data and data users that occur in a storage network, for which storage virtualization aims to provide a solution (Section 5.2). We will then define the term 'storage virtualization' and consider the concept of storage virtualization in more detail (Section 5.3). We will see that for storage virtualization a virtualization entity is required. The requirements for

Storage Networks Explained   U. Troppens R. Erkens W. Müller
© 2004 John Wiley & Sons, Ltd   ISBN: 0-470-86182-7

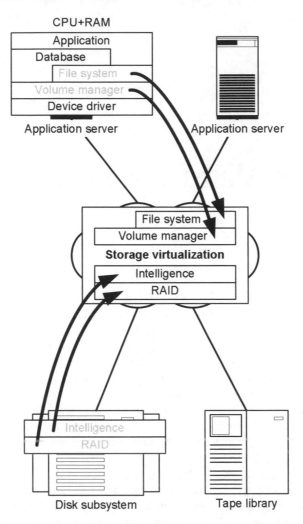

CPU+RAM

Figure 5.1 The storage virtualization in the storage network moves virtualization functions from servers and storage devices into the storage network. This creates a new virtualization entity which, as a result of its central position in the storage network, spans all servers and storage systems and can thus centrally manage all available storage resources

this virtualization entity are defined and some implementation considerations investigated (Section 5.4). Then we will consider the two different forms of virtualization (on block and file level) (Section 5.5), before going on to consider on which different levels a virtualization entity can be positioned in the storage network (server, storage device or network) and the advantages and disadvantages of each (Section 5.6). We will back this up by reintroducing some examples of virtualization methods that have already been discussed. Finally, we will introduce two new virtualization approaches – symmetric and asymmetric storage virtualization – in which the virtualization entity is positioned in the storage network (Section 5.7).

5.1   ONCE AGAIN: VIRTUALIZATION IN THE I/O PATH

The structure of Chapters 2, 3 and 4 was based upon the I/O path from the hard disk to the main memory (Figure 1.7). Consequently, several sections of these chapters discuss different aspects of virtualization. This section consolidates the various realization locations for storage virtualization which we have presented so far. After that we will move on to the virtualization inside of the storage network.

Virtualization is the name given to functions such as RAID, caching, instant copies and remote mirroring. The objectives of virtualization are:

- improvement of availability (fault-tolerance)
- improvement of performance
- improvement of scalability
- improvement of maintainability.

At various points of the previous chapters we encountered virtualization functions. Figure 5.2 illustrates the I/O path from the CPU to the storage system and shows at what points of the I/O path virtualization is realized. We have already discussed in detail virtualization within a disk subsystem (Chapter 2) and, based upon the example of volume manager and file system, in the main memory and CPU (Chapter 4). The host bus adapter and the storage network itself should be mentioned as further possible realization locations for virtualization functions.

Virtualization in the disk subsystem has the advantage that tasks are moved from the computer to the disk subsystem, thus freeing up the computer. The functions are realized at the point where the data is stored: at the hard disks. Measures such as mirroring (RAID 1) and instant copies only load the disk subsystem itself (Figure 5.3). This additional cost is not even visible on the I/O channel between computer and disk subsystem. The communication between servers and other devices on the same I/O bus is thus not impaired.

Virtualization in the storage network has the advantage that the capacity of all available storage resources (e.g. disks and tapes) is centrally managed (Figure 5.4). This reduces the costs for the management of and access to storage resources and permits a more

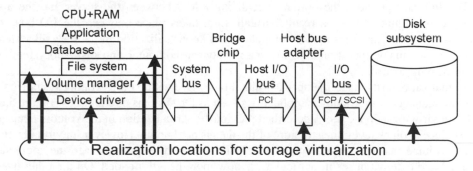

Figure 5.2   Virtualization functions can be realized at various points in the I/O path

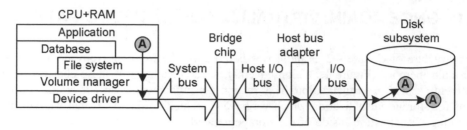

Figure 5.3   Virtualization in the disk subsystem frees up the server and storage network

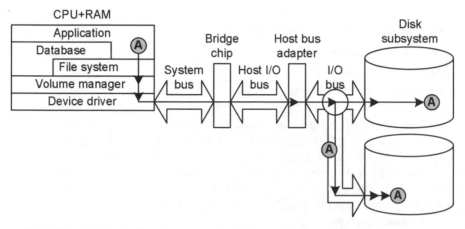

Figure 5.4   Virtualization in the storage network is not visible to the server

efficient utilization of the available hardware. For example, a cache server installed in the storage network can serve various disk subsystems. Depending upon the load on the individual disk subsystems, sometimes one and sometimes the other requires more cache. If virtualization is realized only within the disk subsystems, the cache of one disk subsystem that currently has a lower load cannot be used to support a different disk subsystem operating at a higher load. A further advantage of virtualization within the storage network is that functions such as caching, instant copy and remote mirroring can be used even with cheaper disk subsystems (JBODs, RAID arrays).

The I/O card provides the option of realizing RAID between the server and the disk subsystem (Figure 5.5). As a result, virtualization takes place between the I/O bus and the host I/O bus. This frees up the computer just like virtualization in the disk subsystem, however, for many operations the I/O buses between computer and disk subsystem are more heavily loaded.

Virtualization in the main memory can either take place within the operating system in the volume manager or in low-level applications such as file systems or databases (Figure 5.6). Like all virtualization locations described previously, virtualization in the volume manager takes place at block level; the structure of the data is not known. However, in virtualization in the volume manager the cost for the virtualization is fully passed on to the computer: internal and external buses in particular are now more heavily loaded. On the other hand, the CPU load for volume manager mirroring can generally be disregarded.

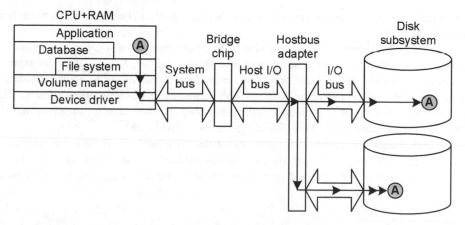

Figure 5.5 Virtualization in the host bus adapter also remains hidden to the server

The alternative approach of realizing copying functions such as remote mirroring and instant copy in system-near applications such as file systems and databases is of interest. The applications know the structure of the data and can therefore sometimes perform the copying functions significantly more efficiently than when the structure is not known.

It is not possible to give any general recommendation regarding the best location for the realization of virtualization. Instead it is necessary to consider the requirements of resource consumption, fault-tolerance, performance, scalability and ease of administration for the specific individual case when selecting the realization location. From the point of view of the resource load on the server it is beneficial to realize the virtualization as close as possible to the hard disk. However, to increase performance when performance requirements are high, it is necessary to virtualize within the main memory: only thus can the load be divided amongst several host bus adapters and host I/O buses (Figure 5.6).

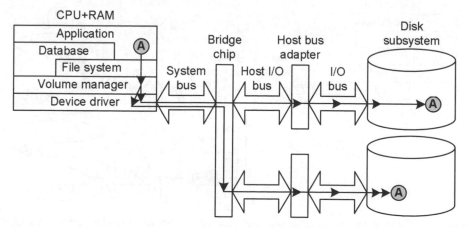

Figure 5.6 Virtualization in the volume manager facilitates load distribution over several buses and disk subsystems

Virtualization in the volume manager is also beneficial from the point of view of fault-tolerance (Section 6.3.3).

As is the case of many design decisions, the requirements of simple maintainability and high performance are in conflict in the selection of the virtualization location. In Section 2.5.3 we discussed how both the performance and also the fault-tolerance of disk subsystems can be increased by the combination of RAID 0 (striping) and RAID 1 (mirroring), with the striping of mirrored disks being more beneficial in terms of fault-tolerance and maintainability than the mirroring of striped disks.

However, things are different if data is distributed over several disk subsystems. In terms of high fault-tolerance and simple maintainability it is often better to mirror the blocks in the volume manager and then stripe them within the disk subsystems by means

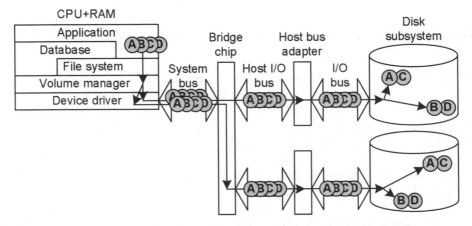

Figure 5.7 Mirroring in the volume manager protects against the failure of a disk subsystem. The blocks are striped within the disk subsystems to increase performance

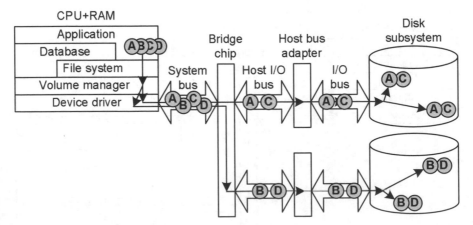

Figure 5.8 Striping in the volume manager for very high write performance: the load is distributed over several disk subsystems and I/O buses. The blocks are not mirrored until they reach the disk subsystems

of RAID 0 or RAID 5 (Figure 5.7). This has the advantage that the application can be kept in operation if an entire disk subsystem fails.

In applications with very high performance requirements for write throughput, it is not always feasible to mirror in the volume manager because the blocks have to be transferred through the host I/O bus twice, as shown in Figure 5.7. If the host I/O bus is the performance bottleneck, then it is better to stripe the blocks in the volume manager and only mirror them within the disk subsystems (Figure 5.8). The number of blocks to be written can thus be halved at the expense of fault-tolerance.

5.2 LIMITATIONS AND REQUIREMENTS

In this section we will first discuss architecture-related (Section 5.2.1) and implementation-related limitations (Section 5.2.2) of storage networks. We will then go on to describe further requirements for an efficient management of storage in large storage networks (Section 5.2.3). Finally, in Section 5.2.4, we will summarize the requirements of storage virtualization.

5.2.1 Architecture-related limitations of non-virtualized storage networks

The storage resources brought together in a storage network are easier to manage than those in a server-centric IT architecture due to the separation of servers and storage devices. In many cases, the number of storage devices to be administered can also be drastically reduced by the introduction of a storage network. As a result, resource management becomes easier and more flexible (Section 1.3).

The flexible assignment of free hard disk capacity (Figure 2.3) alone is not, however, enough to fully exploit the savings potential of the storage-centric IT architecture such as resource and data sharing and the simplification of the management of storage resources. Without storage virtualization in the storage network there remains a direct connection between the storage device that provides the storage and the server that uses it. If, for example, changes are made to the configuration of the storage devices, then these remain visible on the server, meaning that appropriate modifications are necessary there. In smaller environments with moderate data quantities this may be acceptable. In large environments the examples mentioned below represent a greater challenge to system administrators.

The replacement of storage devices in the event of a defect or an upgrade to newer, more powerful devices can only be performed at significant extra cost because the data from the old media must be transferred to the new. Additionally, administrators often are faced with an impossible task if this is to take place in a 24×7 environment without application failures. The modifications that have to be carried out on servers and applications to use the new storage devices after a replacement give rise to additional costs.

Without storage virtualization, every change to the storage resources requires changes to the operating system and to the applications on the servers that use this. In many configurations a volume manager shields changes to the storage hardware from the applications. We will see later that a volume manager represents a form of storage virtualization. In addition to storage virtualization on the server by a volume manager we will also discover further possibilities for storage virtualization, which solve the problem of the direct influence of storage devices and servers.

Often there is also an inefficient use of the storage resources. For example, the following situation can occur (Figure 5.9): a storage network has two servers, A and B, which own disk space allocated on a disk subsystem. If the disks on server A have been filled, this server cannot simply share the free storage space on the drives of server B.

This is because the volumes on a disk subsystem are still statically assigned to a server and no suitable mechanisms have been implemented in the disk subsystems for the sharing of block-level resources. So, although on most disk subsystems it is possible to assign the same volume to several servers, the possible data inconsistencies that could arise as a

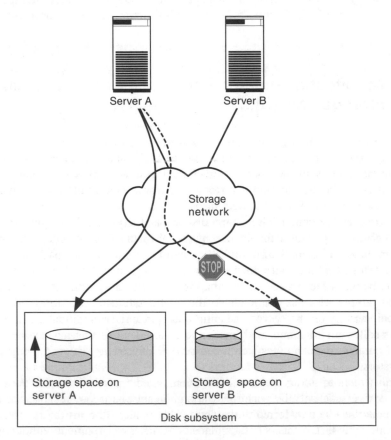

Figure 5.9 The storage space on server A is full. It cannot utilize the free storage space which is available on the volumes for server B

result of such disk sharing are not rectified by the disk subsystem itself. The consequence of this is that additional new storage must be purchased or at least further storage devices allocated in order to solve the space problems of server A, even though the capacity allocated to server B has not yet been used up. Storage virtualization software can realize the sharing of resources in a storage network. The shared disk file systems introduced in Section 4.3 represent one approach to this. However, the complexity of the software to be used for this increases the administrative cost.

5.2.2 Implementation-related limitations of storage networks

In previous sections we discussed only the conceptual boundaries of storage networks. In real environments matters are even worse. Incompatibilities between the storage systems of different manufacturers represent the main evil. For example, the manufacturers of disk subsystems are currently (2003) supplying special device drivers for their storage devices which provide advanced functions like handling multiple paths between a server and the storage device (Section 6.3.1). Unfortunately these disk subsystem specific device drivers only work with *one* disk subsystem type. To make matters worse, the installation of the device drivers for different disk subsystems onto one computer at the same time is usually not supported.

This incompatibility between disk subsystem specific device drivers means that each server is linked to a very specific disk subsystem model or a very specific range of disk subsystem models, depending upon the respective device driver (Figure 5.10). As a result, one advantage of storage networks that has been mentioned several times in this book – namely the flexible allocation of free storage – only works on paper and in homogeneous storage landscapes. In real systems, a server can only use free storage capacity if this exists on a storage device with a compatible device driver. It currently (2003) looks as though the functionality of device drivers will, to an increasing degree, be integrated into operating systems, so that this limitation will very probably be rectified in a few years. Furthermore, some disk subsystem vendors are working on the interoperability of their device drivers and they can thus be installed in parallel on the same server.

In practice this leads directly to economic disadvantages: let us assume that high performance requirements exist for 20% of the data of an application, whilst only average performance requirements exist for the remaining 80%. In this case it would be desirable to put just the 20% of the data on a high-end disk subsystem and store the rest of the data on a cheaper mid-range disk subsystem. Due to the incompatibility of the disk subsystem device drivers, however, the application server can only be connected to one type of disk subsystem, which means that all data must be stored on the high-end disk subsystem. Ultimately, this means that 80% of the data is taking up storage capacity that is more expensive than necessary.

A further interoperability problem in the practical use of storage systems is the lack of standardization of the interfaces for the disk subsystem-based remote mirroring (Section 2.7.2). As a result of this, the data cannot currently (2003) be mirrored between

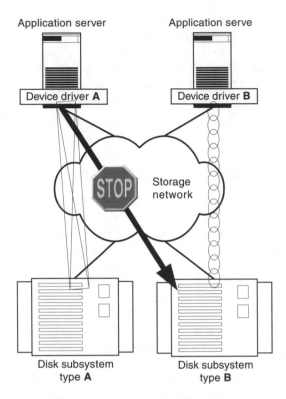

Figure 5.10 The incompatibilities that currently (2003) exist between the device drivers for different disk subsystems mean that a server can only use the storage capacity of the corresponding disk subsystems

any two storage systems. Usually, remote mirroring is only possible between two disk subsystems of the same type, only very exceptionally is it possible between different models or between two devices from different manufacturers. Here too, economic disadvantages result because this restricts the choice of disk subsystems that can be combined, meaning that it is not always possible to use the most economical storage system.

The inadequate interoperability of disk subsystem device drivers and remote mirroring gives rise to very real difficulties when replacing an old disk subsystem with a new one: this operation requires that the data from the old device is copied to the new device. However, it is precisely this copying process that can be very difficult in practice. Data mirroring by the volume manager would be preferable, so that the data could be copied to the new disk subsystem largely without interruptions. However, it is precisely this that is not possible if the device drivers of the two participating disk subsystems are not compatible with each other. In this situation, remote mirroring does not offer an alternative due to the lack of interoperability. Ultimately, economic disadvantages arise here, too, because it is not always possible to choose the most economical new storage system.

5.2.3 Increasing complexity in the administration of large storage networks

The introduction of storage networks is a first step towards the efficient management of storage resources, but it alone cannot solve the problems associated with the data explosion. In large environments with several dozens of servers, each working on several disks, a storage administrator has to deal with hundreds of virtual and even more physical disks. In the following we wish to describe some difficulties associated with the administration of storage resources and the requirements of data and data users in such large environments.

Storage networks offer the possibility of realizing requirements such as scalability, availability, performance, data protection and migration. Often, however, this calls for complex configurations, the administration of which again requires additional time and expense. Furthermore, requirements regarding availability, performance, data protection or migration are different for different data. For example, certain data has to be available even in the event of the failure of its storage resources, whereas it is possible to temporarily manage without other data. Some data has to be available to applications quickly, for example in order to keep the response times of a database low. For other data the response time is not so critical, but it may have to be backed up frequently. Still other data tends to change so seldom that frequent back-ups are not required. All this has to be taken into consideration when distributing the data on the resources. Data that requires a high throughput should therefore be stored on faster – and thus more expensive – media such as hard disks, whereas other data can be moved to slower – and thus cheaper – tapes.

A storage administrator is not able to match the requirements for the data to the physical storage devices. In large environments it would be too much to deal with the needs of every single virtual disk which is assigned to a server. Therefore, corresponding data profiles have to be created that specify the requirements of the data. An entity is required here that creates such data profiles automatically based particularly upon the data usage, and realizes these accordingly. In this manner load peaks in the use of individual data can be recognized so that this data can be moved to fast media or can be distributed over several resources in order to achieve a balanced resource utilization.

Furthermore, users of storage do not want to think about the size, type and location of the storage media when using their applications. They demand an intuitive handling of the storage media. The actual processes that are necessary for the administration of storage should remain hidden and run so that they are invisible to users. Users of storage space are, however, very interested in response times, data throughput and the availability of their applications. In short: users only think about what is related to their applications and not to the physical aspects of their data. The creation of this user-friendliness and the respective service level agreements for storage resources imposes additional requirements on storage administrators.

5.2.4 Proposed solution: storage virtualization

To sum up, we can say that the implementation of a storage network alone does not meet the requirements for the management of large quantities of data. This requires additional mechanisms that simplify administration and at the same time make it possible to make full use of the storage resources. The use of storage virtualization software offers the appropriate possibilities for, on the one hand, simplifying the administration of data and storage resources and, on the other, making their use by the users easier.

The objectives of storage virtualization can be summed up by the following three points:

- simplification of the administration and access of storage resources;
- full utilization of the possibilities of a storage network: the possibilities of a storage network should be fully utilized with regard to the efficient use of resources and data, the improvement of performance and protection in the event of failures by a high level of data availability;
- realization of advanced storage functions that are oriented towards the data profiles and run automatically, such as data back-ups and archiving, data migration, data integrity, access controls and data sharing.

5.3   DEFINITION OF STORAGE VIRTUALIZATION

The term 'storage virtualization' is generally used to mean the separation of the storage into the physical implementation level of the storage devices and the logical representation level of the storage for use by operating systems, applications and users.

In the following we will also use the term 'virtualization', i.e. dropping the word 'storage'. This is always used in the sense of the above definition of storage virtualization. Various uses of the term 'storage virtualization' and 'virtualization' are found in the literature depending upon which level of the storage network the storage virtualization takes place on. The various levels of the storage network here are the server, the storage devices and the network. Some authors only speak of storage virtualization if they explicitly mean storage virtualization within the network. They use the term virtualization, on the other hand, to mean the storage virtualization in the storage devices (for example, in the disk subsystems) or on servers (such as in a volume manager). However, these different types of storage virtualization are not fundamentally different. Therefore, we do not differentiate between the two terms and always use 'storage virtualization' and 'virtualization' in the sense of the above definition.

In Section 5.1 ('Once Again: Virtualization in the I/O Path') we revised various types of storage virtualization on the various levels of the storage network and we will pick these up again later. First of all, however, we want to deal in detail with the conceptual realization of storage virtualization.

Storage virtualization inserts – metaphorically speaking – an additional layer between storage devices and storage users (Figure 5.11). This forms the interface between virtual and physical storage, by mapping the physical storage onto the virtual and conversely the virtual storage onto the physical. The separation of storage into the physical implementation level and the logical representation level is achieved by abstracting the physical

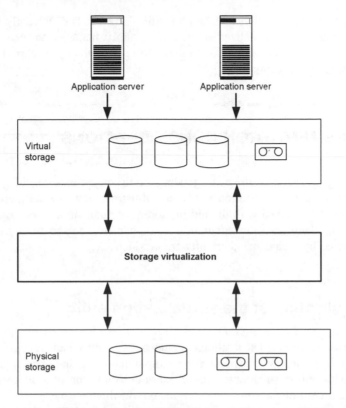

Figure 5.11 In storage virtualization an additional layer is inserted between the storage devices and servers. This forms the interface between virtual and physical storage

storage to the logical storage by aggregating several physical storage units to form one or more logical, so-called virtual, storage units. The operating system or applications no longer have direct access to the physical storage devices, they use exclusively the virtual storage. Storage accesses to the physical storage resources take place independently and separately from the storage accesses to the virtual storage resources.

For example, the physical hard disks available on a disk stack (JBOD) are brought together by the volume manager of a server to form a large logical volume. In this manner the volume manager thus forms an additional layer between the physical disks of the disk stack and the logical and thus virtual volume with which the applications (e.g. filesystems and databases) of the server work. Within this layer, the mapping of physical hard disks onto logical volumes and vice versa is performed.

This means that storage virtualization always calls for a virtualization entity that maps from virtual to physical storage and vice versa. On the one hand it has to make the virtual storage available to the operating system, the applications and the users in usable form and, on the other, it has to realize data accesses to the physical storage medium. This entity can be implemented both as hardware and software on the various levels in a storage network.

It is also possible for several virtualization entities to be used concurrently. For example, an application can use the virtualized volume of a volume manager on server level, which for its part is formed from a set of virtualized volumes which are exported by one or more disk subsystems (Section 5.1).

5.4 IMPLEMENTATION CONSIDERATIONS

In the following we want to draw up general requirements and considerations for the implementation of the virtualization entity and illustrate how the difficulties described in Section 5.2 can be solved with the aid of storage virtualization. For example, storage virtualization also facilitates the integration of higher storage functions that previously had to be realized by means of other software products.

5.4.1 Realization of the virtualization entity

First of all, it is important that a storage virtualization entity can be administered from a central console regardless of whether it is implemented as hardware or software and where it is positioned in the storage network. It is desirable for all tools that are required for the administration of the storage device to run via this console.

All operations performed by the virtualization entity should take place in a rule-based manner and orientate themselves to the applicable data profiles. Policy-based operation allows the storage administrator to configure and control the operations of the virtualization entity. Profile-orientation makes it possible for the data to be automated according to its specific properties and requirements.

Because virtualization always intervenes in the data stream, correct implementation is indispensable if data corruption is to be avoided. The virtualization entity itself should therefore also be backed up so that access to the virtualized storage resources is still possible in the event of a failure. The concepts for server-clustering introduced in Section 6.3.2 are suitable here.

In order to achieve the greatest possible degree of compatibility to servers and applications and also to win acceptance amongst users it is necessary for a virtualization entity to remain hidden from its users. Servers, applications and users must always have the impression that they are working with physical storage media and must not notice the existence of a virtualization entity. Furthermore, for reasons of compatibility, access on both file and block level, including the required protocols, must be supported (Section 5.5).

In addition to virtualized storage, the classical non-virtualized storage access options should continue to exist. This facilitates first of all an incremental introduction of the virtualization technique into the storage network and second, allows applications, servers and storage devices that are incompatible with virtualization to continue to be operated in the same storage network. For example, in our practical work during the testing of virtualization software we found that the connection of a Windows server functioned perfectly, whilst the connection of a Solaris server failed. This was because of minor deviations from the Fibre Channel standard in the realization of the Fibre Channel protocol in the virtualization software used.

5.4.2 Exchange of storage devices

When using storage virtualization the exchange of storage devices is relatively easy to perform, since the servers no longer access the physical devices directly, instead only working with virtual storage media. The exchange of a storage device in this case involves the following steps:

1. Connection of the new storage device to the storage network.
2. Configuration and connection of the new storage device to the virtualization entity.
3. Migration of the data from the old to the new device by the virtualization entity whilst the applications are running.
4. Removal of the old storage device from the configuration of the virtualization entity.
5. Removal of the old storage device from the storage network.

The process requires no configuration changes to the applications. These continue to work on their virtual hard disks throughout the entire process.

5.4.3 Efficient use of resources by dynamic storage allocation

Certain mechanisms, such as the insertion of a volume manager within the virtualization entity, permit the implementation of various approaches for the efficient use of resources. First, all storage resources can be shared. Furthermore, the virtualization entity can react dynamically to the capacity requirements of virtual storage by making more physical capacity available to a growing data set on virtual storage and, in the converse case, freeing up the storage once again if the data set shrinks. Such concepts can be more easily developed on the file level than on the block level since on the file level a file system holds the information on unoccupied blocks, whereas on the block level this information is lacking. Even if such concepts have not previously been realized, they can be realized with storage virtualization.

In this manner it is possible to practically imitate a significantly larger storage, of which only part is actually physically present. By the dynamic allocation of the physical storage, additional physical storage can be assigned to the virtual storage when needed. Finally by dynamic, data-oriented storage allocation it is possible to achieve a more efficient utilization of resources.

5.4.4   Efficient use of resources by data migration

If a virtualization entity is oriented towards the profiles of the data that it administers, it can determine which data is required and how often. In this manner it is possible to control the distribution of the data on fast and slow storage devices in order to achieve a high data throughput for frequently required data. Such data migration is also useful if it is based upon the data type. In the case of video data, for example, it can be worthwhile to store only the start of the file on fast storage in order to provide users with a short insight into the video file. If the user then accesses further parts of the video file that are not on the fast storage, this must first be played back from the slower to the fast storage.

5.4.5   Performance increase

Performance can be increased in several ways with the aid of storage virtualization. First of all, caching within the virtualization entity always presents a good opportunity for reducing the number of slow physical accesses (Section 2.6).

Techniques such as striping or mirroring within the virtualization entity for distributing the data over several resources can also be used to increase performance (Section 2.5).

Further options for increasing performance are presented by the distribution of the I/O load amongst several virtualization entities working together and amongst several data paths between server and virtual storage or virtual storage and physical storage devices (Section 5.1).

5.4.6   Availability due to the introduction of redundancy

The virtualization entity can ensure the redundancy of the data by itself since it has complete control over the resources. The appropriate RAID techniques are suitable here (Section 2.5). For example, in the event of the failure of a storage device, operation can nevertheless be continued. The virtualization entity can then immediately start to mirror the data once again in order to restore the redundancy of the data. As a result, a device failure is completely hidden from the servers – apart from possible temporary reductions in performance.

It is even more important that information about a device failure is reported to a central console so that the device is replaced immediately. The message arriving at the console can also be forwarded by e-mail or pager to the responsible person (Section 8.3).

Multiple access paths, both between servers and virtual storage and also between virtual storage and physical storage devices can also contribute to the improvement of fault-tolerance in storage virtualization (Section 6.3.1).

5.4.7 Back-up and archiving

A virtualization entity is also a suitable data protection tool. By the use of appropriate rules the administrator can, for example, define different back-up intervals for different data. Since the virtualization entity is responsible for the full administration of the physical storage it can perform the back-up processes in question independently. All network back-up methods (Chapter 7) can be integrated into storage virtualization.

5.4.8 Data sharing

Data sharing can be achieved if the virtualization entity permits access to the virtual storage on file level. In this case, the virtualization entity manages the file system centrally. By means of appropriate protocols, the servers can access the files in this file system in parallel. Currently this is permitted primarily by classical network file systems such as NFS and CIFS (Section 4.2) and fast shared disk file systems (Section 4.3). Some manufacturers are working on cross-platform shared disk file systems with the corresponding protocol mechanisms that permit the fast file sharing even in heterogeneous environments.

5.4.9 Privacy protection

The allocation of user rights and access configurations can also be integrated into a virtualization entity, since it forms the interface between virtual and physical storage and thus prevents direct access to the storage by the user. In this manner, the access rights of the data can be managed from a central point.

5.5 STORAGE VIRTUALIZATION ON BLOCK OR FILE LEVEL

In Section 5.3 we saw that the virtualization of storage requires an entity that maps between virtual and physical storage and vice versa. The virtualization entity can be located on the servers (for example, in the form of a volume manager), on the storage devices (for example, in a disk subsystem) or in the network (for example, as a special device). Regardless of which level of the storage network (server, network or storage device) the virtualization entity is located on, we can differentiate between two basic types of virtualization: virtualization on block level and virtualization on file level.

Virtualization on block level means that storage capacity is made available to the operating system or the applications in the form of virtual disks (Figure 5.12). Operating system and applications on the server then work to the blocks of this virtual disk. To this

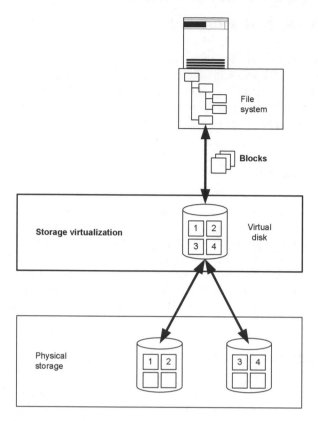

Figure 5.12 In virtualization on block level the virtualization entity provides the virtual storage to the servers in the form of a virtual hard disk

end, the blocks are managed as normal – like the blocks of a physical disk – by a file system or by a database on the server. The task of the virtualization entity is to map these virtual blocks to the physical blocks of the real storage devices. It can come about as part of this process that the physical blocks that belong to the virtual blocks of a file in the file system of the operating system are stored on different physical storage devices or that they are virtualized once more by a further virtualization entity within a storage device.

By contrast, virtualization on file level means that the virtualization entity provides virtual storage to the operating systems or applications in the form of files and directories (Figure 5.13). In this case, the applications work with files instead of blocks and the conversion of the files to virtual blocks is performed by the virtualization entity itself. The physical blocks are presented in the form of a virtual file system and not in the form of virtual blocks. The management of the file system is shifted from the server to the virtualization entity.

To sum up, virtualization on block or file level can be differentiated as follows: in virtualization on block level, access to the virtual storage takes place by means of blocks, in virtualization on file level it takes place by means of files. In virtualization on block

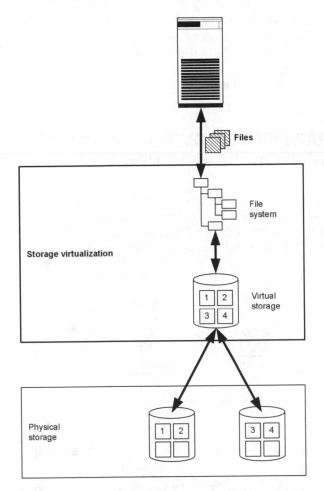

Figure 5.13   In virtualization on file level the virtualization entity provides the virtual storage to the servers in the form of files and directories

level the task of file system management is the responsibility of the operating system or the applications, whereas in virtualization on file level this task is performed by the virtualization entity.

Virtualization on block level is suitable if the storage is to be virtualized for as many different operating systems and applications as possible. Virtualization on block level is actually necessary when dealing with applications that handle their storage access on block level and cannot work on file level. Classic representatives of this category are, for example, databases that can only work with raw devices.

Virtualization on file level, on the other hand, is indispensable for those who want to establish data sharing between several servers. To achieve this, the virtualization entity must allow several servers access to the same files. This can only be achieved if the file system is implemented in the form of a shared resource as in a network file system

(Section 4.2) or a shared disk file system (Section 4.3) or, just like virtualization on file level, is held centrally by the virtualization entity.

In this chapter we constrain the virtualization on block level to the virtualization of disks. Later on in Chapter 9 we will expand this approach and discuss the virtualization of removeable media like tapes and opticals.

5.6 STORAGE VIRTUALIZATION ON VARIOUS LEVELS OF THE STORAGE NETWORK

In the following we will concern ourselves with the points at which a virtualization entity can be positioned in the storage network. The following three levels can be defined here (Figure 5.14): the server (Section 5.6.1) the storage devices (Section 5.6.2) and the network (Section 5.6.3). This will be explained in what follows.

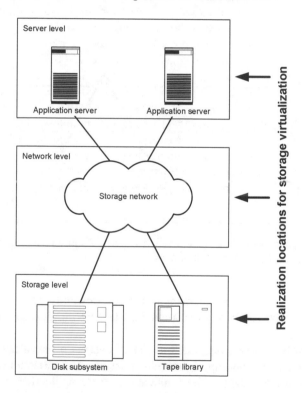

Figure 5.14   A virtualization entity can be positioned on various levels of the storage network

5.6.1   Storage virtualization in the server:

A classic representative of virtualization in the server is the combination of file system and volume manager (Section 4.1.4). A volume manager undertakes the separation of the storage into logical view and physical implementation by encapsulating the physical hard disk into logical disk groups and logical volumes. These are then made available to the applications via file systems. File systems and databases positioned on the server now work with these logical volumes and cease to work directly with the physical hard disks. Some volume managers additionally have further storage functions such as RAID, snapshots or dynamic reconfiguration options, which permit the addition and removal of storage during operation. With shared disk file systems (Section 4.3) storage virtualization can be expanded to several servers, in order to allow fast file sharing among several servers. These cannot, however, be used in a straightforward manner in heterogeneous environments due to the incompatibilities that prevail.

Virtualization on block level can be performed on a server by the host bus adapter itself. Virtualization on block level is found, for example, in the use of a RAID controller. This performs the mapping of the logical blocks that are used by the file system or the volume manager of the operating system to the physical blocks of the various drives.

The benefits of virtualization on server level are:

- Tried and tested virtualization techniques are generally used.
- The virtualization functions can link in several storage systems.
- No additional hardware is required in the storage network to perform the virtualization. Thus additional error sources can be ruled out. The approach remains cost-effective.

The disadvantages of a virtualization on server level are:

- The administration of the storage virtualization must take place on every single server. To achieve this, the appropriate software must be installed and maintained upon the computers.
- The storage virtualization software running on the server can cost system resources and thus have a negative impact upon the server performance.
- Incompatibilities may occur between the virtualization software and certain applications.
- The virtualization extends only to those areas of a storage network that are accessible or assigned to those servers running a virtualization entity.
- The virtualization only ever takes place on individual servers. This disadvantage can be remedied by complex cluster approaches, which, however, come at an additional administration cost.

5.6.2   Storage virtualization in storage devices

Virtualization on block level in storage devices is, for example, found within intelligent disk subsystems (Section 2.7). These storage systems make their storage available to several servers via various I/O channels by means of LUN masking and RAID. The physical hard disks are brought together by the storage devices to form virtual disks, which the servers access using protocols such as SCSI, Fibre Channel FCP or iSCSI. In this manner, the mapping of virtual to physical blocks is achieved.

Virtualization on file level in storage devices is, for example, achieved by NAS servers (Section 4.2.2). The file system management is the responsibility of the NAS server. Access by the server to the storage resources takes place on file level by means of protocols such as NFS and CIFS.

The advantages of virtualization on storage device level are:

- The majority of the administration takes place directly upon the storage device, which is currently perceived as easier and more reliable since it takes place very close to the physical devices.

- Advanced storage functions such as RAID and instant copies are realized directly at the physical storage resources, meaning that servers and I/O buses are not loaded.

- The uncoupling of the servers additionally eases the work in heterogeneous environments since a storage device is able to make storage available to various platforms.

- The servers are not placed under additional load by virtualization operations.

The disadvantages of virtualization on storage device level are:

- Configuration and implementation of virtualization are manufacturer-specific and may thus become a proprietary solution in the event of certain incompatibilities with other storage devices.

- It is very difficult – and sometimes even impossible – to get storage devices from different manufacturers to work together.

- Here too, virtualization takes place only within a storage system and cannot effectively be expanded to include several such storage devices without additional server software.

5.6.3 Storage virtualization in the network

Storage virtualization by a virtualization entity in the storage network is realized by symmetric or asymmetric storage virtualization (Section 5.7). First, however, we want to discuss the general advantages and disadvantages of storage virtualization in the network.

The advantages of virtualization in the storage network are:

- The virtualization can extend over the storage devices of various manufacturers.

- The virtualization is available to servers with different operating systems that are connected to the storage network.

- Advanced storage functions, such as mirroring or snapshots can be used on storage devices that do not themselves support these techniques (for example, JBODs and low cost RAID arrays).

- The administration of storage virtualization can be performed from a central point.
- The virtualization operations load neither the server nor the storage device.

The disadvantages are:

- Additional hardware and software are required in the storage network.
- A virtualization entity in the storage network can become a performance bottleneck.
- Storage virtualization in the storage network is currently (2003) still a new product category. Hardly any such systems have been used in production environments for a long period of time.

5.7 SYMMETRIC AND ASYMMETRIC STORAGE VIRTUALIZATION IN THE NETWORK

The symmetric and asymmetric virtualization models are representatives of storage virtualization in the network. In both approaches it is possible to perform virtualization both on block and on file level. In both models the virtualization entity that undertakes the separation between physical and logical storage is placed in the storage network in the form of a specialized server or a device. This holds all the meta-information needed for the virtualization. The virtualization entity is therefore also called the metadata controller. Its duties also include the management of storage resources and the control of all storage functions that are offered in addition to virtualization.

Symmetric and asymmetric virtualization differ primarily with regard to their distribution of data and control flow. Data flow is the transfer of the application data between the servers and storage devices. The control flow consists of all metadata and control information necessary for virtualization between virtualization entity and storage devices and servers. In symmetric storage virtualization the data flow and the control flow travel down the same path. By contrast, in asymmetric virtualization the data flow is separated from the control flow.

5.7.1 Symmetric storage virtualization

In symmetric storage virtualization the data and control flow go down the same path (Figure 5.15). This means that the abstraction from physical to logical storage necessary for virtualization must take place within the data flow. As a result, the metadata controller is positioned precisely in the data flow between server and storage devices, which is why symmetric virtualization is also called in-band virtualization.

In addition to the control of the virtualization, all data between servers and storage devices now flow through the metadata controller. To this end virtualization is

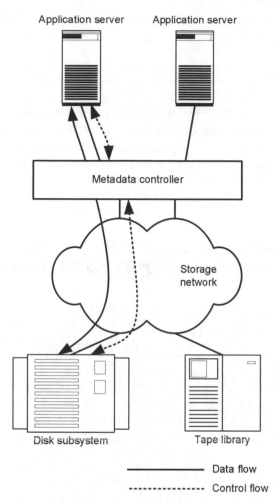

Figure 5.15 In symmetric virtualization, data and control flow travel down the same path. The abstraction from physical to logical storage takes place within the data stream

logically structured in two layers: the layer for the management of the logical volumes and the data access layer (Figure 5.16):

1. The volume management layer is responsible for the management and configuration of the storage devices that can be accessed directly or via a storage network and it provides the aggregation of these resources into logical disks.

2. The data access layer makes the logical drives available for access either on block or file level, depending upon what degree of abstraction is required. These logical drives can thus be made available to the application servers by means of appropriate protocols. In the case of virtualization on block level, this occurs in the form of a

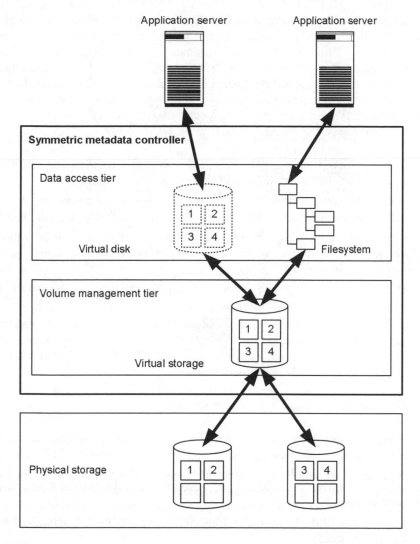

Figure 5.16 In symmetric virtualization the metadata controller consists of a data access layer and a volume management layer

virtual disk and in the case of virtualization on file level it takes place in the form of a file system.

In symmetric virtualization all data flow through the metadata controller, which means that this represents a potential bottleneck. To increase performance, therefore, the metadata controller is upgraded by the addition of a cache. With the use of caching and symmetric virtualization it is even possible to improve the performance of an existing storage network as long as exclusively write-intensive applications are not used.

A further issue is fault-tolerance. A single metadata controller represents a single point of failure. The use of cluster technology (Section 6.3.2) makes it possible to remove the single point of failure by using several metadata controllers in parallel. In addition, a corresponding load distribution provides a performance increase. However, a configuration failure or a software failure of that cluster can lead to data loss on all virtualized resources. In the case of a network-based virtualization spanning several servers and storage devices, this can halt the activity of a complete data centre (Section 6.3.4).

Thus the advantages of symmetric virtualization are evident:

- The application servers can easily be provided with data access both on block and file level, regardless of the underlying physical storage devices.
- The administrator has complete control over which storage resources are available to which servers at a central point. This increases security and eases the administration.
- Assuming that the appropriate protocols are supported, symmetric virtualization does not place any limit on specific operating system platforms. It can thus also be used in heterogeneous environments.
- The performance of existing storage networks can be improved by the use of caching and clustering in the metadata controllers.
- The use of a metadata controller means that techniques such as snapshots or mirroring can be implemented in a simple manner, since they control the storage access directly. They can also be used on storage devices such as JBODs or simple RAID arrays that do not provide to these techniques themselves.

The disadvantages of a symmetric virtualization are:

- Each individual metadata controller must be administered. If several metadata controllers are used in a cluster arrangement, then the administration is relatively complex and time-consuming particularly due to the cross-computer data access layer. This disadvantage can, however, be reduced by the use of a central administration console for the metadata controller.
- Several controllers plus cluster technology are indispensable to guarantee the fault-tolerance of data access.
- As an additional element in the data path, the controller can lead to performance problems, which makes the use of caching or load distribution over several controllers indispensable.
- It can sometimes be difficult to move the data between storage devices if this is managed by different metadata controllers.

5.7.2 Asymmetric storage virtualization

In contrast to symmetric virtualization, in asymmetric virtualization the data flow is separated from the control flow. This is achieved by moving all mapping operations from logical to physical drives to a metadata controller outside the data path (Figure 5.17). The metadata controller now only has to look after the administrative and control tasks of virtualization, the flow of data takes place directly from the application servers to the storage devices. As a result, this approach is also called out-band virtualization.

The communication between metadata controller and agents generally takes place via the LAN (out-band) but can also be realized in-band via the storage network. Hence, in our opinion the terms 'in-band virtualization' and 'out-band virtualization' are a little misleading. Therefore, we use instead the terms 'symmetric virtualization' and 'asymmetric virtualization' to refer to the two network-based virtualization approaches.

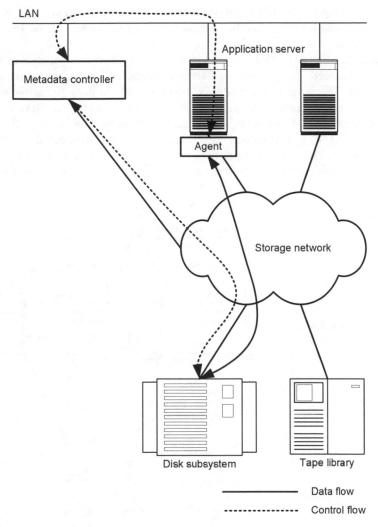

Figure 5.17 In contrast to symmetric virtualization, in asymmetric virtualization the data flow is separated from the control flow. The abstraction of physical to logical storage thus takes place outside the data flow

Like the symmetric approach, the metadata controller is logically structured in two layers (Figure 7.9). The volume management layer has the same duties as in the symmetric approach. The second layer is the control layer, which is responsible for the communication with an agent software that runs on the servers.

The agent is required in order to enable direct access to the physical storage resources. It is made up of a data access layer with the same tasks as in symmetric virtualization and a control layer (Figure 5.18). Via the latter it loads the appropriate location and access information about the physical storage from the metadata controller when the virtual storage is accessed by the operating system or an application. In this manner, access control to the physical resources is still centrally managed by the metadata controller.

An agent need not necessarily run in the memory of the server. It can also be integrated into a host bus adapter. This has the advantage that the server can be freed from the processes necessary for virtualization.

In asymmetric storage virtualization – as is also the case for symmetric storage virtualization – advanced storage functions such as snapshots, mirroring or data migration can be realized. The asymmetric model is, however, not so easy to realize as the symmetric one, but performance bottlenecks as a result of an additional device in the data path do not occur here. If we want to increase performance by the use of caching for both application as well as metadata, this caching must be implemented locally on every application server. The caching algorithm to be used becomes very complex since it is a distributed environment, in which every agent holds its own cache (Section 4.3).

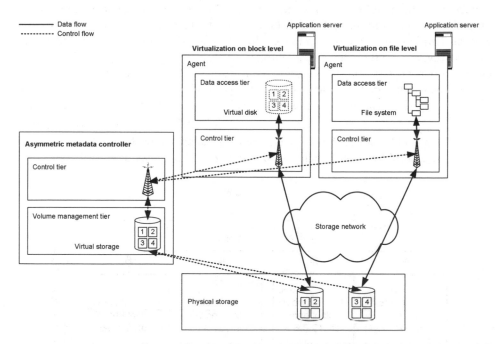

Figure 5.18 In asymmetric virtualization the metadata controller takes on only the administrative control tasks for the virtualization. Access to the physical storage is realized by means of an agent software

Data inconsistencies as a result of different cache contents for the same underlying physical storage contents must be avoided and error situations prevented in which an application crashes, that still has data in the cache. Therefore, additional mechanisms are necessary to guarantee the consistency of the distributed cache. Alternatively, the installation of a dedicated cache server in the storage network that devotes itself exclusively to the caching of the data flow would also be possible. Unfortunately, such products are not currently (end of 2003) available on the market.

Metadata controllers can also be constructed as clusters for the load distribution of the control flow and to increase fault-tolerance. The implementation is, however, easier with the asymmetric approach than it is with the symmetric since only the control flow has to be divided over several computers. In contrast to the symmetric approach, the splitting of the data flow is dispensed with.

The following advantages of asymmetric virtualization can be established:

- Complete control of storage resources by an absolutely centralized management on the metadata controller.
- Maximum throughput between servers and storage devices by the separation of the control flow from the data flow, thus avoiding additional devices in the data path.
- In comparison to the development and administration of a fully functional volume manager on every server, the porting of the agent software is associated with a low cost.
- As in the symmetric approach, advanced storage functions such as snapshots or mirroring can be used on storage devices that do not themselves support these functions.
- To improve fault-tolerance, several metadata controllers can be brought together to form a cluster. This is easier than in the symmetric approach, since no physical connection from the servers to the metadata controllers is necessary for the data flow.

The disadvantages of asymmetric virtualization are:

- A special agent software is required on the servers or the host bus adapters. This can make it more difficult to use this approach in heterogeneous environments, since such software or a suitable host bus adapter must be present for every platform. Incompatibilities between the agent software and existing applications may sometimes make the use of asymmetric virtualization impossible.
- The agent software must be absolutely stable in order to avoid errors in storage accesses. In situations where there are many different platforms to be supported, this is a very complex development and testing task.
- The development cost increases further if the agent software and the metadata controller are also to permit access on file level in addition to access on block level.
- A performance bottleneck can arise as a result of the frequent communication between agent software and metadata controller. These performance bottlenecks can be remedied by the caching of the physical storage information.
- Caching to increase performance requires an ingenious distributed caching algorithm to avoid data inconsistencies. A further option would be the installation of a dedicated cache server in the storage network.

- In asymmetric virtualization there is always the risk of a server with no agent software being connected to the storage network. In certain cases it may be possible for this server to access resources that are already being used by a different server and to accidentally destroy these. Such a situation is called a rogue host condition.

5.8 SUMMARY

By the separation of storage into physical implementation and logical view, storage virtualization opens up a number of possibilities for simplifying administration. In addition, it makes it possible to fully utilize the capabilities of a storage network. In this manner, resources can be used more efficiently in order to increase performance and improve fault-tolerance due to higher availability of the data. In addition, more extensive functions such as data protection, data migration, privacy protection and data sharing can be integrated into the storage virtualization, making the use of additional software for these functions unnecessary. The storage virtualization itself is performed by a virtualization entity, which forms the interface between virtual and physical storage. Virtualization takes place in two different forms: on block or on file level. The virtualization entity can be positioned on different levels of the storage network such as at the servers, storage devices or network. The advantages and disadvantages of the individual levels come to bear here. In particular, symmetric and asymmetric virtualization have great potential, since due to the positioning in the storage network they can provide their services to different servers and at the same time are also able to integrate the various storage devices into the virtualization.

In the previous chapters we introduced all the necessary techniques for storage networks. In the chapters that follow we will discuss how the previously discussed techniques can be used in order to realize requirements such as storage pooling and clustering (Chapter 6) or back-up (Chapter 7). Furthermore, in Chapter 9 we will broaden the concept of storage virtualization by including the virtualization of tapes and other removeable media.

Part II
Application and Management of Storage Networks

6

Application of Storage Networks

In the first part of the book we introduced the fundamental building blocks of storage networks such as disk subsystems, file systems, virtualization and transmission techniques. In the second part of the book our objective is to show how these building blocks can be combined in order to fulfil the requirements of IT systems such as flexibility, fault-tolerance and maintainability. As a prelude to the second part, this chapter discusses the fundamental requirements that are imposed independently of a particular application.

First of all, Section 6.1 contrasts the characteristics of various kinds of networks in order to emphasize the shape of a storage network. Section 6.2 introduces various possibilities in the storage network for device sharing and data sharing among several servers. The final part of the chapter deals with the two fundamental requirements of IT systems: availability of data (fault-tolerance, Section 6.3) and adaptability (Section 6.4).

6.1 DEFINITION OF THE TERM 'STORAGE NETWORK'

In our experience, ambiguities regarding the definition of the various transmission techniques for storage networks crop up again and again. This section therefore illustrates networks and storage networks once again from various points of view. It considers the layering of the various protocols and transmission techniques (Section 6.1.1), discusses once again at which points in the I/O path networks can be implemented (Section 6.1.2) and it again defines the terms LAN, MAN, WAN and SAN (Section 6.1.3).

Storage Networks Explained   U. Troppens R. Erkens W. Müller
© 2004 John Wiley & Sons, Ltd   ISBN: 0-470-86182-7

6.1.1 Layering of the transmission techniques and protocols

If we greatly simplify the OSI reference model, then we can broadly divide the protocols for storage networks into three layers that build upon one another: transmission techniques, transport protocols and application protocols (Figure 6.1). The transmission techniques provide the necessary physical connection between several end devices. Building upon these, transport protocols facilitate the data exchange between end devices via the underlying networks. Finally, the application protocols determine which type of data the end participants exchange over the transport protocol.

Transmission techniques represent the necessary prerequisite for data exchange between several participants. In addition to the already established Ethernet, the first part of the book introduces Fibre Channel and InfiniBand. They all define a medium (cable, radio frequency) and the encoding of data in the form of physical signals, which are transmitted over the medium.

Transport protocols facilitate the exchange of data over a network. In addition to the use of the tried and tested and omnipresent TCP protocol the first part of the book introduces Fibre Channel and the Virtual Interface Architecture (VIA). Transport protocols can either be based directly upon a transmission technique such as, for example, Virtual Interfaces over Fibre Channel, InfiniBand or Ethernet or they can use an alternative transport protocol as a medium. Examples are Fibre Channel over IP (FCIP) and IP over Fibre Channel (IPFC). Additional confusion is caused by the fact that Fibre

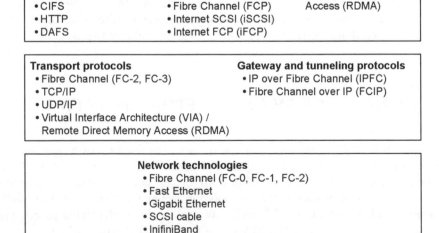

Figure 6.1 The communication techniques introduced in the first part of the book can be divided into transmission techniques, transport protocols and application protocols

Channel defines both a transmission technique (FC-0, FC-1, FC-2) and a transport protocol (FC-2, FC-3) plus various application protocols (FC-4).

Application protocols define the type of data that is transmitted over a transport protocol. With regard to storage networks we differentiate between block-oriented and file-oriented application protocols. SCSI is the mother of all block-oriented application protocols for block-oriented data transfer. All further block-oriented application protocols such as FCP, iFCP and iSCSI were derived from the SCSI protocol. File-oriented application protocols transmit files or file fragments. Examples of file-oriented application protocols discussed in this book are NFS, CIFS, FTP, HTTP and DAFS.

6.1.2 Networks in the I/O path

The logical I/O path offers a second point of view for the definition of transmission techniques for storage networks. Figure 6.2 illustrates the logical I/O path from the disk to the application and shows at which points in the I/O path networks can be used. Different application protocols are used depending upon location. The same transport protocols and transmission techniques can be used regardless of this.

Below the volume manager, block-oriented application protocols are used. Depending upon technique these are SCSI and SCSI offshoots such as FCP, iFCP and iSCSI. Today, block-oriented storage networks are found primarily between computers and storage systems. However, within large disk subsystems too the SCSI cable is increasingly being replaced by a network transmission technique (Figure 6.3).

Above the volume manager and file system, file-oriented application protocols are used. Here we find application protocols such as NFS, CIFS, HTTP, FTP and DAFS. In Chapter 4 three different fields of application for file-oriented application protocols were discussed: traditional file sharing, high-speed LAN file sharing and the World Wide Web. Shared disk file systems, which realize the network within the file system, should also be mentioned as a special case.

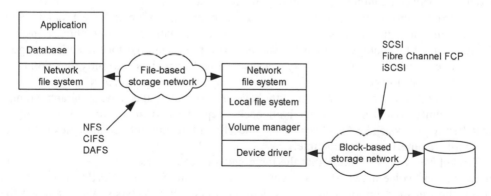

Figure 6.2 Storage networks in the I/O path

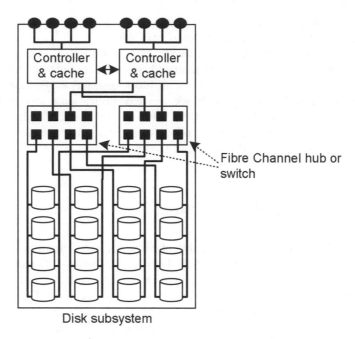

Disk subsystem

Figure 6.3 A storage network can be hidden within a disk subsystem

6.1.3 Data networks, voice networks and storage networks

Today we can differentiate between three different types of communication networks: data networks, voice networks and storage networks. The term 'voice network' hides the omnipresent telephone network. Data networks describe the networks developed in the 1990s for the exchange of application data. Data networks are subdivided into LAN, MAN and WAN, depending upon range. Storage networks were defined in the first chapter as networks that are installed in addition to the existing LAN and are primarily used for data exchange between computers and storage devices.

In introductions to storage networks, storage networks are often called SANs and compared with conventional LANs (a term for data networks with low geographic extension). Fibre Channel technology is often drawn upon as a representative for the entire category of storage networks. This is clearly because Fibre Channel is currently the dominant technology for storage networks. Two reasons lead us to compare LAN and SAN: first, LANs and Fibre Channel SANs currently have approximately the same geographic range. Second, quite apart from capacity bottlenecks, separate networks currently have to be installed for LANs and SANs because the underlying transmission technologies (Ethernet or Fibre Channel) are incompatible.

We believe it is very likely that the three network categories – storage networks, data networks and voice networks – will converge in the future, with TCP/IP, or at least IP, being the transport protocol jointly used by all three network types. We discussed the economic advantages of storage networks over Ethernet in Section 3.5 ('IP Storage').

We see it as an indication of the economic advantages of voice transmission over IP (Voice over IP, VoIP) that more and more reputable network manufacturers are offering VoIP devices.

6.2   STORAGE SHARING

In Part I of the book you heard several times that one advantage of storage networks is that several servers can share storage resources via the storage network. In this context, storage resources mean both storage devices such as disk subsystems and tape libraries and also the data stored upon them. This section discusses various variants of storage device sharing and data sharing based upon the examples of disk storage pooling (Section 6.2.1), dynamic tape library sharing (Section 6.2.2) and data sharing (Section 6.2.3).

6.2.1   Disk storage pooling

Disk storage pooling describes the possibility that several servers share the capacity of a disk subsystem. In a server-centric IT architecture each server *possesses* its own storage: Figure 6.4 shows three servers with their own storage. Server 2 needs more storage space, but the free space in the servers 1 and 3 cannot be assigned to server 2. Therefore, further storage must be purchased for server 2, even though free storage capacity is available on the other servers.

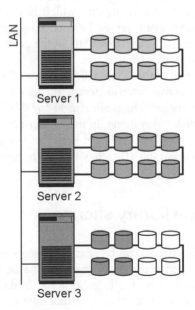

Figure 6.4   Inflexible: storage assignment in server-centric systems. Server 2 cannot use the free storage space of servers 1 and 3

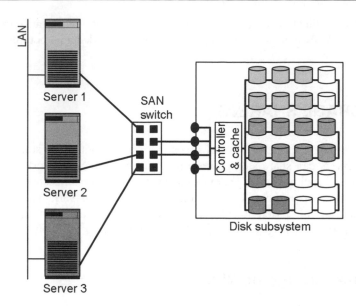

Figure 6.5 Better: storage pooling in storage-centric IT systems. Free storage capacity can be assigned to all servers

In a server-centric IT architecture the storage capacity available in the storage network can be assigned much more flexibly. Figure 6.5 shows the same three servers as Figure 6.4. The same storage capacity is installed in the two figures. However, in Figure 6.5 only one storage system is present, which is shared by several servers (disk storage pooling). In this arrangement, server 2 can be assigned additional storage capacity by the reconfiguration of the disk subsystem without the need for changes to the hardware or even the purchase of a new disk subsystem.

In Section 5.2.2 ('Implementation-related limitations of storage networks') we discussed how storage pooling across several storage devices from various manufacturers is currently (2003) no simple matter. The main reason for this is the incompatibility of the device drivers for various disk subsystems. In the further course of Chapter 5 we showed how virtualization in the storage network can help to overcome these incompatibilities and, in addition, further increase the efficiency of the storage pooling.

6.2.2 Dynamic tape library sharing

Tape libraries, like disk subsystems, can be shared among several servers. In tape library sharing we distinguish between static partitioning of the tape library and dynamic tape library sharing. In static partitioning the tape library is broken down into several virtual tape libraries; each server is assigned its own virtual tape library (Figure 6.6). Each tape drive and each tape in the tape library are unambiguously assigned a virtual tape library; all virtual tape libraries share the media changer that move the tapes cartridges back and

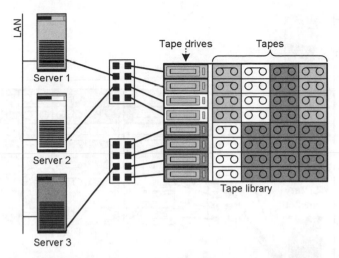

Figure 6.6 The partitioning of a tape library breaks down the tape library statically into several virtual tape libraries. Each server is assigned its own virtual tape library. The servers only share the media changer for the moving of the tapes

for between slots and tape drives. The reconfiguration of the assignment of tapes and tape drives to a certain virtual tape library is expensive in comparison to tape library sharing.

Tape library sharing offers greater flexibility (Figure 6.7). In this approach, the various servers dynamically negotiate which servers use which tape drives and tapes. To this end one server acts as library master, all others as library clients. The library master coordinates access to the tapes and tape drives of the tape library. If a library client wishes to write data to a new tape then it first of all requests a free tape from the library master. The library master selects a tape from the store of free tapes (scratch pool) and places it in a free drive. Then it makes a note in its database that this tape is now being used by the library client and it informs the library client which drive the tape is in. Finally, the library client can write the data directly to the tape via the storage network.

In contrast to the conventional partitioning of tape libraries in which each tape and each tape drive are statically assigned to a certain server, the advantage of the tape library sharing is that tapes and drives are dynamically assigned. Depending upon requirements, sometimes one and sometimes another server can use a tape or a tape drive.

This requires that all servers access the tape library according to the same rules. Tape library sharing is currently an important component of network back-up over storage networks (Section 7.8.4). But today, different applications – either on the same server or on different servers – cannot participate in the tape library sharing of a network back-up system because there is no common synchronization protocol. However, some tape libraries with built-in library managers support dynamic tape library sharing, but this requires that the applications integrate the proprietary API of the respective library manager. In the long term, these proprietary APIs need to be standardized to reduce the costs for library sharing across heterogeneous application and heterogeneous tape library boundaries. The IEEE 1244 Standard for Media Management Systems (Section 9.5) specifies exactly such an interface for tape library sharing.

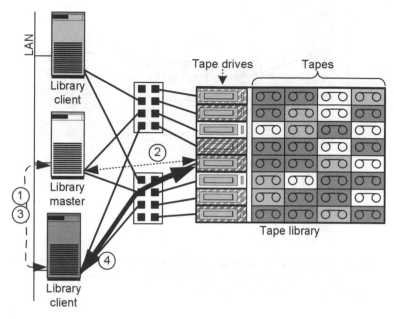

Figure 6.7   Tape library sharing: the library client informs the library master that it wants to write to a free tape (1). The library master places a free tape in a free drive (2) and sends the corresponding information back to the library client (3). The library client then writes directly via the storage network (4)

6.2.3   Data sharing

In contrast to device sharing (disk storage pooling, tape library partitioning and tape library sharing) discussed earlier, in which several servers share a storage device at block level, data sharing is the use of data by several applications. In data sharing we differentiate between data copying and real time data sharing.

In data copying, as the name suggests, data is copied. This means that several versions of the data are kept, which is fundamentally a bad thing: each copy of the data requires storage space and care must be taken to ensure that the different versions are copied according to the requirements of the applications at the right times. Errors occur in particular in the maintenance of the various versions of the data set, so that subsequent applications repeatedly work with the wrong data.

Despite these disadvantages, data copying is used in production environments. The reasons for this can be:

- Generation of test data
  Copies of the production data are helpful for the testing of new versions of applications and operating systems and for the testing of new hardware. In Section 1.3 we used the example of a server upgrade to show how test data for the testing of new hardware could be generated using instant copies in the disk subsystem. The important point

here was that the applications are briefly interrupted so that the consistency of the copied data is guaranteed. As an alternative to instant copies the test data could also be generated using snapshots in the file system.

- Data protection (back-up)
  The aim of data protection is to keep up-to-date copies of data at various locations as a precaution to protect against the loss of data by hardware or operating errors. Data protection is an important application in the field of storage networks. It is therefore dealt with separately in Chapter 7.

- Data replication
  Data replication is the name for the copying of data for access to data on computers that are far apart geographically. The objective of data replication is to accelerate data access and save network capacity. There are many applications that automate the replication of data. Within the World Wide Web the data is replicated at two points: first, every web browser caches local data in order to accelerate access to pages called up frequently by an individual user. Second, many Internet Service Providers (ISPs) install a so-called proxy server. This caches the contents of web pages that are called up by many users. Other examples of data replication are the mirroring of FTP servers (FTP mirror), replicated file sets in the Andrew File System (AFS) or the Distributed File System (DFS) of the Distributed Computing Environment (DCE), and the replication of mail databases.

- Conversion into more efficient data formats
  It is often necessary to convert data into a different data format because certain calculations are cheaper in the new format. In the days before the pocket calculator logarithms were often used for calculations because, for example, the addition of logarithms yielded the same result as the multiplication in the origin space only more simply. For the same reasons, in modern IT systems data is converted to different data formats. In data mining, for example, data from various sources is brought together in a database and converted into a data format in which the search for regularities in the data set is simpler.

- Conversion of incompatible data formats
  A further reason for the copying of data is the conversion of incompatible data formats. A classic example is when applications originally developed independently of one another are being brought together over time.

Real-time data sharing represents an alternative to data copying. In real-time data sharing all applications work on the same data set. Real-time data sharing saves storage space, avoids the cost and errors associated with the management of several data versions and all applications work on the up-to-date data set. For the reasons mentioned above for data copying it is particularly important to replace the conversion of incompatible data sets by real-time data sharing.

The logical separation of applications and data is continued in the implementation. In general, applications and data in the form of file systems and databases are installed on different computers. This physical separation aids the adaptability, and thus the maintainability, of overall systems. Figure 6.8 shows several applications that work on the same

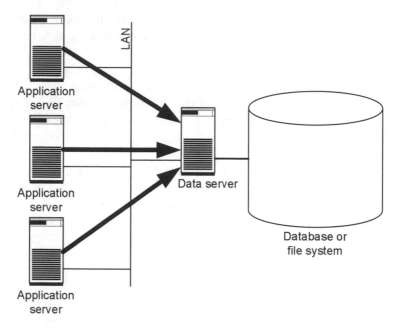

Figure 6.8   Real-time data sharing leads to the separation of applications and data: several applications work on the same data set

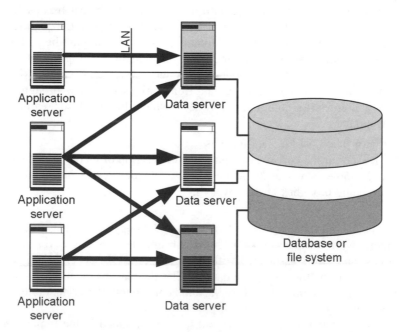

Figure 6.9   Static load distribution of the data server by the partitioning of the data set

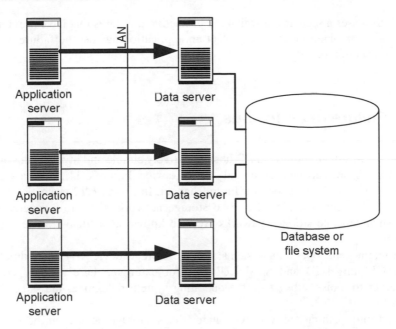

Figure 6.10 Dynamic load distribution of the data server by parallel databases and shared disk file systems

data set, with applications and data being managed independently of one another. This has the advantage that new applications can be introduced without existing applications having to be changed.

However, in the configuration shown in Figure 6.8 the applications may generate so much load that a single data server becomes a bottleneck and the load has to be divided amongst several data servers. There are two options for resolving this bottleneck without data copying: first, the data set can be partitioned (Figure 6.9) by splitting it over several data servers. If this is not sufficient, then several parallel access paths can be established to the same data set (Figure 6.10). Parallel databases and shared disk file systems such as the General Parallel File System (GPFS) introduced in Section 4.3.1 provide the functions necessary for this.

6.3 AVAILABILITY OF DATA

Nowadays, the availability of data is an important requirement made of IT systems. This section discusses how the availability of data and applications can be maintained in various fault situations. Individually, the following will be discussed: the failure of an I/O bus (Section 6.3.1), the failure of a server (Section 6.3.2), the failure of a disk subsystem (Section 6.3.3), and the failure of a storage virtualization instance which is placed in the storage network (Section 6.3.4). The case study 'protection of an important database' discusses a scenario in which the protective measures that have previously been discussed are combined in order to protect an application against the failure of an entire data centre (Section 6.3.5).

6.3.1   Failure of an I/O bus

Protection against the failure of an I/O bus is relatively simple and involves the installation of several I/O buses between server and storage device. Figure 6.11 shows a scenario for SCSI and Figure 6.12 shows one for Fibre Channel. In Figure 6.12 protection against the failure of an I/O bus is achieved by two storage networks that are independent of one another. Such separate storage networks are also known as a 'dual storage network' or 'dual SAN'.

The problem here: operating systems manage storage devices via the triple host bus adapter, SCSI target ID and SCSI LUN. If, for example, there are two connections from a server to a disk subsystem, the operating system recognizes the same disk twice (Figure 6.13).

So-called multipathing software recognizes that a storage device can be reached over several paths. Figure 6.14 shows how multipathing software reintegrates the disk found

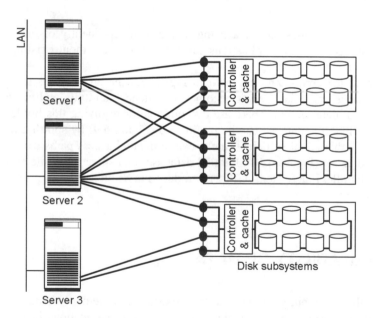

Figure 6.11   Redundant SCSI cable between server and disk subsystem protects against the failure of a SCSI cable, a SCSI host bus adapter or a connection port in the disk subsystem

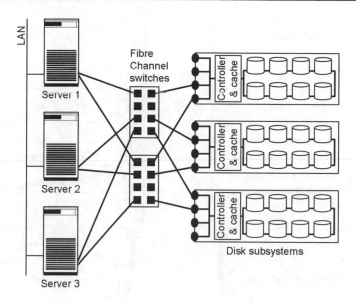

Figure 6.12 So-called dual SANs expand the idea of redundant SCSI cable to storage networks

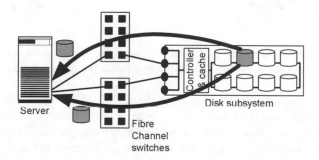

Figure 6.13 Problem: as a result of the redundant I/O path the operating system recognizes a single physical or virtual disk several times

twice in Figure 6.13 to form a single disk again. Multipathing software can act at various points depending upon the product:

- in the volume manager (Figure 6.14, right);
- as an additional virtual device driver between the volume manager and the device driver of the disk subsystem (Figure 6.14, left);
- in the device driver of the disk subsystem;
- in the device driver of the host bus adapter card.

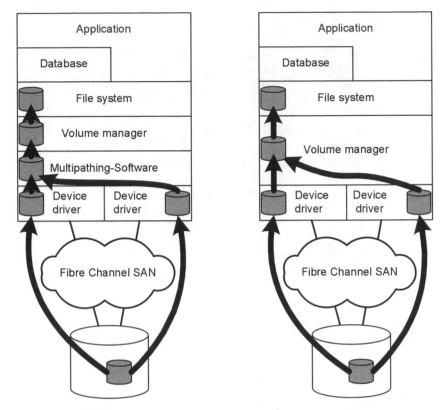

Figure 6.14 Solution: multipathing software brings the multiply recognized disks back together. Multipathing software can be realized at various points in the operating system

Fibre Channel plans to realize this function in the FC-3 layer. However, this part of the Fibre Channel standard has not yet been realized in real products. We believe it is rather unlikely that these functions will ever actually be realized within the Fibre Channel protocol stack. In the past the principle of keeping the network protocol as simple as possible and realizing the necessary intelligence in the end devices has prevailed in networks.

The multipathing software currently available on the market differs in the mode in which it uses redundant I/O buses:

- Active/passive mode
  In active/passive mode the multipathing software manages all I/O paths between server and storage device. Only one of the I/O paths is used for actual data traffic. If the active I/O path fails, the multipathing software activates one of the other I/O paths in order to send the data via this one instead.

- Active/active mode
  In active/active mode the multipathing software uses all available I/O paths between server and storage device. It distributes the load evenly over all available I/O channels.

In addition, the multipathing software continuously monitors the availability of the individual I/O paths; it activates or deactivates the individual I/O paths depending upon their availability.

It is obvious that the active/active mode utilizes the underlying hardware better than the active/passive mode, since it combines fault-tolerance with load distribution.

6.3.2 Failure of a server

Protection against the failure of an entire server is somewhat trickier. The only thing that can help here is to provide a second server that takes over the tasks of the actual application server in the event of its failure. So-called cluster software monitors the state of the two computers and starts the application on the second computer if the first computer fails.

Figure 6.15 shows a cluster for a file server, the disks of which are connected over Fibre Channel SAN. Both computers have access to the disks, but only one computer actively accesses them. The file system stored on the disks is exported over a network file system such as NFS or CIFS. To this end a virtual IP address is configured for the cluster. Clients access the file system via this virtual IP address.

If the first computer fails, the cluster software automatically initiates the following steps:

1. Activation of the disks on the stand-by computer.
2. File system check of the local file system stored on the disk subsystem.
3. Mounting of the local file system on the stand-by computer.
4. Transfer of the virtual cluster IP address.
5. Export of the local file system via the virtual cluster IP address.

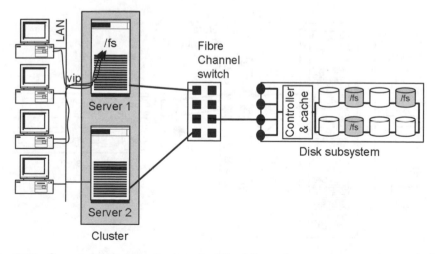

Figure 6.15 Server cluster to protect against the failure of a server: server 1 exports the file system '/fs' over the virtual IP address 'vip'

This process is invisible to clients of the file server apart from the fact that they cannot access the network file system for a brief period so file accesses may possibly have to be repeated (Figure 6.16).

Server clustering and redundant I/O buses are two measures that are completely independent of each other. In practice, as shown in Figure 6.17, the two measures are nevertheless combined. The multipathing software reacts to errors in the I/O buses significantly more quickly than the cluster software so the extra cost of the redundant I/O buses is usually justified.

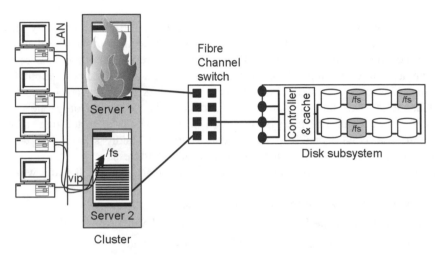

Figure 6.16 Failure of the primary server. The stand-by server activates the disks, checks the consistency of the local file system and exports this over the virtual IP address 'vip'

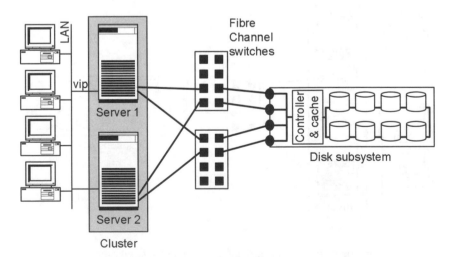

Figure 6.17 Server cluster and redundant I/O buses are independent concepts

6.3.3 Failure of a disk subsystem

In Chapter 2 we discussed how disk subsystems implement a whole range of measures to increase their own fault-tolerance. Nevertheless, disk subsystems can sometimes fail, for example in the event of physical impairments such as fire or water damage or due to faults that should not happen at all according to the manufacturer. The only thing that helps in the event of faults in the disk subsystem is to mirror the data on two disk subsystems.

Mirroring (RAID 1) is a form of virtualization, for which various realization locations were discussed in Section 5.1. In contrast to classical RAID 1 within the disk subsystem for protection against its failure, the data is mirrored on two different disk subsystems, which are wherever possible separated by a fire protection wall and connected to two independent electric circuits. From the point of view of reducing the load on the server, the realization of the mirroring by the disk subsystem in the form of remote mirroring is optimal (Figure 6.18, cf. also Section 2.7.2 and Section 5.1.)

From the point of view of fault-tolerance, however, remote mirroring through the disk subsystem represents a single point of failure: if the data in the disk subsystem is falsified on the way to the disk subsystem (controller faults, connection port faults), the copy of the data is also erroneous. Therefore, from the point of view of fault-tolerance, mirroring in the volume manager or in the application itself is optimal (Figure 6.19). In this approach the data is written to two different disk subsystems via two different physical I/O paths.

A further advantage of volume manager mirroring compared to remote mirroring is due to the way the two variants are integrated into the operating system. Volume manager mirroring is a solid component of every good volume manager: the volume manager reacts automatically to the failure and the restarting of a disk subsystem. On the other hand, today's operating systems in the Open System field are not yet good at handling copies of disks created by a disk subsystem. Switching to such a copy generally requires manual support. Although, technically, an automated reaction to the failure or the restarting of a disk subsystem is possible, this currently (2003) requires specially written scripts due to lack of integration in the operating system.

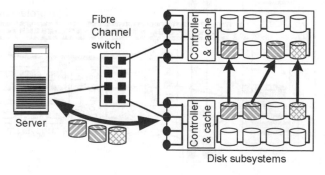

Figure 6.18 Remote mirroring of the disk subsystems protects against the failure of a disk subsystem

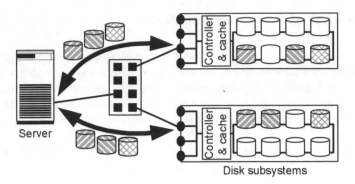

Figure 6.19   Volume manager mirroring is often a favourable alternative to disk subsystem remote mirroring for protection against the failure of a disk subsystem

On the other hand, there are some arguments in favour of remote mirroring. In addition to the performance benefits discussed above, we should also mention the fact that remote mirroring is supported over greater distances than volume manager mirroring. As a rule of thumb, volume manager can be used up to a maximum distance of six to ten kilometres between server and disk subsystem; for greater distances remote mirroring currently has to be used.

Figure 6.20 shows how volume manager mirroring, server clustering and redundant I/O buses can be combined. In this configuration the management of the disks is somewhat more complicated: each server sees each disk made available by the disk subsystem four

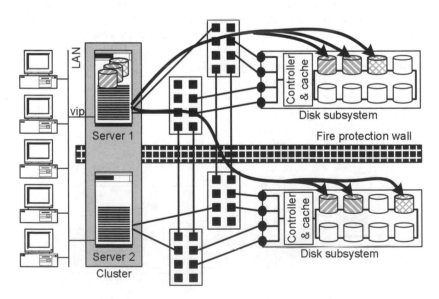

Figure 6.20   Combined use of server clustering, volume manager mirroring and redundant I/O buses

times because each host bus adapter finds each disk over two connection ports of the disk subsystem. In addition, the volume manager mirrors the data on two disk subsystems. Figure 6.21 shows how the software in the server brings the disks recognized by the operating system back together again: the file system writes the data to a logical disk provided by the volume manager. The volume manager mirrors the data on two different virtual disks, which are managed by the multipathing software. The multipathing software also manages the four different paths of the two disks. It is not visible here whether the disks exported from the disk subsystem are also virtualized within the disk subsystem.

The configuration shown in Figure 6.20 offers good protection against the failure of various components, whilst at the same time providing a high level of availability of data and applications. However, this solution comes at a price. Therefore, in practice, sometimes one and sometimes another protective measure is dispensed with for cost reasons. Often, for example, the following argument is used: 'The data is mirrored within

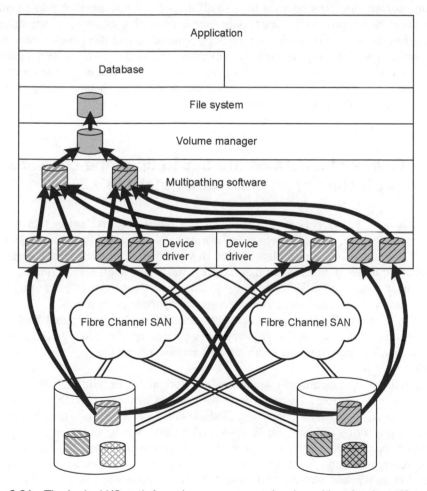

Figure 6.21 The logical I/O path for volume manager mirroring with redundant I/O buses

the disk subsystem by RAID and additionally protected by means of network back-up. That should be enough.'

6.3.4 Failure of virtualization in the storage network

Virtualization in the storage network is currently (2003) treated as *the* solution for the consolidation of storage resources in large storage networks, with which the storage resources of several disk subsystems can be centrally managed (Chapter 5). However, it is necessary to be clear about the fact that precisely such a central virtualization instance represents a single point of failure. Even if the virtualization instance is protected against the failure of a single component by measures such as clustering, the data of an entire data centre can be lost as a result of configuration errors or software errors in the virtualization instance, since the storage virtualization aims to span all the storage resources of a data centre.

Therefore, the same considerations apply for the protection of a virtualization instance positioned in the storage network (Section 5.7, 'Symmetric and Asymmetric Storage Virtualization in the Network') against the failure as the measures to protect against the failure of a disk subsystem discussed in the previous section. Therefore, the mirroring of important data from the server via two virtualization instances should also be considered in the case of virtualization in the storage network.

6.3.5 Failure of a data centre based upon the case study 'protection of an important database'

The measures of server clustering, redundant I/O buses and disk subsystem mirroring (volume manager mirroring or remote mirroring) discussed above protect against the failure of a component within a data centre. However, these measures are useless in the event of the failure of a complete data centre (fire, water damage). To protect against the failure of a data centre it is necessary to duplicate the necessary infrastructure in a back-up data centre for the operation of the most important applications.

Figure 6.22 shows the interaction between the primary data centre and back-up data centre based upon the case study 'protection of an important database'. In the case study, all the measures discussed in this section for protection against the failure of a component are used.

In the primary data centre all components are designed with built-in redundancy. The primary server is connected via two independent Fibre Channel SANs (Dual SAN) to two disk subsystems, on which the data of the database lies. Dual SANs have the advantage that even in the event of a serious fault in a SAN (defective switch, which corrupts the SAN with corrupt frames), the connection via the other SAN remains intact. The redundant paths between servers and storage devices are managed by appropriate multipathing software.

Each disk subsystem is configured using a RAID procedure so that the failure of individual physical disks within the disk subsystem in question can be rectified. In addition,

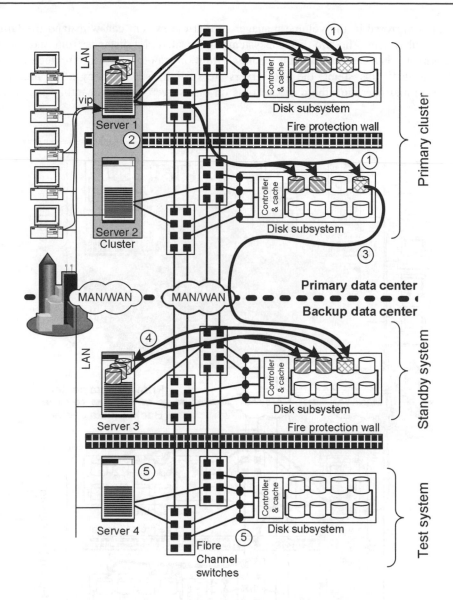

Figure 6.22 For the protection of an important database the volume manager mirrors data files and log files on two different disk subsystems (1). The database computer and the I/O buses between database computers and disk subsystems are designed with built-in redundancy (2). In the back-up data centre only the log files are mirrored (3). There, the log files are integrated into the data set with a delay (4). In normal operation the second computer and the second disk subsystem in the back-up data centre are used for other tasks (5)

the data is mirrored in the volume manager so that the system can withstand the failure of a disk subsystem. The two disk subsystems are located at a distance from one another in the primary data centre. They are separated from one another by a fire protection wall.

Like the disk subsystems, the two servers are spatially separated by a fire protection wall. In normal operation the database runs on one server; in the meantime the second

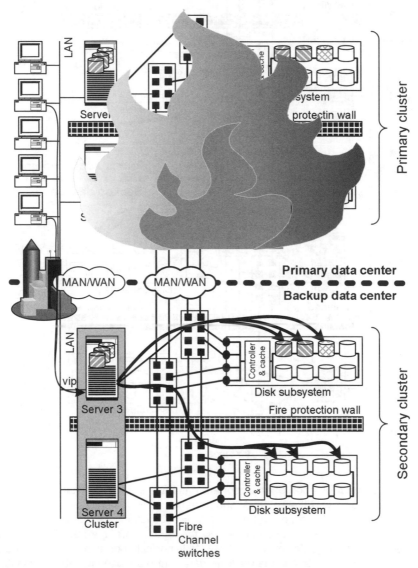

Figure 6.23 In the event of failure of the primary data centre the two computers in the back-up data centre are configured as a cluster. Likewise, the data of the database is mirrored to the second disk subsystem via the volume manager. Thus the same configuration is available in the back-up data centre as in the primary data centre

server is used for other, less important tasks. If the primary server fails, the cluster software automatically starts the database on the second computer. It also terminates all other activities on the second computer, thus making all its resources fully available to the main application.

Remote mirroring takes place via an IP connection. Mirroring utilizes knowledge of the data structure of the database: in a similar manner to journaling in file systems (Section 4.1.2), databases write each change into a log file before then integrating it into the actual data set. In the example, only the log files are mirrored in the back-up data centre. The complete data set was only transferred to the back-up data centre once at the start of mirroring. Thereafter this data set is only ever adjusted with the aid of the log files.

This has two advantages: the powerful network connection between the primary data centre and the remote back-up data centre is very expensive. The necessary data rate for this connection can be halved by only transferring the changes to the log file. This cuts costs.

In the back-up data centre the log files are integrated into the data set after a delay of two hours. As a result, a copy of the data set that is two hours old is always available in the back-up data centre. This additionally protects against application errors: if a table space is accidentally deleted in the database then the user has two hours to notice the error and interrupt the copying of the changes in the back-up data centre.

A second server and a second disk subsystem are also operated in the back-up data centre, which in normal operation can be used as a test system or for other, less time-critical tasks such as data mining. If the operation of the database is moved to the back-up data centre, these activities are suspended (Figure 6.23). The second server is configured as a stand-by server for the first server in the cluster; the data of the first disk subsystem is mirrored to the second disk subsystem via the volume manager. Thus a completely redundant system is available in the back-up data centre.

The realization of the case study discussed here is possible with current technology. However, it comes at a price; for most applications this cost will certainly not be justified. The main point of the case study is to highlight the possibilities of storage networks. In practice you have to decide how much failure protection is necessary and how much this may cost. At the end of the day, protection against the loss of data or the temporary non-availability of applications must cost less than the data loss or the temporary non-availability of applications itself.

6.4 ADAPTABILITY AND SCALABILITY OF IT SYSTEMS

A further requirement of IT systems is that of adaptability and scalability: successful companies have to adapt their business processes to new market conditions in ever shorter cycles. Along the same lines, IT systems must be adapted to new business processes so that they can provide optimal support for these processes. Storage networks are also required to be scalable: on average the storage capacity required by a company doubles in the course of each year. This means that anyone who has 1 terabyte of data to manage today will have 32 terabytes in five years time. A company with only 250 gigabytes today will reach 32 terabytes in seven years time.

This section discusses the adaptability and scalability of IT systems on the basis of clusters for load distribution (Section 6.4.1), the five-tier architecture for web application servers (Section 6.4.2) and the case study 'structure of a travel portal' (Section 6.4.3).

6.4.1   Clustering for load distribution

The term 'cluster' is very frequently used in information technology, but which is not clearly defined. The meaning of the term 'cluster' varies greatly depending upon context. As the greatest common denominator we can only state that a cluster is a combination of components or servers that perform a common function in one form or another.

This section expands the cluster concept for protection against the failure of a server introduced in Section 6.3.2 to include clustering for load distribution. We discuss three different forms of clusters based upon the example of a file server. The three different forms of cluster are comparable to the modes of multipathing software.

The starting point is the so-called shared-null configuration (Figure 6.24). The components are not designed with built-in redundancy. If a server fails, the file system itself

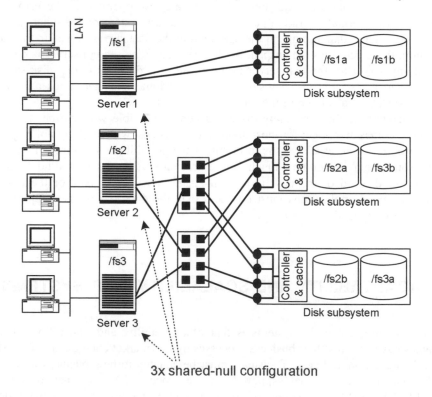

3x shared-null configuration

Figure 6.24   Shared-null configuration: the server is not designed with built-in redundancy

is no longer available, even if the data is mirrored on two different disk subsystems and redundant I/O buses are installed between server and disk subsystems (Figure 6.25).

In contrast to the shared-null configuration, shared-nothing clusters protect against the failure of a server. The basic form of the shared-nothing cluster was discussed in Section 6.3.2 in relation to the protection of a file server against the failure of a server. Figure 6.26 once again shows two shared-nothing clusters each with two servers.

Shared-nothing clusters can be differentiated into active/active and active/passive configurations. In the active/active configuration, applications run on both computers; for example, the computers 'server 1' and 'server 2' in Figure 6.26 each export a file system. If one of the two computers fails, the other computer takes over the tasks of the failed computer in addition to its own (Figure 6.27, top).

This taking over of the applications of the failed server can lead to performance bottlenecks in active/active configurations. The active/passive configuration can help in this situation. In this approach the application runs only on the primary server, the second computer in the cluster (stand-by server) does nothing in normal operation. It is exclusively there to take over the applications of the primary server if this fails. If the primary server fails, the stand-by server takes over its tasks (Figure 6.27, bottom).

The examples in Figures 6.26 and 6.27 show that shared-nothing clusters with only two servers are relatively inflexible. More flexibility is offered by shared-nothing clusters with

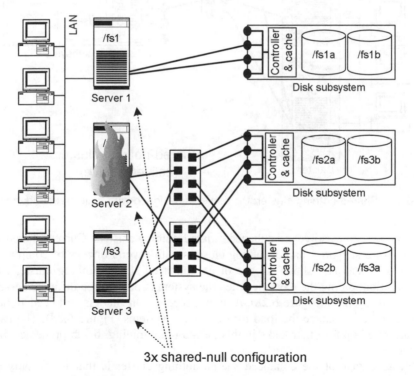

3x shared-null configuration

Figure 6.25 Shared-null configuration: in the event of the failure of a server, the file system '/fs2' can no longer be accessed despite redundant disk subsystems and redundant I/O paths

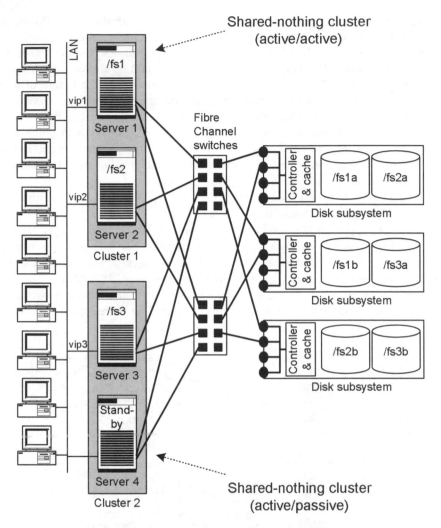

Figure 6.26 Shared-nothing cluster: the server is designed with built-in redundancy

more than two servers, so-called enhanced shared-nothing clusters. Current shared-nothing cluster software supports shared-nothing clusters with several dozens of computers.

Figures 6.28 and 6.29 show the use of an enhanced shared-nothing cluster for static load distribution: during the daytime when the system is busy, three different servers each export two file systems (Figure 6.28). At night, access to the data is still needed; however, a single server can manage the load for the six file systems (Figure 6.28). The two other servers are freed up for other tasks in this period (data mining, batch processes, back-up, maintenance).

One disadvantage of the enhanced shared-nothing cluster is that it can only react to load peaks very slowly. Appropriate load balancing software can, for example, move the file system '/fs2' to one of the other two servers even during the day if the load on the

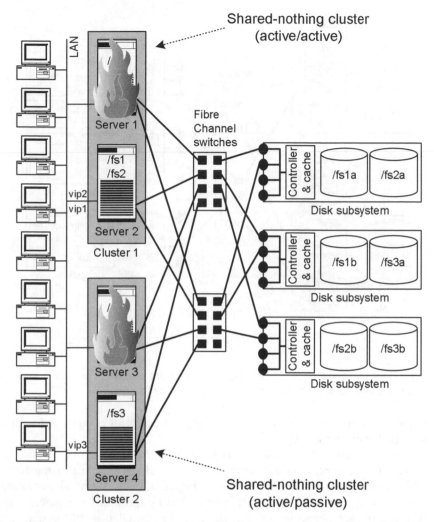

Figure 6.27   Shared-nothing cluster: in the event of the failure of a server, the other server takes over the applications of the failed server

file system '/fs1' is higher. However, this takes some time, which means that this process is only worthwhile for extended load peaks.

A so-called shared-everything cluster offers more flexibility in comparison to enhanced shared-nothing clusters. For file servers, shared disk file systems are used as local file systems here, so that all servers can access the data efficiently over the storage network. Figure 6.30 shows a file server that is configured as a shared-everything cluster with three servers. The shared disk file system is distributed over several disk subsystems. All three servers export this file system to the clients in the LAN over the same virtual IP address by means of a conventional network file system such as NFS or CIFS. Suitable load balancing software distributes new incoming accesses on the network file system equally

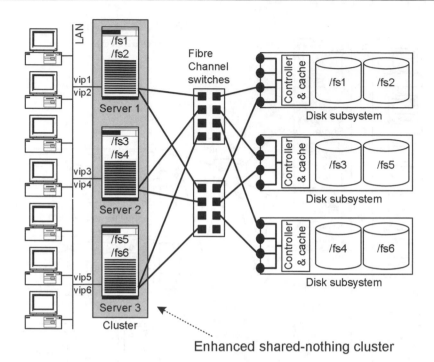

Enhanced shared-nothing cluster

Figure 6.28 Enhanced shared-nothing cluster: the servers are designed with built-in redundancy and the server cluster consists of more than two computers

amongst all three servers. If the three servers are not powerful enough, a fourth server can simply be linked to the cluster.

The shared-everything cluster also offers advantages in the event of the failure of a single server. For example, the file server in Figure 6.30 is realized in the form of a distributed application. If one server fails, as in Figure 6.31, recovery measures are only necessary for those clients that have just been served by the failed computer. Likewise, recovery measures are necessary for the parts of the shared disk file system and the network file system have just been managed by the failed computer. None of the other clients of the file server notice the failure of a computer apart from a possible reduction in performance.

Despite their advantages, shared-everything clusters are very seldom used. The reason for this is quite simply that this form of cluster is the most difficult to realize, so most cluster products and applications only support the more simply realized variants of shared-nothing or enhanced shared-nothing.

6.4.2 Web architecture

In the 1990s the so-called three-tier architecture established itself as a flexible architecture for IT systems (Figure 6.32). The three-tier architecture isolates the tasks of data

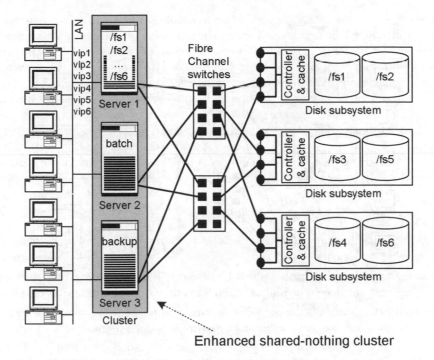

Enhanced shared-nothing cluster

Figure 6.29 Enhanced shared-nothing cluster: for the purpose of load balancing, applications from one server can be moved to another server

management, applications and representation into three separate layers. Figure 6.33 shows a possible implementation of the three-tier architecture.

Individually the three layers have the following tasks:

- Data

  Information in the form of data forms the basis for the three-tier architecture. Databases and file systems store the data of the applications on block-oriented disks or disk subsystems. In addition, the data layer can provide interfaces to external systems and legacy applications.

- Applications

  Applications generate and process data. Several applications can work on the same databases or file systems. Depending upon changes to the business processes, existing applications are modified and new applications added. The separation of applications and databases makes it possible for no changes, or only minimal changes, to have to be made to the underlying databases or file systems in the event of changes to applications.

- Representation

  The representation layer provides the user interface for the end user. In the 1990s the user interface was normally realized in the form of the graphical interface on a PC.

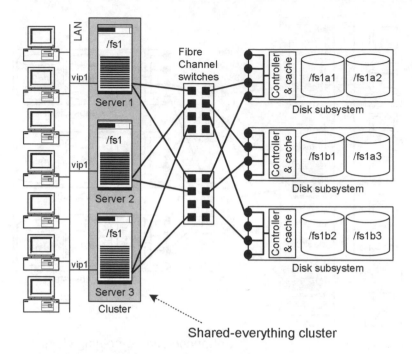

Shared-everything cluster

Figure 6.30 Shared-everything cluster: parallel applications run on several computers. Incoming requests from the client are dynamically and uniformly distributed to all computers in the cluster

The corresponding function calls of the application are integrated into the graphical interface so that the application can be controlled from there.

Currently, the two outer layers can be broken down into sublayers so that the three-tier architecture is further developed into a five-tier architecture Figure 6.34 and Figure 6.35:

- Splitting of the representation layer
  In recent years the representation layer has been split up by the World Wide Web into web servers and web browsers. The web servers provide statically or dynamically generated websites that are represented in the browsers. Websites with a functional scope comparable to that of conventional user interfaces can currently be generated using Java and various script languages.
     The arrival of mobile end devices such as mobile phones and PDAs has meant that web servers had to make huge modifications to websites to bring them into line with the properties of the end devices. In future there will be user interfaces that are exclusively controlled by means of the spoken word – for example navigation systems for use in the car, that are connected to the Internet for requesting up-to-date traffic data.
- Splitting of the data layer
  In the 1990s, storage devices for data were closely coupled to the data servers (storage-centric IT architecture). In the previous chapters storage networks were discussed in

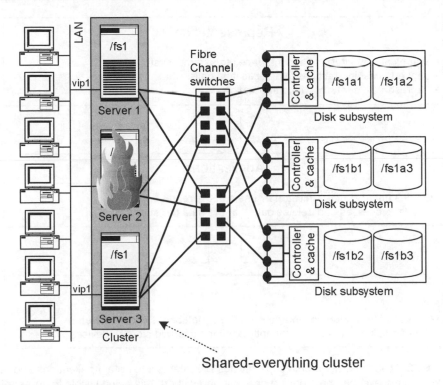

Figure 6.31 Shared-everything cluster: in the event of the failure of a server only the parts of the local shared disk file system and the network file system that have just been managed by the failed computer have to be resynchronized. None of the other clients notice the failure of the computer, apart from possible reductions in performance

detail, so at this point of the book it should be no surprise to learn that the data layer is split into the organization of the data (databases, file servers) and the storage space for data (disk subsystems).

6.4.3 Web applications based upon the 'travel portal' case study

This section uses the 'travel portal' case study to demonstrate the implementation of a so-called web application. The case study is transferable to web applications for the support of business processes. It thus shows the possibilities opened up by the Internet and highlights the potential and the change that stand before us with the transformation to e-business. Furthermore, the example demonstrates once again how storage networks, server clusters and the five-tier architecture can fulfil requirements such as the fault-tolerance, adaptability and scalability of IT systems.

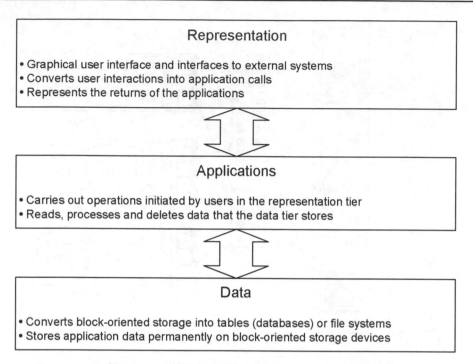

Representation

• Graphical user interface and interfaces to external systems
• Converts user interactions into application calls
• Represents the returns of the applications

Applications

• Carries out operations initiated by users in the representation tier
• Reads, processes and deletes data that the data tier stores

Data

• Converts block-oriented storage into tables (databases) or file systems
• Stores application data permanently on block-oriented storage devices

Figure 6.32 The three-tier architecture divides IT systems into data, applications and representation. Each layer can be modified or expanded without this being visible to another layer

Figure 6.36 shows the realization of the travel portal in the form of a web application. Web application means that users can use the information and services of the travel portal from various end devices such as PC, PDA and mobile phone if these are connected to the Internet. The travel portal initially supports only editorially prepared content (including film reports, travel catalogues, transport timetable information) and content added by the users themselves (travel tips and discussion forums), which can be called up via conventional web browsers. Figure 6.37 shows the expansion of the travel portal by further end devices such as mobile phones and PDAs and by further services.

To use the travel portal, users first of all build up a connection to the representation server by entering the URL. Depending upon its type, the end device connects to a web server (HTTP server) or, for example, to a WAP server. The end user only perceives the web server as being a single web server. In fact, a cluster of representation servers is working in the background. The load balancer of the representation server accepts the request to build up a connection and passes it on to the computer with the lowest load.

Once a connection has been built up the web browser transfers the user identifier, for example, in the form of a cookie or the mobile number, and the properties of the end device (for example, screen resolution). The web server calls up the user profile from the user management. Using this information the web server dynamically generates websites (HTML, WML or iMode) that are optimally oriented towards the requirements of the user. Thus the representation of content can be adjusted to suit the end device in use at

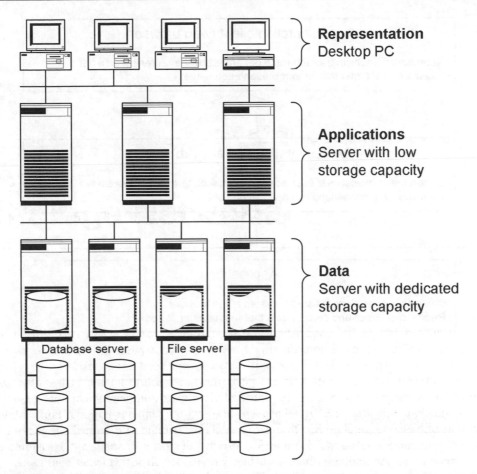

Figure 6.33 A separate LAN can be installed between application servers and data servers for the implementation of a three-tier architecture, since the clients (representation layer) communicate only with the application servers

the time. Likewise, content, adverts and information can be matched to the preferences of the user; one person may be interested in the category of city tips for good restaurants, whilst another is interested in museums.

The expansion of the travel portal to include the new 'hotel tips' application takes place by the linking of the existing 'city maps' and 'hotel directory' databases (Figure 6.37). The application could limit the selection of hotels by a preferred price category stored in the user profile or the current co-ordinates of the user transmitted by a mobile end device equipped with GPS.

Likewise, the five-tier architecture facilitates the support of new end devices, without the underlying applications having to be modified. For example, in addition to the conventional web browsers and WAP phones shown in Figure 6.37 you could also implement mobile PDAs (low resolution end devices) and a pure voice interface for car drivers.

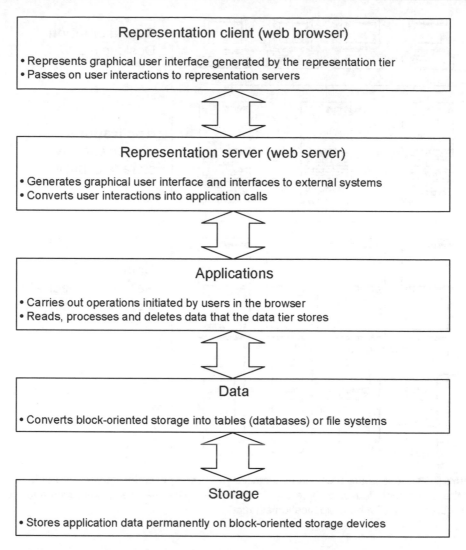

Figure 6.34 In the five-tier architecture the representation layer is split up into representation server and representation client and the data layer is split into data management and storage devices

All server machines are connected together via a fast network. Today primarily Gigabit Ethernet is used; in future InfiniBand will presumably also be used. With the aid of appropriate cluster software, applications can be moved from one computer to another. Further computers can be added to the cluster if the overall performance of the cluster is not sufficient.

Storage networks bring with them the flexibility needed to provide the travel portal with the necessary storage capacity. The individual servers impose different requirements on the storage network:

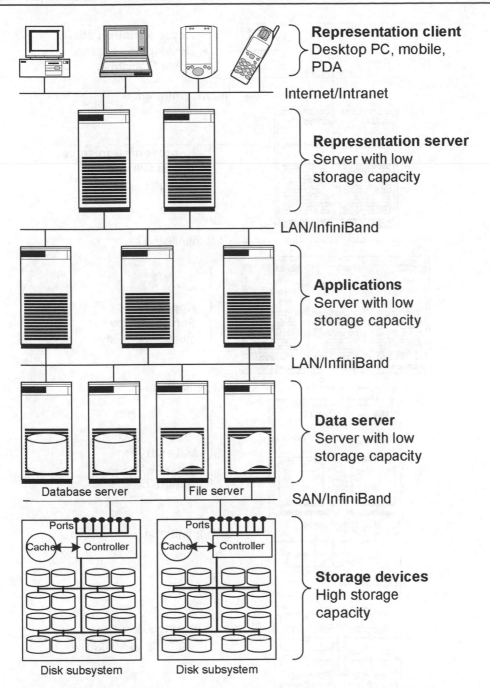

Figure 6.35 The web architecture (five-tier architecture) supports numerous different end devices. Furthermore, a storage network is inserted between the data management and the storage devices so that the IT architecture is transformed from a server-centric to a storage-centric architecture

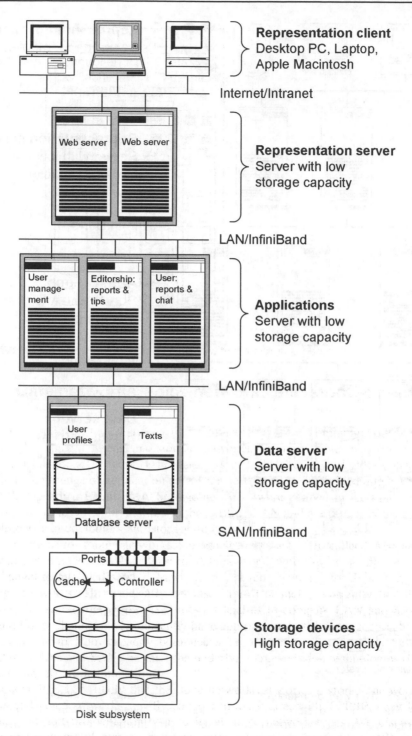

Figure 6.36   Realization of the travel portal with the web architecture

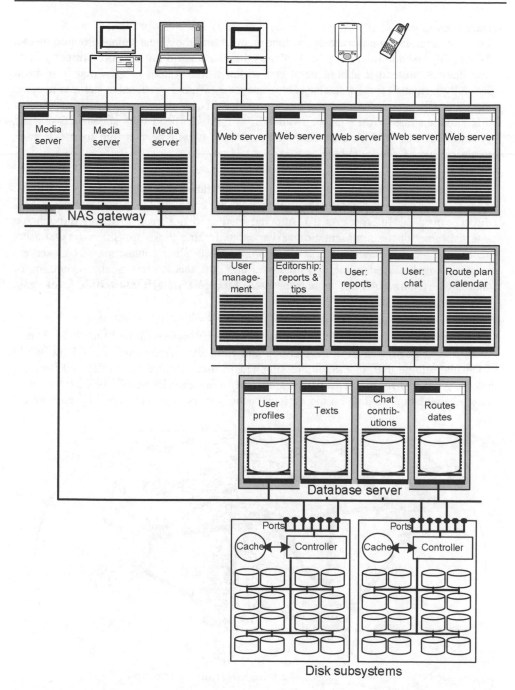

Figure 6.37 The five-tier architecture facilitates the flexible expansion of the travel portal: each layer can be expanded independently without this having major consequences for the other layers

- Databases
  The databases require storage space that meets the highest performance requirements. To simplify the administration of databases the data should not be stored directly upon raw devices, instead it should be stored within a file system in files that have been specially formatted for the database. Nowadays (2003), only disk subsystems connected via Fibre Channel are considered storage devices. NAS servers cannot yet be used in this situation due to the lack of availability of standardized high-speed network file systems such as RDMA enabled NFS. In future, it will be possible to use storage virtualization on file level here.

- Representation server and media servers
  The representation servers augment the user interfaces with photos and small films. These are stored on separate media servers that the end user's web browser can access directly over the Internet. As a result, the media do not need to travel through the internal buses of the representation servers, thus freeing these up. Since the end users access the media over the Internet via comparatively slow connections, NAS servers are very suitable. Depending upon the load upon the media servers, shared-nothing or shared-everything NAS servers can be used. Storage virtualization on file level again offers itself as an alternative here.

- Replication of the media servers
  The users of the travel portal access it from various locations around the globe. Therefore, it is a good idea to store pictures and films at various sites around the world so that the large data quantities are supplied to users from a server located near the user (Figure 6.38). This saves network capacity and generally accelerates the transmission of the data. The data on the various cache servers is synchronized by appropriate

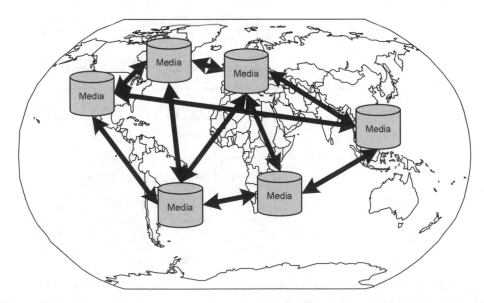

Figure 6.38 The content of the media servers is replicated at various locations in order to save network capacity

replication software. Incidentally, the use of the replication software is independent of whether the media servers at the various sites are configured as shared-nothing NAS servers, shared-everything NAS servers, or as a storage virtualization on the file-level.

6.5 SUMMARY

In the first part of the book the building blocks of storage networks were introduced. Building upon these, this chapter has explained the fundamental principles of the use of storage networks and shown how storage networks help to increase the availability and the adaptability of IT systems.

As an introduction to the use of storage networks, we elaborated upon the characteristics of storage networks by illustrating the layering of the techniques for storage networks, investigated various forms of storage networks in the I/O path and defined storage networks in relation to data networks and voice networks. Storage resource sharing was introduced as a first application of storage networks. Individually, disk storage pooling, tape library partitioning, tape library sharing and data sharing were considered. We described the redundant I/O buses and multipathing software, redundant server and cluster software, redundant disk subsystems and volume manager mirroring or disk subsystem remote mirroring to increase the availability of applications and data, and finally redundant storage virtualization. Based upon the case study 'protection of an important database' we showed how these measures can be combined to protect against the failure of a data centre. With regard to adaptability and scalability, the term 'cluster' was expanded to include the property of load distribution. Individually, shared-null configurations, shared-nothing clusters, enhanced shared-nothing clusters and shared-everything clusters were introduced. We then introduced the five-tier architecture – a flexible and scalable architecture for IT systems. Finally, based upon the case study 'travel portal', we showed how clusters and the five-tier architecture can be used to implement flexible and scalable web applications.

As a further important application of storage networks, the next chapter discusses network back-up (Chapter 7). A flexible and adaptable architecture for data protection is introduced and we show how network back-up systems can benefit from the use of disk subsystems and storage networks.

7

Network Back-up

Network back-up systems can back up heterogeneous IT environments incorporating several thousands of computers largely automatically. In the classical form, network back-up systems move the data to be backed up via the LAN; this is where the name 'network back-up' comes from. This chapter explains the basic principles of network back-up and shows typical performance bottlenecks for conventional server-centric IT architectures. Finally, it shows how storage networks and intelligent storage systems help to overcome these performance bottlenecks.

Before getting involved in technical details, we will first discuss a few general conditions that should be taken into account in back-up (Section 7.1). Then the back-up, archiving and hierarchical storage management services will be discussed (Section 7.2) and we will show which components are necessary for their implementation (Sections 7.3 and 7.4). This is followed by a summary of the measures discussed up to this point that are available to network back-up systems to increase performance (Section 7.5). Then, on the basis of network back-up, further technical boundaries of server-centric IT architectures will be described (Section 7.6) that are beyond the scope of Section 1.1, and we will explain why these performance bottlenecks can only be overcome to a limited degree within the server-centric IT architecture (Section 7.7). Then we will show how data can be backed up significantly more efficiently with a storage-centric IT architecture (Section 7.8). Building upon this, the protection of file servers (Section 7.9) and databases (Section 7.10) using storage networks and network back-up systems will be discussed. Finally, organizational aspects of data protection will be considered (Section 7.11). The consideration of network back-up concludes the use of storage networks.

Storage Networks Explained   U. Troppens R. Erkens W. Müller
© 2004 John Wiley & Sons, Ltd   ISBN: 0-470-86182-7

7.1 GENERAL CONDITIONS FOR BACK-UP

Back-up is always a headache for system administrators. Increasing amounts of data have to be backed up in ever shorter periods of time. Although modern operating systems come with their own back-up tools, these tools only represent isolated solutions, which are completely inadequate in the face of the increasing number and heterogeneity of systems to be backed up. For example, there may be no option for monitoring centrally whether all back-ups have been successfully completed overnight or there may be a lack of overall management of the back-up media.

Changing preconditions represent an additional hindrance to data protection. There are three main reasons for this:

1. As discussed in Chapter 1, installed storage capacity doubles every four to twelve months depending upon the company in question. The data set is thus often growing more quickly than the infrastructure in general (personnel, network capacity). Nevertheless, the ever-increasing quantities of data still have to be backed up.
2. Nowadays, business processes have to be adapted to changing requirements all the time. As business processes change, so the IT systems that support them also have to be adapted. As a result, the daily back-up routine must be continuously adapted to the ever-changing IT infrastructure.
3. As a result of globalization, the Internet and e-business, more and more data has to be available around the clock: it is no longer feasible to block user access to applications and data for hours whilst data is backed up. The time window for back-ups is becoming ever smaller.

Network back-up can help us to get to grips with these problems.

7.2 NETWORK BACK-UP SERVICES

Network back-up systems such as Arcserve (Computer Associates), NetBackup (Veritas), Networker (EMC/Legato) and Tivoli Storage Manager (IBM) provide the following services:

- back-up
- archive
- hierarchical storage management.

The main task of network back-up systems is to back data up regularly. To this end, at least one up-to-date copy must be kept of all data, so that it can be restored after a hardware or application error ('file accidentally deleted or destroyed by editing', 'error in the database programming').

The purpose of archiving is to freeze a certain version of the data so that this precise version can be restored later on. For example, after the conclusion of a project its data can be archived on the back-up server and then deleted from the local hard disk. This saves local disk space and accelerates back-up and restore processes, since only the data that is actually being worked with has to be backed up or restored.

Hierarchical storage management (HSM) finally leads the end user to believe that any desired size of hard disk is present. HSM moves files that have not been accessed for a long time from the local disk to the back-up server; only a directory entry remains in the local file server. The entry in the directory contains meta information such as file name, owner, access rights, date of last modification and so on. The metadata takes up hardly any space in the file system compared to the actual file contents, so space is actually gained by moving the file content from the local disk to the back-up server.

If a process accesses the content of a file that has been moved in this way, HSM blocks the accessing process, copies the file content back from the back-up server to the local file system and only then gives clearance to the accessing process. Apart from the longer access time, this process remains completely hidden to the accessing processes and thus also to end users. Older files can thus be automatically moved to cheaper media (tapes) and, if necessary, fetched back again without the end user having to alter his behaviour.

Strictly speaking, HSM and back-up and archive are separate concepts. However, HSM is a component of many network back-up products, so the same components (media, software) can be used both for back-up, archive and also for HSM. When HSM is used, the back-up software used must at least be HSM-capable: it must back up the metadata of the moved files and the moved files themselves, without moving the file contents back to the client. HSM-capable back-up software can speed up back-up and restore processes because only the meta-information of the moved files has to be backed up and restored, not their file contents.

A network back-up system realizes the above-mentioned functions of back-up, archive and hierarchical storage management by the co-ordination of back-up server and a range of back-up clients (Figure 7.1). The server provides central components such as the management of back-up media that are required by all back-up clients. However, different back-up clients are used for different operating systems and applications. These are specialized in the individual operating systems or applications in order to increase the efficiency of data protection or the efficiency of the movement of data.

The use of terminology regarding network back-up systems is somewhat sloppy: the main task of network back-up systems is the back-up of data. Server and client instances of network back-up systems are therefore often known as the back-up server and back-up client, regardless of what tasks they perform or what they are used for. A particular server instance of a network back-up system could, for example, be used exclusively for HSM, so that this instance should actually be called a HSM server – nevertheless this instance would generally be called a back-up server. A client that provides the back-up function

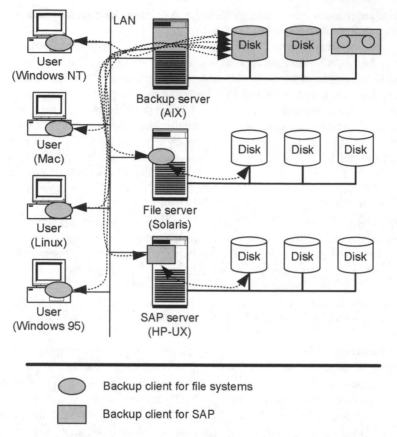

Figure 7.1   Network back-up systems can automatically back-up heterogeneous IT environments via the LAN. A platform-specific back-up client must be installed on all clients to be backed up

usually also supports archive and the restore of back-ups and archives – nevertheless this client is generally just known as a back-up client. In this book we follow the general, untidy conventions, because the phrase 'back-up client' reads better than 'back-up-archive-HSM and restore client'.

The two following sections discuss details of the back-up server (Section 7.3) and the back-up client (Section 7.4). We then turn our attention to the performance and the use of network back-up systems.

7.3   SERVER COMPONENTS

Back-up servers consist of a whole range of component parts. In the following we will discuss the main components: job scheduler (Section 7.3.1), error handler (Section 7.3.2), metadata database (Section 7.3.3) and media manager (Section 7.3.4).

7.3.1   Job scheduler

The job scheduler determines what data will be backed up when. It must be carefully configured; the actual back-up then takes place automatically.

With the aid of job schedulers and tape libraries many computers can be backed up overnight without the need for a system administrator to change tapes on site. Small tape libraries have a tape drive, a magazine with space for around ten tapes and a media changer that can automatically move the various tapes back and forth between magazine and tape drive. Large tape libraries have several dozen tape drives, space for several thousands of tapes and a media changer or two to insert the tapes in the drives.

7.3.2   Error handling

If a regular automatic back-up of several systems has to be performed, it becomes difficult to monitor whether all automated back-ups have run without errors. The error handler helps to prioritize and filter error messages and generate reports. This avoids the situation in which problems in the back-up are not noticed until a back-up needs to be restored.

7.3.3   Metadata database

The metadata database and the media manager represent two components that tend to be hidden. The metadata database is the brain of a network back-up system. It contains the following entries for every back-up up object: name, computer of origin, date of last change, date of last back-up, name of the back-up medium, etc. For example, an entry is made in the metadata database for every file to be backed up.

The cost of the metadata database is worthwhile: in contrast to back-up tools provided by operating systems, network back-up systems permit the implementation of the incremental-forever strategy in which a file system is only fully backed up in the first back-up. In subsequent back-ups, only those files that have changed since the previous back-up are backed up. The current state of the file system can then be calculated on the back-up server from database operations from the original full back-up and from all subsequent incremental back-ups, so that no further full back-ups are necessary. The calculations in the metadata database are generally performed faster than a new full back-up.

Even more is possible: if several versions of the files are backed up on the back-up server, a whole file system or a subdirectory dated three days ago, for example, can be restored (point-in-time restore) – the metadata database makes it possible.

7.3.4   Media manager

Use of the incremental-forever strategy can considerably reduce the time taken by the back-up in comparison to the full back-up. The disadvantage of this is that over time the backed up files can become distributed over numerous tapes. This is critical for the restoring of large file systems because tape mounts cost time. This is where the media manager comes into play. It can ensure that only files from a single computer are located on one tape. This reduces the number of tape mounts involved in a restore process, which means that the data can be restored more quickly.

A further important function of the media manager is so-called tape reclamation. As a result of the incremental-forever strategy, more and more data that is no longer needed is located on the back-up tapes. If, for example, a file is deleted or changed very frequently over time, earlier versions of the file can be deleted from the back-up medium. The gaps on the tapes that thus become free cannot be directly overwritten using current techniques. In tape reclamation, the media manager copies the remaining data that is still required from several tapes, of which only a certain percentage is used, onto a common new tape. The tapes that have thus become free are then added to the pool of unused tapes.

There is one further technical limitation in the handling of tapes: current tape drives can only write data to the tapes at a certain speed. If the data is transferred to the tape drive too slowly this interrupts the write process, the tape rewinds a little and restarts the write process. The repeated rewinding of the tapes costs performance and causes unnecessary wear to the tapes so they have to be discarded more quickly. It is therefore better to send the data to the tape drive quickly enough so that it can write the data onto the tape in one go (streaming).

The problem with this is that in network back-up the back-up clients send the data to be backed up via the LAN to the back-up server, which forwards the data to the tape drive. On the way from back-up client via the LAN to the back-up server there are repeated fluctuations in the transmission rate, which means that the streaming of tape drives is repeatedly interrupted. Although it is possible for individual clients to achieve streaming by additional measures (such as the installation of a separate LAN between back-up client and back-up server) (Section 7.7), these measures are expensive and technically not scalable at will, so they cannot be realized economically for all clients.

The solution: the media manager manages a storage hierarchy within the back-up server. To achieve this, the back-up server must be equipped with hard disks and tape libraries. If a client cannot send the data fast enough for streaming, the media manager first of all stores the data to be backed up to hard disk. When writing to a hard disk it makes no difference what speed the data is supplied at. When enough of the data to be backed up has been temporarily saved to the hard disk of the back-up server, the media manager automatically moves large quantities of data from the hard disk of the back-up server to its tapes. This process only involves recopying the data within the back-up server, so that streaming is guaranteed when writing the tapes.

This storage hierarchy is used, for example, for the back-up of user PCs (Figure 7.2). Many user PCs are switched off overnight, which means that back-up cannot be guaranteed overnight. Therefore, network back-up systems often use the midday period to back up user PCs. Use of the incremental-forever strategy means that the amount of data to be backed up every day is so low that such a back-up strategy is generally feasible. All user PCs are first of all backed up to the hard disk of the back-up server in the time window from 11 : 15 to 13 : 45. The media manager in the back-up server then has a good twenty hours to move the data from the hard disks to tapes. Then the hard disks are once

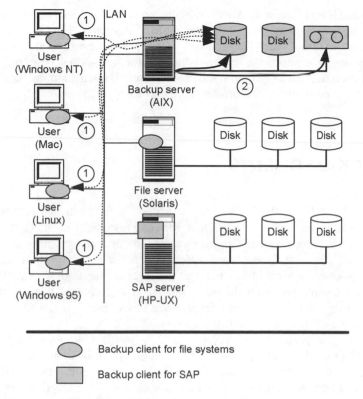

Figure 7.2 The storage hierarchy in the back-up server helps to back user PCs up efficiently. First of all, all PCs are backed up to the hard disks of the back-up server (1) during the midday period. Before the next midday break the media manager copies the data from the hard disks to tapes (2)

again free so that the user PCs can once again be backed up to hard disk in the next midday break.

In all operations described here the media manager checks whether the correct tape has been placed in the drive. To this end, the media manager writes an unambiguous signature to every tape, which it records in the metadata database. Every time a tape is inserted the media manager compares the signature on the tape with the signature in the metadata database. This ensures that no tapes are accidentally overwritten and that the correct data is written back during a restore operation.

Furthermore, the media manager monitors how often a tape has been used and how old it is, so that old tapes are discarded in good time. If necessary, it first copies data that is still required to a new tape. Older tape media formats also have to be wound back and forwards now and then so that they last longer; the media manager can also automate the winding of tapes that have not been used for a long time.

A further important function of the media manager is the management of data in a so-called off-site store. To this end, the media manager keeps two copies of all data to be backed up. The first copy is always stored on the back-up server, so that data can be quickly restored if it is required. However, in the event of a large-scale disaster (fire in the data centre) the copies on the back-up server could be destroyed. For such cases the media manager keeps a second copy in an off-site store that can be several kilometres away. The media manager supports the system administrator in moving the correct tapes back and forwards between back-up server and off-site store. It even supports tape reclamation for tapes that are currently in the off-site store and it.

7.4   BACK-UP CLIENTS

A platform-specific client (back-up agent) is necessary for each platform to be backed up. The base client can back up and archive files and restores them if required. The term platform is used here to mean the various operating systems and the file systems that they support. Furthermore, some base clients offer HSM for selected file systems.

The back-up of file systems takes place at file level as standard. This means that each changed file is completely retransferred to the server and entered there in the metadata database. By using back-up at volume level and at block level it is possible to change the granularity of the objects to be backed up.

When back-up is performed at volume level, a whole volume is backed up as an individual object on the back-up server. We can visualize this as the output of the Unix command 'dd' being sent to the back-up server. Although this has the disadvantage that free areas, on which no data at all has been saved, are also backed up, only very few metadata database operations are necessary on the back-up server and on the client side it is not necessary to spend a long time comparing which files have changed since the last back-up. As a result, back-up and restore operations can sometimes be performed more quickly at volume level than they can at file level. This is particularly true when restoring large file systems with a large number of small files.

Back-up on block level optimizes back-up for members of the external sales force, who only connect up to the company network now and then by means of a laptop via a dial-up line. In this situation the performance bottleneck is the low transmission capacity of modem or ISDN connections. If only one bit of a large file is changed, the whole file must once again be forced down the dial-up connection. When backing up on block level the back-up client additionally keeps a local copy of every file backed up. If a file has changed, it can establish which parts of the file have changed. The back-up client sends only the changed data fragments (blocks) to the back-up server. This can then reconstruct the complete file. As is the case for back-up on file level, each file backed up is entered in the metadata database. Thus, when backing up on block level the quantity of data to be transmitted is reduced at the cost of storage space on the local hard disk.

In addition to the standard client for file systems, most network back-up systems provide special clients for various applications. For example, there are special clients for MS Exchange or Lotus Domino that make it possible to back up and restore individual documents. We will discuss the back-up of file systems and NAS servers (Section 7.9) and databases (Section 7.10) in more detail later on.

7.5   PERFORMANCE GAINS AS A RESULT OF NETWORK BACK-UP

The underlying hardware components determine the maximum throughput of network back-up systems. The software components determine how efficiently the available hardware is actually used. At various points of this chapter we have already discussed how network back-up systems can help to better utilize the existing infrastructure:

- Performance increase by the archiving of data: deleting data that has already been archived from hard disks can accelerate the daily back-up because there is less data to back up. For the same reason, file systems can be restored more quickly.
- Performance increase by hierarchical storage management (HSM): by moving file contents to the HSM server, file systems can be restored more quickly. The directory entries of files that have been moved can be restored comparatively quickly; the majority of the data, namely the file contents, do not need to be fetched back from the HSM server.
- Performance increase by the incremental-forever strategy: after the first back-up, only the data that has changed since the last back-up is backed up. On the back-up server the metadata database is used to calculate the latest state of the data from the first back-up and all subsequent incremental back-ups, so that no further full back-ups are necessary. The back-up window can thus be significantly reduced.
- Performance increase by reducing tape mounts: the media manager can ensure that data that belongs together is only distributed amongst a few tapes. The number of time-consuming tape changes for the restoring of data can thus be reduced.
- Performance increase by streaming: the efficient writing of tapes requires that the data is transferred quickly enough to the tape drive. If this is not guaranteed the back-up server can first temporarily store the data on a hard drive and then send the data to the tape drive in one go.
- Performance increase by back-up on volume level or on block level: as standard, file systems are backed up on file level. Large file systems with several hundreds of thousands of files can sometimes be backed up more quickly if they are backed up at volume level. Laptops can be backed up more quickly if only the blocks that have changed are transmitted over the modem to the back-up server.

7.6   PERFORMANCE BOTTLENECKS OF NETWORK BACK-UP

At some point, however, the technical boundaries for increasing the performance of back-up are reached. When talking about technical boundaries, we should differentiate between application-specific boundaries (Section 7.6.1) and those that are determined by server-centric IT architecture (Section 7.6.2).

7.6.1   Application-specific performance bottlenecks

Application-specific performance bottlenecks are all those bottlenecks that can be traced back to the 'network back-up' application. These performance bottlenecks play no role for other applications.

The main candidate for application-specific performance bottlenecks is the metadata database. A great deal is demanded of this. Almost every action in the network back-up system is associated with one or more operations in the metadata database. If, for example, several versions of a file are backed up, an entry is made in the metadata database for each version. The back-up of a file system with several hundreds of thousands of files can thus be associated with a whole range of database operations.

A further candidate for application-specific performance bottlenecks is the storage hierarchy: when copying the data from hard disk to tape the media manager has to load the data from the hard disk into the main memory via the I/O bus and the internal buses, only to forward it from there to the tape drive via the internal buses and I/O bus. This means that the buses can get clogged up during the copying of the data from hard disk to tape. The same applies to tape reclamation.

7.6.2   Performance bottlenecks due to server-centric IT architecture

In addition to these two application-specific performance bottlenecks, some problems crop up in network back-up that are typical of a server-centric IT architecture. Let us mention once again as a reminder the fact that in a server-centric IT architecture storage devices only exist in relation to servers; access to storage devices always takes place via the computer to which the storage devices are connected. The performance bottlenecks described in the following apply for all applications that are operated in a server-centric IT architecture.

Let us assume that a back-up client wants to back data up to the back-up server (Figure 7.3). The back-up client loads the data to be backed up from the hard disk into the main memory of the application server via the SCSI bus, the PCI bus and the system bus, only to forward it from there to the network card via the system bus and the PCI bus. On the back-up server the data must once again be passed through the buses twice. In back-up, large quantities of data are generally backed up in one go. During back-up, therefore, the buses of the participating computers can become a bottleneck, particularly if the application server also has to bear the I/O load of the application or the back-up server is supposed to support several simultaneous back-up operations.

The network card transfers the data to the back-up server via TCP/IP and Ethernet. Previously the data exchange via TCP/IP was associated with a high CPU load. However, the CPU load caused by TCP/IP data traffic can be disregarded with the increasing use of TCP/IP offload engines (TOE) (Section 3.5.2 'TCP/IP and Ethernet as an I/O technology').

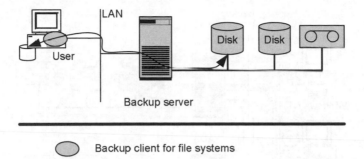

Backup client for file systems

Figure 7.3   In network back-up, all data to be backed up must be passed through both computers. Possible performance bottlenecks are: internal buses, CPU and the LAN

7.7   LIMITED OPPORTUNITIES FOR INCREASING PERFORMANCE

Back-up is a resource-intensive application that places great demands upon storage devices, CPU, main memory, network capacity, internal buses and I/O buses. The enormous amount of resources required for back-up is not always sufficiently taken into account during the planning of IT systems. A frequent comment is 'the back-up is responsible for the slow network' or 'the slow network is responsible for the restore operation taking so long'. The truth is that the network is inadequately dimensioned for end user data traffic and back-up data traffic. Often, data protection is the application that requires the most network capacity. Therefore, it is often sensible to view back-up as the primary application for which the IT infrastructure in general and the network in particular must be dimensioned.

In every IT environment, most computers can be adequately protected by a network back-up system. In almost every IT environment, however, there are computers – usually only a few – for which additional measures are necessary in order to back them up quickly enough or, if necessary, to restore them. In the server-centric IT architecture there are three approaches to taming such data monsters: the installation of a separate LAN for the network back-up between back-up client and back-up server (Section 7.7.1), the installation of several back-up servers (Section 7.7.2) and the installation of back-up client and back-up server on the same physical computer (Section 7.7.3).

7.7.1   Separate LAN for network back-up

The simplest measure to increase back-up performance more of heavyweight back-up clients is to install a further LAN between back-up client and back-up server in addition to the existing LAN and to use this exclusively for back-up (Figure 7.4). An expensive, but powerful, transmission technology such as ATM, FDDI or Gigabit Ethernet can also help here.

The concept of installing a further network for back-up in addition to the existing LAN is comparable to the basic idea of storage networks. In contrast to storage networks,

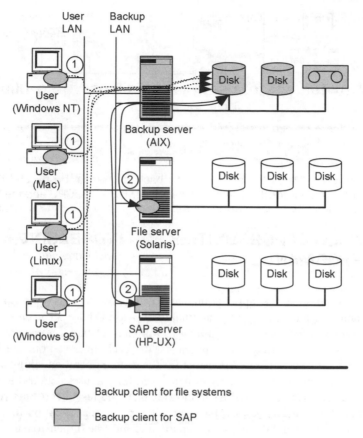

Backup client for file systems

Backup client for SAP

Figure 7.4 Approach 1: the throughput of the network back-up can be increased by the installation of a second LAN. Normal clients are still backed up via the User LAN (1). Only heavyweight clients are backed up via the second LAN (2)

however, in this case only computers are connected together; direct access to all storage devices is not possible. All data thus continues to be passed via TCP/IP and through application server and back-up server which leads to a blockage of the internal bus and the I/O buses.

Individual back-up clients can thus benefit from the installation of a separate LAN for network back-up. This approach is, however, not scalable at will: due to the heavy load on the back-up server this cannot back up any further computers in addition to the back-up of one individual heavyweight client.

Despite its limitations, the installation of a separate back-up LAN is sufficient in many environments. With Fast-Ethernet you can still achieve a throughput of over 10 MByte/s. The LAN technique is made even more attractive by Gigabit Ethernet, 10Gigabit Ethernet and the above-mentioned TCP/IP offload engines that free up the server CPU significantly with regard to the TCP/IP data traffic.

7.7.2 Several back-up servers

Installing multiple back-up servers distributes the load of the back-up server over more hardware. For example, it would be possible to assign every heavyweight back-up client a special back-up server installed exclusively for the back-up of this client (Figure 7.5). Furthermore, a further back-up server is required for the back-up of all other back-up clients. This approach is worthwhile in the event of performance bottlenecks in the metadata database or in combination with the first measure, the installation of a separate LAN between the heavyweight back-up client and back-up server.

The performance of the back-up server can be significantly increased by the installation of multiple back-up servers and a separate LAN for back-up. However, from the point of view of the heavyweight back-up client the problem remains that all data to be backed up must be passed from the hard disk into the main memory via the buses and from there must again be passed through the buses to the network card. This means that back-up still heavily loads the application server. The resource requirement for back-up could be in conflict with the resource requirement for the actual application.

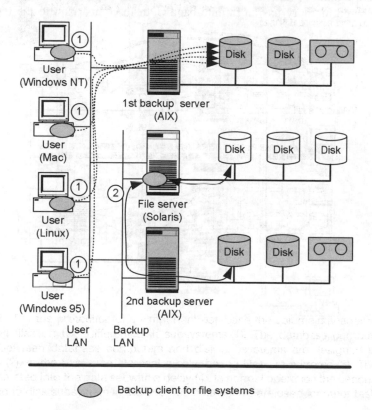

Figure 7.5 Approach 2: dedicated back-up servers can be installed for heavyweight back-up clients. Normal clients continue to be backed up on the first back-up server (1). Only the heavyweight client is backed up on its own back-up server over the separate LAN (2)

A further problem is the realization of the storage hierarchy within the individual back-up server since every back-up server now requires its own tape library. Many small tape libraries are more expensive and less flexible than one large tape library. Therefore, it would actually be better to buy a large tape library that is used by all servers. In a server-centric IT architecture it is, however, only possible to connect multiple computers to the same tape library to a very limited degree.

7.7.3 Back-up server and application server on the same physical computer

The third possible way of increasing performance is to install the back-up server and application server on the same physical computer (Figure 7.6). This results in the back-up client also having to run on this computer. Back-up server and back-up client communicate over Shared Memory (Unix), Named Pipe or TCP/IP Loopback (Windows) instead of via LAN. Shared Memory has an infinite bandwidth in comparison to the buses, which

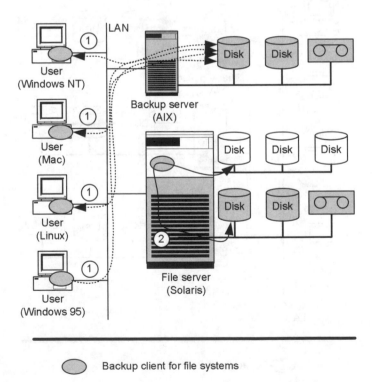

⬭ Backup client for file systems

Figure 7.6 Approach 3: application server, back-up server and back-up client are installed on one computer. Normal clients continue to be backed up on the first back-up server (1). Only the heavyweight client is backed up within the same computer (2)

means that the communication between back-up server and back-up client is no longer the limiting factor.

However, the internal buses continue to get clogged up: the back-up client now loads the data to be backed up from the hard disk into the main memory via the buses. The back-up server takes the data from the main memory and writes it, again via the buses, to the back-up medium. The data is thus once again driven through the internal bus twice. Tape reclamation and any copying operations within the storage hierarchy of the back-up server could place an additional load on the buses.

Without further information we cannot more precisely determine the change to the CPU load. Shared Memory communication (or Named Pipe or TCP/IP Loopback) dispenses with the CPU-intensive operation of the network card. On the other hand, a single computer must now bear the load of the application, the back-up server and the back-up client. This computer must incidentally possess sufficient main memory for all three applications.

One problem with this approach is the proximity of production data and copies on the back-up server. SCSI permits a maximum cable length of 25 m. Since application and back-up server run on the same physical computer, the copies are a maximum of 50 m away from the production data. In the event of a fire or comparable damage, this is disastrous. Therefore, either a SCSI extender should be used or the tapes taken from the tape library every day and placed in an off-site store. The latter goes against the requirement of largely automating data protection.

7.8 NEXT GENERATION BACK-UP

Storage networks open up new possibilities for getting around the performance bottlenecks of network back-up described above. They connect servers and storage devices, so that during back-up production data can be copied directly from the source hard disk to the back-up media, without passing it through a server (server-free back-up, Section 7.8.1). LAN-free back-up (Section 7.8.2) and LAN-free back-up with shared disk file systems (Section 7.8.3) are two further alternative methods of accelerating back-up using storage networks. The introduction of storage networks also has the side-effect that several back-up servers can share a tape library (Section 7.8.4). The use of instant copies (Section 7.8.5) and remote mirroring (Section 7.8.6) provide further possibilities for accelerating back-up and restore operations.

7.8.1 Server-free back-up

The ultimate goal of back-up over a storage network is so-called server-free back-up (Figure 7.7). In back-up, the back-up client initially determines which data has to be backed up and then sends only the appropriate metadata (file name, access rights, etc.) over the LAN to the back-up server. The file contents, which make up the majority of the data quantity to be transferred, are then written directly from the source hard disk

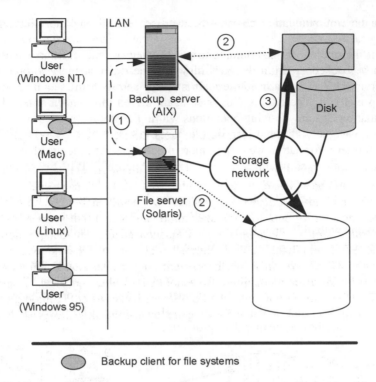

Backup client for file systems

Figure 7.7 In server-free back-up, back-up server and back-up client exchange lightweight metadata via the LAN (1). After it has been determined which data blocks have to be backed up, the network back-up system can configure the storage devices for the data transfer via the storage network (2). The heavyweight file contents are then copied directly from the source hard disk to the back-up medium via the storage network (3)

to the back-up medium (disk, tape, optical) over the storage network, without a server being connected in between. The network back-up system co-ordinates the communication between source hard disk and back-up medium. A shorter transport route for the back-up of data is not yet in sight with current storage techniques.

The performance of server-free back-up is predominantly determined by the performance of the underlying storage systems and the connection in the storage network. Shifting the transport route for the majority of the data from the LAN to the storage network without a server being involved in the transfer itself means that the internal buses and the I/O buses are freed up on both the back-up client and the back-up server. The cost of co-ordinating the data traffic between source hard disk and back-up medium is comparatively low.

A major problem in the implementation of server-free back-up is that the SCSI commands have to be converted en route from the source hard disk to the back-up medium. For example, different blocks are generally addressed on source medium and back-up medium. Or, during the restoration of a deleted file in a file system, this file has to be restored to a different area if the space that was freed up is now occupied by other files.

In the back-up from hard disk to tape, even the SCSI command sets are slightly different. Therefore, software called 3rd-Party SCSI Copy Command is necessary for the protocol conversion. It can be realized at various points: in a SAN switch, in a box specially connected to the storage network that is exclusively responsible for the protocol conversion, or in one of the two participating storage systems themselves.

Server-free back-up is running in the laboratories and demo centres of many manufacturers. Many manufacturers claim that their back-up products already support server-free back-up. In our experience, however, server-free back-up is almost never used in production environments, although it has now been available for some time (2003). In our opinion this proves that server-free back-up is still very difficult to configure and operate at the current level of technology.

7.8.2 LAN-free back-up

LAN-free back-up dispenses with the necessity for the 3rd-Party SCSI Copy Command by realizing comparable functions within the back-up client (Figure 7.8). As in server-free

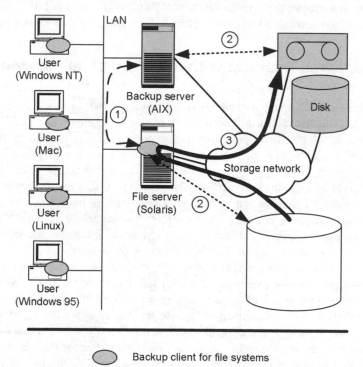

Figure 7.8 In LAN-free back-up, too, back-up servers and back-up clients exchange lightweight metadata over the LAN (1). The back-up server prepares its storage devices for the data transfer over the storage network and then hands control of the storage devices over to the back-up client (2). This then copies heavyweight file contents directly to the back-up medium via the storage network (3)

back-up, metadata is sent via the LAN. File contents, however, no longer go through the back-up server: for back-up the back-up client loads the data from the hard disk into the main memory via the appropriate buses and from there writes it directly to the back-up medium via the buses and the storage network. To this end, the back-up client must be able to access the back-up server's back-up medium over the storage network. Furthermore, back-up server and back-up client must synchronize their access to common devices. This is easier to realize than server-free back-up and thus well proven in production environments.

In LAN-free back-up the load on the buses of the back-up server is reduced but not the load on those of the back-up client. This can impact upon other applications (databases, file and web servers) that run on the back-up client at the same time as the back-up.

LAN-free back-up is already being used in production environments. However, the manufacturers of network back-up systems only support LAN-free back-up for certain applications (databases, file systems, e-mail systems), with not every application being supported on every operating system. Anyone wanting to use LAN-free back-up at the moment must take note of the manufacturer's support matrix (see Section 3.4.6). It can be assumed that in the course of the next one to two years the number of the applications and operating systems supported will increase significantly.

7.8.3   LAN-free back-up with shared disk file systems

Anyone wishing to back up a file system now for which LAN-free back-up is not supported can sometimes use shared disk file systems to rectify this situation (Figure 7.9). Shared disk file systems are installed upon several computers. Access to data is synchronized over the LAN; the individual file accesses, on the other hand, take place directly over the storage network (Section 4.3). For back-up the shared disk file system is installed on the file server and the back-up server. The prerequisite for this is that a shared disk file system is available that supports the operating systems of back-up client and back-up server. The back-up client is then started on the same computer on which the back-up server runs, so that back-up client and back-up server can exchange the data via Shared Memory (Unix) or Named Pipe or TCP/IP Loopback (Windows).

In LAN-free back-up using a shared disk file system, the performance of the back-up server must be critically examined. All data still has to be passed through the buses of the back-up server; in addition, the back-up client and the shared disk file system run on this machine. LAN data traffic is no longer necessary within the network back-up system; however, the shared disk file system now requires LAN data traffic for the synchronization of simultaneous data accesses. The data traffic for the synchronization of the shared disk file system is, however, comparatively light. At the end of the day, you have to measure whether back-up with a shared disk file system increases performance for each individual case.

Although the performance of LAN-free back-up with the aid of a shared disk file system is not as good as the performance of pure LAN-free back-up, it can be significantly better than that of back-up over the LAN. Therefore, this approach has proved its worth in

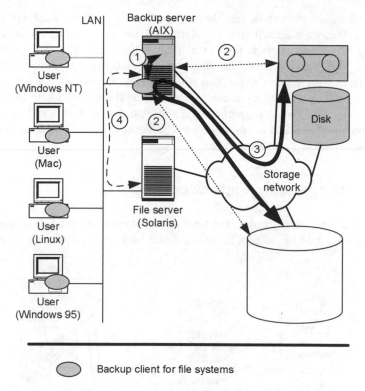

Figure 7.9 When backing up using shared disk file systems, back-up server and back-up client run on the same computer (1). Production data and back-up media are accessed on the back-up server (2), which means that the back-up can take place over the storage network (3). The shared disk file system requires a LAN connection for the lightweight synchronization of parallel data accesses (4)

production environments, so that it can be viewed as an interesting transitional solution until LAN-free (or even server-free) back-up becomes available.

7.8.4 Tape library sharing

Server-free back-up and LAN-free back-up can significantly reduce the load upon the back-up server. However, the problem remains that a large number of objects to be backed up can break the metadata database. The only effective remedy is to distribute the load amongst several back-up servers (Section 7.7.2). All back-up servers can share a large tape library via the storage network by means of tape library sharing (Section 6.2.2). An alternative would be to purchase each back-up server its own smaller tape library. However, many small tape libraries are more expensive to purchase and more difficult to manage than one large one.

Figure 7.10 shows the use of tape library sharing for network back-up: one back-up server acts as library master, all others as library clients. If a back-up client backs up data to a back-up server that is configured as a library client, then this first of all requests a free tape from the library master. The library master selects the tape from its pool of free tapes and places it in a free drive. Then it notes in its metadata database that this tape is now being used by the library client and it informs the library client of the drive that the tape is in. Finally, the back-up client can send the data to be backed up via the LAN to the back-up server, which is configured as the library client. This then writes the data directly to tape via the storage network.

7.8.5   Back-up using instant copies

Instant copies can practically copy even terabyte-sized data sets in a few seconds, and thus freeze the current state of the production data and make it available via a second access

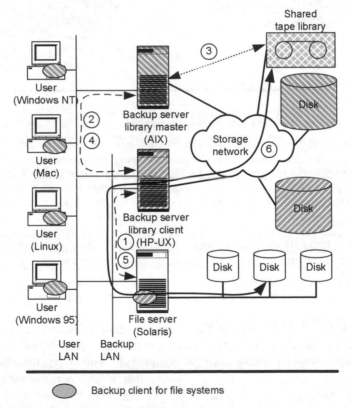

Figure 7.10   In tape library sharing two back-up servers share a large tape library. If a client wants to back data up directly to tape with the second back-up server (library client) (1) then this initially requests a tape and a drive from the library master (2). The library master places a free tape in a free drive (3) and returns the information in question to the library client (4). The library client now informs the back-up client (5) that it can back the data up (6)

path. The production data can still be read and changed over the first access path, so that the operation of the actual application can be continued, whilst at the same time the frozen state of the data can be backed up via the second access path.

Instant copies can be realized on three different levels:

1. Instant copy in the block layer (disk subsystem or block-based virtualization)
   Instant copy in the disk subsystem was discussed in detail in Section 2.7.1: intelligent disk subsystems can practically copy all data of a hard disk onto a second hard disk within a few seconds. The frozen data state can be accessed and backed up via the second hard disk.

2. Instant copy in the file layer (local file system, NAS server or file-based virtualization)
   Many file systems also offer the possibility of creating instant copies. Instant copies on file system level are generally called snapshots (Section 4.1.3). In contrast to instant copies in the disk subsystem the snapshot can be accessed via a special directory path.

3. Instant copy in the application
   Finally, databases in particular offer the possibility of freezing the data set internally for back-up, whilst the user continues to access it (hot back-up, online back-up).

Instant copies in the local file system and in the application have the advantage that they can be realized with any hardware. Instant copies in the application can utilize the internal data structure of the application and thus work more efficiently than file systems. On the other hand, applications do not require these functions if the underlying file system already provides them. Both approaches consume system resources on the application server that one would sometimes prefer to make available to the actual application. This is the advantage of instant copies in external devices (e.g., disk subsystem, NAS Server, network-based virtualization instance): although it requires special hardware, application server tasks are moved to the external device thus freeing up the application server.

Back-up using instant copy must be synchronized with the applications to be backed up. Databases and file systems buffer write accesses in the main memory in order to increase their performance. As a result, the data on the hard disk is not always in a consistent state. Data consistency is the prerequisite for restarting the application with this data set and being able to continue operation. For back-up it should therefore be ensured that an instant copy with consistent data is first generated. The procedure looks something like this:

1. Shut down the application.

2. Perform the instant copy.

3. Start up the application again.

4. Back up the data of the instant copy.

Despite the shutting down and restarting of the application the production system is back in operation very quickly.

Data protection with instant copies is even more attractive if the instant copy is controlled by the application itself: in this case the application must ensure that the data on disk is consistent and then initiate the copying operation. The application can then continue operation after a few seconds. It is no longer necessary to stop and restart the application.

Instant copies thus make it possible to back-up business-critical applications every hour with only very slight interruptions. This also accelerates the restoring of data after application errors ('accidental deletion of a table space'). Instead of the time-consuming restore of data from tapes, the frozen copy that is present in the storage system can simply be put back.

With the aid of instant copies in the disk subsystem it is possible to realize so-called application server-free back-up. In this, the application server is put at the side of a second server that serves exclusively for back-up (Figure 7.11). Both servers are directly connected to the disk subsystem via SCSI; a storage network is not absolutely necessary. For back-up the instant copy is first of all generated as described above: (1) shut down application; (2) generate instant copy; and (3) restart application. The instant copy can

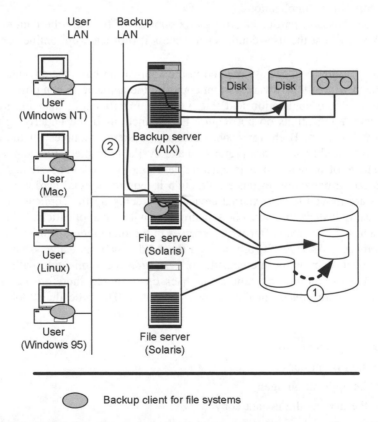

Backup client for file systems

Figure 7.11 Application server-free back-up utilizes the functions of an intelligent disk subsystem. To perform a back-up the application is operated for a short period in such a manner as to create a consistent data state on the hard disks, so that data can be copied by means of instant copy (1). The application can immediately switch back to normal operation; in parallel to this the data is backed up using the instant copy (2)

then be accessed from the second computer and the data is backed up from there without placing a load on the application server. If the instant copy is not deleted in the disk subsystem, the data can be restored using this copy in a few seconds in the event of an error.

7.8.6 Data protection using remote mirroring

Instant copies help to quickly restore data in the event of application or operating errors; however, they are ineffective in the event of a catastrophe: after a fire the fact that there are several copies of the data on a storage device does not help. Even a power failure can become a problem for a 24×7 operation.

The only thing that helps here is to mirror the data by means of remote mirroring on two disk subsystems, which are at least separated by a fire protection barrier. The protection of applications by means of remote mirroring has already been discussed in detail in Sections 6.3.3 and 6.3.5.

Nevertheless, the data still has to be backed up: in remote mirroring the source disk and copy are always identical. This means that if data is destroyed by an application or operating error then it is also immediately destroyed on the copy. The data can be backed up to hard disk by means of instant copy or by means of classical network back-up to tapes. Since storage capacity on hard disks is more expensive than storage capacity on tapes, only the most important data is backed up using instant copy and remote mirroring. For most data, back-up to tapes is still the most cost effective.

7.9 BACK-UP OF FILE SYSTEMS

Almost all applications store their data in file systems or in databases. Therefore, in this section we will examine the back-up of file servers (Section 7.9) and in the next section we will look more closely at that of databases (Section 7.10). The chapter concludes with organizational aspects of network back-up (Section 7.11).

This section first of all discusses fundamental requirements and problems in the back-up of file servers (Section 7.9.1). Then a few functions of modern file systems will be introduced that accelerate the incremental back-up of file systems (Section 7.9.2). Limitations in the back-up of NAS servers will then be discussed (Section 7.9.3). We will then introduce the Network Data Management Protocol (NDMP), a standard that helps to integrate the back-up of NAS servers into an established network back-up system (Section 7.9.4).

7.9.1 Back-up of file servers

We use the term file server to include computers with a conventional operating system such as Windows or Unix that exports part of its local file systems via a network file system or makes it accessible as service (Novell, FTP, HTTP). The descriptions in this section can be transferred to all types of computers, from user PCs through classical file servers to the web server.

File servers store three types of information:

- data in the form of files;
- metadata on these files such as file name, creation date and access rights; and
- metadata on the file servers such as any authorized users and their groups, size of the individual file systems, network configuration of the file server and names, components and rights of files or directories exported over the network.

Depending upon the error situation, different data and metadata must be restored. The restoring of individual files or entire file systems is relatively simple: in this case only the file contents and the metadata of the files must be restored from the back-up server to the file server. This function is performed by the back-up clients introduced in Section 7.4.

Restoring an entire file server is more difficult. If, for example, the hardware of the file server is irreparable and has to be fully replaced, the following steps are necessary:

1. Purchasing and setting up of appropriate replacement hardware.
2. Basic installation of the operating system including any necessary patches.
3. Restoration of the basic configuration of the file server including LAN and storage network configuration of the file server.
4. If necessary, restoration of users and groups and their rights.
5. Creation and formatting of the local file systems taking into account the necessary file system sizes.
6. Installation and configuration of the back-up client.
7. Restoration of the file systems with the aid of the network back-up system.

This procedure is very labour-intensive and time-consuming. The methods of so-called Image Restore (also known as Bare Metal Restore) accelerate the restoration of a complete computer: tools such as 'mksysb' (AIX), 'Web Flash Archive' (Solaris) or various disk image tools for Windows systems create a complete copy of a computer (image). Only a boot diskette or boot CD and an appropriate image is needed to completely restore a computer without having to work through steps 2–7 described above. Particularly advantageous is the integration of image restore in a network back-up system: to achieve this the network back-up system must generate the appropriate image. Furthermore, the boot diskette or boot CD must create a connection to the network back-up system.

7.9.2 Back-up of file systems

For the classical network back-up of file systems, back-up on different levels (block level, file level, file system image) has been discussed in addition to the incremental-forever strategy. The introduction of storage networks makes new methods available for the back-up of file systems such as server-free back-up, application server-free back-up, LAN-free back-up, shared disk file systems and instant copies.

The importance of the back-up of file systems is demonstrated by the fact that manufacturers of file systems are providing new functions specifically targeted at the acceleration of back-ups. In the following we introduce two of these new functions – the so-called archive bit and block level incremental back-up.

The archive bit supports incremental back-ups at file level such as, for example, the incremental-forever strategy. One difficulty associated with incremental back-ups is finding out quickly which files have changed since the previous back-up. To accelerate this decision, the file system adds an archive bit to the metadata of each file: the network back-up system sets this archive bit immediately after it has backed a file up on the back-up server. Thus the archive bits of all files are set after a full back-up. If a file is altered, the file system automatically clears its archive bit. Newly generated files are thus not given an archive bit. In the next incremental back-up the network back-up system knows that it only has to back up those files for which the archive bits have been cleared.

The principle of the archive bit can also be applied to the individual blocks of a file system in order to reduce the cost of back-up on block level. In Section 7.4 a comparatively expensive procedure for back-up on block level was introduced: the cost of the copying and comparing of files by the back-up client is greatly reduced if the file system manages the quantity of altered blocks itself with the aid of the archive bit for blocks and the network back-up system can call this up via an interface.

Unfortunately, the principle of archive bits cannot simply be combined with the principle of instant copies: if the file system copies uses instant copy to copy within the disk subsystem for back-up (Figure 7.11), the network back-up system sets the archive bit only on the copy of the file system. In the original data the archive bit thus remains cleared even though the data has been backed up. Consequently, the network back-up system backs this data up at the next incremental back-up because the setting of the archive bit has not penetrated through to the original data.

7.9.3 Back-up of NAS servers

NAS servers are preconfigured file servers; they consist of one or more internal servers, preconfigured disk capacity and usually a stripped-down or specific operating system (Section 4.2.2). NAS servers generally come with their own back-up tools. However, just like the back-up tools that come with operating systems, these tools represent an isolated solution (Section 7.1). Therefore, in the following we specifically consider the linking of the back-up of NAS servers into an existing network back-up system.

The optimal situation would be if there were a back-up client for a NAS server that was adapted to suit both the peculiarities of the NAS server and also the peculiarities of the network back-up system used. Unfortunately, it is difficult to develop such a back-up client in practice:

- If the NAS server is based upon a specific operating system the manufacturers of the network back-up system sometimes lack the necessary interfaces and compilers to develop such a client. Even if the preconditions for the development of a specific back-up client were in place, it is doubtful whether the manufacturer of the network back-up system would develop a specific back-up client for all NAS servers: the necessary development cost for a new back-up client is still negligible in comparison to the testing cost that would have to be incurred for every new version of the network back-up system.

- Likewise, it is difficult for the manufacturers of NAS servers to develop such a client. The manufacturers of network back-up systems publish neither the source code nor the interfaces between back-up client and back-up server, which means that a client cannot be developed. Even if such a back-up client already exists because the NAS server is based upon on a standard operating system such as Linux, Windows or Solaris, this does not mean that customers may use this client: in order to improve the Plug&Play-capability of NAS servers, customers may only use the software that has been tested and certified by the NAS manufacturer. If the customer installs non-certified software, then he can lose support for the NAS server. Due to the testing cost, manufacturers of NAS servers may be able to support some, but certainly not all network back-up systems.

Without further measures being put in place, the only possibility that remains is to back the NAS server up from a client of the NAS server (Figure 7.12). However, this approach, too, is doubtful for two reasons:

- First, this approach is only practicable for smaller quantities of data: for back-up the files of the NAS server are transferred over the LAN to the network file system client on which the back-up client runs. Only the back-up client can write the files to the back-up medium using advanced methods such as LAN-free back-up.

- Second, the back-up of metadata is difficult. If a NAS server supports the export of the local file system both via CIFS and also via NFS then the back-up client only accesses one of the two protocols on the files – the metadata of the other protocol is lost. NAS servers would thus have to store their metadata in special files so that the network back-up system can back these up. There then remains the question of the cost for the restoring of a NAS server or a file system. The metadata of NAS servers and files has to be re-extracted from these files. It is dubious whether network back-up systems can automatically initiate this process.

As a last resort for the integration of NAS servers and network back-up systems, there remains only the standardization of the interfaces between the NAS server and the network back-up system. This would mean that manufacturers of NAS servers would only have to develop and test one back-up client that supports precisely this interface. The back-up systems of various manufacturers could then back up the NAS server via this interface. In such an approach the extensivity of this interface determines how well the back-up of NAS servers can be linked into a network back-up system. The next section introduces a standard for such an interface – the Network Data Management Protocol (NDMP).

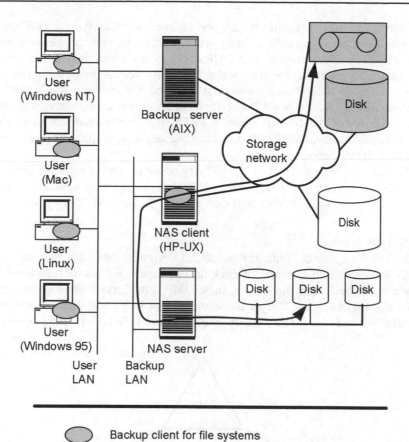

Backup client for file systems

Figure 7.12 When backing up a NAS server over a network file system, the connection
between the NAS server and back-up client represents a potential performance bottleneck.
Back-up over a network file system makes it more difficult to back up and restore the metadata
of the NAS server

7.9.4 The Network Data Management Protocol (NDMP)

The Network Data Management Protocol (NDMP) defines an interface between NAS
servers and network back-up systems that makes it possible to back up NAS servers without providing a specific back-up client for them. More and more manufacturers – both of
NAS servers and network back-up systems – are supporting NDMP. The current version
of NDMP is Version 4; Version 5 is in preparation.

NDMP uses the term 'data management operations' to describe the back-up and restoration of data. A so-called data management application (DMA) – generally a back-up
system – initiates and controls the data management operations, with the execution of a
data management operation generally being called an NDMP session. The DMA cannot

directly access the data; it requires the support of so-called NDMP services (Figure 7.13). NDMP services manage the current data storage, such as file systems, back-up media and tape libraries. The DMA creates an NDMP control connection for the control of every participating NDMP service; for the actual data flow between source medium and back-up medium a so-called NDMP data connection is established between the NDMP services in question. Ultimately, the NDMP describes a client-server architecture, with the DMA taking on the role of the NDMP client. An NDMP server is made up of one or more NDMP services. Finally, the NDMP host is the name for a computer that accommodates one or more NDMP servers.

NDMP defines different forms of NDMP services. All have in common that they only manage their local state. The state of other NDMP services remains hidden to an NDMP service. Individually, NDMP Version 4 defines the following NDMP services:

- NDMP Data Service
  The NDMP data service forms the interface to primary data such as a file system on a NAS server. It is the source of back-up operations and the destination of restore operations. To back-up a file system, the NDMP Data Service converts the content of the file system into a data stream and writes this in an NDMP data connection, which is generally created by means of a TCP/IP connection. To restore a file system it reads

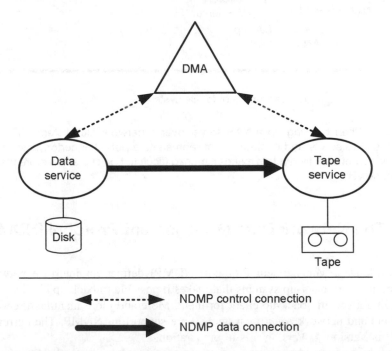

Figure 7.13 NDMP standardizes the communication between the data management application (DMA) – generally a back-up system – and the NDMP services (NDMP data service, NDMP tape service), which represent the storage devices. The communication between the NDMP services and the storage devices is not standardized

the data stream from an NDMP data connection and from this reconstructs the content of a file system. The Data Service only permits the back-up of complete file systems; it is not possible to back up individual files. By contrast, individual files or directories can be restored in addition to complete file systems.

The restoration of individual files or directories is also called 'direct access recovery'. To achieve this, the Data Service provides a so-called file history interface, which it uses to forward the necessary metadata to the DMA during the back-up. The file history stores the positions of the individual files within the entire data stream. The DMA cannot read this so-called file locator data, but it can forward it to the NDMP tape service in the event of a restore operation. The NDMP tape service then uses this information to wind the tape to the appropriate position and read the files in question.

- NDMP Tape Service
  The NDMP Tape Service forms the interface to the secondary storage. Secondary storage, in the sense of NDMP, means computers with connected tape drive, connected tape library or a CD burner. The Tape Service manages the destination of a back-up or the source of a data restoration operation. For a back-up, the Tape Service writes an incoming data stream to tape via the NDMP data connection; for a restoration it reads the content of a tape and writes this as a data stream in a NDMP data connection. The Tape Service has only the information that it requires to read and write, such as tape size or block size. It has no knowledge of the format of the data stream. It requires the assistance of the DMA to change tapes in a tape library.

- NDMP SCSI Pass Through Service
  The SCSI Pass Through Service makes it possible for a DMA to send SCSI commands to a SCSI device that is connected to a NDMP server. The DMA requires this service, for example, for the changing of tapes in a tape library.

The DMA holds the threads of an NDMP session together: it manages all state information of the participating NDMP services, takes on the management of the back-up media and initiates appropriate recovery measures in the event of an error. To this end the DMA maintains an NDMP control connection to each of the participating NDMP services, which – like the NDMP data connections – are generally based upon TCP/IP. Both sides – DMA and NDMP services – can be active within an NDMP session. For example, the DMA sends commands for the control of the NDMP services, whilst the NDMP services for their part send messages if a control intervention by the DMA is required. If, for example, an NDMP Tape Service has filled a tape, it informs the DMA. This can then initiate a tape change by means of an NDMP SCSI Pass Through Service.

The fact that both NDMP control connections and NDMP data connections are based upon TCP/IP means that flexible configuration options are available for the back-up of data using NDMP. The NDMP architecture supports back-up to a locally connected tape drive (Figure 7.14) and likewise to a tape drive connected to another computer, for example a second NAS server or a back-up server (Figure 7.15). This so-called remote back-up has the advantage that smaller NAS servers do not need to be equipped with a tape library. Further fields of application of remote back-up are the replication of file systems (disk-to-disk remote back-up) and of back-up tapes (tape-to-tape remote back-up).

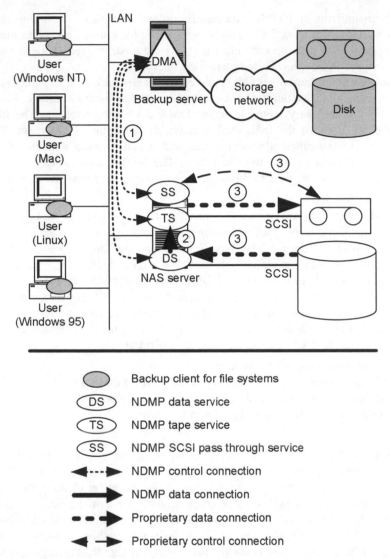

Figure 7.14 NDMP data service, NDMP Tape Service and NDMP SCSI Pass Through Service all run on the same computer in a local back-up using NDMP. NDMP describes the protocols for the NDMP control connection (1) and the NDMP data connection (2). The communication between the NDMP services and the storage devices is not standardized (3)

In remote back-up the administrator comes up against the same performance bottlenecks as in conventional network back-up over the LAN (Section 7.6). Fortunately, NDMP local back-up and LAN-free back-up of network back-up systems complement each other excellently: a NAS server can back up to a tape drive available in the storage network, with the network back-up system co-ordinating access to the tape drive outside of NDMP by means of tape library sharing (Figure 7.16).

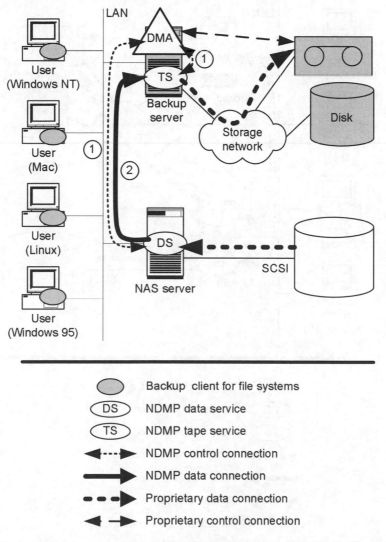

Figure 7.15   In a back-up over the LAN (remote back-up) the NDMP tape service runs on the computer to which the back-up medium is connected. The communication between the remote services is guaranteed by the fact that NDMP control connections (1) and NDMP data connections (2) are based upon TCP/IP. The back-up server addresses the tape library locally, which means that the NDMP SCSI Pass Through Service is not required here

In Version 5, NDMP will have further functions such as multiplexing, compressing and encryption. To achieve this, NDMP Version 5 expands the architecture to include the so-called translator service (Figure 7.17). Translator services process the data stream (data stream processor): they can read and change one or more data streams. The implementation of translator services is in accordance with that of previous NDMP services. This means that the control of the translator service lies with the DMA; other participating NDMP

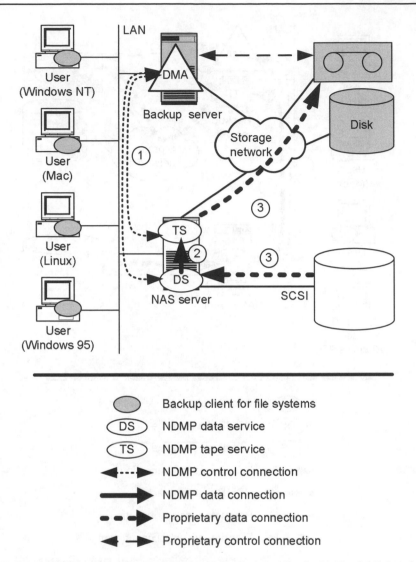

Figure 7.16 NDMP local back-up can be excellently combined with the LAN-free back-up of network back-up systems

services cannot tell whether an incoming data stream was generated by a translator service or a different NDMP service. NDMP Version 5 defines the following translator services:

- Data stream multiplexing
  The aim of data stream multiplexing is to bundle several data streams into one data stream (N:1-multiplexing) or to generate several data streams from one (1:M-multiplexing). Examples of this are the back-up of several small, slower file systems onto a faster tape drive (N:1-multiplexing) or the parallel back-up of a large file system onto several tape drives (1:M-multiplexing).

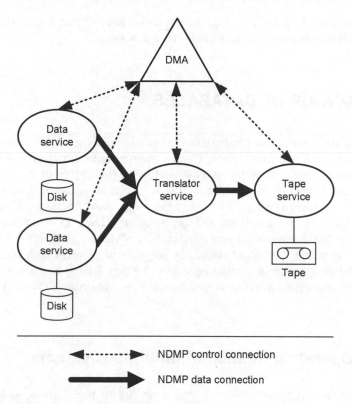

Figure 7.17 NDMP Version 5 expands the NDMP services to include translator services, which provide functions such as multiplexing, encryption and compression

- Data stream compression
  In data stream compression the translator service reads a data stream, compresses it and sends it back out. Thus the data can be compressed straight from the hard disk, thus freeing up the network between it and the back-up medium.

- Data stream encryption
  Data stream encryption works on the same principle as data stream compression, except that it encrypts data instead of compressing it. Encryption is a good idea, for example, for the back-up of small NAS servers at branch offices to a back-up server in a data centre via a public network.

NDMP offers many opportunities to connect NAS servers to a network back-up system. The prerequisite for this is NDMP support on both sides. NDMP data services cover approximately the functions that back-up clients of network back-up systems provide. One weakness of NDMP is the back-up of the NAS server metadata, which makes the restoration of a NAS server after the full replacement of hardware significantly more difficult (Section 7.9.1). Furthermore, there is a lack of support for the back-up of file systems with the aid of snapshots or instant copies. Despite these missing functions

NDMP has established itself as a standard and so we believe that it is merely a matter of time before NDMP is expanded to include these functions.

7.10   BACK-UP OF DATABASES

Databases are the second most important organizational form of data after the file systems discussed in the previous section. Despite the measures introduced in Section 6.3.5, it is sometimes necessary to restore a database from a back-up medium. The same questions are raised regarding the back-up of the metadata of a database server as for the back-up of file servers (Section 7.9.1). On the other hand, there are clear differences between the back-up of file systems and databases. The back-up of databases requires a fundamental understanding of the operating method of databases (Section 7.10.1). Knowledge of the operating method of databases helps us to perform both the conventional back-up of databases without storage networks (Section 7.10.2) and also the back-up of databases with storage networks and intelligent storage subsystems (Section 7.10.3) more efficiently.

7.10.1   Operating method of database systems

One requirement of database systems is the atomicity of transactions, with transactions bringing together several write and read accesses to the database to form logically coherent units. Atomicity of transactions means that a transaction involving write access should be performed fully or not at all.

Transactions can change the content of one or more blocks that can be distributed over several hard disks or several disk subsystems. Transactions that change several blocks are problematic for the atomicity. If the database system has already written a few of the blocks to be changed to hard disk and has not yet written others and then the database server goes down due to a power failure or a hardware fault, the transaction has only partially been performed. Without additional measures the transaction can neither be completed nor undone after a reboot of the database server because the information necessary for this is no longer available. The database would therefore be inconsistent.

The database system must therefore store additional information regarding transactions that have not yet been concluded on the hard disk in addition to the actual database. The database system manages this information in so-called log files. It first of all notes every pending change to the database in a log file before going on to perform the changes to the blocks in the database itself. If the database server fails during a transaction, the database system can either complete or undo incomplete transactions with the aid of the log file after the reboot of the server.

Figure 7.18 shows a greatly simplified version of the architecture of database systems. The database system fulfils the following two main tasks:

- Database: storing the logical data structure to block-oriented storage
  First, the database system organizes the data into a structure suitable for the applications and stores this on the block-oriented hard disk storage. In modern database systems the relational data model, which stores information in interlinked tables, is the main model used for this. To be precise, the database system stores the logical data directly onto the hard disk, circumventing a file system, or it stores it to large files. The advantages and disadvantages of these two alternatives have already been discussed in Section 4.1.1.

- Transaction machine: changing the database
  Second, the database system realizes methods for changing the stored information. To this end, it provides a database language and a transaction engine. In a relational database the users and applications initiate transactions via the database language

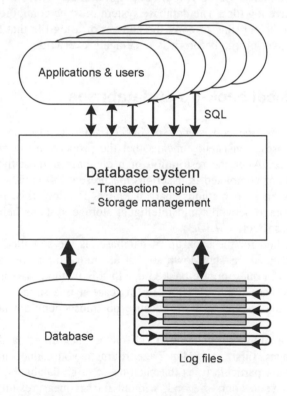

Figure 7.18 Users start transactions via the database language (SQL) in order to read or write data. The database system stores the application data in block-oriented data (database) and it uses log files to guarantee the atomicity of the transactions

SQL and thus call up or change the stored information. Transactions on the logical, application-near data structure thus bring about changes to the physical blocks on the hard disk. The transaction system ensures, amongst other things, that the changes to the data set caused by a transaction are either completed or not performed at all. As described above, this condition can be guaranteed with the aid of log files even in the event of computer or database system crashes.

The database system changes blocks in the data area, in no specific order, depending on how the transactions occur. The log files, on the other hand, are always written sequentially, with each log file being able to store a certain number of changes. Database systems are generally configured with several log files written one after the other. When all log files have been fully written, the database system first overwrites the log file that was written first, then the next, and so on.

A further important function for the back-up of databases is the back-up of the log files. To this end, the database system copies full log files into a file system as files and numbers these sequentially: logfile 1, logfile 2, logfile 3, etc. These copies of the log files are also called archive log files. The database system must be configured with enough log files that there is sufficient time to copy the content of a log file that has just been fully written into an archive log file before it is once again overwritten.

7.10.2   Classical back-up of databases

As in all applications, the consistency of backed up data also has to be ensured in databases. In databases, consistency means that the property of atomicity of the trans- actions is maintained. After the restoration of a database it must therefore be ensured that only the results of completed transactions are present in the data set. In this section we discuss various back-up methods that guarantee precisely this. In the next section we explain how storage networks and intelligent storage systems help to accelerate the back-up of databases (Section 7.10.3).

The simplest method for the back-up of databases is the so-called cold back-up. For cold back-up, the database is shut down so that all transactions are concluded, and then the files or volumes in question are backed up. In this method, databases are backed up in exactly the same way as file systems. In this case it is a simple matter to guarantee the consistency of the backed up data because no transactions are taking place during the back-up.

Cold back-up is a simple to realize method for the back-up of databases. However, it has two disadvantages. First, in a 24×7 environment you cannot afford to shut down databases for back-up, particularly as the back-up of large databases using conventional methods can take several hours. Second, without further measures all changes since the last back-up would be lost in the event of the failure of a disk subsystem. For example, if a database is backed up overnight and the disk subsystem fails on the following evening all changes from the last working day are lost.

With the aid of the archive log file the second problem, at least, can be solved. The latest state of the database can be recreated from the last back-up of the database, all archive log files backed up since and the active log files. To achieve this, the last back-up of the database must first of all be restored from the back-up medium – in the example above the back-up from the previous night. Then all archive log files that have been created since the last back-up are applied to the data set, as are all active log files. This procedure, which is also called forward recovery of databases, makes it possible to restore the latest state even a long time after the last back-up of the database. However, depending upon the size of the archive log files this can take some time.

The availability of the archive log files is thus an important prerequisite for the successful forward recovery of a database. The file system for the archive log files should, therefore, be stored on a different hard disk to the database itself (Figure 7.19) and additionally protected by a redundant RAID procedure. Furthermore, the archive log files should be backed up regularly.

Log files and archive log files form the basis of two further back-up methods for databases: hot back-up and fuzzy back-up. In hot back-up, the database system writes pending changes to the database to the log files only. The actual database remains

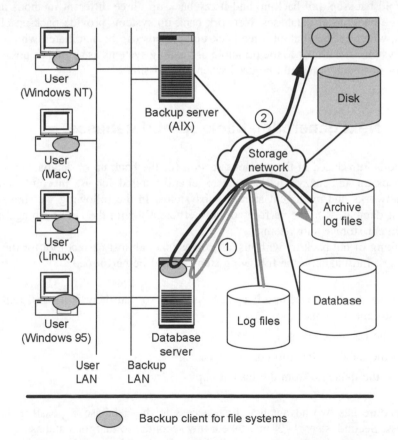

Backup client for file systems

Figure 7.19 The database system copies the archive log files into a file system (1) located on a different storage system to the database and its log files. From there, the archive log files can be backed up using advanced techniques such as LAN-free back-up

unchanged at this time, so that the consistency of the back-up is guaranteed. After the end of the back-up, the database system is switched back into the normal state. The database system can then incorporate the changes listed in the log files into the database.

Hot back-up is suitable for situations in which access to the data is required around the clock. However, hot back-up should only be used in phases in which a relatively low number of write accesses are taking place. If, for example, it takes two hours to back up the database and the database is operating at full load, the log files must be dimensioned so that they are large enough to be able to save all changes made during the back-up. Furthermore, the system must be able to complete the postponed transactions after the back-up in addition to the currently pending transactions. Both together can lead to performance bottlenecks.

Finally, fuzzy back-up allows changes to be made to the database during its back-up so that an inconsistent state of the database is backed up. The database system is nevertheless capable of cleaning the inconsistent state with the aid of archive log files that have been written during the back-up.

With cold back-up, hot back-up and fuzzy back-up, three different methods are available for the back-up of databases. Network back-up systems provide back-up clients for databases, which means that all three back-up methods can be automated with a network back-up system. According to the principle of keeping systems as simple as possible, cold back-up or hot back-up should be used whenever possible.

7.10.3   Next generation back-up of databases

The methods introduced in the previous section for the back-up of databases (cold back-up, hot back-up and fuzzy back-up) are excellently suited for use in combination with storage networks and intelligent storage subsystems. In the following we show how the back-up of databases can be performed more efficiently with the aid of storage networks and intelligent storage subsystems.

The linking of hot back-up with instant copies is an almost perfect tool for the back-up of databases. Individually, the following steps should be performed:

1. Switch the database over into hot back-up mode so that there is a consistent data set in the storage system.
2. Create the instant copy.
3. Switch the database back to normal mode.
4. Back up the database from the instant copy.

This procedure has two advantages: first, access to the database is possible throughout the process. Second, steps 1–3 only take a few seconds, so that the database system only has to catch up comparatively few transactions after switching back to normal mode.

Application server-free back-up expands the back-up by instant copies in order to additionally free up the database server from the load of the back-up (Section 7.8.5). The concept shown in Figure 7.11 is also very suitable for databases. Due to the large quantity of data involved in the back-up of databases, LAN-free back-up is often used – unlike in the figure – in order to back up the data generated using instant copy.

In the previous section (Section 7.10.2) we explained that the time of the last back-up is decisive for the time that will be needed to restore a database to the last data state. If the last back-up was a long time ago, a lot of archive log files have to be reapplied. In order to reduce the restore time for a database it is therefore necessary to increase the frequency of database back-ups.

The problem with this approach is that large volumes of data are moved during a complete back-up of databases. This is very time-consuming and uses a lot of resources, which means that the frequency of back-ups can only be increased to a limited degree. Likewise, the delayed copying of the log files to a second system (Section 6.3.5) and the holding of several copies of the data set on the disk subsystem by means of instant copy can only seldom be economically justified due to the high hardware requirement and the associated costs.

In order to nevertheless increase the back-up frequency of a database, the data volume to be transferred must therefore be reduced. This is possible by means of an incremental back-up of the database on block level. The most important database systems offer back-up tools for this by means of which such database increments can be generated. Many network back-up systems provide special adapters (back-up agents) that are tailored to the back-up tools of the database system in question. However, the format of the increments is unknown to the back-up software, so that the incremental-forever strategy cannot be realized in this manner. This would require manufacturers of database systems to publish the format of the increments.

The back-up of databases using the incremental-forever strategy therefore requires that the back-up software knows the format of the incremental back-ups, so that it can calculate the full back-ups from them. To this end, the storage space of the database must be provided via a file system that can be incrementally backed up on block level using the appropriate back-up client. The back-up software knows the format of the increments so the incremental-forever strategy can be realized for databases via the circuitous route of file systems.

7.11 ORGANIZATIONAL ASPECTS OF BACK-UP

In addition to the necessary technical resources, the personnel cost of backing data up is also often underestimated. We have already discussed (1) how the back-up of data has to be continuously adapted to the ever-changing IT landscape; and (2) that it is necessary to continuously monitor whether the back-up of data is actually performed according to plan. Both together quite simply take time, with the time cost for these activities often being underestimated.

As is the case for any activity, human errors cannot be avoided in back-up, particularly if time is always short due to staff shortages. However, in the field of data protection these human errors always represent a potential data loss. The costs of data loss can be enormous: for example, Marc Farley (Building Storage Networks, 2000) cites a figure of US$ 1000 per employee as the cost for lost e-mail databases. Therefore, the personnel requirement for the back-up of data should be evaluated at least once a year. As part of this process, personnel costs must always be compared to the cost of lost data.

The restoration of data sometimes fails due to the fact that data has not been fully backed up, tapes have accidentally been overwritten with current data or tapes that were already worn and too old have been used for back-ups. The media manager can prevent most of these problems.

However, this is ineffective if the back-up software is not correctly configured. One of the three authors can well remember a situation more than ten years ago in which he was not able to restore the data after a planned repartitioning of a disk drive. The script for the back-up of the data contained a single typing error. This error resulted in an empty partition being backed up instead of the partition containing the data.

The restoration of data should be practised regularly so that errors in the back-up are detected before an emergency occurs, in order to practise the performance of such tasks and in order to measure the time taken. The time taken to restore data is an important cost variable: for example, a multi-hour failure of a central application such as SAP R/3 can involve significant costs.

Therefore, staff should be trained in the following scenarios, for example:

- restoring an important server including all applications and data to equivalent hardware;
- restoring an important server including all applications and data to new hardware;
- restoring a subdirectory into a different area of the file system;
- restoring an important file system or an important database;
- restoring several computers using the tapes from the off-site store;
- restoring old archives (are tape drives still available for the old media?).

The cost in terms of time for such exercises should be taken into account when calculating the personnel requirement for the back-up of data.

7.12 SUMMARY

Storage networks and intelligent storage subsystems open up new possibilities for solving the performance problems of network back-up. However, these new techniques are significantly more expensive than classical network back-up over the LAN. Therefore, it is first necessary to consider at what speed data really needs to be backed up or restored. Only then is it possible to consider which alternative is the most economical: the new techniques will be used primarily for heavyweight clients and for 24 × 7 applications. Simple clients will continue to be backed up using classical methods of network back-up and for medium-sized clients there remains the option of installing a separate LAN for the back-up of data. All three techniques are therefore often found in real IT systems nowadays.

Data protection is a difficult and resource-intensive business. Network back-up systems allow the back-up of data to be largely automated even in heterogeneous environments. This automation takes the pressure off the system administrator and helps to prevent errors such as the accidental overwriting of tapes. The use of network back-up systems is indispensable in large environments. However, it is also worthwhile in smaller environments. Nevertheless, the personnel cost of back-up must not be underestimated.

This chapter started out by describing the general conditions for back-up: strong growth in the quantity of data to be backed up, continuous adaptation of back-up to ever-changing IT systems and the reduction of the back-up window due to globalization. The transition to network back-up was made by the description of the back-up, archiving and hierarchical storage management (HSM). We then discussed the server components necessary for the implementation of these services (job scheduler, error handler, media manager and meta-data database) plus the back-up client. At the centre was the incremental-forever strategy and the storage hierarchy within the back-up server. Network back-up was also considered from the point of view of performance: we first showed how network back-up systems can contribute to using the existing infrastructure more efficiently. CPU load, the clogging of the internal buses and the inefficiency of the TCP/IP/Ethernet medium were highlighted as performance bottlenecks. Then, proposed solutions for increasing performance that are possible within a server-centric IT architecture were discussed, including their limitations. This was followed by proposed solutions to overcome the performance bottlenecks in a storage-centric IT architecture. Finally, the back-up of large file systems and databases was described and organizational questions regarding network back-up were outlined.

This chapter ends our consideration of the use of storage networks. In the remaining three chapters we concern ourselves with management of storage networks, removable media management, and the SNIA Shared Storage Model.

8

Management of Storage Networks

In the course of this book we have dealt with the different techniques that are used in storage networks and the benefits that can be derived from them. As we did so it became clear that storage networks are complex architectures, the management of which imposes stringent demands on administrators. In this chapter we therefore want to look at the management of storage networks Our primary objective here is to show how the management of a storage network can be supported by appropriate software.

To this end we will first consider new requirements of the system management that arise as a result of the developmental transition from server-centric to storage-centric IT architecture (Section 8.1). It is evident that various technical fields impose different requirements that should be taken into account in a management system (Section 8.2). Therefore, a management system must provide a range of functions (Section 8.3) and operate existing interfaces such as in-band and out-band interfaces (Section 8.4). These interfaces are provided via proprietary and standardized mechanisms (Section 8.5). Then we want to deal in more detail with the possibilities that the standardized methods offer by means of in-band (Section 8.6) and out-band (Section 8.7) interfaces. Finally, we discuss operational aspects of the management of storage networks (8.8).

8.1 SYSTEM MANAGEMENT

In the conventional server-centric IT architecture it is assumed that a server has directly connected storage. From the perspective of system management, therefore, there are two

Storage Networks Explained   U. Troppens R. Erkens W. Müller
© 2004 John Wiley & Sons, Ltd   ISBN: 0-470-86182-7

units to manage: the server on the one hand and the storage on the other. The connection between server and storage does not represent a unit to be managed. It is primarily a question of how and where the data is stored and not how it is moved.

The transition to storage-centric IT architecture – i.e. the introduction of storage networks – has greatly changed the requirements of system management. In a storage network the storage is no longer local to the servers but can instead be located in different buildings or even different parts of the city. In the network between the servers and storage devices, numerous devices (host bus adapters, hubs, switches, gateways) are used, which can each change the data flow. In a storage network there are thus many more units to manage than in a server-centric IT architecture. Now administrators have to think not only about their data on the storage devices, but also about how the data travels from the servers to the storage devices. The management of a storage network is therefore comparable to the management of a LAN. However, LAN management methods are better known than the methods for the management of new technologies such as Fibre Channel SAN, iSCSI or InfiniBand.

The manufacturers of these new storage technologies are still involved in implementing suitable management functions and integrating these into the management tools for LAN and servers. The objective is to develop a central management system in which all resources of a data center from hardware to the applications can be managed. Therefore, in the management of storage networks we meet long familiar representatives from the LAN and the server world. The most prominent example is the SNMP protocol (Section 8.7.1), which has already been used for a long time in the field of LAN.

8.2   REQUIREMENTS OF MANAGEMENT SYSTEMS

The management of storage networks is of different significance to various technical fields. For example, the classical network administrator is interested in the question of how the data should be transported and how it is possible to ensure that the transport functions correctly. Further aspects for him are the transmission capacity of the transport medium, redundancy of the data paths or the support for and operation of numerous protocols (Fibre Channel FCP, iSCSI, NFS, CIFS, etc.). In short: to a network administrator it is important how the data travels from A to B and not what happens to it when it finally arrives at its destination.

This is where the field of interest of a storage administrator begins. He is more interested in the organization and storage of the data when it has arrived at its destination. He is concerned with the allocation of LUNs to the servers (LUN mapping) of intelligent storage systems or the RAID levels used. A storage administrator therefore assumes that the data has already arrived intact at point B and concerns himself with aspects of storage. The data transport in itself has no importance to him.

An industrial economist, on the other hand, assumes that A, B and the route between them function correctly and concerns himself with the question of how long it takes for the individual devices to depreciate or when an investment in new hardware and software must be made.

A balanced management system must ultimately live up to all these different requirements equally. It should cover the complete bandwidth from the start of the conceptual phase through the implementation of the storage network to its daily operation. Therefore, right from the conception of the storage network, appropriate measures should be put in place to subsequently make management easier in daily operation.

A good way of taking into account all aspects of such a management system for a storage network is to orientate ourselves with the requirements that the individual components of the storage network will impose upon a management system. These components include:

- Applications
  These include all software that processes data in a storage network.

- Data
  Data is the term used for all information that is processed by the applications, transported over the network and stored on storage resources.

- Resources
  The resources include all the hardware that is required for the storage and the transport of the data and the operation of applications.

- Network
  The term network is used to mean the connections between the individual resources.

Diverse requirements can now be formulated for these individual components with regard to monitoring, availability, performance or scalability. Some of these are requirements such as monitoring that occur during the daily operation of a storage network, others are requirements such as availability that must be taken into account as early as the implementation phase of a storage network. For reasons of readability we do not want to investigate the individual requirements in more detail at this point. In Appendix B you will find a detailed elaboration of these requirements in the form of a checklist. We now wish to turn our attention to the possibilities that a management system can offer in daily operation.

8.3   SUPPORT BY MANAGEMENT SYSTEMS

As explained in the previous section, a storage network raises numerous questions for and imposes many requirements upon a management system. Many software manufacturers tackle individual aspects of this problem and offer various management systems that address the various problem areas. Some management systems concern themselves more with the commercial aspects, whereas others tend to concentrate upon administrative interests. Still other management systems specialize in certain components of the storage network such as applications, resources, data or the network itself. This results in numerous different system management products being used in a complex and heterogeneous storage network. The lack of a comprehensive management system increases the complexity of and the costs involved in system management. Analysts therefore assume that in addition to the simple costs for hardware and software of a storage network, up to ten times these costs will have to be spent upon its management.

In this context it makes sense to develop a management system which makes it possible for as many aspects of the storage network as possible to be managed from a central point by means of a management console. In order to guarantee the management of all components, a management system must operate the existing interfaces of applications and resources and – where this is not possible – try to integrate existing management mechanisms into the central software or to re-establish them.

In order to permit the full management of a storage network in daily operation, a management system should have the following five core components:

- Discovery
  The task of a discovery component is to recognize the applications and resources used in the storage network. It collects information about the properties and the current configuration of resources. Finally, it correlates and evaluates all gathered information and supplies the data for the representation of the network topology.

- Monitoring
  The monitoring components are used to monitor the status of the applications and resources of the network. In the event of an application crash or the failure of a resource, it must take appropriate measures to raise the alert based upon the severity of the error that has occurred. The monitoring components operate error isolation by trying to find the actual cause of the fault in the event of the failure of part of the storage network.

- Configuration
  The configuration of applications and resources can be changed by the configuration components. They further make it possible to simulate in advance the effects of changing the configuration.

- Analysis
  This allows trend analyses, in particular of the commercial aspects, to be called up. It also evaluates the availability and scalability requirements of the storage network. However, it can also be used to track down single points of failure within the storage network.

- Data control
  These components are concerned with all aspects of data such as performance, backups, archiving or migration and thus control the efficient use and availability of data and resources. By using policies it allows the administrator to control the flow and placement of data.

In the following we want to deal in more detail with the mechanisms that are needed for the first three core components: discovery, monitoring and configuration. Due to the complexity of the methods used in the analysis component it is not possible to deal with these in detail. A model – storage virtualization – has already been introduced to deal with the requirements that crop up for the data control component (Chapter 5).

8.4   MANAGEMENT INTERFACES

Storage networks consist of two main types of devices (Figure 8.1):

- Connection devices
  Connection devices include the switches, hubs and bridges that are used to create the connections in the storage network.
- Endpoint devices
  Endpoint devices are the servers and storage devices that are connected to the connection devices.

Devices – i.e. connection devices and endpoint devices – in a storage network are also called nodes because they seem to form the nodes of the network. Endpoint devices are correspondingly called end nodes.

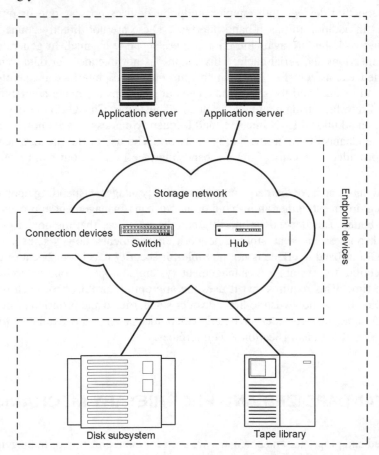

Figure 8.1   There are two main types of device in the storage network: connection devices and endpoint devices. Devices are also called nodes since they seemingly form the nodes of the network

The interfaces for the management of endpoint devices and connection devices are differentiated into in-band and out-band interfaces:

- In-band
  All devices of a storage network have an in-band interface as standard. Devices are connected to the storage network via the in-band interface and data transfer takes place through this interface. In addition, management functions for discovery, monitoring and configuration of connection devices and endpoint devices are made available on this interface. These are generally realized in the form of components of the current protocol of the in-band interface. Thus, for example, in a Fibre Channel SAN the Fibre Channel protocol makes the appropriate in-band management functions available. The use of these services for the management of storage networks is then called in-band management.

- Out-band
  Most connection devices and complex endpoint devices possess one or more further interfaces in addition to the in-band interface. These are not directly connected to the storage network, but are available on a second, separate channel. In general, these are LAN connections and serial cable. This channel is not intended for data transport, but is provided exclusively for management purposes. This interface is therefore called out-of-band or out-band for short. Management functions are made available over this additional interface using a suitable protocol. Thus Fibre Channel SAN devices generally have an additional LAN interface and frequently possess a serial port in addition to their Fibre Channel ports to the storage network. The use of the management services that are provided by means of the out-band interface is called out-band management.

In-band and out-band have their advantages and disadvantages. Depending upon the implementation environment, either an in-band or an out-band management approach will fulfil its purpose better. This depends primarily upon the interfaces that the devices in the storage network possess. In some storage network environments, however, even the use of an additional out-band interface is not possible for security reasons or because there is no LAN connection, for example. A management system can operate one or both interfaces at the same time. This requires that it uses the appropriate protocol for each interface.

In the following we now wish to first consider standardized and proprietary mechanisms (Section 8.5) and then consider in detail which mechanisms are available for in-band (Section 8.6) and out-band (Section 8.7) interfaces.

8.5 STANDARDIZED AND PROPRIETARY MECHANISMS

Standardized and proprietary mechanisms are used for the realization of management functions on in-band and out-band interfaces. Standardized mechanisms offer the advantage in relation to proprietary interfaces that management systems can address various devices via a unified interface. This means that the developer of a management system does not need to implement a proprietary mechanism in the software for each device, which is complicated and thus expensive. Proprietary mechanisms, on the other hand, have the advantage over standardized mechanisms that they can provide more management functions for a certain device and thus permit deeper and more device-specific management interventions.

8.5.1 Standardized mechanisms

Many standardization organizations invest a great deal of development work in the standardization of management interfaces. For in-band management the developments occur on different protocol levels:

- In-band transport levels
  The management interfaces for Fibre Channel, TCP/IP and InfiniBand are defined on the in-band transport levels. In Section 8.6.1 we will discuss in detail the management interface of the transport levels of the Fibre Channel protocol.
- In-band upper layer protocols (ULP)
  Primarily SCSI variants such as Fibre Channel FCP and iSCSI are used as an upper layer protocol. SCSI has its own mechanisms for requesting device and status information: the so-called SCSI Enclosure Services (SES). In addition to the management functions on transport levels a management system can also operate these ULP operations in order to identify an end device and request status information.

Special protocols such as SNMP (Section 8.7.1) and WBEM with CIM (Section 8.7.2) as well as SMI-S (Section 8.7.3) are used for the out-band management.

8.5.2 Proprietary mechanisms

The proprietary (this generally means manufacturer-specific and usually even device-specific) mechanisms fall into three categories:

- APIs
  In this approach, individual devices have programming interfaces – so-called Application Programming Interfaces (APIs) – which they can use to call up special management functions. They are generally implemented out-band. It requires a considerable development and testing cost to be able to use these APIs in a central management system. The manufacturers of management systems must develop appropriate software modules for various device APIs in order to access the management functions of each. This increases the complexity and the costs of such a management system. Some manufacturers do not shy away from this cost. The advantage of such an approach can be a device-near support of the management system. Thus such a management system can supply better results than one that only operates standardized mechanisms.

- Telnet

  Many devices can also be configured out-band via Telnet. Although Telnet itself is
  not a proprietary mechanism, it is subject to the same problems as an API regarding
  connection to a central management system. For this reason we will count it amongst
  the proprietary mechanisms.

- Element manager

  An element manager is a device-specific management interface. It is frequently found
  in the form of a GUI (graphical user interface) on a further device or in the form of
  a WUI (web user interface) implemented over a web server integrated in the device
  itself. Since the communication between element manager and device generally takes
  place via a separate channel next to the data channel, element managers are classified
  amongst the out-band management interfaces. Element managers have largely the same
  disadvantages in a large heterogeneous storage network as the proprietary APIs. However, element managers can be more easily integrated into a central management system
  than can an API. To achieve this, the element manager only needs to know and call
  up the appropriate start routines. WUIs are started by means of the Internet browser.
  To call up a GUI this must be installed upon the computer on which the management
  system runs. In that way element managers to a certain degree form the device-specific
  level in the software architecture of the management system.

In the following we will look in more detail at the standardized mechanisms and how
these are used for in-band (Section 8.6) and out-band management (Section 8.7). Let us
begin with in-band management.

8.6 IN-BAND MANAGEMENT

In-band management runs over the same interface as the one that connects devices to the
storage network and over which normal data transfer takes place. This interface is thus
available to every end device node and every connection node within the storage network.
The management functions are implemented as services that are provided by the protocol
in question via the nodes.

In-band services can be divided into the following two groups:

- Operational services

  Operational services serve to fulfil the actual tasks of the storage network such as
  making the connection and data transfer.

- Management-specific services

  Management-specific services supply the functions for discovery, monitoring and the
  configuration of devices.

However, not only the management-specific services are of interest from a management
point of view. The operational services can also be used for system management.

In order to be able to use in-band services, a so-called management agent is normally needed that is installed in the form of software upon a server connected to the storage network. This agent communicates with the local host bus adapter over an API in order to call up appropriate in-band management functions from an in-band management service (Figure 8.2).

For Fibre Channel, the Storage Networking Industry Association (SNIA) has already released the Fibre Channel Common HBA API, which gives a management agent easy and cross-platform access to in-band management services. The computer on which this management agent runs is also called the management agent.

For a central management system, this either means that it acts as such a management agent itself and must be connected to the storage network or that within the storage network there must be computers upon which – in addition to the actual applications – a management agent software is installed, since the in-band management services

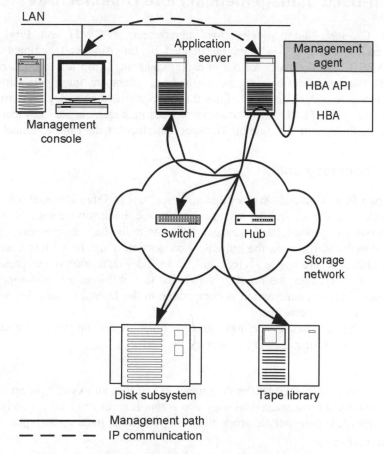

Figure 8.2 In-band management runs through the same interface that connects devices to the storage network and via which the normal data transfer takes place. A management agent accesses the in-band management services via the HBA API

otherwise could not be used. If the management system uses such a decentral agent, then a communication between the central management console and the management agent must additionally be created so that the management information can travel from the agents to the central console (Figure 8.2). Normally this takes place over a LAN connection.

Typically, the management agent is also used for more services than merely to provide access to the management services of the in-band protocol. Some possibilities are the collection of information about the operating system, about the file systems or about the applications of the server. This information can then also be called up via the central console of the management system.

In the following we will explain which management functions can be realized with in-band management based upon the example of the in-band management of a Fibre Channel SAN.

8.6.1 In-band management in Fibre Channel SAN

The Fibre Channel Methodologies for Interconnects (FC-MI) and Fibre Channel Generic Services 4 (FC-GS-4) standards defined by the American National Standards Institute (ANSI) form the basis for the in-band management in the Fibre Channel SAN. The FC-MI standard describes general methods to guarantee interoperability between various devices. In particular, this defines the prerequisites that a device must fulfil for in-band management. The FC-GS-4 standard defines management services that are made available over the so-called Common Transport Interface of the Fibre Channel protocol.

Services for management

There are two Fibre Channel services that are important to Fibre Channel SAN management: the directory service and the management service. Each service defines one or more so-called servers. In general, these servers – split into individual components – are implemented in distributed form via the individual connection nodes of a Fibre Channel SAN but are available as one single logical unit. If an individual component cannot answer a management query, then the query is forwarded to a different server component on a different node. This implementation is comparable to the Domain Name Services (DNS) that we know from IP networks.

The Fibre Channel standard defines, amongst other things, the following servers that are of interest for the management of storage networks:

- Name server
  The name server is defined by the directory service. It is an example of an operational service. Its benefit for a management system is that it reads out connection information and the Fibre Channel specific properties of a port (node name, port type).

- Configuration server
  The configuration server belongs to the class of management-specific services. It is provided by the management service. It allows a management system to recognize the topology of a Fibre Channel SAN.

- Zone server
  The zone server performs both an operational and an administrative task. It permits the zones of a Fibre Channel SAN fabric to be configured (operational) and recognized (management-specific).

These services make it possible for a management system to recognize and configure the devices, the topology and the zones of the SAN.

Discovery

The configuration server is used to identify devices in the Fibre Channel SAN and to recognize the topology. The so-called RNID function (Request Node Identification Data) is also available to the management agent via its host bus adapter API, which it can use to request identification information from a device in the Fibre Channel SAN. The RTIN function (Request Topology INformation) allows information to be called up about connected devices.

Suitable chaining of these two functions finally permits a management system to recognize the entire topology of the Fibre Channel SAN and to identify all devices and properties. If, for example, a device is also reachable out-band via a LAN connection, then its IP address can be requested in-band in the form of a so-called management address. This can then be used by the software for subsequent out-band management.

Monitoring

Since in-band access always facilitates communication with each node in a Fibre Channel SAN, it is simple to also request link and port state information. Performance data can also be determined in this manner. For example, a management agent can send a request to a node in the Fibre Channel SAN so that this transmits its counters for error, retry and traffic. With the aid of this information, the performance and usage profile of the Fibre Channel SAN can be derived. This type of monitoring requires no additional management entity on the nodes in question and also requires no out-band access to them.

The FC-GS-4 standard also defined extended functions that make it possible to call up state information and error statistics of other nodes. Two commands that realize the collection of port statistics are: RPS (Read Port Status Block) and RLS (Read Link Status Block).

Messages

In addition to the passive management functions described above, the Fibre Channel protocol also possesses active mechanisms such as the sending of messages, so-called events. Events are sent via the storage network in order to notify the other nodes of status changes of an individual node or a link.

Thus, for example, in the occurrence of the failure of a link at a switch, a so-called Registered State Change Notification (RSCN) is sent as an event to all nodes that have registered for this service. This event can be received by a registered management agent and then transmitted to the management system.

The zoning problem

The identification and monitoring of a node in the Fibre Channel SAN usually fail if this is located in a different zone than the management agent since in this situation direct access is no longer permitted. This problem can be rectified by the setting up of special management zones, the placing of a management agent in several zones or the placing of further management agents.

The Fibre Channel protocol, however, has an even more elegant method of solving this problem. It defines services that permit the collection or entering of information. A management agent is capable of requesting the necessary information about these services, since these are not affected by the zoning problem. Two examples are:

- Platform registration
  This service is offered by the fabric configuration server and makes it possible for an end node, such as a server or a storage device, to enter information about itself in the configuration server.
- End point node information
  This is a new proposal for the Fibre Channel protocol, which was entered under the name of fabric device management interface and which allows the fabric itself to collect information about the properties and state statistics via ports.

8.7   OUT-BAND MANAGEMENT

Out-band management goes through a different interface than the interface used by data traffic. In Fibre Channel SANs, for example, most devices have a separate IP interface for connection to the LAN, over which they offer management functions (Figure 8.3).

For out-band management an IP connection must exist between the computer of the central management system and the device to be managed. For security reasons it can be a good idea to set up a separate LAN for the management of the storage network in addition to the conventional LAN for the data transfer.

The protocol that is currently (end of 2003) most frequently used for out-band management is the Simple Network Management Protocol (SNMP, Section 8.7.1). In addition there are more recent developments such as the Common Information Model (CIM) and the Web Based Enterprise Management (WBEM), which can be used instead of SNMP (Section 8.7.2). Finally, SMI-S represents a further development of WBEM and CIM that is specially tailored to the management of storage networks (Section 8.7.3). Furthermore,

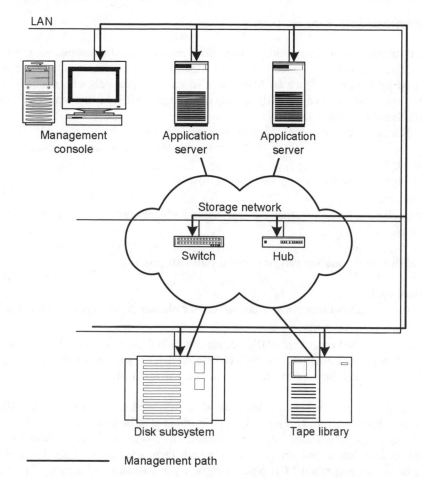

Figure 8.3 Out-band management goes through a different interface than the interface used by the data traffic. In order to operate out-band management from a central management system the management consoles and the device to be managed generally have to be able to make contact via an interface provided by IP

there are other protocols such as CMIP and DMI that specialize in server monitoring (Section 8.7.4).

8.7.1 Use of SNMP

The Simple Network Management Protocol (SNMP) was ratified by the Internet Engineering Task Force (IETF) and was originally a standard for the management of IP networks. Although there are, even now, protocols for this field that can be better adapted to the devices to be managed, SNMP is still the most frequently used protocol due to its simple architecture. Perhaps this is also the reason why SNMP has gained such great importance in the field of storage networks.

Management information bases

In SNMP, management information is organized into so-called management information bases (MIBs). An MIB is a collection of so-called managed objects. Managed objects are represented by variables. Since an MIB can also exist as precisely one managed object, managed objects are also called MIB objects or even just MIB. In this manner a managed object is identified with its MIB.

We differentiate between two types of managed objects:

- Scalar objects
  Scalar objects define precisely one object instance.

- Tabular objects
  Tabular objects bring together several related object instances to form a so-called MIB table.

All the MIBs on the market can be divided into two groups:

- Standard MIBs
  General management functions of certain device classes are covered by standard MIBs.

- Private or enterprise MIBs
  Private or so-called enterprise MIBs permit individual companies to develop their own MIBs. Management functions can thus be offered that are specially tailored to individual devices and extend beyond the functions of the standard MIBs.

In order to differentiate between the individual managed objects there is an MIB hierarchy with a tree structure (Figure 8.4). The various standardization organizations form the top level of the tree. From there, the tree branches to the individual standards of this organization and then to the actual objects, which form the leaves of the hierarchy tree. In this manner an individual MIB object can be clearly defined by means of its position within the MIB hierarchy. In addition, each managed object is given a unique identification number, the so-called object identifier. The object identifier is a sequence of digits that are separated by points. Each individual digit stands for a branch in the MIB tree and each point for a junction. The full object identifier describes the route from the root to the MIB object in question. For example, all MIB objects defined by the IBM Corporation hang under the branch 1.3.6.1.4.1.2 or in words iso.org.dod.internet.private.enterprises.ibm (Figure 8.4). Thus all object identifiers of the MIB objects that have been defined by IBM Corporation begin with this sequence of numbers.

SNMP architecture

SNMP defines three components (Figure 8.5):

- Managed device
  A managed device is a connection device or an end device that carries an SNMP agent. Managed devices collect and save their management data in an MIB.

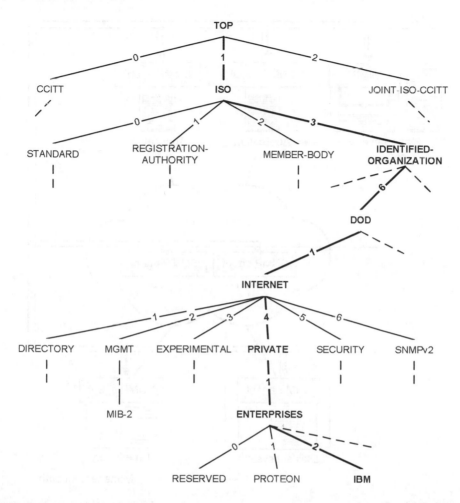

Figure 8.4 The MIBs are kept in an MIB hierarchy. The section of this tree structure represented shows the path through the tree to the MIB object that has been defined by the IBM Corporation. The actual MIB objects – the leaves of the tree – are not shown

- SNMP agent
  The SNMP agent is a software module that runs on a managed device. Its task is to translate the MIB information collected by the managed device into an SNMP-compatible form upon request.

- Network management system (NMS)
  An application for the monitoring and configuration of various managed devices runs on the NMS. If the NMS knows the MIB of the device to be managed, then it can interrogate or change individual MIB objects by appropriate requests to the SNMP agent. The information regarding the MIB in question is loaded into the NMS in advance by means of a so-called MIB file. In our context the NMS corresponds with

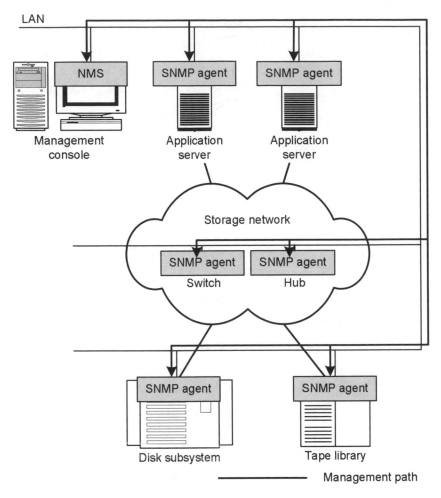

Figure 8.5 An SNMP agent can be installed upon extremely different devices in the storage network. This allows MIB information to be read via IP from a network management system (NMS)

the management system. However, even the Syslog-Daemon of a Unix system can be used as an NMS.

SNMP operations

SNMP defines four operations for the monitoring and configuration of managed devices:

- Get
  Get is used by NMS in order to request the values of one or more MIB object instances from an agent.

- GetNext
  GetNext allows the NMS to request the next value of an object instance within an MIB
  table from an agent after a prior Get request.

- Set
  Set allows the NMS to set the value of an object instance.

- Trap
  The Trap operation allows the SNMP agent to inform the NMS independently about
  value changes of object instances.

Security with SNMP

SNMP has no secure authentication options. Only so-called community names are issued.
Each NMS and each SNMP agent is allocated such a community name. The allocation of
community names creates individual administrative domains. Two communication partners (an NMS and an SNMP agent) may only talk to each other if they have the same
community name. The most frequently used community name is 'public'.

If, for example, an NMS makes a Set request of an SNMP agent, then it sends its
community name with it. If the community name of the NMS corresponds with that of
the SNMP agent, then this performs the Set operation. Otherwise it is rejected. Thus
anyone who knows the community name can make changes to the values of an object
instance. This is one reason why many providers of SNMP-capable devices avoid the
implementation of Set operations on their SNMP agent, because community names only
represent a weak form of authentication. In addition, they are transmitted over the network
unencrypted.

Application in storage networks

An SNMP agent can be installed upon the various devices such as servers, storage
devices or connection devices. SNMP thus covers the entire range of devices of a storage
network.

- Discovery
  A management system can address the SNMP agent on a connection device in order
  to interrogate the properties of a device and to obtain information from it about the
  connected devices. It thus also gets to know the immediate neighbours and with that
  information can continue scanning the end devices insofar as all devices lying on this
  route support SNMP. In this manner a management system finally obtains the topology
  of a storage network.

- Monitoring
  SNMP also supports the management system in the monitoring of the storage network.
  The SNMP agents of the end nodes can be addressed in order to ask for device-specific

status information. Corresponding error and performance statistics can thus be requested from the SNMP agent of a connection node, for example, from a Fibre Channel switch.

- Messages
  Due to the Trap operation SNMP is also familiar with the concept of messages. In SNMP jargon these are called traps. In this manner an SNMP agent on a device in the storage network can send the management system information via IP if, for example, the status has changed. To achieve this only the IP address of the so-called trap recipient has to be registered on the SNMP agent. In our case, the trap recipient would be the management system. In contrast to the RSCN, in the in-band management of a Fibre Channel SAN, in which all registered nodes are informed about changes to a device by means of a message, an SNMP trap only reaches the trap recipients registered in the SNMP agent. In addition, the connection-free User Datagram Protocol (UDP) is used for sending a trap, which does not guarantee the message delivery to the desired recipient.

- Configuration
  SNMP also offers the option of changing the configuration of devices. If the device MIB is known, this can be performed by changing the value of the MIB variables on a managed device by means of the Set operation.

Standard MIBs for Fibre Channel SAN

There are two important standard MIBs for the management of a Fibre Channel SAN:

- Fabric element MIB
  This standard MIB developed by the Storage Networking Industry Association (SNIA) is specialized for Fibre Channel switches and supplies detailed information on port states and port statistics. Likewise, connection information can be read over this.

- Fibre Channel management MIB
  This MIB was developed by the Fibre Alliance. It can be used to request connection information, information on the device configuration or the status of a device. Access to the fabric name server and thus the collection of topology information is also possible.

8.7.2 CIM and WBEM

Today, numerous techniques and protocols are used for system management that, when taken together, are very difficult to integrate into a single, central management system. Therefore, numerous tools are currently used for system management that all address only a subsection of the system management. Web Based Enterprise Management (WBEM) is an initiative by the Distributed Management Task Force (DMTF), the aim of which is to

make possible the management of the entire IT infrastructure of a company (Figure 8.6).
WBEM uses web techniques such as XML and HTTP to access and represent management
information. Furthermore, it defines interfaces for integrating conventional techniques such
as SNMP.

WBEM defines three columns that standardize the interfaces between resources and
management tools (Figure 8.7):

- Common Information Model (CIM)
  The Common Information Model (CIM) defines an object-oriented model that can
  describe all aspects of system management. It is left up to the components participating

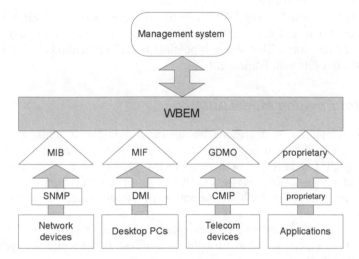

Figure 8.6 The objective of Web Based Enterprise Management (WBEM) is to develop
integrated tools that can manage the entire IT infrastructure of a company

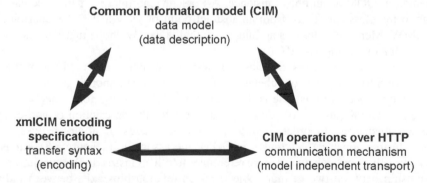

Figure 8.7 The three columns of WBEM standardize the modelling language (CIM), the
transfer syntax (xmlCIM) and the transport mechanism (CIM operations over HTTP)

in a WBEM environment how they realize this model, for example in C++ or in Java. The only important thing is that they provide the semantics of the model, i.e. provide the defined classes and objects plus the corresponding methods outwards to other components.

- xmlCIM Encoding Specification
  The xmlCIM Encoding Specification describes the transfer syntax in a WBEM environment. It thus defines precisely the XML formats in which method calls of the CIM objects and the corresponding returned results are encoded and transmitted. As a result, it is possible for two components to communicate with each other in the WBEM architecture, regardless of how they locally implement the CIM classes and CIM objects.

- CIM operations over HTTP
  Finally, CIM operations over HTTP provide the transport mechanism in a WBEM environment that makes it possible for two components to send messages encoded in xmlCIM back and forth. This makes it possible to call up methods of CIM objects that are located on a different component.

Common Information Model (CIM)

CIM itself is a method of describing management data for systems, applications networks, devices, etc. CIM is based upon the concept of object-oriented modelling (OOM). Understanding CIM requires knowledge of OOM. OOM is based upon the concept of object-oriented programming. However, OOM is not a programming language, but a formal modelling language for the description of circumstances of the real world on abstract level.

In OOM, real existing objects are represented by means of instances. An instance has certain properties, which are called attributes, and allows for execution of specific actions, which are called methods.

A class in OOM is the abstract description of an instance, i.e. it is the instance type. To illustrate: a Porsche Cabriolet in a car park is an object of the real world and is represented in OOM as an object instance. A Porsche Cabriolet is of the type car, thus it belongs to the class car. Thus, from an abstract point of view a Porsche Cabriolet – just like a BMW, Mercedes, etc. – is nothing more than a car. We hope that Porsche fans will forgive us for this comparison!

Classes can have subclasses. Subclasses inherit the attributes and methods of the parent class (Figure 8.8). Examples of subclasses of the class car are sports cars or convertibles. An inherited property in this case is that they have a chassis and four wheels.

As we see, OOM can also be used to great effect for the description of non-computer-related circumstances. In order to describe complex states of affairs between several classes, a further construct is required in OOM: the association (Figure 8.8). An association is a class that contains two or more references to other classes. In that way it represents a relationship between two or more objects. Such relationships exist between individual classes and can themselves possess properties. Let us consider the class 'person'. In the language of OOM 'man' and 'woman' are subclasses of the parent class 'person'. A relationship between the class 'man' and the class 'woman' could be 'marriage'. A property of this relationship would be the date of the wedding, for example.

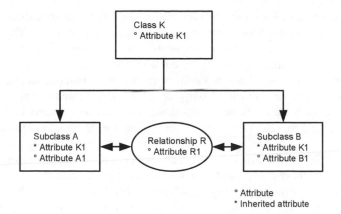

° Attribute
* Inherited attribute

Figure 8.8 Classes pass on their attributes to subclasses. Connections between classes are described as relationships, which again have their own attributes

Complex management environments can be described in abstract terms with the aid of the class and relationship constructs. An abstract description of a management environment using OOM is called a schema in CIM. CIM has three different types of schema: the Core Schema (also known as Core Model), the Common Schema (also known as Common Model) and further Extension Schemas (Figure 8.9).

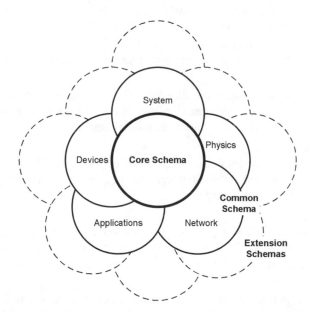

Figure 8.9 The basis of the CIM model is the Core Schema. The Common Schema supplies abstract classes and relationships on the basis of the Core Schema for all those components that the different management environments have in common. By means of Extension Schemas the abstract basic Core Schema and Common Schema can be concretized and expanded

The Core Schema defines the abstract classes and their relationships necessary for the description and analysis of complex management environments. The Core Schema specifies the basic vocabulary for management environments. For example, the Core Schema specifies that in a management environment elements to be managed exist, which themselves have logical and physical components. A strict differentiation is always made between logical and physical units or properties. Systems, applications or networks represent such elements to be managed and can be realized in CIM as extensions of this Core Schema. The Core Schema thus yields the conceptual template for all extensions.

The Common Schema builds upon the Core Schema to supply the abstract classes and relationships for all those components that the different management environments have in common, regardless of the underlying techniques or implementations. The abstract classes of the Common Schema all arise by inheritance from the classes of the Core Schema. The Common Schema defines the following submodels:

- System model
  The system model brings together all objects that belong in a management environment.

- Device model
  The device model represents the logical units of such a system that provide the system functions on a purely logical level in order to remain independent of the physical implementation. This makes sense because physical aspects of devices change but their importance on a logical level generally remains the same for the management of a system as a whole. For example, a Fibre Channel switch differs from an iSCSI switch only in terms of its physical properties. The logical property of acting as a connection node to connect other nodes in the network together is common to both components.

- Application model
  The application model defines the aspects that are required for the management of applications. The model is designed so that it can be used to describe both single location applications and also complex distributed software.

- Network model
  The network model describes the components of the network environment such as topology, connections and the various services and protocols that are required for the operation of and access to a network.

- Physical model
  The physical model makes it possible to also describe the physical properties of a management environment. However, these are of low importance for the management, since the important aspects for the management are on a logical and not a physical level.

Extension Schemas permit the abstract basic Core Schema and Common Schema to be further concretized and expanded. The classes of the Extension Schema must be formed by inheritance from the classes of the Core and Common Schemas and the rules of the CIM model have to be applied. In this manner it is possible to use CIM for the description of the extremely different management data of the components of a storage network, which can be used for management by means of the following WBEM architecture.

WBEM architecture

WBEM describes the architecture of a WBEM management system using the three pillars CIM, xmlCIM and CIM operations over HTTP. To this end, WBEM defines the following elements (Figure 8.10):

- CIM managed object
  The object to be managed is called a CIM managed object. This can, for example, be a storage device or an application.

- CIM provider
  The CIM provider supplies the management data of a managed object. In the terminology of CIM this means that it provides the instances of the object that are defined in the CIM model for the managed device. The interface between CIM provider and CIM managed object is not described by WBEM, with this interface being the starting point for the integration of other protocols such as SNMP.

- CIMOM – CIM object manager
  The CIM object manager implements the CIM repository and provides interfaces for CIM provider and CIM clients (e.g. central management applications). The specification of the interfaces between CIM provider and CIMOM is also not part of WBEM, so manufacturer-specific mechanisms are used here too.

- CIM repository
  The CIM repository contains templates for CIM models and object instances.

- CIM client
  The CIM client corresponds to a management system. The CIM client contacts the CIMOM in order to recognize managed objects and to receive management data from the CIM provider. The communication between CIM client and CIMOM is based upon the techniques xmlCIM and CIM operations over HTTP described above. These should facilitate interoperability between CIM clients and CIMOMs of different manufacturers.

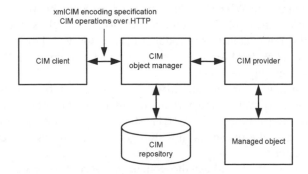

Figure 8.10   Data on a managed object is made available via a CIM provider. CIM clients can access this data by means of the CIM object manager

The CIM specification also provides a mechanism for sounding an alert in case of a state change of an object. The recognition of a state change such as creation, deletion, update or access of a class instance is called a Trigger. A Trigger will result in the creation of a short-living object called Indication which is used to communicate the state change information to a CIM client through the WBEM architecture. For that the CIM client needs to subscribe for indications with the CIMOM previously.

The use of CIM and WBEM for the management of storage networks

In the past, WBEM/CIM has proved itself useful in the management of homogeneous environments. For example, the management of Windows servers is based upon these techniques. Storage networks, on the other hand, contain components from very different manufacturers. Experience from the past has shown that WBEM and CIM alone are not sufficient to guarantee the interoperability between CIM clients, i.e. management systems, and CIMOMs in the field of storage networks. In the next section we will introduce Bluefin, a technique that aims to fill this gap.

8.7.3 Storage Management Initiative Specification (SMI-S)

At the start of this chapter we sketched out the necessity of a central management system from which all components of a storage network can be managed from different points of view. The so-called Bluefin initiative aimed to close the gaps of WBEM/CIM with the objective of defining an open and manufacturer-neutral interface (API) for the discovery, monitoring and configuration of storage networks. Bluefin thus aimed to define a standardized management interface for heterogeneous storage networks, so that they can be managed in a consistent manner. The Bluefin initiative was set up in 2001 by a group of manufacturers under the name of Partner Development Process (PDP). Since August 2002 the further development of Bluefin has been in the hands of the SNIA. The standardization itself is now being driven forward by the SNIA Storage Management Initiative (SMI) under the name Storage Management Initiative Specification (SMI-S).

SMI-S is based upon the WBEM architecture and expands this in two directions. First, it refines the classes of the CIM Common Schemas to include classes for the management of storage networks. For example, it introduces classes for host, fabric, LUN, zoning, etc. Second, it extends the WBEM architecture by two new services: the Directory Manager and the Lock Manager (Figure 8.11).

The Directory Manager aims to simplify discovery in a storage network. SMI-S also defines how resources (physical and virtual) report to the Directory Manager by means of the Service Location Protocol (SLP, IETF standard since 1997), so that management systems can interrogate the resources in a storage network through a central service, i.e. the Directory Manager.

The Lock Manager aims to assist the concurrent access to resources from different management applications in a storage network. Access to CIM objects can be protected by locks, so that a transaction model can be implemented. To this end, SMI-S-compliant

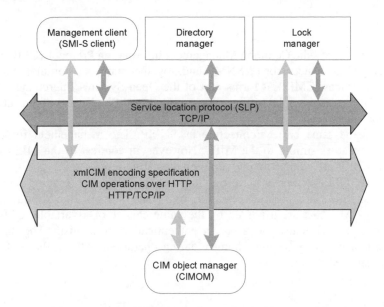

Figure 8.11   SMI-S expands the WBEM architecture: the Directory Manager and the Service Location Protocol aim to simplify the location of resources (discovery) in the storage network. The Lock Manager helps to synchronize parallel accesses to protected methods of CIM objects

management systems must demand the corresponding rights from the Lock Manager in the role of the lock management client, in order to be allowed to call up the protected methods.

The SMI is a working group that co-ordinates the various subgroups of the SNIA that are working on the standardization of various aspects of storage networks. In the opinion of SNIA around 70% of the required functions for the management of a storage network have already been passed. The current standard (end of 2003) primarily describes the components of a Fibre Channel SAN. SMI-S still has to be expanded for techniques such as NAS and iSCSI. Reference implementations already exist for the Directory Manager, but there are still none for the Lock Manager. As the next step, the CIM classes that are still lacking must be defined and the interoperability of the implementations from different manufacturers tested. Therefore SNIA has established the Interoperability Conformance Testing Program (ICTP), which provides unique test standards for all participating products to demonstrate proven interoperability and standard compliance.

8.7.4   CMIP and DMI

For the sake of completeness we will now list two further protocol standards for out-band management: the Common Management Information Protocol (CMIP) and the Desktop Management Interface (DMI). However, neither protocol has as yet made any inroads into storage networks and they have up until now been used exclusively for the monitoring of servers.

CMIP

At the end of the 1980s the Common Management Information Protocol (CMIP) was originally developed as a successor of SNMP and, together with the Common Management Information Services (CMIS), it forms part of the Open Systems Interconnect Specification (OSI). Due to its complexity it is, however, very difficult to program and for this reason is not widespread today.

CMIP uses the same basic architecture as SNMP. The management information is also held in variables similar to the MIBs. However, in contrast to the MIBs in SNMP, variables in CMIP are comparatively complex data structures.

Like SNMP, CMIP provides corresponding operations for the reading and changing of variables and also incorporates messaging by means of traps. In addition, actions can be defined in CMIP that are triggered by the value change of a variable. CMIP has the advantage over SNMP that it has a proper authentication mechanism. The disadvantage of CMIP is that it is very resource-hungry during operation, both on the NMS side and also at the managed device.

DMI

The Desktop Management Interface was also specified by the DMTF. It describes a mechanism by means of which management information can be sent to a management system over a network. The architecture of the DMI consists of a service layer, a database in the management information format (MIF), a management interface (MI) and a component interface (Figure 8.12). The service layer serves to exchange information between the managed servers and a management system. All properties of a managed server are stored in the MIF database. A DMI-capable management system can access a server and its components via the management interface. The component information is provided to the management interface by component interfaces. DMI thus provides an open standard for the management of servers, but is nowhere near as widespread as SNMP.

8.8 OPERATIONAL ASPECTS OF THE MANAGEMENT OF STORAGE NETWORKS

In large heterogeneous environments the introduction of a management system appears indispensable for those wishing to take control of management costs and make full use of the storage network. For small environments, the implementation of a management system is recommended if the environment is expected to grow strongly in the medium term. Entry in a small environment offers the additional advantage that the management system grows with the environment and you have plenty of time to get used to the product in question. If the storage network reaches its critical size at a later date you will already be better prepared for the more difficult management. Because, by this time, the installed tools will already be well known, the optimal benefit can be drawn from them.

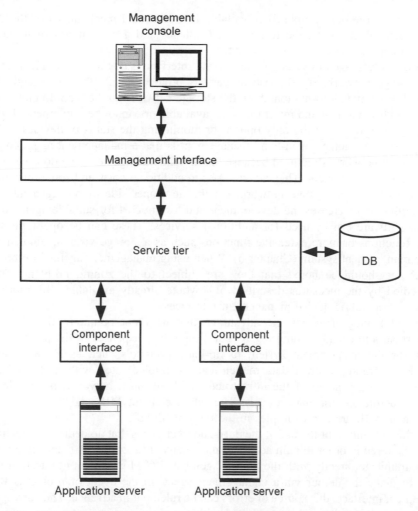

Figure 8.12   The DMI architecture allows a management system to access information of servers and their components

If you have the choice between standardized or proprietary mechanisms, then you should go for standardized mechanisms. Many device manufacturers have already built support for the standards in question into their products. Other manufacturers will follow this example. When purchasing new devices, the devices' support for standards is a critical selection criterion and should thus be checked in advance. When choosing a management system you should ensure corresponding support for the various standards. It should, however, also have interfaces for the support of proprietary mechanisms. The calling up of element managers from the management console is the minimum requirement here. Only thus can many older devices be integrated into the management system.

Which strategies should a management system use: in-band or out-band? This question cannot be answered in a straightforward manner since the success of a management system depends to a large degree upon the available interfaces and mechanisms of the devices used. In general, however, the following advantages and disadvantages of in-band and out-band management can be worked out.

The main advantage of the use of the in-band interface is that it is available as standard in the storage network. By the use of various protocol levels (transport and ULP) a great deal of detailed information about the storage network can be read. In environments where an additional out-band interface is not available or cannot be implemented, in-band monitoring may represent the only option for monitoring the status of devices.

The great disadvantage of in-band management is that a management agent connected to the storage network is required because the in-band management functions can only be used through such an agent. This can give rise to additional costs and sometimes increase the complexity of the storage network. On the developer side of management systems this naturally also increases the development and testing cost for suitable agent software.

Agent software can be used for additional services. These can be operating system-specific functions or more extensive functions such as a storage virtualization integrated into the management system (Chapter 5). When using management agents in Fibre Channel SAN, it should be noted that they are subject to the zoning problem. This can be remedied by the measures described or – where already available – by more recent options such as fabric device management interfaces.

Out-band management has the advantage that it is not bound to the storage network infrastructure and technology in question. This dispenses with the necessity of support for the management system by in-band protocols such as Fibre Channel or iSCSI. Furthermore, abstract data models can be implemented with SNMP-MIBs and CIM that are independent of the infrastructure. These must, however, be supplemented by infrastructure-specific data models. The fabric element MIB and the Fibre Channel management MIB are two examples in the field of SNMP.

A further advantage of the use of the out-band interface is that no dedicated management agent is required in order to gain access to management functions. A management system can communicate directly with the SNMP agents and CIM providers in question without having to make the detour via a management agent. In the event of problems with the management interface, this source of errors can be ruled out in advance. The corresponding costs and administrative effort associated with the management agent are therefore also not incurred.

A great disadvantage of out-band management is that up until now there has been no access to the operational services that are available in-band. Although this would be technically possible it has not yet been implemented. Finally, even the additional interface that is required can prevent the use of out-band management in cases where the implementation of a further interface is not possible or not desirable.

Therefore, a management system should, where possible, support both interfaces in order to get the best of both worlds. This means that it is also capable of integrating devices that only have one of the two interfaces. For devices that have access to both in-band and out-band interfaces an additional connection can be very helpful, particularly for error isolation. If, for example, the in-band connection to a device has failed, then an in-band management system would report both the failure of the line and also the failure of the device. A management system that operates both interfaces would still be able to reach the device out-band and thus trace the error to the failed connection.

8.9 SUMMARY

In this chapter we have dealt with the requirements and the possibilities that exist for the management of storage networks. The realization of these comprehensive requirements in a management system implies a complexity that should not be underestimated. In general, storage networks impose higher requirements on management than do storage-centric IT architectures. The objective of effective storage management is the use of a central management system that is capable of integrating both the proprietary and the standardized management mechanisms of the individual devices. Both in-band and out-band management mechanisms are offered. We discussed the Fibre Channel Generic Services for the in-band management of a Fibre Channel SAN. Out-band, standardized management mechanisms are available in the form of the important protocols SNMP, CIM/WBEM and SMI-S. Today (end of 2003) SNMP is an important protocol for the management of storage networks. As development progresses and the power of CIM/WBEM and SMI-S increases, the SNMP MIBs may gradually be forced from the market. Suitable extensively implemented CIM providers could then also supersede the in-band interface. From an operational point of view it is to be hoped that, on the one hand, the management techniques continue to be further developed in an open and standardized – and thus interoperable – manner and, on the other, that even more manufacturers feel obliged to establish corresponding standards for their devices.

In the next chapter we continue the discussion of storage management: Removable media and large tape libraries are central components of large data centres and we have not covered them so far. Thus the next chapter deals with the management of removable media.

9

Removable Media Management

Removable media is a central component of the storage architectures of large data centers. The use of storage networks means that several servers – and thus various different applications – can now use media and libraries jointly. The management of removable media in storage networks is therefore becoming increasingly important. Hence this chapter describes the network based virtualization of tape libraries and other removable media resources.

In the following section we first of all explain why, in spite of the ever-increasing capacity of hard disks and intelligent disk subsystems, removable media is indispensable (Section 9.1). Then we consider various types of removable media (Section 9.2) and libraries (Section 9.3), giving special consideration to media management. We then discuss the problems and requirements related to the management of removable media (Section 9.4). Finally, we introduce the IEEE 1244 Standard for Removable Media Management – an approach that describes both the architecture of a system for the management of removable media and also its communication with applications.

9.1 THE SIGNIFICANCE OF REMOVABLE MEDIA

Articles with such titles as 'Tapes Have No Future' or 'Is Tape Dead?' keep appearing in the press. Some storage manufacturers proclaimed the end of tapes as early as twenty years ago. Then it was to have been all over in the last few years ... After all, they said, hard disks (e.g. serial ATA disks) have now become so cheap that it is unnecessary to move data to other data carriers. In our opinion (in 2003), removable media is, and will remain, an important building block in the storage architectures of data center.

Storage Networks Explained   U. Troppens R. Erkens W. Müller
© 2004 John Wiley & Sons, Ltd   ISBN: 0-470-86182-7

In addition to their high capacity and low price, for many companies the fact that removable media can be stored separately from read and write devices and thus withdrawn from direct access is particularly relevant. Viruses, worms and other 'animals' are thus denied the possibility of propagating themselves uncontrollably, as they could on storage that is continuously available online. Furthermore, with removable media a very large quantity of data can be stored in a very small and possibly well-protected area at low storage costs. WORM (Write Once Read Multiple) properties, which are now available not only for optical media but also for magnetic tapes, additionally increase security. Furthermore, the requirement for storage capacity is increasing continuously. Progress in storage density and the capacity of cartridges can scarcely keep up with the ever-growing requirement, which means that the number of cartridges is also growing continuously.

For the film *The Lord of the Rings* alone, 160 computer animators generated and edited a data volume of one terabyte every day, which was stored to tape. At the end of the three-year production period, the digital material for the final version of the film – 150 terabytes in size – was stored on tape.

In the scientific field, and also in the field of medicine and bioinformation, data volumes in the petabyte range have been handled for a long time. This immense requirement for storage space cannot be provided exclusively in the form of storage that is available online, such as hard disks. Power consumption, heat and space requirements would drive the costs of this so high that this type of storage could not currently be justified by the shorter access time. For example, the power consumption of an average 120 GB S-ATA drive is currently (mid-2003) approximately 13 Watts. An installation with 400 terabytes of storage thus has a power consumption of more than 42 kW! This corresponds with approximately the average power consumption for 120 german single family homes.

A further important advantage of removable media in comparison to hard disks is their robustness. They are less sensitive to impact and a service life of up to 30 years is possible for media in the field of high-end tapes stored in the correct manner.

9.2   REMOVABLE MEDIA

Various types of removable media are currently in use. These are primarily magnetic tapes (Section 9.2.1), optical media such as CDs and DVDs and magneto-optical media (Section 9.2.2). In these sections we are primarily interested in how the special properties of the various media types should be taken into consideration in the management of removable media.

9.2.1   Tapes

Tapes have firmly established themselves as a back-up and archiving medium for large data quantities due to their very low costs per megabyte storage space in comparison to other media. However, tapes can only be accessed sequentially. The position of the head of a tape drive cannot, therefore, be chosen at will, but must be determined by the appropriate fast-forwarding and rewinding of the tape. This movement of the tape costs significantly more time than the movement of the head of a hard disk drive and an optimal speed can, therefore, only be achieved if as many associated data blocks as possible are read and written one after the other, i.e. sequentially.

Access to back-up and archive data at will is often unnecessary. The speed at which the large quantities of data can be backed up and restored is likely to be a significantly more important factor than the random access to individual files. Back-up and archiving applications available today utilize this special property of tapes by aggregating the data to be backed up into a stream of blocks and then writing these blocks onto tapes sequentially (cf. Section 9.3.1). Such programs use an internal management system to ensure that they are capable of identifying at any time both the tape on which a file or database is saved and also the position of the start of the file or database on the tape (cf. Section 7.3.4)

Today (end of 2003), the term 'removable media' is primarily used to refer to tapes and tape libraries. In almost all large data centres, tape libraries with several drives and a great many tape cartridges are used. They are currently the most commonly used medium for back-up and archiving purposes. Therefore, systems for the management of removable media are currently used primarily where tapes have to be managed and tape libraries have to be controlled. Nevertheless, in view of future developments of new storage technologies, current management systems should also support media that possess several sides and several partitions.

9.2.2   CD, DVD and magneto-optical media

When writing to CDs, DVDs and magneto-optical media, a file system (e.g. ISO-9660) is generally applied. When writing to these media, the same limitations apply as for tapes, since only one application can write to the data carrier at any one time. Normally, this application also writes a large portion – if not the whole – of the available storage space.

However, once these data carriers have been written, applications can access them like hard disk drives. As a result, the applications have available to them the full support of the operating system for the read access to optical media, which is why in this case they behave like write-protected hard disks and can be shared accordingly. Magneto-optical media are generally readable and writeable on both sides.

Depending upon the drive, the cartridge may have to be turned over in order to access the second side. This property makes it necessary for management systems to be able to manage a second side of a cartridge and control the changing mechanism so that the cartridge can be turned over. Furthermore, the WORM properties must be suitably represented for these data carriers.

9.2.3   Management features of removable media

In what follows we give an overview of the most important features and terms, plus a brief explanation:

Cartridge   A cartridge is a physical medium upon which storage space is available. A cartridge can be moved and has one or more sides.

External cartridge label   A label that is applied to the outside of a cartridge and serves to identify the cartridge, for example, a mechanically readable barcode.

Internal cartridge label   A dataset in a certain format at a certain position on the data carrier that serves to identify the cartridge.

Side   A physical part of a cartridge that provides storage space. A side contains one or more partitions. Tapes normally have only one side. DVDs and magneto-optical media are also available in double-sided variants.

Partition   Part of a side that provides storage space as a physical unit of the cartridge.

Volume   A volume is a logical data container. It serves to reserve storage space for applications on data carriers. A partition can hold as many volumes as desired. Please note that the term *volume* may have different meanings depending on the context it is used: in terms of the SNIA Shared Storage Model (Chapter 10) a tape volume is called a tape extent and may span multiple physical tape cartridges. In terms of back-up software and mainframes a *volume* is often used synonymously with *cartridge*.

Scratch tape   A new tape without any content or a tape, the content of which is no longer of interest, and the entire storage capacity of which can be used for new purposes.

Access handle   An identifier that an application can use to access the data of a volume. Under UNIX operating systems an access handle is equivalent to the name of a device special file (for example: /dev/rmt0).

Mount request   The command to place a certain cartridge in a drive.

Audit trail   Audit trails consist of a series of data sets, which describe the processes that have been performed by a computer system. Audit trails are used primarily in security-critical fields in order to record and check access to data.

As already mentioned, a system for the management of removable media should also be able to represent the logical and physical properties and features of a cartridge. Ideally a cartridge can consist of as many sides as desired (tapes generally have only one side, optical media often have two, holographic media could, at least theoretically, provide even more sides). Each side can hold one or more partitions, and any desired number of volumes can be allocated to each partition.

9.3   LIBRARIES AND DRIVES

Operating systems and applications that use removable data carriers must be able to deal with a large amount of different library hardware. In general, libraries possess a media changer, slots to accept cartridges, and drives with which the cartridges can be read and written. The media changer takes cartridges from the slots and transports them to the drives.

In automatic libraries, the media changer can be controlled via an interface. This interface can be realized in the form of an in-band interface (e.g. SCSI) or an out-band interface depending upon the device (cf. Section 9.3.3). The bandwidth of these automatic libraries ranges from individual small autoloaders with 1–2 drives and a few slots through to large automatic tape libraries, in which one or more media changers can transport thousands of cartridges in dozens or possibly even hundreds of drives.

In addition to automatic libraries, a removable media management system should also consider manually operated libraries. In these, an operator takes on the function of the media changer and inserts the cartridges in the drives accordingly. It is thus possible to include even individual (standalone) drives in the system as a whole.

Depending upon the level of abstraction, a shelf or a safe filled with cartridges and without any drives can also be viewed as a library. These libraries are also called *vaults* or *vaulting locations*. Particularly if both automatic libraries and vaults are used, it is wise to choose the level of abstraction for the management of the media so that vaults can also be handled like manual libraries without drives. This means that, for all libraries of whatever type, the same procedures can be applied for auditing (the requesting of all components, particularly the cartridges of a library), export (the removal of a cartridge from a less library) and import (the insertion of a cartridge into a library).

In what follows we will consider the individual components of libraries.

9.3.1 Drives

Like hard drives, drives for removable media are currently equipped with a SCSI or Fibre Channel interface in the Open Systems environment and are connected to the storage network via these. In the mainframe field, ESCON and FICON are dominant.

As already mentioned, tape drives in particular can only work at full speed if they read and write many blocks one after the other (streaming). Although it is possible, and in the mainframe environment totally normal, to write individual files consisting of just one logical block to tape, or to read them from tape, different drives are necessary for this than those used in the Open Systems back-up operation. These enterprise drives have larger motors and can position the read-write heads significantly more quickly and precisely over a certain logical block.

9.3.2 Media changers

Media changers have the job of transporting cartridges within a library. The start and end of a transport operation can either be a slot or a drive. To this end, a library has an inventory in which all elements of the library and their attributes are noted. The media changer has access to this inventory. Like drives, media changers have an interface for the control and checking of their functions. It is normal to use this interface for requesting data from the inventory, as well as for controlling the transport operations. The following information can therefore be requested via the media changer interface:

- the number of drives and their properties (addresses, type, etc.);
- the number of slots and their properties;
- the number of cartridges and their properties (slot, label, etc.);
- the number of further media changers and their properties.

9.3.3   Control of the media changer

Applications must be able to control the media changers in automatic libraries. To this end, these libraries are equipped with suitable interfaces, which the applications use to send commands and receive return messages. In the Open Systems environment the direct connection via SCSI or Fibre Channel (in-band interface) is the most widespread. On the other hand, proprietary out-band interfaces tend to be used more in the mainframe environment.

SCSI and Fibre Channel interface

Two procedures have established themselves for the control of the media changer via the SCSI or Fibre Channel FCP interface. In one case the media changer is equipped with its own controller and can be addressed as a separate device over its own SCSI target ID. In the other case the media changer shares the controller with the tape drives (Figure 9.1). Then it is either visible as an independent device with separate LUN (independent media changer) or is controlled via the drive LUN using special commands (attached media changer).

As is often the case in the IT world, there are two contrasting philosophies here, that reveal their specific advantages and disadvantages depending upon the application case. If the media changer shares the same controller with the tape drive, then the bandwidth available to the drive is reduced. However, as only a relatively small number of commands are transferred and carried out for media changers, the reduction of the bandwidth available for the drive is low. This is particularly true in the Open Systems environment, where tapes are predominantly used in streaming mode.

If, on the other hand, access is mainly file-based and if the files are located on several tapes, the ratio of media changer to drive commands increases correspondingly. In this case it can be worthwhile conducting the communication with the media changer over an additional controller. However, both this additional controller and the additional SAN components make such a solution more expensive and involve additional management costs.

The addressing of the media changer over a second LUN of the drive controller has a further major advantage in addition to the low costs. Normally, several drives are fitted in a large library. Additional access paths make it possible to also control the media changer over the second LUN of a different drive controller. If a drive should fail, the media changer remains accessible. Furthermore, drives are often provided with a redundant power supply or the controllers possess an additional port, which can automatically be used if the first path fails.

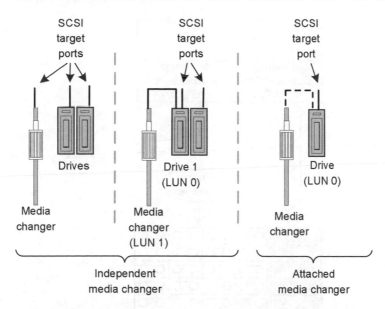

Figure 9.1 Independent media changers either possess their own SCSI target port or they can be reached as an additional device with a different LUN over the SCSI port of the drive. Attached media changers form a unit with the drive. In order to move the media changer, special SCSI commands such as READ ELEMENT STATUS ATTACHED and MOVE MEDIUM ATTACHED must be used

Proprietary interfaces

In addition to SCSI interfaces, further interfaces have established themselves, particularly in the mainframe environment. These interfaces offer a higher level of abstraction than SCSI and often also a rudimentary management of the media. Typically, such interfaces are out-of-band, i.e. not accessible over the data path (SCSI or Fibre Channel connection), but instead over TCP/IP or RS-232 (Figure 9.2).

The commands that are exchanged over such interfaces are generally executed by a control unit that is fitted in the library. This control unit can usually accept and execute commands from several applications at the same time, without this leading to conflicts. Likewise, additional services such as the management of scratch pools can be made available to all applications.

9.4 PROBLEMS AND REQUIREMENTS RELATED TO REMOVABLE MEDIA MANAGEMENT

The problems and requirements relating to the integration of removable media in the storage network can be divided into two areas:

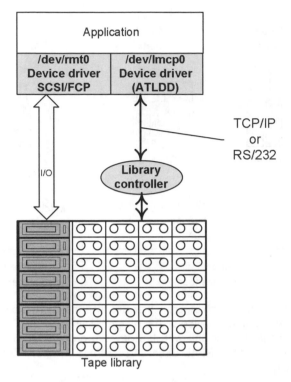

Figure 9.2 Tape library with a proprietary media changer interface. The media changer is controlled over a TCP/IP or an RS/232 interface, depending upon configuration

1. the management of removable media; and
2. the sharing of the associated resources.

In large environments, removable media management must be able to catalogue hundreds of thousands of media, storing not only the media and their attributes, but also accessing these media with corresponding data about errors, duration of use, etc.

In contrast to hard disk storage, it is possible to store the media separately from drives, which means that the system must additionally know the location of a medium at all times. Since this location can be a manually-managed store or an automatic library in which the cassettes are automatically located, special solutions are required that take these requirements into account.

The second important field of application for a removable media management system in the storage network is the sharing of libraries, drives and media. This sharing between several applications connected to the storage network requires corresponding mechanisms for access control, access synchronization and access prioritization. These mechanisms control who may access which hardware when, so that potentially all applications can access all resources available in the storage network.

In order to be able to fulfil these requirements, there is an increasing need for management layers for removable media in storage networks. These layers link existing

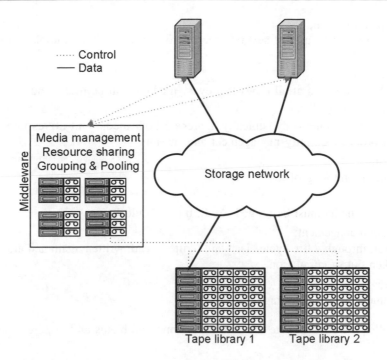

Figure 9.3 The middleware interface provides media management services, synchronizes access to the hardware and permits the grouping of drives and cartridges

applications to the hardware connected via the storage network (Figure 9.3). They control and synchronize all accesses and should remain as transparent as possible to the applications. As a central interface, this middleware should therefore be capable of managing all resources and also the sharing, i.e. the sharing of libraries, drives and cartridges by various applications.

We already discussed in Section 6.2.2 the various options for realizing library and drive sharing for removable media in storage networks. As also mentioned at that point, we believe that an architecture that shields the applications from the complex internal processes during management and sharing represents the best and most promising solution. After all, the management is familiar with all components and their interaction. Therefore, an optimal control over the use of resources can also be implemented there.

Individually, the following problems and requirements can be defined:

- Resource Utilization:
  Efficient use of all available resources by intelligent sharing.
- Access control:
  Applications and users must be authenticated. Applications and users may only be given access to the media for which suitable authorization exists.
- Access synchronization:
  Accesses to libraries and drives must be synchronized.

- Access prioritization:
  Prioritization can be used if several accesses to a resource, for example a drive, are to be performed.
- Media tracking:
  It must be guaranteed at all times that every medium can be found and accessed.
- Grouping, pooling:
  It should be possible to dynamically aggregate both media and drives into groups or pools in order to simplify management and sharing.
- Monitoring:
  Automatic monitoring of the system.
- Reporting:
  Accesses to media must be logged. Audit trails should be possible.
- Life cycle management:
  Media run through a life cycle. They are written, read, written again and after a certain time taken out of circulation.
- Vaulting:
  Management of offline storage locations.

In what follows we investigate the above-mentioned problems and requirements further.

9.4.1   Efficient use of the available resources

A great advantage of the use of well-designed storage networks is the fact that the available hardware resources are better utilized. In contrast to directly connected devices, the available storage space is available to many applications and can therefore be used significantly more effectively. In the field of removable media this is achieved by the better utilization of the free storage capacity and the sharing of drives.

Efficient use of the storage capacity

The disk storage pooling described in Section 6.2.1 is transferable to removable media one-to-one. In this case, free storage space should be taken to mean both unused removable media and also free slots for removable media, which must be kept in reserve due to the continuous growth in data. Ideally, this takes place in a cross-library manner. To this end, all free cartridges from all libraries are managed in a so-called scratch pool (Section 9.4.6), which is available to all applications, so that the remaining free storage capacity can be flexibly assigned.

Efficient use of the drives

What applies for the effective use of the free storage capacity also applies in the same way for the use of the drives. If drives are directly connected to servers they cannot be used by other servers, even if they currently have no cartridge loaded into them.

By contrast, drives in storage networks can be assigned to the applications that need them at the time. Thus, it can be ensured that all drives that are installed are also actually used.

The utilization of drives can be further increased by mount request queuing. However, more time is then required to perform the mount requests in the queue. This is a typical time-versus-space optimization problem. With more drives, more mount requests can be carried out in the same time. If, however, a lot of mount requests are not urgent, fewer drives can execute the requests one after the other. Ideally, the mount requests in the queues are prioritizable, so that urgent tasks are actually performed sooner.

9.4.2 Access control

Reliable control to prevent unauthorized access to media is indispensable. Users and applications must be authenticated. Successfully authenticated users can then be given suitable authorization to access certain resources.

Authentication

Users, and also applications, that want to make use of removable media management services must be registered with the system. A sufficiently strict authentication mechanism should ensure that only users and applications that have been unambiguously identified can use the system.

Authorization

Authorization is necessary to prevent unauthorized users from being able to view, or even change, data belonging to other users. Authorization can both apply for certain operations and also arrange access to certain objects (cartridges, partitions, volumes, drives, etc.). A successful authentication is a necessary prerequisite for authorization.

By means of an appropriate authorization, users or applications can be assigned the following rights regarding certain objects in the management system:

- generation and deleting of objects (e.g. the allocation and deallocation of volumes);
- read access to objects (e.g. read access to own volumes);
- write access to objects (e.g. addition of cartridges to a scratch pool);
- mount and unmount of cartridges, sides, partitions or volumes;
- moving of cartridges within libraries;
- import and export of cartridges;
- activation and deactivation of libraries or drives.

The use of various authorization levels allows access control to be modified according to the user's role. The following roles and activities are currently used in systems for the management of removable media and can be provided with different authorizations. This list serves as an example only. These roles and activities can also be assigned differently depending upon the specific requirements.

The *system administrator* is responsible for:

- installation of the system
- installation/deinstallation of libraries
- user and application management
- management of disk and cartridge groups.

The *storage administrator* is responsible for:

- management of disk and cartridge groups
- cartridge life cycle management
- planning of the future requirements for resources.

The *library administrator* is responsible for:

- management of disk and cartridge groups for individual libraries
- planning of the future requirements for resources
- starting and continuance of the operation of individual libraries
- starting and continuance of the operation of individual drives.

The *library operator* is responsible for:

- starting and continuance of the operation of individual libraries
- monitoring the operation of libraries
- starting and continuance of the operation of individual drives
- monitoring of the operation of drives in the libraries
- manual import and export of cartridges into and out of libraries
- performance of mount/unmount operations in manually operated libraries
- moving cartridges within a library.

The *users/applications* may:

- allocate and de-allocate volumes to cartridges
- mount and unmount volumes
- read and write volumes
- list and display volumes that they have allocated
- list and display cartridges upon which volumes they have allocated have been put
- list and display scratch cartridges, which are included in cartridge groups to which there is an access right
- list and display drives that are included in drive groups to which there is an access right.

The list makes clear that 'simple' users, for example, are not capable of managing cartridge groups or drive groups. If they were, it might be possible for a user to gain unauthorized access to foreign data. Likewise, a library operator should only have access to libraries for which he is responsible. In this manner, the smooth operation of the system as a whole can be ensured.

Authorization for access to individual objects

It is currently still common to use authorization procedures for entire cartridges only and not for their components. However, in order to be prepared for future developments, such as the 1-terabyte tape cartridge, a management system should, even now, have appropriately detailed access protection for subdivisions of cartridges such as sides, partitions and volumes.

All components of a cartridge are suitable for access control. The application purpose determines whether the user receives access to a side, a partition or a volume. An authorization is always applicable to all elements of the authorized object. If, for example, the right to access a cartridge is granted, this right also applies to all sides, partitions and volumes of this cartridge.

It is not only cartridges that should be provided with access control. For example, it is a good idea to restrict applications' access to cartridges that are still available. To this end, the available cartridges are combined into one or more scratch pools. The applications are then granted the right to access only certain scratch pools. Usually, access control is less important here than an optimal utilization of the free storage capacity.

Drives are also suitable for access control. However, here, too, it is usually the optimal utilization of the drives that is sought. An allocation of drives to certain users or applications should, however, be possible. As a result, users can be granted exclusive access to drives. Naturally, the grouping of drives is again an option here for simplifying management and increasing drive utilization.

9.4.3 Access synchronization

As already mentioned several times, a library or a drive cannot receive and process several commands from various applications in parallel. Therefore, synchronization is required that serializes all commands received at the same time and forwards them to the drives one after the other. As a result of this functionality, devices can be used 'quasi' simultaneously, in the same way as operating systems allow a single processor to be made available to several processes one after the other for a limited duration. This type of synchronization corresponds with dynamic tape library sharing and has already been described in Section 6.2.1.

9.4.4 Access prioritization and mount request queuing

Despite intelligent access control, there may be more mount requests than available drives at a certain point in time. Ideally, a system should collect requests into a request queue in

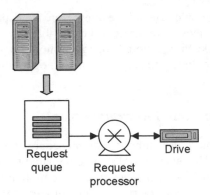

Figure 9.4   The mount requests are stored in a queue and processed one after the other by the request processor

this case (Figure 9.4). This queue can be available for each drive and also for each group of drives and collect all mount requests that cannot be carried out immediately. Once a drive becomes available again, the system can perform the next request and remove this from the queue in question. In the search for the next request to be carried out, a scheduler can sometimes also evaluate the priority of requests and change their sequence accordingly.

Request queues that are not bound to drives have the advantage that several free drives may be available for each new request that is taken out of the queue. The assignment of mount request and drive must be re-evaluated accordingly, taking into account utilization and priority in order to increase the utilization of the system as a whole. Depending upon realization, this can also lead to an application being again withdrawn from a drive, so that it has to interrupt the access to the tape.

It should be possible to remove requests from a queue and change the priorities of requests via an administrative interface.

9.4.5   Media tracking

As an integral part of a disaster recovery solution, a management system must ensure that all removable media plus the appropriate metadata remain in the system until they are deleted by an appropriately authorized user. Thus, under no circumstances may tapes be 'lost' or removed from the system without authorization. Furthermore, it must be possible to determine the storage location of each medium at all times.

If access is available to the media online, for example, in automatic tape libraries in which tapes can be automatically identified by the reading of a barcode label by a scanner, a suitable audit can be performed at any time. In such an audit, the content of the inventory is compared with the real existing tapes. Such libraries also automatically report the opening of a door. After the door has been closed an audit should once again be automatically performed in order to ensure that no media has been removed from the system without authorization.

If a part of the media is withdrawn from direct access, either to a well-protected safe or to another manually-operated library, this storage place must be managed with appropriate care by the responsible administrators. Ideally, the management software provides an interface for this vaulting.

In order to increase the reliability of a disaster recovery concept and to fulfil statutory provisions, a two-stage or multi-stage strategy made up of online and offline storage is often performed. Storage media are first written in automatic libraries, then stored offline for a certain period of time and subsequently either taken out of circulation or reused (Figure 9.5). Media that are in transit from an online library to an offline storage place must be identified.

A management system for removable media should serve both as a central repository for all resources and as a universal interface for applications. It should not be possible for any application to withdraw itself from the control of the system and access or move media in an uncontrolled manner. Only thus is it actually guaranteed that all media in the system can be located at any time.

Such a central interface is always in danger of becoming a single point of failure. It is therefore very wise to use appropriate measures to guarantee a high level of availability for the entire solution. Consequently, care must be taken to ensure that all components of the entire system, from the hardware through the operating systems used with the media management to the back-up software, are designed to have a high level of availability. The hardware often offers suitable options. Drives and media changers are available with a redundant power supply and redundant access paths. Modern operating systems such as AIX or Solaris can automatically use such redundantly designed access paths in the event of a fault.

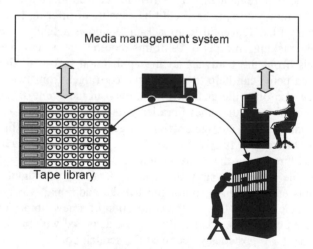

Figure 9.5 The integration of offline storage space requires manual support

9.4.6 Grouping, pooling

Systems for the management of removable media must be able to deal with a great many media and facilitate access to many applications. In order to plan and execute access control in a sensible manner and to guarantee its effective use, it is necessary to combine cartridges and drives into groups. Grouping also allows budgets for storage capacities or drives to be created, which are made available to the applications.

Scratch pools

A scratch pool contains unused cartridges that are available to authorized applications so that they can place volumes upon them. As soon as an application has placed a volume upon a cartridge from such a scratch pool, this cartridge is no longer available to all other applications and is thus removed from the scratch pool.

If several scratch pools are available, they cannot only be grouped for different media, it is also possible to define groups for certain application purposes. For example, an administrator should be able to make a separate pool of cartridges available for important back-up jobs, whilst cartridges from a different scratch pool are used for 'normal' back-up jobs. The back-up application can choose which pool it would like to have a cartridge from. If it is possible to assign priorities to scratch pools on the basis of which the management system can decide from which pool a new cartridge will be provided, then such a request can be automated to a certain degree without the back-up application having to know all available pools. To this end, the request for a new tape must be given an appropriate priority, whereupon the management system searches for a cartridge from a scratch pool with a suitably high priority.

In addition to the requirement that all cartridges can be located at all times, a management system for removable media should be capable of offering free storage space to an application at any time. Only thus can back-up windows actually be adhered to. As is the case for media tracking, in order to fulfil this requirement a high-availability solution covering all levels, from the hardware to the application software, should be pursued. In addition, scratch pools can help to contain the cartridges from two or more libraries (Figure 9.6). They also offer the guarantee that, even in the event of the failure of individual libraries, cartridges in the other libraries will remain usable. It is precisely in this case that the advantages of a storage network, together with an intelligent management system for removable media, fully come to bear in the optimal utilization of resources that are distributed throughout the entire system.

In order to be able to react flexibly to changes, scratch pools should be dynamically expandable. To this end, an administrator must make additional storage space available to the system dynamically, whether by the connection of a new library or by the addition of previously unused cartridges. Ideally, this can be achieved without making changes to the applications that have previously accessed the scratch pool.

An adjustable minimum size (low water mark) makes the management of a scratch pool easier. If this threshold is reached, measures must be taken to increase the size of the

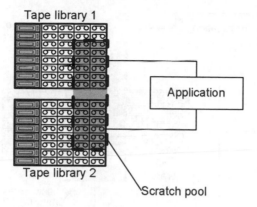

Figure 9.6 A scratch pool that contains the free cartridges from two libraries. A free cartridge is still available to the application even if one library has failed

pool, as otherwise there is the danger that the system will cease to be able to provide free storage space in the foreseeable future. The management system can help here by flexibly offering more options. Many actions are possible here, from the automatic enlargement of the scratch pools – as long as free media are available in the libraries – to the 'call home' function, in which an administrator is notified.

If a cartridge has several partitions, then it would occasionally be desirable to collect just the free partitions – rather than the complete cartridges – into a scratch pool. Then it would be possible to manage free storage capacity with a finer granularity and thus achieve an optimal utilization of the total amount of available storage capacity. Since, however, the individual partitions of a medium cannot be accessed at the same time, a cartridge is currently generally managed and allocated to an application as the smallest unit of a scratch pool. As capacity increases, however, the additional use of partitions for this may also be required.

Drive pools

The mere fact that cartridges are available does not actually mean that the storage space can be used. In addition, drives must be available that can mount the cartridges for reading or writing.

Similarly to cartridges, it is also possible to combine drives into pools. A pool of high-priority drives can, for example, always be kept to fulfil mount requests if all other drives are fully utilized. In order to save the applications from having to know and request all drive pools, it is a good idea to have a priority attribute that is used by the management system to automatically locate a drive with an appropriate priority.

If several libraries are available, drive pools should include drives from several libraries (Figure 9.7). This ensures that drives are still available even if one library has failed. At the very least, this helps when writing new data if free cartridges are still available.

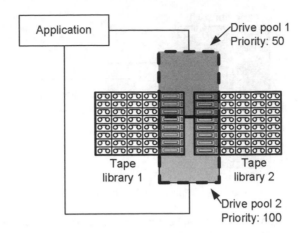

Figure 9.7 The application gets a drive from the drive pool with the highest priority

9.4.7 Monitoring

The large number of devices and media that have to be monitored in a data centre makes it almost impossible for monitoring to be performed exclusively by administrators. Automatic control of the system, or at least of parts of it, is therefore absolutely necessary for installations above a certain size. For removable media, in particular, it is important that monitoring is well constructed because in daily operation there is too little time to verify every back-up. If errors creep in whilst the system is writing to tape this may not be recognized until the data needs to be restored – when it is too late. If there is no second copy, the worst conceivable incident for the datacenter has occurred: data loss!

Modern tape drives permit a very good monitoring of their state. This means that the number of read-write errors that cannot be rectified by the built-in firmware, and also the number of load operations, are stored in the drive. Ideally, this data will be read by the management system and stored so that it is available for further evaluations.

A further step would be to have this data automatically analyzed by the system. If certain error states are reached, actions can be triggered automatically so that at least no further error states are permitted. Under certain circumstances, errors can even be rectified automatically, for example by switching a drive off and back on again. In the worst case, it is only possible to mark the drive as defective so that it is not used further. In these tasks, too, a mechanism controlled by means of rules can help and significantly take the pressure off the administrator.

The data stored on the drives not only provides information on the drives themselves, but also on the loaded tapes. This data can be used to realize a tape quality management, which, for example, monitors the error rates when reading and writing and, if necessary, copies the data to a new tape if a certain threshold is exceeded.

9.4.8 Reporting

In addition to media management and drive and library sharing a powerful system requires the recording of all actions. For certain services it is even a legal requirement that so-called security audits are performed. Therefore, all actions must be precisely logged. In addition, the log data must be protected against manipulation in an appropriate manner.

With the aid of a powerful interface, it should be possible to request data including the following:

- When was a cartridge incorporated into the system?
- Who allocated which volume to which cartridge when?
- Who accessed which volume when?
- Was this volume just read or also written?
- Which drive was used?
- Was this an authorized access or was access refused?

The following requirements should be fulfilled by the reporting module of a removable media management system:

- Audit trails
  As already mentioned, it should be possible to obtain a complete list of all accesses to a medium. Individual entries in this list should give information about who accessed a medium, for how long, and with what access rights.
- Usage statistics
  Data about when the drives were used, and for how long they were used, is important in order to make qualitative statements about the actual utilization of all drives. At any point in time, were sufficient drives available to carry out all mount requests? Are more drives available than the maximum amount needed at same time over the last twelve months? The answers to such questions can be found in the report data. Like the utilization of the drives, the available storage space is, of course, also of interest. Was enough free capacity available? Were there bottlenecks?
- Error statistics
  Just like the data on the use of resources, data regarding the errors that occurred during use is also of great importance for the successful use of removable media. Have the storage media of manufacturer X caused less read-write errors in the drives of manufacturer Y than the media of manufacturer Z? Appropriate evaluations help considerably in the optimization of the overall performance of a system.
- Future planning
  Predictions for the future can be made from the above-mentioned statistics. How will the need for storage grow? How many drives will be used in twelve months? And

how many slots and cartridges? A management system should be able to help in the search for answers to these questions. In order that future changes can also be simply carried out, the addition of further drives or cartridges must also be possible without any problems and must not require any changes to the existing applications that use the management services.

9.4.9   Life cycle management

The life cycle of a cartridge describes a series of states that a cartridge can take on over the course of time. Essentially, the following events, which lead to state transitions, can be observed in the life cycle:

- Initialization
  Cartridges are announced to the system.
- Allocation of access rights
  Applications are permitted to access certain cartridges.
- Use
  Cartridges are used for reading and writing.
- deallocation
  The data on a cartridge is no longer needed; the storage space can once again be made available to other applications.
- Retirement
  The cartridge has reached the end of its life cycle and is removed from the system.

These events directly yield a series of states for cartridges.

States of media

In addition to the location of the media, it is also important that storage administrators are aware of the state of the media. For example, a cartridge may not be removed from the system until no more logical volumes have been allocated to it. Otherwise, there is a danger of data loss, because back-up software can no longer access this volume.
   During its life cycle (Figure 9.8) a cartridge can take on the following states:

- Undefined (unknown)
  No further information is known about a cartridge. This is the initial state of a cartridge before it is taken into a management system.
- Defined
  A cartridge is announced to the system. Information about the type, cartridge label, etc. are given, and the cartridge is thus described.
- Available
  In addition to the information that a cartridge exists in the system, information about whether, and where, data can be still written to the cartridge is also important. If this information is known, the cartridge is available for applications

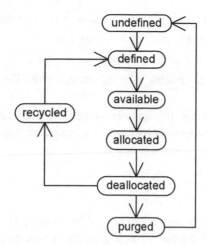

Figure 9.8   States in the life cycle of a cartridge

- Allocated
  In order that an application can use a cartridge, suitable storage space on a cartridge must be allocated by the system. This allocation of storage space generally leads to the placing of a volume on a partition of a cartridge. The application should be able to freely choose the identification of the volume. In general, the state of the first volume placed determines the state of the entire cartridge. To this end, as soon as the first volume has been placed on a cartridge, the state of the cartridge is set to 'allocated'.

- deallocated
  If the storage space (the volume) is no longer required by an application, the volume can be de-allocated. The system should then delete all information about the volume. The application should continue to be able to reallocate the same storage space. If the storage space is to be made available to other applications, a cartridge must be recycled.

- Recycled
  Depending upon system configuration, once all volumes have been removed from a cartridge the entire storage space can be made available to other applications.

- Purged
  A cartridge, and all information about this cartridge, is completely removed from the system. In general, this state is reached at the end of a cartridge's life cycle. Typically, this state exists only for a short time, since the cartridge is immediately placed in the undefined state.

Policy-based life cycle management

Certain tasks should be automated so that as little manual intervention as possible is required during the management of the data carriers. In life cycle management, some tasks positively demand to be performed automatically. These include:

- the monitoring of retention periods;

- transportation to the next storage location (movement or rotation);
- the copying of media when it reaches a certain age;
- the deletion of media at the end of the storage period;
- the recycling or automatic removal of the cartridge from the system.

The individual parameters for the automated tasks are specified by suitable policies. Individual cartridges, or groups of cartridges, are assigned suitable policies.

9.4.10   Vaulting

The term 'vaulting', or 'vault management' describes the possibility of managing media that is located in a remote and possibly well-protected room. Such locations are also called offsite locations, since media in these locations cannot be immediately accessed (online).

A management system should also be capable of managing such offsite locations. To this end, the media must be moved back and forth between automatic libraries and offsite locations. Automatic control must ensure that all media that is removed from a library actually arrives at the other library. Since this usually only works with manual support, a suitable operator interface is necessary. This first of all, notifies the responsible personnel of the tasks that have to be performed and, second, accepts manual inputs with which the personnel can acknowledge the tasks.

In order to automate, as far as possible, the tasks that arise, the above-mentioned policies are recommended. With a rotation or movement policy it can, for example, be specified that a cartridge is located in a safe after the next mount, stored there for 10 years, and then taken out of circulation.

9.5   THE IEEE 1244 STANDARD FOR REMOVABLE MEDIA MANAGEMENT

As early as 1990, the IEEE Computer Society set up the 1244 project for the development of standards for storage systems. The Storage System Standards Working Group was also established with the objective of developing a reference model for mass storage systems (Mass Storage System Reference Model/MSSRM). This reference model has significantly influenced the design of some storage systems that are in use today. The model was then revised a few times and in 1994 released as the IEEE Reference Model for Open Storage Systems Interconnection (OSSI). Finally, in the year 2000, after further revisions, the 1244 Standard for Media Management Systems was released.

This standard consists of a series of documents that describe a platform-independent, distributed management system for removable media. It also defines both the architecture for a removable media management system and its interfaces towards the outside world. The architecture makes it possible for software manufacturers to implement very scalable, distributed software systems, which serve as generic middleware between application software and library and drive hardware. The services of the system can thus be consolidated in a central component and from there made available to all applications. The specification paid particular attention to platform-independence and the heterogeneous environment of current storage networks was thus taken into account amazingly early on.

Systems that build upon this standard can manage different types of media. In addition to the typical media for the computer field such as magnetic tape, CD, DVD or optical media, audio and video tapes, files and video disks can also be managed. In actual fact, there are no assumptions about the properties of a medium in IEEE 1244-compliant systems. Their characteristic features (number of sides, number of partitions, etc.) must be defined for each media type that the system is to support. There is a series of predefined types, each with their own properties. This open design makes it possible to specify new media types and their properties at any time and to add them to the current system.

In addition to neutrality with regard to media types, the standard permits the management of both automatic and manually-operated libraries. An operator interface, which is also documented, and with which messages are sent to the appropriate administrators of a library, serves this purpose.

In the following sections we wish to examine more closely the architecture and functionality of a system based upon the IEEE standard.

9.5.1 Media management system architecture

The IEEE 1244 standard describes a client/server architecture (Figure 9.9). Applications such as network back-up systems take on the role of the client that makes use of the services of the removable media management system. The following components are individually defined:

- a media management component, which serves as a central repository for the metadata and provides mechanisms for controlling and co-ordinating the use of media, libraries and drives;

- a library manager component, which controls the library hardware on behalf of the media manager and transmits the properties and the content of the library to the media manager;

- a drive manager component, which manages the drive hardware on behalf of the media manager and transmits the properties of the drives to the media manager.

In addition, the standard defines the interfaces for the communication with these components:

- the Media Management Protocol (MMP) for the communication between application (client) and media manager (server);

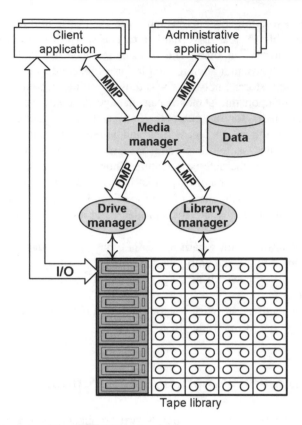

Figure 9.9   Architecture of the IEEE 1244 standard

- the Library Management Protocol (LMP) for the communication between library manager and media manager;
- the Drive Management Protocol (DMP) for the communication between drive manager and media manager.

These protocols use TCP/IP as the transport layer. As in the popular Internet applications HTTP, FTP or SMTP, commands are sent via TCP/IP in the form of text messages. These protocols can be implemented and used just as simply on different platforms.

The advantage of this approach is that the media manager can implement components as a generic application, i.e. independently of the specific library and drive hardware used. The differences, in particular with the control, are encapsulated in the library manager or drive manager for the hardware in question. For a new tape library, therefore, only a new library manager component needs to be implemented that converts the specific interface of the library into the library management protocol, so that this can be linked into an existing media manager installation.

The next sections describe how communication takes place between clients and servers and how the media manager processes the commands.

Operational characteristics of the media manager

From the point of view of the client, the media manager works as a server that waits for MMP commands, which the client sends via a TCP/IP connection. The media manager executes these commands, generates appropriate responses and sends these back to the clients. All commands are given unambiguous task identifiers. The responses contain the task identifier of the command in question.

The response takes place in two stages. First, the successful receipt of the command is acknowledged. In a second response, the application is informed whether the command has been successfully executed and which responses the system has supplied.

Example 1   An application wants to mount the volume with the name back-up-1999-12-31. To this end it, sends the following command to the media manager:

```
mount  task["1"] volname ["back-up-1999-12-31"]
       report [MOUNTLOGICAL."MountLogicalHandle"];
```

The media manager has recognized the command and accepted it for processing and therefore sends the following response:

```
response  task["1"] accepted;
```

Now the media manager will transport the cartridge containing the volume into a drive to which the application has access. Once the cartridge has been successfully inserted, a response is generated that could look like this:

```
response  task["1"] success text ["/dev/rmt0"];
```

The media manager stores all commands in a task queue until all resources required for execution are available. Once all the resources are available, the media manager removes the command from the task queue and executes it. If several commands are present that require the same resources, the media manager selects the next command to be carried out on the basis of priorities or on a first come, first served basis. All other commands remain in the task queue until the resources in question become free again. In this manner, libraries, drives and also cartridges can be shared.

Commands that are in the task queue can be removed again using the Cancel command.

Operational characteristics of the library and drive managers

The library manager receives the media manager's commands via the library management protocol (LMP) and converts these into the specific commands for the hardware in question. From the point of view of the media manager, a unified abstract interface that conceals the properties of the hardware in question thus exists for all libraries. New hardware can thus be integrated into the management system using a suitable library manager, without having to make changes to the whole system.

Accordingly, drive manager implementations of the abstract drive management protocol (DMP) are interfaces for a certain drive hardware. However, drive management must also take into account the specific properties of the various client platforms upon which the applications that want to use the media management system run. If such an application is running on a UNIX-compatible platform, the drive manager must provide the corresponding names of a device special file for access to the drive. Under Windows, such a drive manager must supply a windows-specific file name, such as \\.\TAPE0.

Privileged and non-privileged clients

The media manager carries out requests from clients that want to take advantage of the media management services. From the point of view of the media manager there are privileged and non-privileged clients:

- Non-privileged clients, such as back-up systems, can only handle objects for which they have been granted an appropriate authorization.
- Privileged clients, usually administrative applications, may perform all actions and manipulate all objects. They serve primarily to include non-privileged applications in the system and to establish suitable access controls.

9.5.2 The IEEE 1244 data model (Table 9.1)

In addition to the architecture and the logs for communication, the standard also describes a complete data model, which includes all objects, and their attributes, that are necessary for the representation of the media management system.

Objects can be provided with additional application-specific attributes. The object model can thus be dynamically and flexibly adapted to the task at hand, without changes being necessary to the underlying management system.

9.5.3 Media Management Protocol (MMP)

The media management protocol (MMP) is used by the applications to make use of the media management services of an IEEE 1244-compatible system. MMP is a text-based protocol, which exchanges messages over TCP/IP. The syntax and semantics of the individual protocol messages are specified in the MMP specification IEEE 1244.3. MMP permits applications to allocate and mount volumes, read and write metadata and to manage and share libraries and drives platform-independently. Due to the additional abstraction levels, the application is decoupled from the direct control of the hardware. Thus, applications can be developed independently of the capability of the connected hardware and can be made available to a large number of different types of removable media.

Table 9.1   The most important objects of the IEEE 1244 data model

Object	Description
APPLICATION	Authorized client application. Access control is performed on the basis of applications. User management is not part of this standard, since it is assumed that it is not individual users, but applications that already manage their users, that will use the services of the media management system.
AI	Authorized instances of a client application. All instances of an application have unrestricted access to resources that are assigned to the application.
LIBRARY	Automatic or manually operated libraries.
LM	Library managers know the details of a library. The library manager protocol serves as a hardware-independent interface between media manager and library manager.
BAY	Part of a LIBRARY (contains DRIVES and SLOTS).
SLOT	Individual storage space for CARTRIDGEs within a BAY.
SLOTGROUP	Group of SLOTS to represent a magazine, for example, within a LIBRARY.
SLOTTYPE	Valid types for SLOTs, for example 'LTO', 'DL-Tor3480', 'QIC' or 'CDROM'.
DRIVE	Drives, which can accept CARTRIDGEs for writing or reading.
DRIVEGROUP	Groups of drives.
DRIVEGROUPAPPLICATION	This object makes it possible for applications to access drives in a DRIVEGROUP. This connection can be assigned a priority so that several DRIVEGROUPs with different priorities are available. The media manager selects a suitable drive according to priority.
DM	Drive manager. Drive managers know the details of a drive and make this available to the media manager. The drive manager protocol serves as a hardware-independent interface between media manager and drive manager.
CARTRIDGE	Removable data carrier; media.
CARTRIDGEGROUP	Group of CARTRIDGEs.
CARTRIDGEGROUPAPPLICATION	This object makes it possible for applications to access CARTRIDGEs in a CARTRIDGEGROUP. This connection can be assigned a priority so that several CARTRIDGEGROUPs with different priorities are available. The media manager selects a suitable CARTRIDGE according to priority in order to allocate a VOLUME, if no further entries are made.

(continued overleaf)

Table 9.1   (*continued*)

Object	Description
CARTRIDGETYPE	Valid types for CARTRIDGEs are for example 'LTO-1', 'LTO-2' or '3592'.
SIDE	CARTRIDGEs can have more than one SIDE, for example magneto-optical disks.
PARTITION	SIDEs can be divided into several separately allocable partitions.
VOLUME	Logical unit with a name to which an application connects an allocated partition.
MOUNTLOGICAL	VOLUMEs currently being accessed.
DRIVECARTRIDGEACCESS	Object for the storage of all accesses to cartridges and drives. Contains time, duration and errors of the accesses. Can be used for the production of error statistics.
SESSION	Describes an existing connection of an application to the media management system.
TASK	Commands, that are currently waiting for the resources to become available again.
MESSAGE	Operator or error message of the system.
REQUEST	Request of an operator.

As already mentioned, MMP, as well as the drive and library management protocol, work asynchronously. An application sends a command and first of all receives the response that the command has been accepted and passed on for processing. Once the application has received this response it can transmit further commands. Commands must have a task identifier so that the system responses can be appropriately assigned.

Example 2   An application wants to mount an LTO cartridge. To this end, it sends the following command to the media manager:

```
mount task["1"]
      match[streq(CartridgeType."CartridgeTypeName" "LTO"]
      report[MOUNTLOGICAL."MountLogicalHandle"];
```

The media manager has recognized the command and accepted it for processing. It therefore sends the following response:

```
response  task["1"] accepted;
```

Now the application can send a further command. For example, a list of the names of all drives that are not loaded can be requested:

```
show   task["2"] report[DRIVE."DriveName"]
       match[streq(DRIVE."DriveStateHard" "unloaded")];
```

The media manager has recognized the command and accepted it for processing. Therefore, it sends the following response:

```
response  task["2"] accepted;
```

Since the mount command takes quite some time, the show command may be carried out first. A response could look like this:

```
response  task["2"] success text  ["LTO-DRIVE-3"
                                    "LTO-DRIVE-7"
                                    "LTO-DRIVE-8"];
```

After a while, all resources for the mount command are available. The media manager instructs the responsible library manager to transport the cartridge, upon which the volume is located, into the appropriate drive. Then the responsible drive manager is requested to load the cartridge and generate an access handle. The application then receives this MountLogical Handle with which it can access the volume:

```
response  task["1"] success text["/dev/tape/LTO123"];
```

The application-specific attribute color of the drive LTO123 should be set to the value red. If this attribute is not available for the drive is it will be dynamically generated. To this end the application sends a further command containing another task identifier, without having waited for the successful performance of the first command:

```
attribute  task["3"] set[DRIVE."Color" "red"];
           match[streq(DRIVE."DriveName" "LTO123")];
```

Due to the property of being able to add any desired optional attributes, manufacturer- and application-specific properties of an object can be modelled very well. For example, a back-up system could set a list of all files on the cartridge as an attribute or a video rental, the number of the customer who last rented the video cassette (cartridge).

The media manager has also recognized this command and accepted it for processing and therefore sends the following response:

```
response  task["3"] accepted;
```

The command has been successfully processed, therefore the media manager sends this response back to the application:

```
response  task["3"] success;
```

For reporting, the MMP includes the show command. Together with a match clause, a powerful interrogation language can thus be implemented.

Example 3   List of all cartridge labels that have been mounted in the drive LTO123 since the beginning of 2003 and in which an error has occurred in this time. The list should be sorted by the number of write errors in descending order:

```
show  task["1"]
      report [DRIVEACARTRIDGEACCESS."CartridgePCL"]
      match[and(streq(DRIVECARTRIDGEACCESS."DriveName"  "LTO123")
              strgt(DRIVECARTRIDGEACCESS."TimeUnmount"
                    "2003 01 01 00 00 00 000")
  or(numgt(DRIVECARTRIDGEACCESS."HardReadErrorCount"  "0")
     numgt(DRIVECARTRIDGEACCESS."SoftReadErrorCount"  "0")
     numgt(DRIVECARTRIDGEACCESS."HardWriteErrorCount"  "0")
     numgt(DRIVECARTRIDGEACCESS."SoftWriteErrorCount"  "0")))]
order[numhilo(DRIVECARTRIDGEACCESS."HardWriteErrorCount")];
```

9.5.4   Library and drive management protocol (LMP/DMP)

These protocols are used by a media manager in order to communicate with library and
drive managers. Like MMP, these protocols use text messages that are exchanged over
TCP/IP. The specified commands, however, serve for the control of the hardware, for
example the transport of a tape (LMP) or the insertion of a tape into a drive (DMP).
Syntax and semantics of the individual LMP messages are set down in the IEEE 1244.5
specification. The DMP messages are specified in IEEE 1244.4.

9.6   SUMMARY

Strong growth in data quantities and increasing cartridge quantities call for improved
solutions for the efficient management of removable media in the storage network. The
requirements of such a system in the storage network are largely comparable with the
requirements that are also made of disk subsystems. However, due to the special properties
of removable media, such as the separate storage of medium and drive, there are additional
problems to master, which we have described individually and will list here once again:

- Centralized administration and control of all resources such as media, drives and
  libraries, make efficient management significantly easier.
- Intelligent sharing of libraries, drives and scratch pools makes the efficient use of the
  available resources easier and can be used to implement highly available solutions
  (cross-library drive and scratch pools).
- Authentication and authorization of users/applications facilitate adherence to data protection guidelines and the allocation of resources.
- Mount request management, including request queuing, increases the robustness of the
  system as a whole and permits prioritized processing and allocation of mount requests
  to drives.
- Uninterrupted tracking of the media ensures that at every point in time the location of
  a medium is known and thus protected against data loss.

- Automated life cycle management of the data carriers greatly frees up the administrators from tasks that occur repeatedly.

- Full integration of online and offline locations permits security concepts in which the data carriers must be stored in a well-protected location.

- Monitoring provides the automatic recording and processing of errors in the system. Rule-based mechanisms can perform suitable actions for error rectification or can signal manual intervention.

Unfortunately, there are currently still no cross-manufacturer and cross-application management layers and interfaces for removable media. As a result, each manufacturer puts their own proprietary system, which is often part of a back-up solution, on the market. Some of these systems are not capable of using several instances of the connected hardware co-operatively and thus do not fully exploit the potential of resource sharing in storage networks. Other solutions are not very scalable, which is why they can only sensibly be used up to a certain number of drives or cartridges. With different applications from several manufacturers, a co-operative use of all removable media resources is currently almost impossible.

The IEEE 1244 Standard for Media Management Systems provides the basis for effectively managing removable media in the storage network and intelligently sharing resources and thus describes the architecture for an asymmetrical virtualization of removable media. Due to the use of text-based protocols over TCP/IP, a lot of platforms can easily make use of the services of a system based upon this standard, in a similar way to the widespread Internet protocol (SMTP, HTTP).

The standard addresses the most important problems in dealing with removable media in the storage network and provides tools for the solution. Of particular importance is the fact that not only not only interfaces are defined for applications (media management protocol (MMP)) and hardware (library management protocol (LMP) and drive management protocol (DMP)) defined, but an architecture is also described that fits in optimally with these interfaces.

10

The SNIA Shared Storage Model

The fact that there is a lack of any unified terminology for the description of storage architectures has already become apparent at several points in previous chapters. There are thus numerous components in a storage network which, although they do the same thing, are called by different names. Conversely, there are many systems with the same name, but fundamentally different functions.

A notable example is the term 'data mover' relating to server-free back-up (Section 7.8.1) in storage networks. When this term is used it is always necessary to check whether the component in question is one that functions in the sense of the 3rd-party SCSI Copy Command for, for example, a software component of back-up software on a special server, which implements the server-free back-up without 3rd-party SCSI.

This example shows that the type of product being offered by a manufacturer and the functions that the customer can ultimately expect from this product are often unclear. This makes it difficult for customers to compare the products of individual manufacturers and find out the differences between the alternatives on offer. There is no unified model for this with clearly defined descriptive terminology.

For this reason, in 2001 the Technical Council of the Storage Networking Industry Association (SNIA) introduced the so-called Shared Storage Model in order to unify the terminology and descriptive models used by the storage network industry. Ultimately, the SNIA wants to use the SNIA Shared Storage Model to establish a reference model, which will have the same importance for storage architectures as the seven-tier OSI model has for computer networks.

In this chapter, we would first like to introduce the disk-based Shared Storage Model (Section 10.1) and then show, based upon examples (Section 10.2), how the model can be

Storage Networks Explained   U. Troppens R. Erkens W. Müller
© 2004 John Wiley & Sons, Ltd   ISBN: 0-470-86182-7

used for the description of typical disk storage architectures. In Section 10.3 we introduce the extension of the SNIA model to the description of tape functions. We then discuss examples of tape-based back-up architectures (Section 10.4). Whilst describing the SNIA Shared Storage Model we often refer to text positions in this book where the subject in question is discussed in detail, which means that this chapter also serves as a summary of the entire book.

10.1   THE MODEL

In this book we have spoken in detail about the advantages of the storage-centric architecture in relation to the server-centric architecture. The SNIA sees its main task as being to communicate this paradigm shift and to provide a forum for manufacturers and developers so that they can work together to meet the challenges and solve the problems in this field. In the long run, an additional reason for the development of the Shared Storage Model by SNIA was the creation of a common basis for communication between the manufacturers who use the SNIA as a platform for the exchange of ideas with other manufacturers. Storage-centric IT architectures are called shared storage environments by the SNIA. We will use both terms in the following.

First of all, we will describe the functional approach of the SNIA model (Section 10.1.1) and the SNIA conventions for graphical representation (Section 10.1.2). We will then consider the model (Section 10.1.3), its components (Section 10.1.4) and the layers 'file/record layer' and 'block layer' in detail (Section 10.1.5 to Section 10.1.8). Then we will introduce the definitions and representation of concepts from the SNIA model, such as access paths (Section 10.1.9), caching (Section 10.1.10), access control (Section 10.1.11), clustering (Section 10.1.12), data (Section 10.1.13) and resource and data sharing (Section 10.1.14). Finally, we will take a look at the service subsystem (Section 10.1.15).

10.1.1   The functional approach

The SNIA Shared Storage Model first of all describes functions that have to be provided in a storage-centric IT architecture. This includes, for example, the block layer or the file/record layer. The SNIA model describes both the tasks of the individual functions and also their interaction. Furthermore, it introduces components such as server ('host computer') and storage networks ('interconnection network').

Due to the separation of functions and components, the SNIA Shared Storage Model is suitable for the description of various architectures, specific products and concrete installations. The fundamental structures, such as the functions and services of a shared storage environment, are highlighted. In this manner, functional responsibilities can be assigned to individual components and the relationships between control and data flows in the storage network worked out. At the same time, the preconditions for interoperability between individual components and the type of interoperability can be identified. In addition to providing a clear terminology for the elementary concepts, the model should be simple to use and, at the same time, extensive enough to cover a large number of possible storage network configurations.

The model itself describes, on the basis of examples, possible practicable storage architectures and their advantages and disadvantages. We will discuss these in Section 10.2 without evaluating them or showing any preference for specific architectures. Within the model definition, however, only a few selected examples will be discussed in order to highlight how the model can be applied for the description of storage-centred environments and further used.

10.1.2   Graphical representations

The SNIA Shared Storage Model further defines how storage architectures can be graphically illustrated. Physical components are always represented as three-dimensional objects, whilst functional units should be drawn in two-dimensional form. The model itself also defines various colours for the representation of individual component classes. In the black and white format of the book, we have imitated these using shades of grey. A coloured version of the illustrations to this chapter can be found on our home page http://www.storage-explained.com. Thick lines in the model represent the data transfer, whereas thin lines represent the metadata flow between the components.

10.1.3   An elementary overview

The SNIA Shared Storage Model first of all defines four elementary parts of a shared storage environment (Figure 10.1):

1. File/record layer
   The file/record layer is made up of database and file system.

2. Block layer
   The block layer encompasses the storage devices and the block aggregation. The SNIA Shared Storage Model uses the term 'aggregation' instead of the often ambiguously used term 'storage virtualization'. In Chapter 5, however, we used the term 'storage virtualization' to mean the same thing as 'aggregation' in the SNIA model, in order to avoid ambiguity.

3. Services subsystem
   The functions for the management of the other components are defined in the services subsystem.

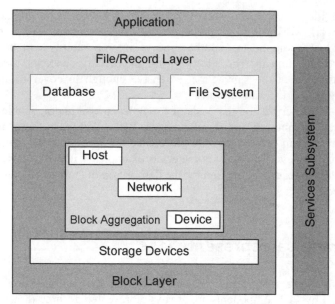

Figure 10.1 The main components of the SNIA Shared Storage Model are the file/record layer, the block layer and the services subsystem. Applications are viewed as users of the model

4. Applications
   Applications are not discussed further by the model. They will be viewed as users of the model in the widest sense.

10.1.4   The components

The SNIA Shared Storage Model defines the following components:

- Interconnection network
  The interconnection network represents the storage network, i.e. the infrastructure, that connects the individual elements of a shared storage environment with one another. The interconnection network can be used exclusively for storage access, but it can also be used for other communication services. Our definition of a storage network (Section 1.2) is thus narrower than the definition of the interconnection network in the SNIA model.
     The network must always provide a high-performance and easily scaleable connection for the shared storage environment. In this context, the structure of the interconnection network – for example redundant data paths between two components to increase fault-tolerance – remains just as open as the network techniques used. It is therefore a prerequisite of the model that the components of the shared storage environment are connected over a network without any definite communication protocols or transmission techniques being specified.

In actual architectures or installations, Fibre Channel, Fast Ethernet, Gigabit Ethernet, InfiniBand and many other transmission techniques are used (Chapter 3). Communication protocols such as SCSI, Fibre Channel FCP, TCP/IP, RDMA, CIFS or NFS are based upon these.

• Host computer
Host computer is the term used for computer systems that draw at least some of their storage from the shared storage environment. According to SNIA, these systems were often omitted from classical descriptive approaches and not viewed as part of the environment. The SNIA shared storage model, however, views these systems as part of the entire shared storage environment because storage-related functions can be implemented on them.

Host computers are connected to the storage network via host bus adapters or network cards, which are operated by means of their own drivers and software. Drivers and software are thus taken into account in the SNIA Shared Storage Model. Host computers can be operated fully independently of one another or they can work on the resources of the storage network in a compound, for example, a cluster (Section 6.4.1).

• Physical storage resource
All further elements that are connected to the storage network and are not host computers are known by the term 'physical storage resource'. This includes simple hard disk drives, disk arrays, disk subsystems and controllers plus tape drives and tape libraries. Physical storage resources are protected against failures by means of redundant data paths (Section 6.3.1), replication functions such as snapshots and mirroring (Section 2.7) and RAID (Section 2.5).

• Storage device
A storage device is a special physical storage resource that stores data.

• Logical storage resource
The term 'logical storage resource' is used to mean services or abstract compositions of physical storage resources, storage management functions or a combination of these. Typical examples are volumes, files and data movers.

• Storage management functions
The term 'storage management function' is used to mean the class of services that monitor and check (Chapter 8) the shared storage environment or implement logical storage resources. These functions are typically implemented by software on physical storage resources or host computers.

10.1.5 The layers

The SNIA Shared Storage Model defines four layers (Figure 10.2):

I. Storage devices
II. Block aggregation layer

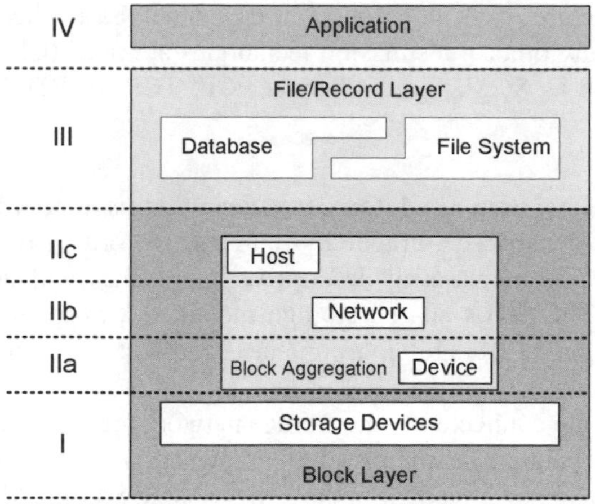

Figure 10.2 The SNIA Shared Storage Model defines four layers

III. File/record layer
  IIIb. Database
  IIIa. File system
IV Applications

Applications are viewed as users of the model and are thus not described in the model. They are, however, implemented as a layer in order to illustrate the point in the model to which they are linked. In the following we'll consider the file/record layer (Section 10.1.6), the block layer (Section 10.1.7) and the combination of both (Section 10.1.8) in detail.

10.1.6 The file/record layer

The file/record layer maps database records and files on the block-oriented volume of the storage devices. Files are made up of several bytes and are therefore viewed as byte vectors in the SNIA model. Typically, file systems or database management systems take over these functions. They operate directories of the files or records, check the access, allocate storage space and cache the data (Chapter 4). The file/record layer thus works on volumes that are provided to it from the block layer below. Volumes themselves consist of several arranged blocks, so-called block vectors. Database systems map one or more records, so-called tuple of records, onto volumes via tables and table spaces:

$$\text{Tuple of records} \longrightarrow \text{tables} \longrightarrow \text{table spaces} \longrightarrow \text{volumes}$$

In the same way, file systems map bytes onto volumes by means of files:

$$\text{Bytes} \longrightarrow \text{files} \longrightarrow \text{volumes}$$

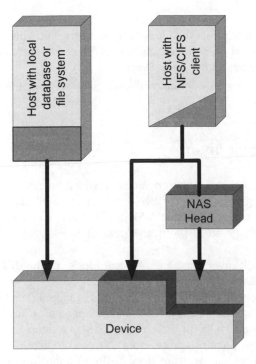

Figure 10.3 The functions of the file/record layer can be implemented exclusively on the host or distributed over a client and a server component

Some database systems can also work with files, i.e. byte vectors. In this case, block vectors are grouped into byte vectors by means of a file system – an additional abstraction level. Since an additional abstraction level costs performance, only smaller databases work in a file-oriented manner. In large databases the additional mapping layer of byte to block vectors is dispensed with for performance reasons.

The functions of the file/record layers can be implemented at various points (Figure 10.3, Section 5.6):

- Exclusively on the host
  In this case, the file/record layer is implemented entirely on the host. Databases and the host-based file systems work in this way.
- Both in the client and also on a server component
  The file/record layer can also be implemented in a distributed manner. In this case the functions are distributed over a client and a server component. The client component is realized on a host computer, whereas the server component can be realized on the following devices:
  - NAS/file server
    A NAS/file server is a specialized host computer usually with a locally connected, dedicated storage device (Section 4.2.2).

- NAS head
  A host computer that offers the file serving services, but which has access to external storage connected via a storage network. NAS heads correspond with the devices called NAS gateways in our book (Section 4.2.2).

In this case, client and server components work over network file systems such as NFS or CIFS (Section 4.2).

10.1.7 The block layer

The block layer differentiates between block aggregation and the block-based storage devices. The block aggregation in the SNIA model corresponds to our definition of the virtualization on block level (Section 5.5). SNIA thus uses the term 'block aggregation' to mean the aggregation of physical blocks or block vectors into logical blocks or block vectors.

To this end, the block layer maps the physical blocks of the disk storage devices onto logical blocks and makes these available to the higher layers in the form of volumes (block vectors). This either occurs via a direct $(1:1)$ mapping, or the physical blocks are first aggregated into logical blocks, which are then passed on to the upper layers in the form of volumes (Figure 10.4). In the case of SCSI, the storage devices of the storage device layer exist in the form of one or more so-called logical units (LU).

Further tasks of the block layer are the labelling of the logical units using so-called logical unit numbers (LUNs), caching and – increasingly in the future – access control. Block aggregation can be used for various purposes, for example:

- Volume/space management
  The typical task of a volume manager is to aggregate several small block vectors to form one large block vector. On SCSI level this means aggregating several logical units

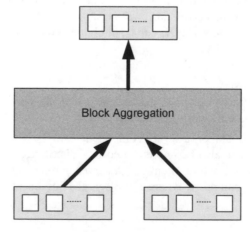

Figure 10.4 The block aggregation layer aggregates physical blocks or block vectors into logical blocks or block vectors

to form a large volume, which is passed on to the upper layers such as the file/record layer (Section 4.1.4).

- Striping
  In striping, physical blocks of different storage devices are aggregated to one volume. This increases the I/O throughput of the read and write operations, since the load is distributed over several physical storage devices (Section 2.5.1).

- Redundancy
  In order to protect against failures of physical data carriers, RAID (Section 2.5) and remote mirroring (Section 2.7.2) are used. Snapshots (instant copies) can also be used for the redundant storage of data (Section 2.7.1).

The block aggregation functions of the block layer can be realized at different points of the shared storage environment (Section 5.6):

- On the host
  Block aggregation on the host is encountered in the form of a logical volume manager software, in device drivers and in host bus adapters.

- On a component of the storage network
  The functions of the block layer can also be realized in connection devices of the storage network or in specialized servers in the network.

- In the storage device
  Most commonly, the block layer functions are implemented in the storage devices themselves, for example, in the form of RAID or volume manager functionality.

In general, various block aggregation functions can be combined at different points of the shared storage environment. In practical use, RAID may, for example, be used in the disk subsystem with additional mirroring from one disk subsystem to another via the volume manager on the host computer (Section 4.1.4). In this setup, RAID protects against the failure of physical disks of the disk subsystem, whilst the mirroring by means of the volume manager on the host protects against the complete failure of a disk subsystem. Furthermore, the performance of read operations is increased in this set-up, since the volume manager can read from both sides of the mirror (Section 2.5.2).

10.1.8 Combination of the block and file/record layers

Figure 10.5 shows how block and file/record layer can be combined and represented in the SNIA shared storage model:

- Direct attachment
  The left-hand column in the figure shows storage connected directly to the server, as is normally the case in a server-centric IT architecture (Section 1.1).

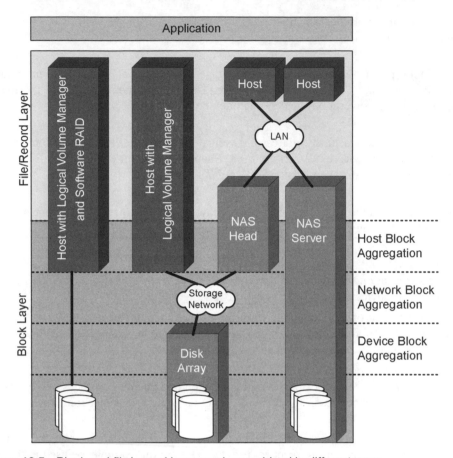

Figure 10.5 Block and file/record layer can be combined in different ways

- Storage network attachment
  In the second column we see how a disk array is normally connected via a storage network in a storage-centric IT architecture, so that it can be accessed by several host computers (Section 1.2).

- NAS head (NAS gateway)
  The third column illustrates how a NAS head is integrated into a storage network between SAN storage and a host computer connected via LAN.

- NAS server
  The right-hand column shows the function of a NAS server with its own dedicated storage in the SNIA Shared Storage Model.

10.1.9 Access paths

Read and write operations of a component on a storage device are called access paths in the SNIA Shared Storage Model. An access path is descriptively defined as the list

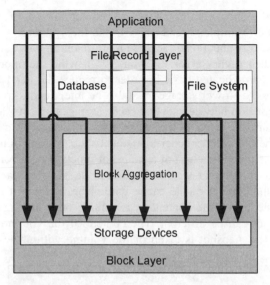

Figure 10.6   In the SNIA Shared Storage Model, applications can access the storage devices via eight possible access paths

of components that are run through by read and write operations to the storage devices and responses to them. If we exclude cyclical access paths, then a total of eight possible access paths from applications to the storage devices can be identified in the SNIA Shared Storage Model (Figure 10.6):

1. Direct access to a storage device.
2. Direct access to a storage device via a block aggregation function.
3. Indirect access via a database system.
4. Indirect access via a database system based upon a block aggregation function.
5. Indirect access via a database system based upon a file system.
6. Indirect access via a database system based upon a file system, which is itself based upon a block aggregation function.
7. Indirect access via a file system.
8. Indirect access via a file system based upon a block aggregation function.

10.1.10   Caching

Caching is the method of shortening the access path of an application – i.e. the number of the components to be passed through – to frequently used data on a storage device. To this end, the data accesses to the slower storage devices are buffered in a faster cache storage. Most components of a shared storage environment can have a cache. The cache can be implemented within the file/record layer, within the block layer or in both.

In practice, several caches working simultaneously on different levels and components are generally used. For example, a read cache in the file system may be combined with a write cache on a disk array and a read cache with pre-fetching on a hard disk (Figure 10.7). In addition, a so-called cache-server (Section 5.7.2), which temporarily stores data for other components on a dedicated basis in order to reduce the need for network capacity or to accelerate access to slower storage, can also be integrated into the storage network.

However, the interaction between several cache storages on several components means that consideration must be given to the consistency of data. The more components that use cache storage, the more dependencies arise between the functions of individual components. A classic example is the use of a snapshot function on a component in the block layer, whilst another component stores the data in question to cache in the file/record layer. In this case, the content of the cache within the file/record layer, which we will assume to be consistent, and the content of a volume on a disk array that is a component of the block layer can be different. The content of the volume on the array is thus inconsistent. Now, if a snapshot is taken of the volume within the disk array, a virtual

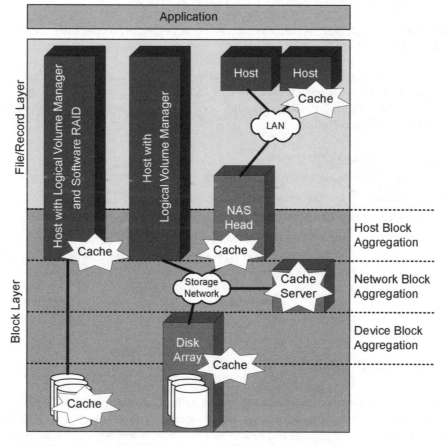

Figure 10.7 Caching functions can be implemented at different levels and at different components of a shared storage environment

copy is obtained of an inconsistent state of the data. The copy is thus unusable. Therefore, before the snapshot is made within the block layer, the cache in the file/record layer on the physical volume must be destaged, so that it can receive a consistent copy later.

10.1.11 Access control

Access control is the name for the technique that arranges the access to data of the shared storage environment. The term access control should thus be clearly differentiated from the term access path, since the mere existence of an access path does not include the right to access. Access control has the following main objectives:

- Authentication
  Authentication establishes the identity of the source of an access.
- Authorization
  Authorization grants or refuses actions to resources.
- Data protection
  Data protection guarantees that data may only be viewed by authorized persons.

All access control mechanisms ultimately use a form of secure channel between the data on the storage device and the source of an access. In its simplest form, this can be a check to establish whether a certain host is permitted to have access to a specific storage device.

Access control can, however, also be achieved by complicated cryptographic procedures, which are secure against the most common external attacks. When establishing a control mechanism it is always necessary to trade off the necessary protection and efficiency against complexity and performance sacrifices.

In server-centric IT architectures, storage devices are protected by the guidelines on the host computers and by simple physical measures. In a storage network, the storage devices, the network and the network components themselves must be protected against unauthorized access, since in theory they can be accessed from all host computers. Access control becomes increasingly important in a shared storage environment as the number of components used, the diversity of heterogeneous hosts and the distance between the individual devices rise.

Access controls can be established at the following points of a shared storage environment:

- On the host
  In shared storage environments, access controls comparable with those in server-centric environments can be established at host level. The disadvantage of this approach is, however, that the access rights have to be set on all host computers. Mechanisms that reduce the amount of work by the use of central instances for the allocation and distribution of rights must be suitably protected against unauthorized access. Database systems and file systems can be protected in this manner. Suitable mechanisms for the block layer are currently being planned. The use of encryption technology for the host's network protocol stack is in conflict with performance requirements. Suitable

offload engines, which process the protocol stack on the host bus adapter themselves, are available for some protocols.

- In the storage network
  Security within the storage network is achieved in Fibre Channel SANs by zoning and virtual storage networks (Virtual SAN (VSAN), Section 3.4.2) and in Ethernet-based storage networks by so-called virtual LANs (VLAN). This is always understood to be the subdivision of a network into virtual subnetworks, which permit communication between a number of host ports and certain storage device ports. These guidelines can, however, also be defined on finer structures than ports.

- On the storage device
  The normal access control procedure on SAN storage devices is the so-called LUN masking, in which the LUNs that are visible to a host are restricted. Thus, the computer sees only those LUNs that have been assigned to it by the storage device (Section 2.7.3).

10.1.12 Clustering

A cluster is defined in the SNIA Shared Storage Model as a combination of resources with the objective of increasing scalability, availability and management within the shared storage environment (Section 6.4.1). The individual nodes of the cluster can share their resources via distributed volume managers (multi-node LVM) and cluster file systems (Figure 10.8, Section 4.3).

10.1.13 Storage, data and information

The SNIA Shared Storage Model differentiates strictly between storage, data and information. Storage is space – so-called containers – provided by storage units, on which the data is stored. The bytes stored in containers on the storage units are called data. Information is the meaning – the semantics – of the data. The SNIA Shared Storage Model names the following examples in which data–container relationships arise (Table 10.1).

10.1.14 Resource and data sharing

In a shared storage environment, in which the storage devices are connected to the host via a storage network, every host can access every storage device and the data stored upon it (Section 1.2). This sharing is called resource sharing or data sharing in the SNIA model, depending upon the level at which the sharing takes place (Figure 10.9).

If exclusively the storage systems – and not their data content – are shared, then we talk of resource sharing. This is found in the physical resources, such as disk subsystems and tape libraries, but also within the network.

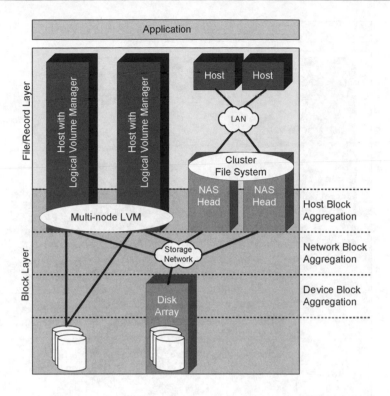

Figure 10.8 Nodes of a cluster share resources via distributed volume managers or cluster file systems

Table 10.1 Data–container relationships

Relationship	Role	Remark
User	Data	Inputs via keyboard
Application	Container	Input buffer
User	Data	Input buffer file
File system	Container	Byte vector
File system	Data	A file
Volume manager	Container	Blocks of a volume
Volume manager	Data	Mirrored stripe set
Disk array	Container	Blocks of a logical unit

Data sharing denotes the sharing of data between different hosts. Data sharing is significantly more difficult to implement, since the shared data must always be kept consistent, particularly when distributed caching is used.

Heterogeneous environments also require additional conversion steps in order to convert the data into a format that the host can understand. Protocols such as NFS or

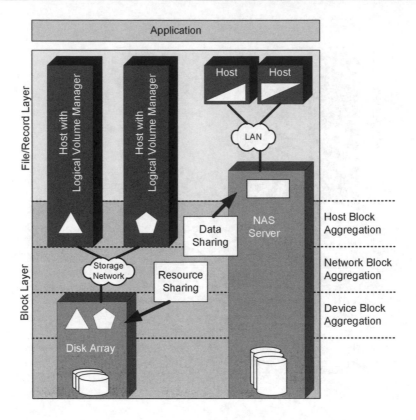

Figure 10.9 In resource sharing, hosts share the physical resources – in this case a disk array – which make a volume available to each host. In data sharing, hosts access the same data – in this case the NAS server and its data

CIFS are used in the more frequently used data sharing within the file/record layers (Section 4.2).

For data sharing in the block layer, server clusters with shared disk file systems or parallel databases are used (Section 4.3, Section 6.2.3).

10.1.15   The service subsystem

Up to now we have concerned ourselves with the concepts within the layers of the SNIA Shared Storage Model. Let us now consider the service subsystem (Figure 10.10). Within the service subsystem we find the management tasks which occur in a shared storage environment and which we have, for the most part, already discussed in Chapter 8.

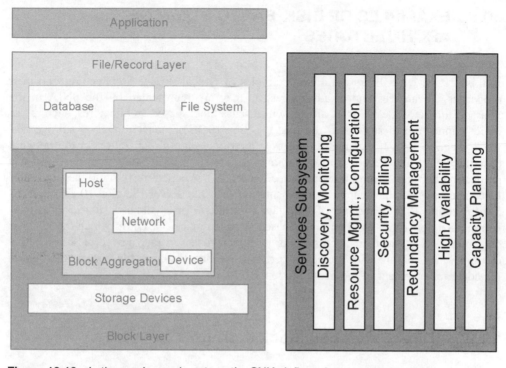

Figure 10.10   In the services subsystem, the SNIA defines the management tasks in a shared storage environment

In this connection, the SNIA Technical Council mention:

- discovery and monitoring
- resource management
- configuration
- security
- billing (charge-back)
- redundancy management, for example, by network back-up
- high availability
- capacity planning.

The individual subjects are not yet dealt with in more detail in the SNIA Shared Storage Model, since the required definitions, specifications and interfaces are still being developed (Section 8.7.3). At this point we expressly refer once again to the check list in the Appendix B, which reflects a cross-section of the questions that crop up here.

10.2 EXAMPLES OF DISK-BASED STORAGE ARCHITECTURES

In this section we will present a few examples of typical storage architectures and their properties, advantages and disadvantages, as they are represented by the SNIA in the Shared Storage Model. First of all, we will discuss block-based architectures, such as the direct connection of storage to the host (Section 10.2.1), connection via a storage network (Section 10.2.2), symmetric and asymmetric storage virtualization in the network (Section 10.2.3 and Section 10.2.4) and a multi-site architecture such as is used for data replication between several locations (Section 10.2.5). We then move on to the file/record layer and consider the graphical representation of a file server (Section 10.2.6), a NAS head (Section 10.2.7), the use of metadata controllers for asymmetric file level virtualization (Section 10.2.8) and an object-based storage device (OSD), in which the position data of the files and their access rights is moved to a separate device, a solution that combines file sharing with increased performance due to direct file access and central metadata management of the files (Section 10.2.9).

10.2.1 Direct attached block storage

Figure 10.11 shows the direct connection from storage to the host in a server-centric architecture. The following properties are characteristic of this structure:

- No connection devices, such as switches or hubs, are needed.
- The host generally communicates with the storage device via a protocol on block level.
- Block aggregation functions are possible both in the disk subsystem and on the host.

10.2.2 Storage network attached block storage

The connection from storage to host via a storage network can be represented in the Shared Storage Model as shown in Figure 10.12. In this case:

- Several hosts share several storage devices.
- Block-oriented protocols are generally used.
- Block aggregation can be used in the host, in the network and in the storage device.

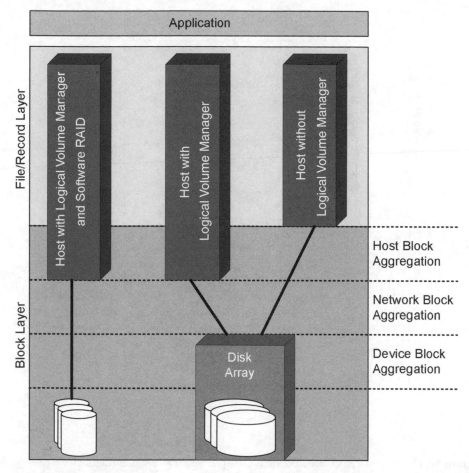

Figure 10.11 In direct attachment, hosts are connected to storage devices directly without connection devices such as switches or hubs. Joint use of data or resources is not possible without additional software

10.2.3 Block storage aggregation in a storage device: SAN appliance

Block aggregation can also be implemented in a specialized device or server of the storage network in the data path between hosts and storage devices, as in the symmetric storage virtualization (Figure 10.13, Section 5.7.1). In this approach:

- Several hosts and storage devices are connected via a storage network.
- A device or a dedicated server – a so-called SAN appliance – is placed in the data path between hosts and storage devices to perform block aggregation, and data and metadata traffic flows through this.

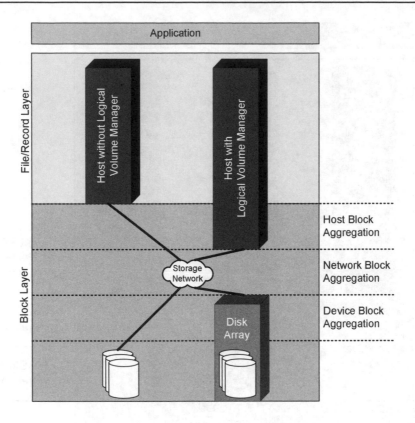

Figure 10.12   In storage connected via a storage network, several hosts share the storage devices, which are accessed via block-oriented protocols

10.2.4   Network attached block storage with metadata server: asymmetric block services

The asymmetric block services architecture is identical to the asymmetric storage virtualization approach (Figure 10.14, Section 5.7.2):

- Several hosts and storage devices are connected over a storage network.
- Host and storage devices communicate with each other over a protocol on block level.
- The data flows directly between hosts and storage devices.
- A metadata server outside the data path holds the information regarding the position of the data on the storage devices and maps between logical and physical blocks.

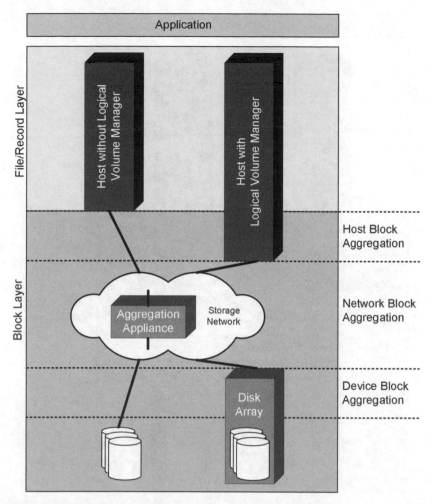

Figure 10.13 In block aggregation on a specialized device or server in the storage network, a SAN appliance maps between logical and physical blocks in the data path in the same way as symmetric virtualization

10.2.5 Multi-site block storage

Figure 10.15 shows how data replication between two locations can be implemented by means of WAN techniques. The data can be replicated on different layers of the model using different protocols:

- between volume managers on the host;
- between specialized devices in the storage network; or
- between storage systems, for example disk subsystems.

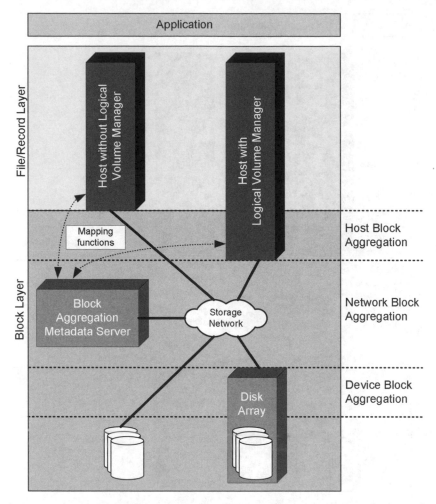

Figure 10.14 In an asymmetric block services architecture a metadata server outside the data path performs the mapping of logical to physical blocks, whilst the data flows directly between hosts and storage devices

If the two locations use different network types or protocols, additional converters can be installed for translation.

10.2.6 File server

A file server (Section 4.2) can be represented as shown in Figure 10.16. The following points are characteristic of a file server:

- the combination of server and normally local, dedicated storage;
- file sharing protocols for the host access;

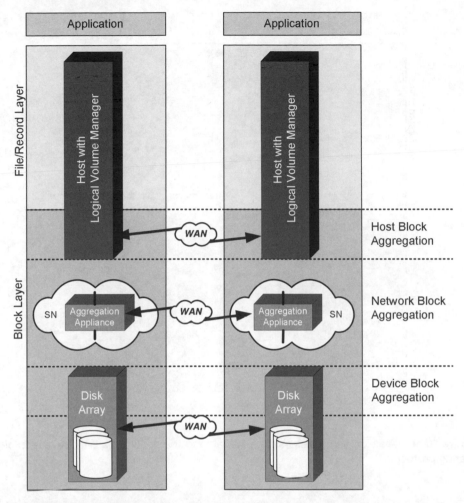

Figure 10.15   Data replication between two locations by means of WAN technology can take place at host level between volume managers, at network level between specialized devices, or at storage device level between disk arrays

- normally the use of a network, for example, a LAN, that is not specialized to the storage traffic;
- optionally, a private storage network can also be used for the control of the dedicated storage.

10.2.7   File server controller: NAS heads

In contrast to file servers, NAS heads (Figure 10.17, Section 4.2.2) have the following properties:

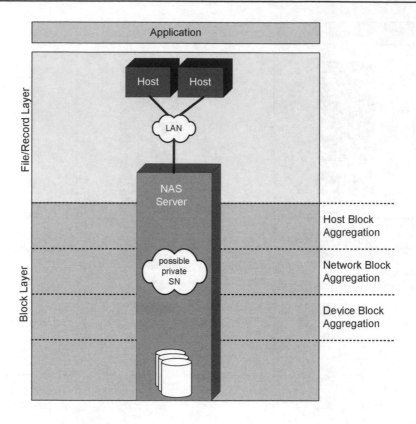

Figure 10.16   A file server makes storage available to the hosts via a LAN by means of file sharing protocols

- They separate storage devices from the controller on the file/record layer, via which the hosts access.

- Hosts and NAS heads communicate over a file-oriented protocol.

- The hosts use a network for this that is generally not designed for pure storage traffic, for example a LAN.

- When communicating downwards to the storage devices, the NAS head uses a block-oriented protocol.

NAS heads have the advantage over file servers that they can share the storage systems with other hosts that access them directly. This makes it possible for both file and block services to be offered by the same physical resources at the same time. In this manner, IT architectures can be designed more flexibly, which in turn has a positive effect upon scalability.

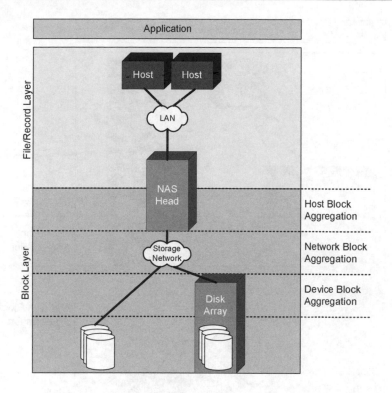

Figure 10.17   A NAS head separates the storage devices from the hosts and thereby achieves better scalability and a more efficient use of resources

10.2.8   Asymmetric file services: NAS/file server metadata manager

A file server metadata manager (Figure 10.18) works in the same way as asymmetric storage virtualization on file level (Section 5.7.2):

- Hosts and storage devices are connected via a storage network.
- A metadata manager positioned outside the data path stores all file position data, i.e. metadata, and makes this available to the hosts upon request.
- Hosts and metadata manager communicate over an expanded file-oriented protocol.
- The actual user data then flows directly between hosts and storage devices by means of a block-oriented protocol.

This approach offers the advantages of fast, direct communication between host and storage devices, whilst at the same time offering the advantages of data sharing on

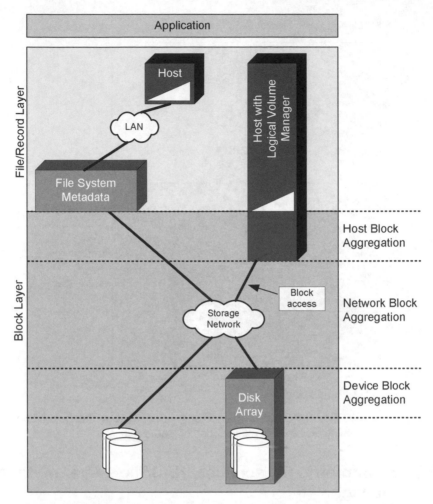

Figure 10.18 A file server metadata manager holds all position data of the files on the storage devices and makes this available to the hosts upon request. Then the hosts can exchange their useful data with the storage devices directly over the storage network. In addition, a metadata manager can offer classical file sharing services in a LAN

file level. In addition, in this solution the classic file sharing services can be offered in a LAN over the metadata manager.

10.2.9   Object-based storage device (OSD)

The SNIA Shared Storage Model defines the so-called object-based storage device (OSD). The idea behind this architecture is to move the position data of the files and the access rights to a separate OSD. OSD offers the same advantages as a file sharing solution, combined with increased performance due to direct access to the storage by the hosts, and central metadata management of the files. The OSD approach functions as follows (Figure 10.19):

- An OSD device exports a large number of byte vectors instead of the LUNs used in block-oriented storage devices. Generally, a byte vector corresponds to a single file.
- A separate OSD metadata manager authenticates the hosts and manages and checks the access rights to the byte vectors. It also provides appropriate interfaces for the hosts.
- After authentication and clearance for access by the OSD metadata manager, the hosts access the OSD device directly via a file-oriented protocol. This generally takes place via a LAN, i.e. a network that is not specialized for storage traffic.

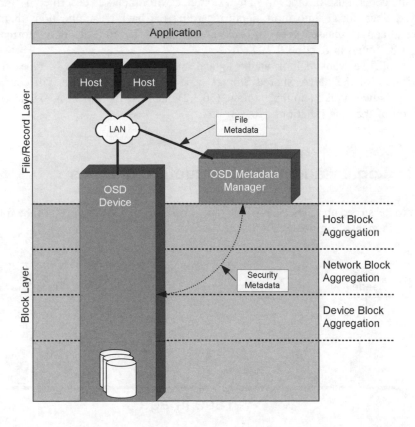

Figure 10.19 Object-based storage devices offer file sharing and facilitate direct I/O between hosts and storage. A metadata manager authenticates the hosts and controls access

10.3   EXTENSION OF THE SNIA SHARED STORAGE MODEL TO TAPE FUNCTIONS

The SNIA Shared Storage Model described previously concentrates upon the modelling of disk-based storage architectures. In a supplement to the original model, the SNIA Technical Council defines the necessary extensions for the description of tape functions and back-up architectures.

The SNIA restricts itself to the description of tape functions in the Open Systems environment, since the use of tapes in the mainframe environment is very difficult to model and differs fundamentally from the Open Systems environment. In the Open Systems field, tapes are used almost exclusively for back-up purposes, whereas in the field of mainframes tapes are used much more diversely. Therefore, the extension of the SNIA model concerns itself solely with the use of tape in back-up architectures.

Only the general use of tapes in shared storage environments is described in the model. The SNIA does not go into more depth regarding the back-up applications themselves. We have already discussed network back-up in Chapter 7. More detailed information on tapes can be found in Section 9.2.1.

First of all, we want to look at the logical and physical structure of tapes from the point of view of the SNIA Shared Storage Model (10.3.1). Then we will consider the differences between disk and tape storage (10.3.2) and how the model is extended for the description of the tape functions (10.3.3).

10.3.1   Logical and physical structure of tapes

Information is stored on tapes in so-called tape images, which are made up of the following logical components (Figure 10.20):

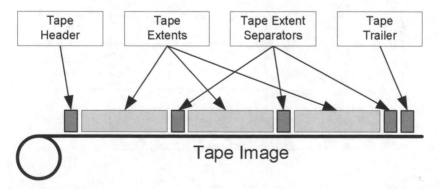

Figure 10.20   Logically, a tape image is made up of tape extents and tape extent separators. A tape header and trailer may optionally mark the start and end of a tape image respectively

- Tape extent
  A tape extent is a sequence of blocks upon the tape. A tape extent is comparable with a volume in disk storage. The IEEE Standard 1244 (Section 9.5) also uses the term volume but it only allows volumes to reside exactly on one tape and not span multiple tapes.

- Tape extent separator
  The tape extent separator is a mark for the division of individual tape extents.

- Tape header
  The tape header is an optional component that marks the start of a tape.

- Tape trailer
  The tape trailer is similar to the tape header and marks the end of a tape. This, too, is an optional component.

In the same way as logical volumes of a volume manager extend over several physical disks, tape images can also be distributed over several physical tapes. Thus, there may be precisely one logical tape image on a physical tape, several logical tape images on a physical tape, or a logical tape image can be distributed over several physical tapes. So-called tape image separators are used for the subdivision of the tape images (Figure 10.21).

10.3.2 Differences between disk and tape

At first glance, disks and tapes are both made up of blocks, which are put together to form long sequences. In the case of disks these are called volumes, whilst in tapes they are called extents. The difference lies in the way in which they are accessed, with

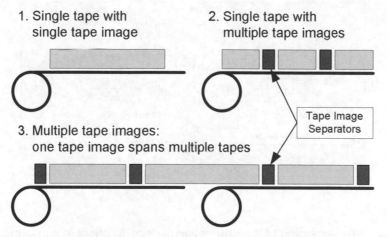

Figure 10.21 Physically, a tape image can take up on precisely one tape (1), several tape images can share a tape (2), or a tape image can extend over several tapes (3). Tape image separators separate the individual tape images

disks being designed for random access, whereas tapes can only be accessed sequentially. Consequently, disks and tapes are also used for different purposes. In the Open Systems environment, tapes are used primarily for back-up or archiving purposes. This is completely in contrast to their use in the mainframe environment, where file structures – so-called tape files – are found that are comparable to a file on a disk. There is no definition of a tape file in the Open systems environment, since several files are generally bundled to form a package, and processed in this form, during back-up and archiving. This concept is, therefore, not required here.

10.3.3   Extension of the model

The SNIA Shared Storage Model must take into account the differences in structure and application between disk and tape and also the different purposes for which they are used. To this end, the file/record layer is expanded horizontally. The block layer, which produces the random access to the storage devices in the disk model, is exchanged for a sequential access block layer for the sequential access to tapes. The model is further supplemented by the following components (Figure 10.22):

- Tape media and tape devices
  Tape media are the storage media upon which tape images are stored. A tape devices is a special physical storage resource, which can process removable tape media. This differentiation between media and devices is particularly important in the context

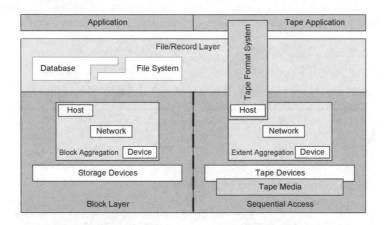

Figure 10.22   The extension of the SNIA model to tape functions expands the file/record layer in the horizontal direction, exchanges the block layer for a sequential access block layer and adds the required components of a tape architecture

of removable media management (Chapter 9). The applicable standard, IEEE 1244, denotes tape media as cartridge and tape device as drive.

- Tape applications
  The SNIA model concentrates upon the use of tapes for back-up and archiving. Special tape applications, for example, back-up software, are used for back-up. This software can deal with the special properties of tapes.

- Tape format system
  In the tape format system, files or records are compressed into tape extents and tape images. Specifically in the Open Systems environment, the host generally takes over this task. However, access to physical tape devices does not always have to go through the tape format system. It can also run directly via the extent aggregation layer described below or directly on the device.

- Extent aggregation layer
  The extent aggregation layer works in the same way as the block aggregation layer (Section 10.1.7), but with extents instead of blocks. However, in contrast to the random access of the block aggregation layer, access to the physical devices takes place sequentially. Like the access paths, the data flows between the individual components are shown as arrows.

10.4 EXAMPLES OF TAPE-BASED BACK-UP TECHNIQUES AND ARCHITECTURES

First of all, we want to examine four examples that illustrate back-up techniques. At the forefront are the access paths and the interaction of the individual components with the UNIX tool *tar* in the file back-up (Section 10.4.1), file system volume back-up using *dump* (Section 10.4.2), the volume back-up using *dd* (Section 10.4.3) and the use of virtual tapes (Section 10.4.4).

We then concentrate upon the data flow between the individual components of a back-up architecture with the disk, first of all discussing the two classical approaches to back up to tape: tape connected directly to the host (Section 10.4.5) and the data flow in a back-up over LAN (Section 10.4.6). We then consider typical approaches for tape sharing in a shared storage environment, such as tape library sharing (10.4.7) and tape library partitioning (Section 10.4.8).

Next we see how tape virtualization by means of a virtual tape controller (Section 10.4.9) and supplemented by a disk cache (Section 10.4.10) changes the data flow. In addition to a virtual tape controller, a data mover can also be positioned in the storage network to permit the realization of server-free back-up. As in LAN-free back-up, in addition to the LAN and the back-up server this also frees up the host performing the back-up (Section 10.4.11).

We will then look at two variants of the NDMP local back-up with local (Section 10.4.12) and external (Section 10.4.13) storage. Finally, we will consider an architecture in which the NDMP is used with a data mover for the realization of server-free back-up (Section 10.4.14).

10.4.1   File back-up

The example shows how a file back-up using the UNIX tool *tar* functions (Figure 10.23):

1. *Tar* reads files from the file system.
2. *Tar* compresses the files in the integral tape format system.
3. It finally writes them to tape.

In the restore case the access paths are turned around:

1. *Tar* reads the file packages from tape.

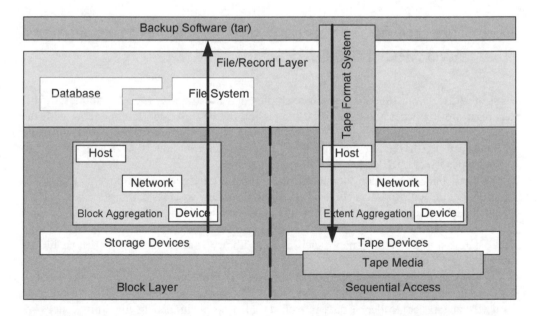

Figure 10.23 *Tar* carries out a file back-up by reading data from the file system, then compressing it in the integral tape format system and writing it to tape. In the restore case, the access paths are reversed

2. *Tar* extracts them by means of the integral tape format system.

3. It writes them into the file system.

10.4.2   File system volume back-up

Using the file system back-up tool *dump* it is possible to use the file system to back up a logical volume – and thus the files contained within it – bypassing the file system (Figure 10.24). The meta information of the file system is also backed up, so that it is possible to restore individual files later. *Dump*, like *tar*, has an integral tape format system for the compression and extraction of the files during back-up or restore.

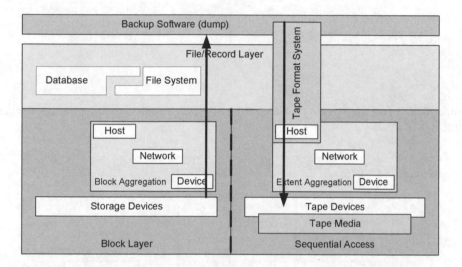

Figure 10.24   With *dump*, files can be backed up directly from a logical volume, bypassing the file system. As is the case for *tar*, an integral tape format system looks after the compression and extraction during restore or back-up

10.4.3   Volume back-up

The program *dd* represents the simplest way of creating a copy of a logical volume and writing it directly to tape (Figure 10.25). *dd* writes the information it has read to tape 1 : 1 without previously sending it through a tape format system. The restore can be represented in a similar way by reversing the access paths.

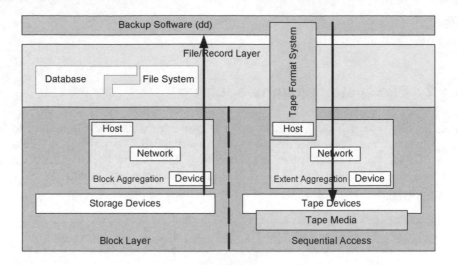

Figure 10.25   The *dd* program creates a copy of a logical volume on tape without the use of a tape format system

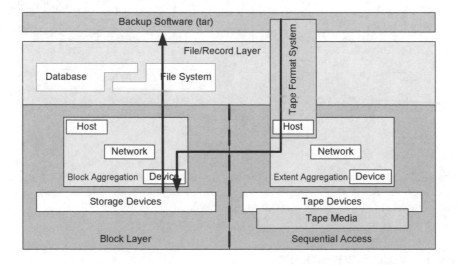

Figure 10.26   By the emulation of a virtual tape, the sequential access of the *tar* command in the extent aggregation layer is diverted into the block aggregation layer of a disk-based storage system, which permits random access

10.4.4   File back-up to virtual tape

The concept of virtual tapes can also be described using the SNIA model. Figure 10.26 uses the example of the *tar* command to show how a disk-based storage system is used to emulate a virtual tape. The sequential tape access of *tar* is diverted via the tape format system in the extent aggregation layer to the block aggregation layer of a disk storage system, where random access can take place.

10.4.5   Direct attached tape

The simplest back-up architecture is the direct connection of the tape to the host, in which the data flows from the disk to the tape library via the host (Figure 10.27).

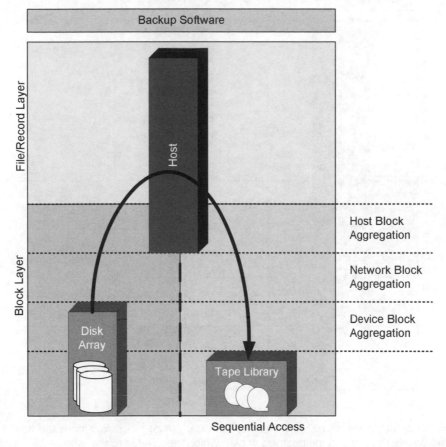

Figure 10.27   In direct attached tape the data flows from the disk to the tape library via the host, as shown by the arrow

10.4.6   LAN attached tape

LAN attached tape is the classic case of a network back-up (Section 7.2), in which a LAN separates the host to be backed up from the back-up server, which is connected to the tape library. The back-up data is moved from the host, via the LAN, to the back-up server, which then writes to the tape (Figure 10.28).

10.4.7   Shared tape drive

In tape library sharing, two hosts use the same tape drives of a library. In this approach, the hosts dynamically negotiate who will use which drives and tape media. To achieve

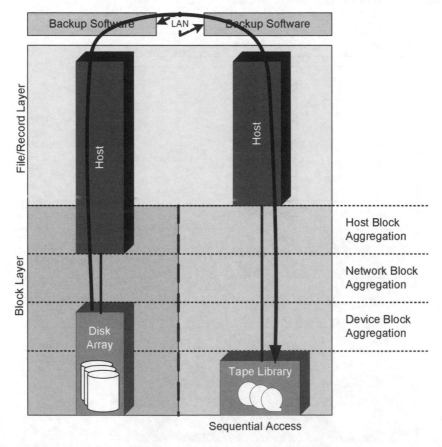

Figure 10.28   In classical network back-up, the data must be moved from the host to be backed up, via the LAN, to the back-up server, which then writes to the tape

this, one server acts as library master, all others as library clients. The library master co-ordinates access to the tapes and the tape drives (Figure 10.29). In this manner, a LAN-free back-up can be implemented, thus freeing up the LAN from back-up traffic (Section 7.8.2).

10.4.8 Partitioned tape library

In library partitioning a library can be broken down into several virtual tape libraries (Section 7.8.4). Each host is assigned its own virtual library to which it works. In this manner, several back-up servers can work to the library's different tape drives simultaneously.

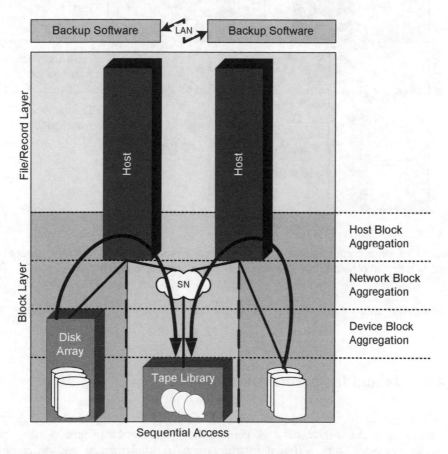

Figure 10.29 A shared tape drive facilitates the implementation of LAN-free back-up, which frees the LAN from back-up traffic

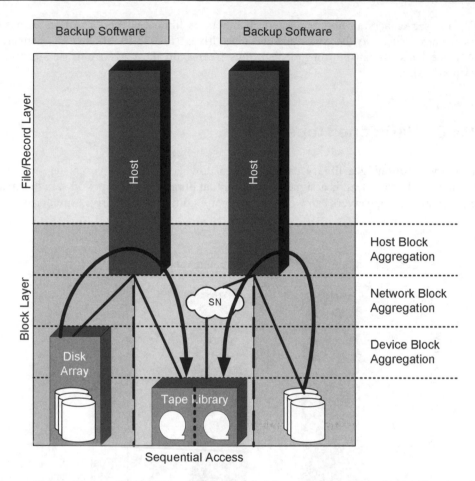

Figure 10.30 In a partitioned tape library, several hosts work to virtual tape libraries that consist of different physical tape drives, but which share a common robot

The library co-ordinates the parallel accesses to the media changer (Figure 10.30) independently.

10.4.9   Virtual tape controller

Additional back-up functionality now comes into play in the storage network! A virtual tape controller in the storage network permits the virtualization of tape devices, media and media changer. Thus, different interfaces can be implemented and different tape devices emulated. However, the back-up data still runs directly from the hosts to the drives (Figure 10.31).

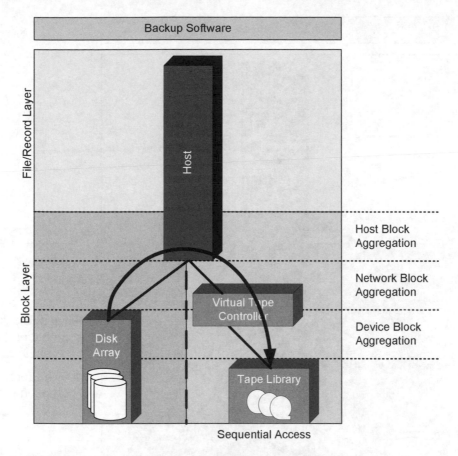

Backup Software

File/Record Layer

Block Layer

Host

Host Block
Aggregation

Network Block
Aggregation

Virtual Tape
Controller

Device Block
Aggregation

Disk
Array

Tape Library

Sequential Access

Figure 10.31   A virtual tape controller virtualizes tape devices, media and media changer

10.4.10   Virtual tape controller with disk cache

The approach using a virtual tape controller can be expanded to include an additional disk cache (Figure 10.32). This yields the following three-stage process for a back-up:

1. First of all, the host reads the data to be backed up from disk.
2. This data is first written to a disk belonging to the virtual tape controller, the so-called disk cache.
3. Finally, the data is moved from the disk cache to tape.

In this manner, a back-up can benefit from the higher performance of the disk storage. This is especially useful when backed up data must be restored: Most restore requests deal with data which was backed up within the last one or two days.

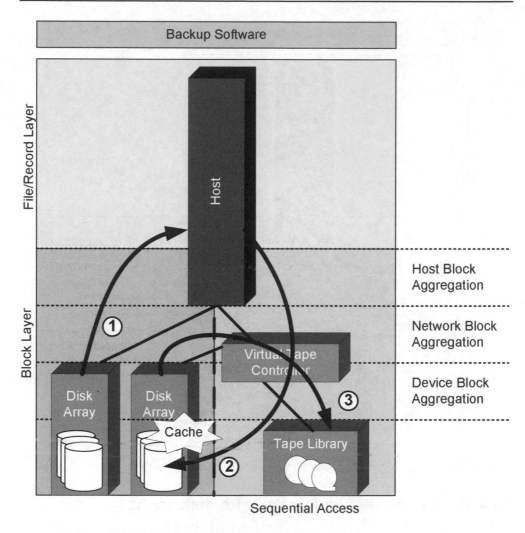

Figure 10.32   If the virtual tape controller is extended to include a disk cache, the back-up software can benefit from the higher disk performance

10.4.11   Data mover for tape

With an additional data mover in the storage network that moves the data from disk to tape, server-free back-up can be implemented. This frees up both the LAN and also the participating hosts from back-up traffic (Section 7.8.1). The back-up servers only have to control and check the operations of the data mover (Figure 10.33).

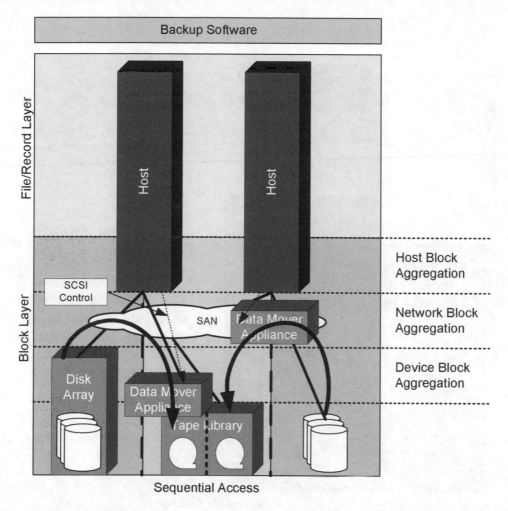

Figure 10.33 Additional data movers in the network implement the server-free back-up, which frees both the LAN and the hosts from back-up traffic at the same time

10.4.12 File server with tape drive

Figure 10.34 shows the implementation of the NDMP local back-up (Section 7.9.4). In this approach, the file server itself transports the data from disk to tape, which in this case is even locally connected. External back-up software checks this process and receives the meta-information of the backed up data via a LAN connection by means of the NDMP protocol.

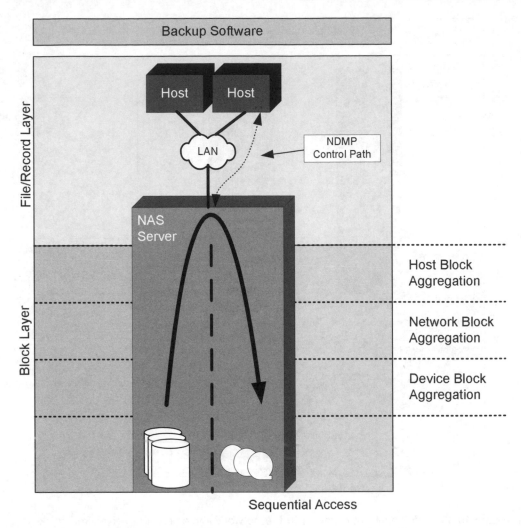

Figure 10.34 In the NDMP local back-up the NAS server takes over the transport of the data from disk to tape, which in this case is even locally connected

10.4.13 File server with external tape

If the NAS server in Section 10.4.12 is exchanged for a NAS head with external disk and tape storage, then the back-up software additionally checks the functions of the tape library on the host. Again, additional meta information on the backed up information flows from the NAS head to the back-up server (Figure 10.35).

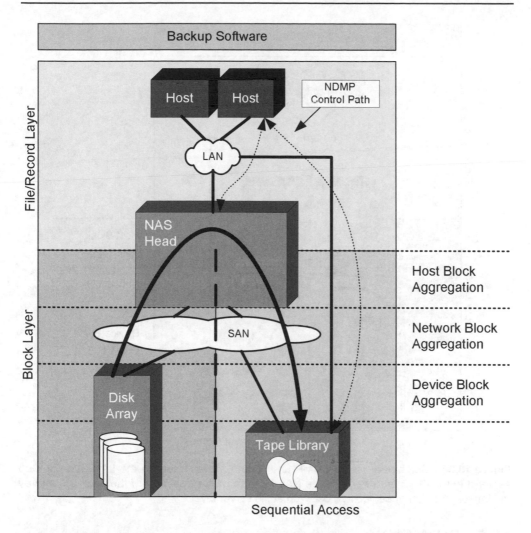

Figure 10.35 The NDMP local back-up can also be implemented for external disk and tape storage on a NAS head

10.4.14 File server with data mover

An additional data mover in the storage network (Figure 10.36), which takes over the transport of the back-up data from the NAS head with external storage, also implements server-free back-up (Section 7.8.1) on file server level. LAN and back-up software are already freed from data transport by the use of NDMP (Section 7.9.4).

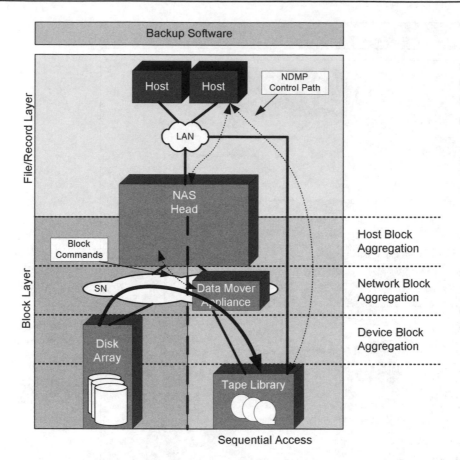

Figure 10.36 Combined use of NDMP and a data mover frees up the LAN, the back-up server due to NDMP, and frees up the NAS head from the transport of the back-up data by the implementation of server-free back-up at file server level

10.5 SUMMARY

The SNIA Shared Storage Model permits architectures to be described and compared with one another in a value-neutral manner and discussed using a consistent vocabulary. This makes it easier for manufacturers to present the differences between their products and competing products to the customer on the basis of a common vocabulary. The customer interested in the actual functionality finds it easier to compare and choose between different product alternatives. He benefits from the function-centred approach of the SNIA Shared Storage Model, which puts the entire functionalities of the Shared Storage environment in the foreground and only highlights the components on the basis of which these are implemented as a secondary consideration.

Glossary

3rd-Party SCSI Copy Command The 3rd-Party SCSI Copy Command is the specification for the use of the SCSI XCOPY command in order to copy blocks from one storage device to another within a storage network. This command is, for example, the basis for server-free back-up.

64b/66b-encoding Variant of 8b/10b-encoding used for 10-Gigabit networks with various cable types.

8b/10b encoding An encoding procedure that converts an eight-bit data byte sequence into a ten-bit transmission word sequence that is optimized for serial transmission. The 8b/10b encoding is used, for example, for Fibre Channel, Gigabit Ethernet and InfiniBand.

Access control The granting or refusal of a request for access to services or resources based upon the identity of the requester.

Access path Descriptively defined as the list of components that are run through by read and write operations to the storage devices and responses to them.

Active An active configuration means a component that is not designed with built-in redundancy.

Active/active An active/active configuration describes a component designed with built-in redundancy, in which both subcomponents are used in normal operation. We differentiate between active/active configurations with and without load sharing.

Storage Networks Explained U. Troppens R. Erkens W. Müller
© 2004 John Wiley & Sons, Ltd ISBN: 0-470-86182-7

Active/passive An active/passive configuration describes a component designed with built-in redundancy, in which the second component is not used in normal operation (stand-by).

Agent In the fields of storage networks and system management the client software of a client-server application is very often referred to as the agent. For example, we talk of the back-up agent for an application-specific back-up client in a network back-up system or the SNMP agent for the management of storage devices.

Aggregation The combining of multiple similar and related objects or operations into a single one. Two or more disks can be aggregated into a single virtual disk or in a RAID array.

AL_PA The Arbitrated Loop Physical Address (AL_PA) is the address of a device (host bus adapter or switch) in a Fibre Channel Arbitrated Loop.

Appliance A device for the execution of a very specific task. Appliances differ from normal computers due to the fact that their software has generally been modified for this very specific purpose.

Application server-free back-up Application server-free back-up refers to the back-up of application data with the aid of an instant copy generated in the disk subsystem and a second server, so that the load for the back-up is offloaded from the application server to the second server.

Arbitrated Loop One of the three Fibre Channel topologies. The other two are point-to-point and fabric.

Archive bit The archive bit is a bit in the metadata of a file, which can be used to accelerate the realization of the incremental-forever strategy.

Archiving Subfunction of a network back-up system used to permanently back up the state of a file system or the state of an application at a certain point in time.

Asymmetric storage virtualization Asymmetric storage virtualization is the form of storage virtualization within a storage network in which the data flow is separated from the control flow. The data flow runs directly between the servers and storage devices whereas the control flow, i.e. the control of the virtualization by a configuration entity, travels outside the data path.

Autoloader Small automatic tape library with few slots and usually just one drive.

Back-up Subfunction of a network back-up system used to regularly back-up the latest state of a file system or an application.

Back-up window Time window that is particularly favourable for the back-up of the data of an application. For some applications the back-up window specifies the maximum period of time that is available for the back-up of data.

Bare Metal Restore   Alternative expression for 'image restore'.

Binary encoding   Physical encoding procedure for the transmission of data.

Block aggregation   The bringing together of physical blocks or block vectors to form logical blocks or block vectors (block-based storage virtualization). Two or more physical disks can thus be aggregated to form one virtual disk.

Block layer   Component of the SNIA Shared Storage Model that includes block-based storage devices and block aggregation.

Block level   This expression refers to the physical or virtual blocks of hard disks and tapes. For example, we talk of back-up or storage virtualization on block level.

Block level incremental back-up   Block level incremental back-up describes the capability of a network back-up system to incrementally back up only those subsections (blocks) of files or of entire files systems that have changed since the previous back-up.

Block orientation   Storage devices and I/O protocols that are organized in blocks are called block-oriented, for example hard disks, SCSI, iSCSI and Fibre Channel FCP. File orientation represents an alternative to this.

Bluefin   see SMI-S.

Bus   Physical I/O medium with several lines for parallel signal transmission.

Cache   Fast storage, in which data accesses to slower storages are buffered.

Cache server   Describes a component in a network that temporarily stores data for other components in order to reduce the consumption of network capacity or to provide damping for accesses to slower storage.

Cartridge   Physical medium on which storage capacity is available. The storage capacity can be distributed over several sides.

CIFS   Common Internet File System (CIFS), the network file system from Microsoft for Windows operating systems.

CIM   The Common Information Model (CIM) is an object-oriented description of systems, applications, networks and devices. CIM is a significant component of the Web Based Enterprise Management (WBEM), a standard developed by the Distributed Management Task Force (DMTF) for the management of storage networks, which is currently viewed as the successor to the Simple Network Management Protocol (SNMP).

Class 1, Class 2, Class 3   Different service classes for transmission in a Fibre Channel network.

Cluster A compound of the same type of resources. The term 'cluster' is often used without being defined more precisely. Sometimes the term 'cluster' also denotes a single node of such a compound. Therefore when talking about clusters you should always ask precisely what is meant by the term.

CMIP The Common Management Information Protocol (CMIP) was designed at the end of the 1980s as the successor to the Simple Network Management Protocol (SNMP). In practise, however, CMIP is hardly ever used.

Co-location Co-location describes the capability of a network back-up system to write several incremental back-ups of a server onto just a few tapes, so that the number of tape mounts is reduced if the data has to be restored.

Cold back-up Cold back-up describes the back-up of a database that has been shut down for the duration of the back-up.

Common Scratch pool Group of cartridges, the storage capacity of which is (or has once again become) completely available and to which all applications have access so that they can reserve a cartridge from it for the purpose in question.

Community name The Simple Network Management Protocol (SNMP) has no secure authentication mechanisms. Instead, so-called community names are used. Two components (for example an SNMP agent and an SNMP-capable management system) can only communicate with each other if they are configured with the same community name.

Copy-on-demand Copy-on-demand is an implementation variant of instant copies and snapshots in which source data is not copied until it has been changed on the source.

Credit The credit model is a procedure for the realization of flow control. Fibre Channel differentiates between buffer-to-buffer credit for link flow control and end-to-end credit for the flow control between two end devices.

Cut-through routing Cut-through routing is the capability of a switch, a director or a router to forward incoming data packets before they have been fully received.

CWDM Coarse Wavelength Division Multiplexing (CWDM) uses similar procedures to DWDM. The two techniques differ mainly in the division of the frequency ranges and the number of payload streams that they can transmit over a single fiber-optic cable. See also DWDM.

DAFS The Direct Access File System (DAFS) is a network file system that is based upon the Virtual Interface Architecture. DAFS aims to achieve lightweight and very fast file access within a data centre.

DAS Direct Attached Storage (DAS) is storage that is directly connected to a server without a storage network, for example over SCSI or SSA.

Data copying   A variant of data sharing, in which common data is copied for each applications.

Data sharing   The use of common data by several applications.

Director   A director is a switch with a higher fault-tolerance than that of a simple switch as a result of redundant components.

Discovery   Discovery is the automatic detection of all resources used in the storage network (hardware, network topology, applications).

Disk subsystems   A disk subsystem is a collection of hard disks installed in a common enclosure. We differentiate between JBODs, RAID systems and intelligent disk subsystems. The storage capacity of a disk subsystem ranges from some 100 GBytes to several ten terabytes.

DMI   The Desktop Management Interface (DMI) is a protocol for the management of servers specified by the Distributed Management Task Force (DMTF). DMI is seldom used in comparison to the Simple Network Management Protocol (SNMP).

DMTF   The Distributed Management Task Force (DMTF) is an association of manufacturers with the objective of driving forward the standardization of the management of IT systems.

Dual SAN   Dual SAN denotes the installation of two storage networks that are completely separate from each other. Dual SANs have the advantage that even in the event of a serious fault in a storage network (configuration error or defective switch, which corrupts the storage network with corrupt frames) the connection over the other storage network is maintained.

DWDM   Dense Wavelength Division Multiplexing (DMWM) increases the capacity of a fiber-optic cable by assigning several incoming optical signals (= payload streams) to certain optical frequency ranges. Metaphorically speaking, each payload stream is transmitted in a different colour. Since the signals are only optically transformed, there are no limitations with regard to data rates or data formats of the payload streams. As a result, very different payload streams such as Fibre Channel, ESCON, Gigabit Ethernet and Sonet/SDH can be transmitted simultaneously over a single fiber-optic cable.

Element manager   The element manager is a device-specific management interface that is classified as an out-band interface. It is often realized in the form of a GUI or web interface.

Enhanced shared-nothing cluster   Server clusters of up to several dozen servers. Enhanced shared-nothing clusters can react to load peaks with a delay.

Emulated loop   Facilitates communication between private loop devices of a Fibre Channel arbitrated loop and devices in a Fibre Channel fabric.

Error handler   Component of a network back-up system. The error handler helps to prioritize and filter error messages and to generate reports.

ESCON   The Enterprise System Connection (ESCON) is a serial I/O technology for mainframes.

Exchange   An exchange is a logical communication connection between two Fibre Channel devices.

External storage   Storage (hard disks, tape drives), which is located outside the computer enclosure.

Fabric   The most flexible and scalable of the three Fibre Channel topologies.

Fabric login (FLOGI)   Fabric login denotes the registration of an N-Port into a fabric topology. It establishes a session between the N-Port and the corresponding F-Port of a Fibre Channel switch.

FC   Abbreviation for Fibre Channel.

FCIA   The Fibre Channel Industry Association (FCIA) is an association of manufacturers from the field of Fibre Channel technology.

FCIP   Tunnelling protocol that transports the Fibre Channel traffic between two Fibre Channel devices via TCP/IP.

FCN   A Fibre Channel Name (FCN) is a 64-bit identifier for a Fibre Channel component, which in contrast to a WWN is not unique world-wide. In practice it has become common practise to refer to WWNs and FCNs simply as WWNs.

FCP   The Fibre Channel Protocol (FCP) is the protocol mapping that maps the SCSI protocol onto the Fibre Channel transmission technology.

Fiber   Alternative name for fiber-optic cable.

Fibre Channel   A technology that can realize both storage networks and data networks. Fibre Channel is currently the predominant technology for the realization of storage networks. We differentiate between three network topologies: arbitrated loop, fabric and point-to-point.

Fibre Channel SAN   A Fibre Channel network that is used as a storage network. Or the other way around: A storage network that is realized with Fibre Channel.

FICON   Fibre Connection (FICON) is the mapping of the ESCON protocol on Fibre Channel.

File level   The files of a file system are the object of the processing. For example, we talk of back-up on file level or storage virtualization on file level.

File orientation   Storage devices and I/O protocols are called file-oriented if they are organized in files or file fragments, for example NAS servers, NFS, CIFS and HTTP. An alternative to this is block orientation.

File/record layer   Component of the SNIA Shared Storage Model that maps the database records and files on the block-oriented volumes of the storage device.

Flow control   Mechanism for the regulation of the data stream between a sender and a receiver. The flow control ensures that the transmitter only sends data at a speed that the receiver can process it at.

Forward recovery   Forward recovery, sometimes also called 'roll forward', denotes the restoring of a database using a back-up copy plus archive log files generated after the back-up copy and the active log files that are still present.

Frame   The data packets that are transmitted in a Fibre Channel network are called frames.

Hard zoning   In hard zoning only the end devices that lie in at least one common zone can communicate with each other. Hard zoning is often confused with port zoning.

HBA   A host bus adapter (HBA) is another term for an adapter card that is fitted in a server. Examples of host bus adapters are SCSI controllers, Fibre Channel cards and iSCSI cards.

HCA   Host channel adapter (HCA) denotes the connection point of a server to an Infini-Band network.

Hierarchical storage management (HSM)   Hierarchical storage management (HSM) denotes the automatic moving and restoring of data that has not been used for a long time from fast storage to slower but cheaper storage, for instance from disk to tape. HSM is commonly a subfunction of network back-up systems.

Host I/O bus   The host I/O bus represents the link between system bus and I/O bus. The most important representative of the host I/O bus is the PCI bus.

Hot back-up   Hot back-up denotes the back-up of a database during operation.

Hot spare disks   In a RAID configuration (RAID array, intelligent disk subsystem) a spare disk is called a hot spare disk.

Hub   A component that is not visible to end devices, which simplifies the physical cabling of a network. In Fibre Channel networks the ring (physical) of the arbitrated loop (logical) is simplified to a star-shape (physical).

I/O bus   Physical communication connection between servers and storage devices, for example SCSI, Fibre Channel or iSCSI. Originally, parallel buses were used for this

such as SCSI or IDE. For historical reasons, serial I/O techniques such as SSA, Fibre
Channel or iSCSI are also often called I/O buses.

I/O path   The path from CPU and main memory to the storage devices via system bus,
host I/O bus and I/O bus.

IETF   The Internet Engineering Task Force (IETF) is a committee that standardizes the
protocols for the Internet. These include TCP/IP-based protocols such as FTP, HTTP,
NFS, iSCSI, FCIP, iFCP and iSNS.

iFCP   Internet FCP (iFCP), a new standard with the objective of replacing the network
layer in a Fibre Channel SAN with a TCP/IP network.

Image restore   Image restore (also known as Bare Metal Restore) denotes the restoration
of a server or a hard disk partition (Windows) or a volume (Unix) from a previously
generated copy of a hard disk partition or volume.

In-band management   We talk of in-band management if the management of a resource
takes place over the same interface over which the actual data is transmitted. Examples
of this are the SCSI Enclosure Services (SES) and the corresponding services of the
Fibre Channel FCP protocol.

In-band virtualization   Alternative name for 'symmetric virtualization'.

Incremental-forever strategy   The incremental-forever strategy relates to the capability of a network back-up system to calculate the last state of the file system from
continuous incremental back-ups of a file system by means of database operations. A
complete back-up of the file system is only necessary the first time. After this, only
incremental back-ups are performed. The metadata database in the back-up server helps
to immediately recreate the last state of the file system when restoring the file system.

InfiniBand   New transmission technology that aims to replace the parallel PCI-bus with
a serial network. InfiniBand may be used for interprocess communication, client-server
communication and server-storage communication.

Instant copy   Instant copy is the capability of a storage system to practically copy large
data sets within a few seconds.

Internal storage   Storage (hard disks, tape drives) located inside the enclosure of the
computer.

IPFC   IP over Fibre Channel (IPFC), the protocol mapping that makes it possible to use
a Fibre Channel network for IP data traffic.

IP storage   General term for storage networks that use TCP/IP as a transmission technique. IP storage includes the protocols iSCSI, FCIP and iFCP.

iSCSI   Internet SCSI (iSCSI) is the protocol mapping of SCSI on TCP/IP.

iSCSI SAN   A storage network that is realized with iSCSI.

iSER   iSCSI Extension for RDMA (iSER) is an application protocol for RDMA over TCP. iSER enables to transmit the SCSI data traffic via the quick and CPU-friendly RDMA over TCP instead of via TCP.

iSNS   The Internet Storage Name Service (iSNS) defines a name service that is used by different IP storage standards such as iSCSI and iFCP.

ISL   The inter switch link (ISL) is a connection cable between two Fibre Channel switches.

JBOD   Just a Bunch of Disks (JBOD) is the term for a disk subsystem without a controller.

Jitter   As a result of physical influences, incoming signal steps at the receiver are not the same length. This bucking within the signal sequence is called jitter.

Job scheduler   Component of a network back-up system. It controls which data is backed up when.

Journaling   Journaling of a file system describes a method in which the file system – in a similar way to a database – first writes changes to a log file and only then enters them in the actual data area. Journaling significantly reduces the time for a file system check after a system crash.

K28.5 symbol   Special transmission symbol of the 8b/10b encoding, which does not represent a data byte. The K28.5 symbol includes a special bit sequence that does not occur in a bit sequence generated with 8b/10b encoding even across symbol boundaries. The K28.5 symbols scattered in a data stream allows to synchronize transmitter and receiver.

Label   A label is both the sticker on the cartridge, which often has a barcode upon it, and a storage area on the tape that holds metadata.

LAN   Local Area Network (LAN), a data network with low geographic extension (maximum several tens of kilometres).

LAN-free back-up   Back-up method of a network back-up system in which the back-up client copies the data directly to the back-up medium via the storage network bypassing the back-up server and the LAN.

Latency   Latency describes the time duration that passes before the input signal becomes visible in an expected output reaction.

Library partitioning   Tape library partitioning statically divides a physical tape library into several logical (=virtual) tape libraries, which are perceived as independent libraries by the connected servers.

Library sharing   In tape library sharing several applications dynamically share the tapes and the drives of a tape library.

Link   Physical connection cable in a Fibre Channel network.

LIP   The loop initialization primitive sequence (LIP) describes the procedure for the initialization of a Fibre Channel arbitrated loop. During the LIP procedure the data traffic on the arbitrated loop is interrupted.

Loop   Abbreviation for Fibre Channel arbitrated loop.

LUN   The SCSI protocol and its derivates such as Fibre Channel FCP and iSCSI address subcomponents of a device (SCSI target) by means of the Logical Unit Number (LUN). It has become common practise to also call these subcomponents LUN. Examples of LUNs are physical or virtual hard disks exported from a disk subsystem and the tape drives and the media changer of a tape library.

LUN masking   LUN masking limits the visibility of disks exported by a disk subsystem. Each computer sees only the disks that are assigned to it. LUN masking thus works as a filter between the disks exported from the disk subsystem and the accessing computers.

LUN zoning   Alternative term for LUN masking. Often used in the context of more modern switches that offer zoning on the basis of LUNs and thus facilitate LUN masking in the storage network.

MAN   Metropolitan Area Network (MAN), a data network with average geographic extension (maximum several 100 kilometres).

Managed hub   Fibre Channel hub with additional management functions.

Management console   Central point, from which all aspects of a storage network, or all aspects of an IT system in general, can be monitored and managed.

Manchester encoding   Encoding procedure that generates at least one signal change for every bit transmitted.

Media changer   Mechanical transport device that can transport media between slots and drives.

Media manager   Component of a network back-up system. The media manager manages the hard disks and the tapes upon which a network back-up system stores the backed up objects (files, file systems, images).

Metadata controller (MDC)   The metadata controller is a management and synchronization entity in a distributed application. For example, we talk of the metadata controller of a shared disk file system or of the metadata controller of the storage virtualization.

Metadata database   The metadata database is the brain of a network back-up system. It includes approximately the following entries for every object backed up: name, computer of origin, date of last change, data of last back-up, name of the back-up medium, etc.

mFCP   Metro FCP (mFCP) is an iFCP variant, which in contrast to iFCP is not based upon TCP but on UDP.

MIB   The term management information base (MIB) stems from SNMP jargon. An MIB is a hierarchically constructed collection of variables, which describes the management options of a resource (server, storage device, network component, application).

MIB file   File that contains an MIB description.

Mirroring   Mirroring of data on two or more hard disks (RAID 1).

Monitoring   Monitoring denotes the monitoring of all resources used in the storage network (hardware, network topology, applications).

Multipathing   Multipathing is the existence of several I/O paths between server and storage system. The objectives are to increase fault-tolerance by means of redundant I/O paths, to increase the I/O throughput by means of the simultaneous use of several I/O paths, or both at the same time.

Name server   In general, the term name server is used to describe an information service in distributed systems. In the case of Fibre Channel the name server (here Simple Name Server) manages information about all N-Ports connected in a fabric such as their WWPN, WWNN, Node_ID and supported service classes and application protocols.

NAS   Network Attached Storage (NAS) refers to the product category of preconfigured file servers. NAS servers consist of one or more internal servers, preconfigured disk capacity and usually a stripped-down or special operating system.

NDMP   The Network Data Management Protocol (NDMP) defines the interface between the client and the server of a network back-up system. The objective of the NDMP is to improve and standardize the integration of NAS servers in a network back-up system.

Network Management System (NMS)   In SNMP jargon a Network Management System is an application that monitors and manages components by means of the SNMP protocol.

Network File System   Network file systems are the natural extension of local file systems: end users and applications can access directories and files over a network file system that physically lie on a different computer – the file server. Examples of network file systems are the Common Internet File System (CIFS), the Network File System (NFS) and the Direct Access File System (DAFS).

Network back-up system   Network back-up systems can back up heterogeneous IT environments incorporating several thousand computers largely automatically.

NFS   Network File System (NFS) is the network file system originally developed by SUN Microsystems, which is currently supplied as standard with all Unix systems.

NIC   Network Interface Controller (NIC), Network Interface Card (NIC); both terms for network cards.

Off-site location   An off-site location is a remote location at which a second copy of data that has been backed up by means of a network back-up system is stored. The second copy of the data in the off-site location serves to protect against major catastrophes.

OOM   Object-oriented modelling (OOM) is an object-oriented specification language, which is used for the description of the Common Information Model (CIM).

Open Systems   Open Systems signifies the world of the non-mainframe server. Unix, Windows NT/2000, OS/400, Novell and MacOS belong to the Open System world. Incidentally, for us 'Unix' also covers the Linux operating system, which is sometimes listed separately in such itemizations.

Ordered set   8b/10b encoded group of four transmission words that begins with the K28.5 symbol.

Out-band management   Out-of-band management (out-band management for short) signifies the management of a resource by means of a second interface, which exists in addition to the data path. An example of out-band management would be the management of a Fibre Channel switch by means of an Ethernet connection and SNMP.

Out-band virtualization   Alternative term for 'asymmetric virtualization'.

Parity   Parity is a binary cross-check sum or check sum. RAID 4 and RAID 5, for example calculate and store additional parity blocks, with which the data stored upon a hard disk can be reconstructed after its failure.

Partition   Part of a side, which provides storage capacity as a physical unit of the cartridge.

PCI   Peripheral Component Interconnect (PCI) is currently the predominant technology for host I/O buses.

Point-in-time restore   Point-in-time restore signifies the capability of a network back-up system to recreate any desired earlier state of a file system.

Point-to-point   The simplest of the three Fibre Channel topologies, which solely connects two end devices (server, storage) together.

Port   A port denotes the physical interface of a device (servers, storage devices, switches, hubs, etc.) to a storage network.

Port login (PLOGI)   Port login denotes the structure of a connection (session) between two Fibre Channel end devices. Port login exchanges service parameters such as service class and end-to-end credit. It is an absolute prerequisite for further data exchange.

Port zoning   Zoning variant, in which the zones are defined by means of port addresses. Port zoning is often confused with hard zoning.

Prefetch hit rate   The prefetch hit rate describes the success rate of a cache in shifting data from a slower storage device before a different component demands precisely this data from the cache.

Private loop   A Fibre Channel arbitrated loop that is not connected to a fabric.

Private loop devices   A private loop device is a device connected to a Fibre Channel arbitrated loop that does not master the fabric protocol. It is not capable of communicating with end devices in the fabric via a Fibre Channel switch connected to the loop.

Protocol mapping   The Fibre Channel standard denotes the mapping of an application protocol such as SCSI or IP on the Fibre Channel transport layer (FC-2, FC-3) as protocol mapping.

Process login (PRLI)   Process login describes the construction of a connection (session) between two processes on the FC-4 layer of Fibre Channel.

Public loop   A Fibre Channel arbitrated loop, which is connected to a fabric via a switch.

Public loop devices   A public loop device denotes a device connected to a Fibre Channel arbitrated loop, which in addition to the loop protocol also masters the fabric protocol. It can communicate with end devices in the fabric via a Fibre Channel switch connected to the loop.

Quickloop   Implementation variant of the emulated loop by the company Brocade.

RAID   Originally RAID was the abbreviation for 'Redundant Array of Inexpensive Disks'. Today RAID stands for 'Redundant Array of Independent Disks'. RAID has two primary objectives: to increase the performance of hard disks by striping and to increase the fault-tolerance of hard disks by redundancy.

RDMA   Remote Direct Memory Access (RDMA) makes it possible for processes to read from or write to memory areas of processes that run on a different computer. RDMA aims to achieve lightweight and very fast interprocess communication within a data centre.

RDMA over TCP   Standardized RDMA variant that uses TCP as the transmission medium.

Real time data sharing   Variant of data sharing in which several applications work on the same data set concurrently.

Remote mirroring   Remote mirroring signifies the capability of a block-based storage system (e.g. a disk subsystem) to copy data sets to a second storage system without the involvement of a server.

Replication   Replication denotes automatic copying and synchronization mechanisms on file level.

RNIC   RDMA enabled NIC (network interface controller), a network card that supports RDMA over TCP and, in addition to RDMA, most likely also realize the functions of a TCP/IP offload engine (TOE).

Roll forward   See forward recovery.

RSCN   The Registered State Change Notification (RSCN) is an in-band mechanism in Fibre Channel networks, by means of which registered end devices are automatically informed of status changes of network components and other end devices.

SAFS   SAN Attached File System (SAFS), an alternative term for shared disk file system.

SAN   SAN is an abbreviation for two different terms. Firstly, SAN is the abbreviation for 'Storage Area Network'. Very often 'storage area networks' or 'SANs' are equated with Fibre Channel technology. The advantages of storage area networks can, however, also be achieved with alternative technologies such as for example iSCSI. In this book we therefore do not use the term SAN or 'Storage Area Network' alone. For general statements on storage area networks we use the term 'storage network'. Otherwise, we always state the transmission technology with which a storage area network is realized, for example Fibre Channel SAN or iSCSI SAN.
Secondly, SAN is an abbreviation for 'System Area Network'. A system area network is a network with a high bandwidth and low latency, which serves as a connection between computers in a distributed computer system. In this book we have never used the abbreviation SAN to mean this. However, it should be noted that the VIA standard uses the abbreviation SAN in this second sense.

SAN router   Alternative name for a Fibre Channel-to-SCSI bridge.

SATA   Serial ATA (SATA) is an economical I/O technology for disk attachment that transmits the conventional parallel ATA protocol serially and thus permits higher transmission rates than IDE/ATA.

Scratch pool   Group of cartridges, the storage capacity of which is (or has once again become) completely available.

Scratch tape   A new tape without content or a tape the content of which is no longer of interest and the whole of the storage capacity of which can be used for new purposes.

SCSI The Small Computer System Interface (SCSI) is an important technology for I/O buses. The parallel SCSI cables are increasingly being replaced by serial I/O techniques such as Fibre Channel, TCP/IP/Ethernet/iSCSI, SATA and InfiniBand. The SCSI protocol, however, lives on in the new serial techniques, for example as Fibre Channel FCP or as iSCSI.

SES The SCSI Enclosure Services (SES) are an in-band management interface for SCSI devices.

SDP The Socket Direct Protocol (SDP) maps the socket API of TCP/IP on RDMA, so that protocols based upon TCP/IP such as NFS and CIFS do not need to be changed. Users of SDP benefit both from the simplicity of the protocol and also from the low latency and low CPU load obtained with RDMA.

Sequence A sequence is a large data unit in the FC-2 layer of Fibre Channel that is transmitted from transmitter to receiver in the form of one or more frames.

Server-centric IT architecture In a server-centric IT architecture, storage devices are only connected to individual servers. Storage only ever exists in relation to the servers to which it is connected. Other servers cannot directly access the data; they must always go through the server to which the storage is connected.

Server consolidation Server consolidation is the replacement of many small servers by a more powerful large server.

Server-free back-up Back-up method of a network back-up system, in which the data is copied from the source disk to the back-up medium via the storage network without a server being connected in between. Server-free back-up makes use of the 3rd-Party SCSI Copy Command.

Service subsystem Component of the SNIA Shared Storage Model in which the management tasks of a shared storage environment are brought together.

Shared disk file system Shared disk file systems are a further development of local file systems in which several computers can directly access the hard disks of the file system at the same time via the storage network. Shared disk file systems must synchronize the write accesses to shared disks in addition to the functions of local file systems.

Shared storage environment SNIA term for storage-centered IT architectures.

Shared-everything cluster The shared-everything cluster is the cluster configuration that permits the greatest flexibility and the best load balancing. In shared-everything clusters, several instances of an application run on different computers, with all instances providing the same services towards the outside. A corresponding load balancing software ensures that all instances are loaded to the same degree.

Shared-nothing cluster   Shared-nothing clusters are a configuration of two servers in which in the event of the failure of one computer the remaining computer takes over the tasks of the failed computer in addition to its own.

Shared-null configuration   The shared-null configuration is a server or an application that is not designed with built-in redundancy. If the server fails the application is no longer available.

Side   Part of a cartridge that provides storage capacity. A side contains one or more partitions. Tapes normally possess only one side. DVDs and magneto-optical media are also available in double-sided variants. Holographic storage may provide even more than two sides.

Single point of failure   Single point of failure signifies a subcomponent of a system, the failure of which leads to the failure of the entire system. Fault-tolerant systems such as server clusters or high-end disk subsystems must not have any single points of failure.

Skew   Skew means the divergence of signals that belong together in a parallel bus.

Slot   Storage location for cartridges that are not being accessed.

SMI-S   The Storage Management Initiative Specification is a further development of WBEM and CIM by SNIA, which is specially tailored to the management of storage networks. Amongst other things, the standardized refinement of the CIM classes aims to guarantee the interoperability of management systems for storage networks.

Snapshot   A snapshot means an instant copy within a file system or a volume manager.

SNIA   Storage Networking Industry Association (SNIA), an association of manufacturers in the field of storage and storage networks.

SNMP   The Simple Network Management Protocol (SNMP) is a standard that was originally developed for the management of IP networks. SNMP is now a widespread standard for the management of IT systems that is also used for the management of storage networks.

Soft zoning   Soft zoning describes a zoning variant that restricts itself to the information of the name server. If an end device asks the name server for further end devices in the Fibre Channel network then it is only informed of the end devices with which it lies in at least one common zone. However, if an end device knows the address of a different device, with which it does not lie in a common zone, then it can nevertheless communicate with the other device. Soft zoning is often confused with WWN zoning.

SoIP   Storage over IP (SoIP), the name of a product from Nishan Technologies (acquired by McData Corporation in September 2003). According to the manufacturer these products are compatible with various IP storage standards.

SRM   Storage Resource Management (SRM) is the category of software products that unifies storage virtualization and storage management.

SSA   Serial Storage Architecture, an alternative I/O technology to SCSI.

SSP   A Storage Service Provider (SSP) is a business model in which a service provider (the SSP) operates a storage network, which is used by many customers. Originally it was hoped that this would result in cost benefits. In practice this business model has failed. However, it is very likely that this approach will experience a renaissance in a modified form with the increasing use of the web architecture and so-called e-business applications.

Storage-centric IT architecture   In contrast to server-centric IT architecture, in storage-centric IT architecture, storage exists completely independently of any computers. A storage network installed between the servers and the storage devices allows several servers to directly access the same storage device without a different server necessarily being involved.

Storage consolidation   Storage consolidation means the replacement of a large number of small storage systems by one more powerful large storage system.

Storage gateway   Alternative term for a Fibre Channel-to-SCSI bridge.

Storage hierarchy   A network back-up system can realize a storage hierarchy on the back-up server consisting of disk subsystems and tape libraries. Depending upon load profile and performance requirements the use of the optimal back-up medium from a technical and economic point of view can be automated.

Storage networks   The idea behind storage networks is to replace the SCSI cable between servers and storage devices by a network, which is installed alongside the existing LAN as an additional network and is primarily used for the data exchange between computers and storage devices.

Storage virtualization   Storage virtualization (often just called virtualization) is generally used to mean the separation of storage into the physical implementation in the form of storage devices and the logical representation of the storage for the use by operating systems, applications and users. A differentiation is made between three levels of storage virtualization: (1) virtualization within a storage system, for example in a RAID disk subsystem or an intelligent disk subsystem, (2) virtualization in the form of an own virtualization entity in the storage network and (3) virtualization on the server by host bus adapter, volume manager, file systems and databases. A further differentiation is made with regard to the granularity of the virtualization (virtualization on block level and virtualization on file level) and, for the virtualization in the storage network, we also differentiate between symmetric and asymmetric virtualization.

Streaming   The reading or writing of large quantities of data to a tape, whereby the data is written in one go with stopping, rewinding an restarting the tape.

Striping   Distribution of data over two or more hard disks (RAID 0).

Support matrix   In heterogeneous storage networks, numerous components from extremely different manufacturers come together. In the support matrix, manufacturers of hardware and software components state which components from other manufacturers their components will work with.

Switch   The switch is the control centre in networks such as Ethernet and the Fibre Channel fabric. It realizes the routing of frames and services such as name server and zoning.

Switched hub   A special kind of Managed hub, which in addition allow for the direct communication between two end devices, so that several end devices can communicate with each other in pairs within a Fibre Channel arbitrated loop at the same time.

Symmetric storage virtualization   Symmetric storage virtualization is the form of storage virtualization within a storage network in which the data flow between servers and storage devices plus the control flow – i.e. the control of the virtualization by a virtualization instance – take place in the data path.

System bus   The I/O bus in a computer that connects, amongst other things, the CPUs to the main memory (RAM).

Tape library partitioning   Tape library partitioning (library partitioning for short) divides a physical tape library statically into several logical (= virtual) tape libraries, which are perceived as independent libraries by the connected servers.

Tape library sharing   In tape library sharing (library sharing) several applications dynamically share the tapes and drives of a tape library.

Tape mount   The inserting of a tape in a tape drive.

Tape reclamation   In a network back-up system over time more and more data is left on a tape that is no longer required. With current technology it is difficult to write new data to these gaps on tapes that have become free. In tape reclamation the data that is still valid from several such tapes with gaps is copied onto one new tape so that these tapes can be rewritten.

Target   The SCSI protocol calls the device connected to a SCSI bus a target. Examples of targets are servers, disk subsystems and tape libraries.

Target_ID   Target_ID is the name for the address of a device (target), which is connected to a SCSI bus.

TCA   InfiniBand calls the connection point of a server to an InfiniBand network a Target Channel Adapter (TCA). The complexity of a TCA is low in comparison to a HCA.

TCP/IP offload engine (TOE)   A network card that realizes the TCP/IP protocol stack completely in firmware on the network card. TOEs significantly reduce the CPU load for TCP/IP data traffic.

Three tier architecture   Further development of the client-server architecture, in which the data, applications and the user interface arc separated into different layers.

Translated Loop   Implementation variant of the emulated loop from CNT/Inrange.

Trap   A trap is a mechanism with which a resource managed by SNMP (or to be more precise its SNMP agent) informs a management system for storage networks or a general management system of state changes.

Trap recipient   The trap recipient is the recipient of SNMP messages (traps). To set up a trap recipient the IP address of the computer that is to receive the trap is entered on the SNMP agent.

Twin-tailed SCSI cabling   Cabling method in which the storage devices are connected to two servers via a SCSI bus for the benefit of fault-tolerance.

ULP   Upper level protocol (ULP). Application protocol of a Fibre Channel network. Examples of ULPs are SCSI and IP.

Unmanaged hub   Fibre Channel hub without management functions.

VI   The Virtual Interface (VI) denotes a communication connection in the Virtual Interface Architecture (VIA).

VIA   The Virtual Interface Architecture (VIA) is a system-near I/O technology, which facilitates the lightweight and fast data exchange between two processes that run on different servers or storage devices within a data centre.

VI NIC   VI-capable network card. Today VI-capable network cards exist for Fibre Channel, Ethernet and InfiniBand.

Virtualization   See Storage virtualization.

Voice over IP (VoIP)   VoIP is the transmission of telephone calls via IP data networks.

Volume   A volume is a logical data container. It serves to reserve storage capacity on storage devices for applications.

Volume level   Back-up mode in which an entire volume (e.g. disk, partition of a disk, or logical volume) is backed up as a single object.

Volume manager   Virtualization layer in the server between disk and file system that can bring together several physical hard disks to form one or more logical hard disks.

VSAN   A virtual SAN (VSAN) makes it possible to operate several virtual Fibre Channel fabrics that are logically separate from one another over one physical Fibre Channel network. In addition, separate fabric services such as name server and zoning are realized for every virtual storage network.

WAN   Wide Area Network (WAN), a data network with large geographical extension (several 1000 kilometres).

WBEM   The Web Based Enterprise Management (WBEM) is a standard developed by the Distributed Management Task Force (DMTF) for IT infrastructure management, which is currently viewed as the successor to the Simple Network Management Protocol. WBEM uses web techniques. A significant part of WBEM is the Common Information Model (CIM).

Web architecture   Further development of the three tier architecture to a five tier architecture for the flexible support of Internet and e-business applications. The representation layer is broken down into the web server and the web browser and the data layer is broken down into the organization of the data (databases, file servers) and storage capacity for data (disk subsystems and tape libraries).

WWN   A World Wide Name (WWN) is a 64-bit identifier for a Fibre Channel component, which in contrast to FCN is unique world-wide. In practice it has become common practise to call WWNs and FCNs simply WWNs.

WWN zoning   Zoning variant in which the zones are defined by WWNs. WWN zoning is often confused with soft zoning.

WWNN   The World Wide Node Name (WWNN) is the WWN for a device (server, storage device, switch, director) in a Fibre Channel network.

WWPN   The World Wide Port Name (WWPN) is the WWN for a connection port of a device (server, storage device, switch, director) in a Fibre Channel network.

XCOPY   SCSI command that realizes the 3rd-Party SCSI Copy Command.

Zoning   Subdivision of a network into virtual sub-networks, which can overlap.

Annotated Bibliography

When we began writing this book in April 2001 there were hardly any books about storage networks. Since then a couple of books have appeared on this subject. In the following we introduce a selection of the sources (books, white papers and websites) that have been helpful to us when writing this book, in addition to our daily work. That means, the following list represents our subjective list of readings – there may be a lot of other useful resources available as well.

GENERAL SOURCES

Marc Farley *Building Storage Networks* (2nd Edition), McGraw-Hill 2001. In our opinion the first comprehensive book on storage networks. When we started to work with storage networks in mid-2000 Farley's book quickly became the 'storage bible' for us. We still use this book as a reference today. The book gives a particularly good overview of the fundamental technologies for storage networks.

Tom Clark *Designing Storage Area Networks: A Practical Reference for Implementing Fibre Channel and IP SANs* (2nd Edition), Addison-Wesley 2003. This book gives a good overview about techniques for storage networking and their application.

InfoStor (http://is.pennet.com), a manufacturer-neutral technical journal on storage and storage networks. For us the companion website is the first port of call for new developments such as IP storage, RDMA, SMI-S or InfiniBand. At InfoStor you can also

Storage Networks Explained   U. Troppens R. Erkens W. Müller
© 2004 John Wiley & Sons, Ltd   ISBN: 0-470-86182-7

order a free weekly e-mail newsletter with up-to-date information on storage and storage networks.

http://searchstorage.techtarget.com and http://www.byteandswitch.com are two other websites with a lot of material about storage and storage networks. At both sides you can order a free e-mail newsletters with up-to-date information on storage and storage networking.

Storage Networking Industry Association (SNIA, http://www.snia.org), the SNIA is an association of manufacturers, system integrators and service providers in the field of storage networks. The website includes a directory of all SNIA members, which at the same time gives a good overview of all important players in the field of 'storage networks'. Furthermore, the SNIA website provides a couple of other useful information including whitepapers, a dictionary, presentations, a link collection and a regular newsletter. In addition to that, Europeans can subscribe the freely distributed *SNS Europe* magazine at http://www.snia-europe.com.

IBM Redbooks (http://www.redbooks.ibm.com): IBM makes technical expertise and material on its products freely available via IBM Redbooks. Many IBM Redbooks deal with the integration, implementation and operation of realistic customer scenarios. They should thus be viewed as a supplement to the pure handbooks. Many Redbooks also deal with product-independent subjects such as RAID or the fundamentals of storage networks. IBM Redbooks can be downloaded free of charge from the website.

http://www.storage-explained.com: The homepage of this book. On this page we will publish corrections and supplements to this book and maintain the bibliography. In addition to this, we have provided the figures from this book and presentations to download.

INTELLIGENT DISK SUBSYSTEMS

We know of no comprehensive representation of disk subsystems. We have said everything of importance on this subject in this book, so that the next step would be to look at specific products. On the subject of RAID we have drawn upon Marc Farley's *Building Storage Networks*, Jon William Togo's *The Holy Grail of Data Storage Management* and various IBM Redbooks.

I/O TECHNIQUES

SCSI: With regard to SCSI, two sources were important to us. Firstly, we must again mention Marc Farley's *Building Storage Networks* and the book by Robert Kembel below. In addition to that you may refer to "The SCSI Bench Reference" by Jeffrey Stai.

Robert Kembel *Fibre Channel: A Comprehensive Introduction*, Northwest Learning Associations, 2000. This book is the first book of a whole series on Fibre Channel. It explains the Fibre Channel standard in bits and bytes and also includes an interesting section on 'SCSI-3 Architectural Model (SAM)'.

IP Storage – iSCSI and related subjects: with regard to IP storage we have drawn upon Marc Farley's *Building Storage Networks*, various articles from InfoStor (http://is.pennet. com) and the relevant standards of the Internet Engineering Task Force (IETF) on http:// www.ietf.org. More and more iSCSI products are coming onto the market, so that more and more information on this subject can be found on the websites of relevant manufacturers. A book has now appeared – Tom Clark's *IP SANs*: An Introduction to iSCSI, iFCP, and FCIP Protocols for Storage Area Networks – that leaves no questions on this subject unanswered.

InfiniBand, Virtual Interface Architecture and RDMA: For InfiniBand, Marc Farley's *Building Storage Networks* and InfoStor (http://is.pennet.com) should again be mentioned. We should also mention the homepage of the InfiniBand Trade Association (http://www.infinibandta.org), the homepage of the Virtual Interface Architecture (http://www.viarch.org), the homepage of the RDMA Consortium (http://www. rdmaconsortium.org) and various white papers from the homepages of relevant manufacturers.

LAN and WAN techniques: We confess that our coverage of LAN techniques like TCP/IP and Ethernet and of WAN techniques like Dark Fiber, DWDM and SONET/SDH must be improved. As general introduction in computer networks and LAN techniques we recommend Andrew S. Tanenbaum's *Computer Networks*. With regard to WAN techniques we recommend the Lightreading's Beginner's Guides at http://www.lightreading.com/section. asp?section_id=29. Lightreading is also a very good starting point for upcoming WAN techniques like the Resilient Packet Ring (RPR) and the Generic Framing Procedure (GFP).

FILE SYSTEMS

For basic information on modern file systems we recommend that you take a look at the handbooks and white papers of relevant products. Particularly worth a mention are the Veritas File System from Veritas (http://www.veritas.com) and the Journaled File System from IBM (http://www.ibm.com, http://www.redbooks.ibm.com).

A good comparison of NFS and CIFS can be found in Marc Farley's *Building Storage Networks*. He gives a very good description of the difficulties of integrating the two protocols in a NAS server. Further information on NAS servers can also be found on the websites of the relevant manufacturers.

For GPFS we primarily used the two IBM Redbooks *Sizing and Tuning GPFS* by Marcello Barrios *et al.* and *GPFS on AIX Clusters: High Performance File System Administration Simplified* by Abbas Farazdel *et al.*

With regard to DAFS we referred to Marc Farley's *Building Storage Networks* and the DAFS homepage http://www.dafscollaborative.com. Also helpful were articles by Boris

Bialek on http://www.db2magazin.com and by Marc Farley on http://storagemagazine.
techtarget.com.

STORAGE VIRTUALIZATION

Some articles at InfoStor (http://is.pennnet.com) deal with the subject of storage virtualization. The IBM Redbook *Storage Networking Virtualization: What's it all about?* is
highly recommended. More and more storage virtualization products are coming onto the
market, which means that an increasing amount of information on the subject can be
found on the websites of the manufacturers in question. There's also a great technical
tutorial booklet on storage virtualization available from SNIA.

SAN APPLICATIONS

With regard to the application and use of storage networks we unfortunately do not
know of any comprehensive book. We can only refer you to the white papers of relevant
manufacturers, various IBM Redbooks and to InfoStor and the SNIA on the Internet.

NETWORK BACK-UP

A good representation of the components of a network back-up system can be found in
Marc Farley's *Building Storage Networks*. For the interaction of network back-up systems
with storage networks and intelligent storage systems, we can again only refer the reader
to the white papers of the products in question.

   With regard to NDMP we can refer the reader to the same sources. In addition, the
NDMP homepage http://www.ndmp.org and the standard itself at the Internet Engineering
Task Force (IETF) on http://www.ietf.org should be mentioned.

MANAGEMENT OF STORAGE NETWORKS

Some articles on the management of storage networks can be found at InfoStor (http://is.
pennnet.com). Some IBM Redbooks (http://www.redbooks.ibm.com) and white papers
also deal with this subject. A detailed representation of the Fibre Channel Generic
Services and the Fibre Channel Methodologies for Interconnects for the in-band
management in the Fibre Channel SAN is provided by the pages of the Technical
Committee T11 (http://www.t11.org). Information on SNMP can be found on the

Internet pages of the SNMP Research Technology Corporation (http://www.snmp.org). A comprehensive description of CIM and WBEM can be found on the websites of the Distributed Management Task Force (DMTF, http://www.dmtf.org). Information on SMI-S can be found on the Storage Networking Industry Association website (SNIA, http://www.snia.org).

REMOVABLE MEDIA MANAGEMENT

The IEEE Standard 1244 documents can be found at http://www.ieee.org. Related documentation and additional reading can be found at the homepage of the Storage Systems Standards Working Group at http://www.ssswg.org. There is an *IBM Journal of Research & Development* volume 47, no 4, 2003: Tape Storage Systems and Technology: http://www.research.ibm.com/journal/rd47-4.html. Some interesting articles on the future of tape storage can be found here:

http://www.enterprisestorageforum.com/technology/features/article.php/
11192_1562851_2
http://www.emaglink.com/newsletter_archive/newsletter_June_2003.htm
http://www.it-director.com/article.php?articleid=2379

THE SNIA SHARED STORAGE MODEL

The SNIA provides a lot of material on the SNIA Shared Storage Model at http://www.snia.org/tech_activities/shared_storage_model. Tom Clark's *Designing Storage Area Networks* (2nd Edition) covers the model as well.

Appendix A

Proof of the Calculation of the Parity Block of RAID 4 and 5

In Section 2.5.4 we stated that during write operations the new parity block can be calculated from the old parity block and the difference Δ between the old data block D and the new data block $\tilde{D}$. In the following we would like to present the proof for the example in Figure 2.16.

Mathematically speaking we state that:

$$\tilde{P}_{ABCD} = P_{ABCD} \text{ XOR } \Delta \text{ where } \Delta = D \text{ XOR } \tilde{D}$$

Taking into account the calculation formula for the parity block we must therefore show that:

$$P_{ABCD} \text{ XOR } D \text{ XOR } \tilde{D} = \tilde{P}_{ABCD} = A \text{ XOR } B \text{ XOR } C \text{ XOR } \tilde{D}$$

The associative law applies to the XOR operation so we do not need to insert any brackets.

We will conduct the proof on the basis of the values table in Table A.1. The parity block will be calculated bit-by-bit by means of the XOR operation. The table therefore shows the occupancy of a bit ('0' or '1') from the various blocks.

The left-hand part of the table shows the possible occupancies for the bits in the old data block D, in the new data block $\tilde{D}$ and the parity bit for the bits in the remaining data blocks (A XOR B XOR C). The values of the individual blocks A, B, and C is insignificant because at the end of the day the parity of these three blocks flows into the parity of all four data blocks. This proof is therefore transferable to arrays with more or less than five hard disks.

Storage Networks Explained   U. Troppens R. Erkens W. Müller
© 2004 John Wiley & Sons, Ltd   ISBN: 0-470-86182-7

Table A.1 Calculation of the parity block for RAID 4 and RAID 5 by two methods

A XOR B XOR C	D	$\tilde{D}$	P_{ABCD}	D XOR $\tilde{D}$	P_{ABCD} XOR D XOR $\tilde{D}$	A XOR B XOR C XOR $\tilde{D}$
0	0	0	0	0	**0**	**0**
0	0	1	0	1	**1**	**1**
0	1	0	1	1	**0**	**0**
0	1	1	1	0	**1**	**1**
1	0	0	1	0	**1**	**1**
1	0	1	1	1	**0**	**0**
1	1	0	0	1	**1**	**1**
1	1	1	0	0	**0**	**0**

The middle section of the table shows the calculation of the new parity block according to the formula given by us $\tilde{P}_{ABCD} = P_{ABCD}$ XOR(D XOR $\tilde{D}$). The end result is printed in bold.

The right-hand column shows the calculation of the new parity by means of the definition $\tilde{P}_{ABCD} = $ (A XOR B XOR C)XOR $\tilde{D}$ and is also printed in bold. The two columns printed in bold show the same value occupancy, which means that our statement is proven.

Appendix B

Checklist for the Management of Storage Networks

In Section 8.2 we discussed the development of a management system for storage networks. As a reminder: a good approach to the management of a storage network is to familiarize yourself with the requirements that the individual components of the storage network impose on such software. These components include:

- Applications
  These include all software that is operated in a storage network and processes the data.
- Data
  Data is the information that is processed by the applications, transported via the network and stored on storage resources.
- Resources
  Resources include all of the hardware that is required for the storage and transport of the data and for the operation of applications.
- Network
  Network means the connections between the individual resources.

Diverse requirements with regard to availability, performance or scalability can be formulated for these individual components. The following checklist should help to specify these requirements more precisely.

Storage Networks Explained   U. Troppens R. Erkens W. Müller
© 2004 John Wiley & Sons, Ltd   ISBN: 0-470-86182-7

B.1   APPLICATIONS

B.1.1   Monitoring

- How can I check the error-free implementation of the applications?
- Which active or passive interfaces will be provided for this by the applications?

B.1.2   Availability

- What availability must I guarantee for which applications?
- What degree of fault-tolerance can and must I guarantee?
- What factors influence the availability of the application?
- What measures should be taken after the failure of the application?
- How can I guarantee availability?
- How can I detect that an application has failed?

B.1.3   Performance

- What data throughput and what response times will users expect?
- How can the performance be measured?
- What usage profiles underlie the applications, i.e. when is there a heavy load and when is there a less heavy load?
- What are my options for adapting to a changing usage profile?

B.1.4   Scalability

- How scalable are the applications?
- Can I use the same applications in the event of an increase in the volume of data?
- What measures may be necessary?

B.1.5   Efficient use

- Can applications be shared across business processes?
- Can one application handle multiple business processes?

B.2 DATA

B.2.1 Availability

- Which data requires what degree of availability?
- How can I guarantee availability?
- In case of a disaster: how quickly must the data be back online?
- What level of data loss is tolerable in the event of a failure?

B.2.2 Performance

- What data must be provided to the applications quickly and must therefore be stored on fast storage devices?
- How can I measure and check the data throughput?

B.2.3 Data protection

- Which data must additionally be backed up?
- How often must such a back-up take place?
- How can I check the back-up process?

B.2.4 Archiving

- Which data must be stored for how long?
- Which statutory provisions should be observed in this connection?
- At what points in time must data be archived?

B.2.5 Migration

- Which data can be moved within the storage hierarchy from expensive media such as hard disks to cheaper media such as tape?
- For which data can a hierarchical storage management (migration) be used?
- How do I check an automatic migration?
- How do I check where the data really is after a certain period of operation?

B.2.6   Data sharing

- Which data sets can be shared by several applications?
- Where do conflicts occur in the event of parallel access?
- How can data sharing use be realized?

B.2.7   Security/access control

- Which users are given what access rights to the data?
- How can access rights be implemented?
- How can I check log and audit accesses?

B.3   RESOURCES

B.3.1   Inventory/asset management and planning

- Which resources are currently used in the storage network?
- Which financial aspects such as depreciation, costs, etc. play a role?
- When is it necessary to invest in new hardware and software?

B.3.2   Monitoring

- How can I determine the failure of a resource?
- Are there possibilities and criteria for checking that would indicate a failure in advance (for example temperature, vibration, failure of a fan, etc.)?

B.3.3   Configuration

- How can I view the current configuration of a resource?
- How can I change the configuration of a resource?
- Which interfaces are available to me for this?
- What consequences does the configuration change of a resource have?
- Can I simulate this in advance?

B.3.4 Resource use

- Which resources are consumed by which applications?
- How can I ensure an equably resource utilization?
- How must I distribute the data over the resources in order to realize availability, efficient use and scalability?
- Which media, for example which tapes, are in use?
- Which media must be renewed, for example on the basis of age?
- How can I transfer the data on media to be replaced onto new media?

B.3.5 Capacity

- How much free capacity is available on which resource?
- Is sufficient storage capacity available for the capacity requirements?
- How many resource failures can be withstood with regard to sufficient storage capacity?
- Which trends can be expected in the capacity requirement?

B.3.6 Efficient resource utilization

- How are the resources utilized?
- Are there unused resources?
- Where have I allocated resources inefficiently?
- Where can several resources be integrated in one?

B.3.7 Availability

- Which resources require a high level of availability?
- How can I guarantee the availability of resources?
- Which technologies exist for this?

B.3.8 Resource migration

- How can I – without interrupting the operation – exchange and expand resources?
- What happens to the data during this process?

B.3.9   Security

- How can I protect resources against unauthorized access?
- Which physical measures are to be taken for this?

B.4   NETWORK

B.4.1   Topology

- Which devices are connected together how?

B.4.2   Monitoring

- How can I recognize the failure of connections?
- Are there criteria for predicting any failures?

B.4.3   Availability

- What level of availability of the network is required?
- How can I guarantee the availability of the network?
- Where are redundant data paths required and how can I provide these?
- Where do single points of failure exist?

B.4.4   Performance

- Where are there bottlenecks in the data path?
- How can I optimize the data path?
- Usage profile: when are which data paths utilized and how?
- Trend analysis: am I coming up against bandwidth limits?

Index

Glossary entries are type set in *italic*.

Storage Networks Explained   U. Troppens R. Erkens W. Müller
© 2004 John Wiley & Sons, Ltd   ISBN: 0-470-86182-7